Over the Horizon Proliferation Threats

Over the Horizon Proliferation Threats

Edited by
James J. Wirtz and Peter R. Lavoy

Stanford Security Studies

An Imprint of Stanford University Press
Stanford, California

Stanford University Press
Stanford, California

© 2012 by the Board of Trustees of the Leland Stanford Junior University.
All rights reserved.

Printed in the United States of America

Library of Congress Cataloging-in-Publication Data

Over the horizon proliferation threats / edited by James J. Wirtz and Peter R. Lavoy.
    pages cm.
Includes bibliographical references and index.
ISBN 978-0-8047-7400-0 (cloth : alk. paper) —
ISBN 978-0-8047-7401-7 (pbk.   )
1. Nuclear nonproliferation. 2. Nuclear weapons—Government policy.
I. Wirtz, James J., editor of compilation.   II. Lavoy, Peter R. (Peter René),
editor of compilation.

JZ5675.O82 2012
327.1'747—dc23   2011036781

Typeset at Stanford University Press in 10/14 Minion

CONTENTS

Contributors

Wyn Q. Bowen is Professor of Non-proliferation and International Security at King's College London, where he also directs the Centre for Science and Security Studies. He is the author of *Libya and Nuclear Proliferation* (2006).

Arthur S. Ding is a Research Fellow of the Institute of International Relations, National Chengchi University, Taipei, Taiwan.

Lewis A. Dunn is a Senior Vice President of Science Applications International Corporation. He also served as Assistant Director of the U.S. Arms Control and Disarmament Agency and as Ambassador to the 1985 Nuclear Non-proliferation Treaty Review Conference.

Isabelle Facon is a Senior Research Fellow at the Paris-based Foundation for Strategic Research. She is the author of *Russie, Les chemins de la puissance* (Artège, 2010).

Christopher A. Ford is a Senior Fellow at Hudson Institute in Washington, DC. He previously served as U.S. Special Representative for Nuclear Nonproliferation, as Principal Deputy Assistant Secretary of State, and as General Counsel to the U.S. Senate Select Committee on Intelligence.

Katsuhisa Furukawa is former Fellow of Research Institute of Science and Technology for Society, of Japan Science and Technology Agency.

Jeffrey W. Knopf is Associate Professor of national security affairs at the Naval Postgraduate School, Monterey, California. He is a former editor of *The Nonproliferation Review* and the author of *Domestic Society and International Cooperation: The Impact of Protest on U.S. Arms Control Policy* (1999).

Peter R. Lavoy is Principal Deputy Assistant Secretary of Defense for Asian and Pacific Security Affairs in the Office of the Secretary of Defense. He previously held positions as the Deputy Director of National Intelligence for Analysis, Chairman of the National Intelligence Council, and National Intelligence Officer for South Asia. He is the editor of *The Causes and Consequences of the Kargil Conflict* (2009).

Michael Malley is a Lecturer in the Department of National Security Affairs at the Naval Postgraduate School, Monterey California.

Tanya Ogilvie-White is a Senior Lecturer in International Relations, University of Canterbury, New Zealand, and a Research Fellow in the Nonproliferation and Disarmament Program, International Institute for Strategic Studies, United Kingdom.

James A. Russell is an Associate Professor in the Department of National Security Affairs at the Naval Postgraduate School in Monterey, California. He is the author of *Innovation, Transformation and War: US Counterinsurgency Operations in Anbar and Ninewa Provinces, Iraq, 2005–2007* (2011).

Andrew Selth is a Research Fellow with the Griffith Asia Institute in Brisbane, Australia. He is the author of *Burma's Armed Forces: Power without Glory* (2002).

Etel Solingen is Chancellor's Professor at the University of California, Irvine. She is the author of *Nuclear Logics: Contrasting Paths in East Asia and the Middle East* (2007).

Noel Stott is a Fellow at the Institute of Security Studies, South Africa. He is the coauthor of *Destroying Surplus Weapons: As Assessment of Experience in South Africa and Lesotho* (2003).

Bruno Tertrais is a Senior Research Fellow at the *Fondation pour la Recherche Stratégique*. He is also a member of the International Institute for Strategic Studies and a contributing editor to *Survival*. He is the author of *War without End* (2005).

James J. Wirtz is Dean of the School of International Graduate Studies, Naval Postgraduate School, Monterey, California, and Director of the Global Center for Security Cooperation, Defense Security Cooperation Agency. He is coeditor of *Complex Deterrence: Strategy in the Global Age* (2009).

Abbreviations

ABAAC	Agency for Accounting and Control of Nuclear Materials
APEC	Asia-Pacific Economic Cooperation
ARF	ASEAN Regional Forum
ASEAN	Association of Southeast Asian Nations
BW	biological weapons
CBW	chemical and biological weapons
CWC	Chemical Weapons Convention
CIS	Commonwealth of Independent States
CTBT	Comprehensive Test Ban Treaty
CSCAP	Council for Security Cooperation in the Asia Pacific
GSDF	Ground Self-Defense Forced
GCC	Gulf Cooperation Council
HEU	highly enriched uranium
IDCs	innovative developing countries
ICBM	intercontinental ballistic missile
IAEA	International Atomic Energy Agency
ICJ	International Court of Justice
IMF	International Monetary Fund
NAS	National Academy of Sciences
CNEN	National Atomic Energy Commission
NNWS	Non Nuclear Weapons States
NPT	Non-proliferation Treaty
NATO	North Atlantic Organization Treaty
NBC	Nuclear, Biological, and Chemical

NWFZ	Nuclear Weapons Free Zone
NWS	Nuclear Weapons States
PLA	People's Liberation Army
P-5	Permanent Five
PDVSA	Petróleos de Venezuela
PSI	Proliferation Security Initiative
SDF	Self-Defense Forces
SAGSI	Standing Advisory Group on Safeguards Implementation
SLORC	State Law and Order Restoration Council
SPDC	State Peace and Development Council
START	Strategic Arms Reduction Treaty
UNSCR 1540	U.N. Security Council Resolution 1540
UNSCR 255	U.N. Security Council Resolution 255
VAEC	Vietnam Atomic Energy Commission
WMD	Weapons of Mass Destruction

Over the Horizon Proliferation Threats

1 Introduction

James J. Wirtz and Peter R. Lavoy

As the first decade of the twenty-first century comes to a close, a feeling of optimism and renewal animates the scholars and practitioners who deal with nuclear nonproliferation. President Barak Obama has embraced nuclear disarmament as a long-term U.S. policy goal, an objective endorsed by other eminent U.S. statesmen.[1] This renewed interest in nuclear disarmament also is reflected in recent scholarly work that seeks to identify practical ways to make total nuclear disarmament a reality.[2] Scholars have suggested that arms control verification, combined with confidence building measures, can reassure the global community that fissile materials, manufacturing facilities, and scientific expertise are not being diverted into clandestine nuclear weapons programs. For many observers, nuclear disarmament is no longer a millenarian dream. Instead, it is a practical objective that should be embraced by national leaders.

Disarmament advocates are quick to identify today's proliferation threats as justification for their position and policies. Topping this list of threats is the possibility that a nuclear weapon could fall into the possession of a violent extremist group or some other nonstate actor. The fear is that a nuclear weapon might be stolen from a stockpile maintained by a state, or that a primitive fission bomb might be crafted from nuclear material obtained on the black market, or that a "dirty bomb" might be built by wrapping high explosive in a blanket of radioactive material.[3] A. Q. Khan's ability to siphon off significant nuclear materials and technology from Pakistan's nuclear program to create a commercial market for nuclear materials, bomb-making equipment, and weapons design information is considered a harbinger of a world in which nuclear trafficking is commonplace.[4] Analysts worry that it is only a matter of time before a terrorist

1

organization detonates a nuclear device or a dirty bomb in an urban area, possibly killing thousands and irradiating large portions of a major city. For those who embrace "the logic of zero," disarmament is the only sure way to head off the threat posed by nonstate actors by eliminating nuclear weapons before they fall into the hands of terrorists and by securing fissile materials and technologies associated with building a nuclear device before they find their way onto black markets.[5]

Iran's ongoing effort to develop nuclear weapons and the emergence of a North Korean nuclear arsenal also are identified as major threats to regional security and the nonproliferation regime. North Korea or Iran might start a "proliferation cascade" as neighboring states initiate their own nuclear programs to counter emerging threats, creating dynamics that can fuel nuclear arms races and crises.[6] There are even signs that this cascade is already occurring. In 2006, thirteen countries in the Middle East initiated or revived plans to pursue civilian nuclear programs, plans that are in part a political response to Iran's nuclear ambitions.[7] Nascent bomb programs also could create a discernible path to open hostilities as regional states contemplate preventive war to block Tehran or Pyongyang from fully deploying a nuclear arsenal. Global disarmament efforts are identified as a response to this threat by helping to create sustained international pressure against these nuclear holdouts. As the nuclear threat recedes elsewhere in the world, disarmament champions believe the existing hard cases will come under increasing international scrutiny and public condemnation. The political and economic price of maintaining an active nuclear weapons program will increase so much in the years ahead that disarmament advocates believe North Korea and Iran will eventually be forced to accept the logic of zero.

By focusing on the international threat environment, however, champions of global nuclear disarmament fail to recognize the underlying political, scientific, and military trends that actually have created the strategic setting whereby the issue of nuclear disarmament can rise to the top of international policy agendas. This is not an unusual situation in diplomatic history or the social sciences. As Geoffrey Blainey reminds us, "For every thousand pages published on the causes of wars there is less than one page directly on the causes of peace."[8] Nevertheless, understanding the nature, duration, and strength of the trends that favor disarmament and other cooperative security measures is important because it can inform policymakers about the impact of their policies on positive international developments. For example, will arms reductions or the atrophy of great power nuclear programs reduce the credibility of extended deterrence, leading smaller states to seek nuclear arms in the face of regional threats? What are the prospects of maintaining a stable nuclear balance and system of strong regional security arrangements as forces are drawn down? Most important, policymakers must have some appreciation of what might reverse positive trends and the steps they can take to prevent deterioration in the international political and military climate that would increase the importance they give to maintaining robust nuclear arsenals or reinvigorating nuclear modernization programs.

When it comes to vertical and horizontal nuclear proliferation over the last thirty years, two generalizations can be offered about these positive trends. In terms of vertical proliferation, the nuclear arms race among the great powers is becoming a distant memory. Their nuclear programs have been scaled back with the end of the Cold War. For the United States, the demise of the Soviet Union quickly eliminated the political and strategic motivation to maintain a robust nuclear modernization and procurement program. Research and development efforts were terminated and aging strategic systems were retired. For Russia, the economic dislocation caused by the end of the Soviet empire led to large reductions in its nuclear arsenal. A de facto nuclear test moratorium also has curtailed nuclear weapons modernization programs, limiting efforts to marry global precision-strike delivery systems with "boutique" weapons designed to maximize electromagnetic pulse and other nuclear effects. The nuclear programs of the United Kingdom, France, the People's Republic of China, the United States, and Russia are either in stasis or decline.[9] In reality, the New START treaty signed by the United States and Russia in April 2010,[10] potential U.S. ratification of the Comprehensive Test Ban Treaty, and growing international support of the Fissile Material Cutoff Treaty will simply formalize the decline of the great powers' nuclear programs. States will still make references to their nuclear deterrent, but in reality nuclear weapons are likely to play a less central role in their defense policies.

In terms of horizontal proliferation, the positive trend can be summarized by the phrase "the situation could be worse." Only a few countries have acquired nuclear arsenals. In fact, in each of the six decades of the nuclear era, only one or two states have obtained nuclear weapons capabilities: the United States and the Soviet Union in the 1940s, the United Kingdom and France in the 1950s, China and Israel in the 1960s, India and South Africa in the 1970s, Pakistan in the 1980s, and North Korea in the 1990s. Iran also seems intent on acquiring a nuclear device despite considerable international pressure and domestic turmoil following its June 2009 presidential elections. Nevertheless, this is a relatively small number of states, especially compared with the number of countries that possess the scientific and industrial capability needed to make nuclear weapons. Additionally, several states that inherited nuclear weapons (such as Ukraine) or developed them (for example, South Africa) have abandoned their arsenals; and Libya has terminated its rudimentary efforts to acquire a nuclear capability. Moreover, with the exception of India and Pakistan, no nuclear powers appear to be locked into an arms race that is producing either a qualitative or quantitative increase in nuclear arsenals.[11]

If these positive trends set the stage for more ambitious disarmament agendas, it would make sense for disarmament advocates to take steps to preserve this strategic setting. An important initiative, related to the issue of horizontal proliferation, would be to identify the reasons why certain governments have decided to forgo developing a nuclear capability and the type of events that might lead to a change in that policy. Lewis Dunn, for instance, notes that "once a country's leadership [has] committed itself to acquire nuclear weapons, little [can] be done to reverse that decision. Attempts to make it technically harder, diplomatic and political jawboning, threats and imposition of sanctions, rougher inspections, legal constraints and/or conventional arms placebos often proved too little, too late." By understanding what strategic developments might prompt a reassessment of policy, the international community could act to allay concerns and emerging threats before they prompt policymakers to embark on a more ominous path. By doing so, according to Dunn, "it then would become possible to pursue a multifaceted approach to influence their calculations while time remains to do so."[12]

If policymakers actually possessed this type of proliferation early warning system, what steps could they take to alter the strategic setting before it forced governments to reassess their nuclear options? In terms of vertical proliferation, policymakers might explore the unilateral and multilateral initiatives that can be undertaken to reduce incentives for states to acquire nuclear weapons. Unbridled regional nuclear arms races or the use of nuclear weapons on some distant battlefield would likely reverse the trend toward de-emphasizing the role of nuclear weapons in great power defense strategies. The United States, Great Britain, or France, for instance, might face political pressure to restart their nuclear weapons programs following Iranian acquisition of a nuclear weapon. By contrast, confidence building measures, positive and negative security guarantees, and multilateral efforts to stop trafficking in illicit material that were sponsored by the great powers might not only strengthen the nonproliferation regime but also build mutual confidence in their commitment to stop the spread of nuclear weapons. Unilateral and multilateral confidence building measures and security guarantees can work to stem proliferation "on the periphery," while providing evidence of the great power commitment to nonproliferation, strengthening the trends toward nuclear disarmament in great power relations. As they work to eliminate potential incentives for other states to develop nuclear weapons, the great powers can also work to coordinate their own policies and build confidence concerning their own ambitions.

DOES NUCLEAR PROLIFERATION HAVE A FUTURE?

This book sets aside the traditional proliferation "hard cases" that gain the lion's share of scholarly attention to explore the reasons why several states have turned away—at least for now—from the opportunity to acquire a nuclear arsenal. We offer no general theory to explain why states might choose to acquire a nuclear capability. Most of our authors are guided by the realist assumption that governments will acquire a nuclear arsenal when they believe that it will improve their security.[13] Etel Solingen in Chapter 8 of this book uses a political-economic model to explain various countries' nuclear trajectories.[14] According to this approach, leaders or ruling coalitions advocating economic growth through integration in the global economy ("internationalizers") have incentives to avoid the costs of nuclearization because a nuclear weapons program impairs domestic economic and political reforms favoring internationalization, including macroeconomic and political stability, economic reforms, and efforts to enhance exports, economic competitiveness, and global access.

A few other of our authors deliberately utilize a "nuclear mythmaking" approach that highlights the beliefs that link the acquisition of nuclear weapons or other types of weapons of mass destruction to the state's enhanced security or influence. According to this perspective, a state is likely to seek nuclear weapons when national elites (*nuclear mythmakers*) who support this strategy: (1) emphasize their country's insecurity or its poor international standing; (2) portray this strategy as the best corrective for these problems; (3) argue for the political, economic, and technical feasibility of acquiring nuclear weapons; (4) successfully associate these beliefs and arguments (*nuclear myths*) with existing cultural norms and political priorities; and, finally, (5) convince senior decision-makers to accept and act on these views.[15] As several authors of this book illustrate, competing myths also may exist and are spread by similar mechanisms. Thus if enterprising and well-connected strategic elites manage to cultivate a national—or at least a governmental—consensus that acquiring nuclear weapons would make the state *less* secure or *less* influential, then the government is not likely to initiate or continue to invest in a nuclear bomb program. At any given time and in any given country, multiple strategic myths may coexist and compete with one another.

In fact, most of the authors of this volume take an empirical approach by identifying the reasons national leaders and governments abandon their nuclear ambitions. The contributors identify the strategic, political, and economic factors that shift national calculations away from the decision to go nuclear. These factors constitute the underlying trends that produce positive developments in the realm of nuclear nonproliferation. If these strategic and political factors evaporate, one might expect that the governments in question could reassess their decision to forgo nuclear weapons, a situation that could spark a fresh round of proliferation. In each of the cases we consider, there are active debates (some relatively open but most quite secret) about developing or redeveloping a nuclear arsenal.

Identifying the factors that shape positive outcomes can improve the ability to estimate the likelihood of future proliferation threats. Early warning that a government might reassess its non-nuclear posture could help the international community take the steps necessary to reverse a deteriorating local or regional strategic setting. The book also alerts policymakers and scholars alike to the fact that people in and around the governments considered here are thinking about their nuclear options, despite the fact that they are not actively pursuing a nuclear capability.

Our first group of contributors—Katsuhisa Furukawa, Arthur Ding, James Russell, Michael Malley, Tanya Ogilvie-White, Etel Solingen, Isabelle Facon, Noel Stott, and Andrew Selth—examine several states that have little in common other than the fact that they possess at least a rudimentary nuclear infrastructure and have at some point made the decision to abandon or not to acquire a nuclear weapons capability. Two of these states—Taiwan and Japan—have significant nuclear capabilities. Japan is often described as a state that could even acquire a modern, lightweight fusion weapon and long-range ballistic missile delivery system within months of a political decision to go nuclear. South Africa and Ukraine actually possessed nuclear weapons, deciding to abandon their arsenals when their leaders found themselves in fundamentally different strategic and political settings. Libya had launched a program to develop a nuclear weapon, but its leaders apparently decided to drop the project when international efforts at dissuasion ramped up following the Second Gulf War. All of these states have attracted some scholarly attention because they once posed or continue to pose a potential for nuclear proliferation.

Those concerned with nuclear proliferation often overlook other states for the very reason that they seem unlikely to exploit their commercial nuclear industries or appear uninterested in developing a nuclear weapon. The governments of Saudi Arabia, Burma, Vietnam, Indonesia, Argentina, Brazil, and Venezuela all possess nuclear infrastructures, and all have at times expressed some degree of interest in further developing their nuclear industries. What keeps these states from more vigorously pursuing their nuclear option? Is it wrong for scholars to take this nuclear restraint for granted? Our contributors describe the nuclear debate in these countries and how governments weigh incentives and disincentives when it comes to developing a capability to build nuclear weapons.

Our second set of contributors describe policies and events that can shape perceptions of the utility of a nuclear arsenal. One emerging issue is an ongoing revolution in the biological and life sciences that is creating the potential for new kinds of biological weapons. As Michael Moodie observes, the widespread availability of these new technologies, especially to nonstate actors, could create an incentive to acquire nuclear weapons to bolster deterrent or even war fighting capabilities. Perceptions of the desirability of acquiring nuclear weapons also can be altered by so-called proliferation shocks, setbacks to the international nonproliferation agenda. Given the continued presence of proliferation "hard cases," Lewis Dunn suggests that it might be prudent to develop plans to exploit these setbacks to strengthen the nonproliferation regime. Chris Ford also explores the way the existing nonproliferation regime can be used to help alter perception of the utility of developing a nuclear arsenal, while Bruno Tertrais explores the role of positive and negative security guarantees in deterring the proliferation of weapons of mass destruction. With an eye toward drawing lessons for the future, Wyn Bowen also describes the diplomatic and intelligence resources brought to bear by the British and U.S. governments to persuade Libyan officials to abandon their chemical, biological, and nuclear weapons programs.

Viewed as a whole, our volume seeks to identify the types of considerations that have led various governments and policymakers to forgo the nuclear option, while suggesting several kinds of policies that can reinforce these perceptions, even in the face of inevitable setbacks to the nonproliferation regime. Our volume thus highlights a key issue in world politics by not treating the decision against acquisition of nuclear weapons as irreversible. Our authors agree that this is not a valid assumption because the strategic and political setting that fostered a specific decision can change, and because scientific and industrial capabilities are constantly advancing. A weapon that was once at the cutting edge of science and technology now appears increasingly within reach of relatively limited programs. And, when held up to close scrutiny, it becomes apparent that in several cases, the decision to abandon a nuclear weapons program was highly contested and controversial. Nuclear advocates still constitute a vocal minority in many "disarmed" polities. And with shifting security circumstances or domestic political fortunes, these minority positions and proponents might yet come out on top.

NOTES

1. Remarks by President Barak Obama, Hradcany Square, Prague, Czech Republic, April 5, 2009, http://www.whitehouse.gov/the_press_office/Remarks-By-President-Barack-Obama-In-Prague-As-Delivered/; and George P. Shultz, William J. Perry, Henry Kissinger, and Sam Nunn, "A World Free of Nuclear Weapons," *Wall Street Journal*, January 4, 2007, A15.

2. Ivo Daalder and Jan Lodal, "The Logic of Zero: Toward a World without Nuclear Weapons," *Foreign Affairs*, 87, No. 6 (November–December 2008): 80–95.

3. Lewis A. Dunn, "Can al Qaeda Be Deterred from Using Nuclear Weapons?" Center for the Study of Weapons of Mass Destruction, National Defense University, Occasional Paper 3, July 2005, available at http://www.ndu.edu/WMDCenter/docUploaded/206-186_CSWMD_OCP3WEB.pdf.

4. Jeremy Bernstein, *Nuclear Weapons: What You Need To Know* (Cambridge: Cambridge University Press, 2008), 255–81.

5. William C. Potter, "Nuclear Terrorism and the Global Politics of Civilian HEU Elimination," *Nonproliferation Review*, 15, No. 2 (July 2008): 135–58.

6. James Clay Moltz, "Future Nuclear Proliferation Scenarios in North East Asia," *Nonproliferation Review*, 13, No. 3 (November 2006): 591–604.

7. Shlomo Brom, "Israeli Perspectives on the Global Elimination of Nuclear Weapons," in *Unblocking the Road to Zero: Perspectives of Advanced Nuclear Nations*, ed. Barry Blechman (Washington, DC: Henry L. Stimson Center, 2009), 47.

8. Geoffrey Blainey, *The Causes of War* (New York: Free Press, 1973), 1.

9. James J. Wirtz, "United States: Nuclear Policy at a Crossroads," in *The Long Shadow: Nuclear Weapons and Security in 21st Century Asia*, ed. Muthiah Alagappa (Stanford: Stanford University Press, 2008), 111–33.

10. U.S. Department of State, "New START," http://www.state.gov/t/avc/newstart/index.htm.

11. Although the term "arms race" is often used as a pejorative term for virtually any expenditure on defense, it implies a self-sustaining, "action-reaction" phenomenon. In reality, this type of event is relatively rare in world politics. See Grant T. Hammond, *Plowshares into Swords* (Columbia: University of South Carolina Press, 1993).

12. Lewis A. Dunn, "Countering Proliferation: Insights from Past Wins, Losses, and Draws," *Nonproliferation Review*, 13, No. 3 (November 2006): 483.

13. Realism—or, more accurately, neorealism—expects states to balance against the most serious military threats to their security; rarely do they *bandwagon*, or appease their adversaries. States can try to balance "internally" by relying on their own military capabilities or "externally" by relying on the military capabilities of allies. Defense planners generally prefer internal balancing because it leaves less to chance and less to the will of others; however, this strategy, especially when it comes to developing nuclear weapons, requires levels of national will and resources beyond the reach of most countries. See Kenneth N. Waltz, *Theory of International Politics* (New York: Random House, 1979), 128, 168; and John J. Mearsheimer, *The Tragedy of Great Power Politics* (New York: W. W. Norton, 2001), 156–57.

14. This argument is developed fully in Etel Solingen, *Nuclear Logics: Contrasting Paths in East Asia and the Middle East* (Princeton, NJ: Princeton University Press, 2007).

15. This approach is developed more fully in Peter R. Lavoy, "Nuclear Proliferation over the Next Decade: Causes, Warning Signs, and Policy Responses," *Nonproliferation Review*, 13, No. 3 (November 2006): 433–54.

PART I:
NATIONAL DECISIONS IN PERSPECTIVE

2 Japan's Nuclear Option

Katsuhisa Furukawa

The possibility that Japan might build a nuclear arsenal has raised international concerns over the last several decades.[1] This chapter identifies the conditions under which Japan might decide to pursue its nuclear option. It first surveys Japan's nuclear policy during the Cold War. It then describes current strategic thinking in Japan, especially in light of the ongoing challenges posed by North Korea and increasing uncertainty about the scope and pace of military modernization in the People's Republic of China. The chapter also explores Japan's efforts to sustain and strengthen a credible deterrent for the future. It concludes by identifying the conditions that could prompt Japanese decision-makers to create an indigenous nuclear deterrent. But readers should be cautioned that the nuclear scenario outlined by this chapter is not a likely course of action for Tokyo. The chances that Japan will "go nuclear" are extremely low as long as current international security trends continue.

JAPAN'S NUCLEAR POLICY

Throughout most of the Cold War, Japan's nuclear policy reflected two guiding concepts. The first was the so-called Three Non-Nuclear Principles, which prohibit Japan from manufacturing, possessing, or permitting the entry of nuclear weapons into the air, land, or sea controlled by Japan. Japanese Prime Minister Eisaku Sato announced these principles during the Diet session in December 1967. The Four Nuclear Policies, announced by Prime Minister Sato in 1968, constitute the second principle that guides Japanese policy. By Four Nuclear Policies, Japanese governments mean that they will (1) adhere to the Three Non-Nuclear Principles, (2) pursue global nuclear disarmament, (3) limit the use of nuclear energy to peaceful purposes as defined by the 1955 Atomic Energy Basic Law, and (4) rely upon U.S. extended deterrence that is codified by the 1960 U.S.-Japan Security Treaty. In keeping with these Four Nuclear Policies, Japanese policymakers have embraced various international treaties and agreements, such as the International Atomic Energy Agency (IAEA) safeguards agreement, the IAEA Additional Protocol, and the Nuclear Suppliers Group London Guidelines for nuclear transfers. In addition, Japan has signed bilateral safeguards agreements with its major nuclear suppliers, including the United States, the United Kingdom, France, Australia, and Canada. These agreements are intended to provide additional safeguards on transferred materials and technologies in the event that Japan should withdraw from the Nuclear Non-proliferation Treaty (NPT). Various Japanese governments have chosen to deeply embed nuclear issues into a network of treaties, laws, and administrative regulations.

Thinking about the Nuclear Option: 1940–70

Despite the general disposition against acquiring a nuclear arsenal, Japan occasionally explored the nuclear option, especially at moments of uncertainty in the international system.[2] In the spring of 1940, the Japanese Army initiated a research project on uranium enrichment technology using a gas diffusion process. As the war situation deteriorated in the summer of 1944, Japan began to devote more attention to developing a nuclear weapon, but its efforts were in vain. After the war, the U.S. government concluded that Japan had possessed only a rudimentary nuclear weapons program, roughly equivalent to the state reached by the U.S. nuclear weapons program in early 1942.[3] Nevertheless, Japanese scientists had determined the amount of uranium required for a bomb, calculated the likely yield of a fission device, and understood how they might go about triggering a fission reaction.[4] With the end of World War II, Japan terminated its exploratory work on developing a nuclear weapon.

As the Cold War deepened in the 1950s, the Dwight Eisenhower administration began to encourage Japan to prepare for nuclear warfare. Tokyo's response was driven by increasing anxiety about potential nuclear attack from the Soviet Union and the possibility that China might test a nuclear weapon. The Japanese military began to explore various battlefield contingencies created by the nuclear age, including tactical use of nuclear weapons. The 1950s were unique in the sense that statements about Japan's nuclear options appeared in the press, reflecting Japan's increasing concern over Soviet nuclear attack and U.S. encouragement to take the problem seriously.[5] As the United States began to encourage Japan's remilitarization in the mid-1950s, Japan's Self-Defense Forces (SDF) initiated research on protection measures in the event of nuclear attack.[6] In March 1955, Japanese Prime Minister Ichiro Hatoyama stated: "There is no reason to oppose the (idea of) U.S. storage of nuclear weapons in Japan if (military) power contributes to the preservation of peace justifiably."[7] He made a similar statement in July 1955.

Starting in 1956, the U.S. Army Command and General Staff College began to accept colonels from Japan's Ground Self Defense Forces (GSDF) as overseas students. These officers were taught U.S. battlefield nuclear doctrine.[8] In February 1957, Japan's defense minister confirmed in the Diet session that the government had initiated an assessment of the potential damage Japan might suffer in the event of nuclear attack. By the late 1950s, Japan also began to procure combat tanks and vessels that offered some protection against fallout (for example, self-contained oxygen systems) and decontamination equipment to prepare for possible operations on a nuclear battlefield.[9]

There also are indications that, during the 1950s, the Japanese GSDF undertook studies on the use of nuclear weapons against the Soviet Union.[10] In May 1957, Japanese Prime Minister Shinsuke Kishi stated, "The Japanese Constitution does not rule out Japan's possession of nuclear weapons for self-defense."[11] In November 1958, during a visit to the United States, Lieutenant-General Kumao Imoto stated that Japan would fare better by possessing nuclear weapons against an enemy equipped with nuclear weapons.[12] In May 1959, Japanese Defense Minister Hanjiro Inou suggested that Japan might possess nuclear armed missiles in the future.[13] In July 1959 Munenori Akagi (who later became defense minister) revealed a draft of the second defense buildup program, which anticipated deployment of missiles that could be armed with conventional or nuclear warheads.[14]

Although Japanese defense officials often spoke favorably in the 1950s about Japan's nuclear option, this enthusiasm was constrained by the public's allergy to nuclear weapons, which became pronounced when the members of a fishing ship, Daigo Fukuryumaru (Lucky Dragon), were exposed to radiation during their operations near the U.S. nuclear testing site on Marshall Island in March 1954. The Japanese public was appalled because this incident rekindled memories of the U.S. nuclear attacks on Japan.[15]

The U.S. military apparently introduced nuclear weapon components into

Japan in 1954: non-nuclear components of nuclear warheads were moved to U.S. bases in the country that year.[16] Japan's bases would play a critical part in any U.S. war effort against the Soviet Union or the People's Republic of China.[17] About 800 nuclear warheads were stored at Kadena Airbase by the end of the 1950s.[18] In August 1955, the United States also deployed Honest John, a U.S. rocket system capable of carrying nuclear warheads, to the U.S. military base in Asaka in Saitama Prefecture, which is close to Tokyo. U.S. military spokesmen, however, would not confirm or deny that the Honest John system was equipped with nuclear warheads.[19] In January 1957, the U.S. media reported that the United States planned on deploying land units armed with tactical nuclear weapons to Japan. Martin E. Weinstein, who became a special advisor to the U.S. ambassador to Japan from 1975 to 1977, admitted that the Eisenhower administration planned to introduce nuclear missiles to Japan as part of its New Look national security policy.[20] The Hatoyama government was concerned about public opposition to the deployments. As a result, it agreed only to introduce the rocket system without nuclear warheads. Nuclear weapons for the system would be brought into Japan only if the global security situation deteriorated.[21]

In April 1957, the U.S. Defense Department produced a report stating that there was a chance that the Japanese public's opposition to nuclear weapons might recede in the coming years and that they might accept nuclear weapons for defensive purpose if they became convinced a Japanese nuclear capability would bolster deterrence and stability in Asia.[22] In February 1959, another U.S. Department of Defense report stated that Japan might approve U.S. nuclear operations against the People's Republic of China from U.S. military bases in Japan if the Japanese government believed that Beijing might use nuclear weapons against Japan.[23] In December 1957, Frank C. Nash, a special advisor to President Eisenhower, recommended to the president that the U.S. military should train the SDF in the use of nuclear weapons so that the SDF could employ them in wartime.[24] Nash also recommended that the United States inform key Japanese figures about the types of nuclear weapons that could be integrated into the Japanese SDF. In 1957, the U.S. government also predicted that there was an "even" chance that the Japanese would acquire a nuclear weapon by 1967.[25] The Eisenhower administration placed more importance on countering the threat posed by the Soviet Union and the People's Republic of China than avoiding the threat produced by nuclear proliferation.

Although the John F. Kennedy administration eventually considered nuclear proliferation to be a serious issue, it continued to view the potential of a nuclear armed Japan with equanimity. In February 1961, the U.S. Air Force recommended a nuclear sharing program with U.S. allies in Asia to counter a nuclear armed China.[26] In December 1962, the Far Eastern Bureau of the U.S. State Department noted that U.S. military assistance to Japan was intended to prepare the country to possess nuclear weapons under the NATO-type safeguards.[27] The U.S. military was prepared to launch nuclear attacks from Japan's main islands in the 1960s in the event of a crisis in the region, according to State Department documents.[28] In November 1961, Prime Minister Hayato Ikeda expressed his interest in acquiring a nuclear capability in his meeting with Secretary of State Dean Rusk.[29] Apparently, Ikeda thought that acquiring a nuclear capability might be a good way to reduce Japan's overall defense budget.[30]

In 1963, Japan's Joint Staff Council and the U.S. military conducted the "Mitsuya Study," a highly classified simulation of a second Korean War. They concluded that the use of strategic nuclear weapons should be avoided as much as possible to prevent the crisis from escalating into an all-out war between the United States and Soviet Union. But the participants did find that the limited use of tactical nuclear weapons against an adversary's missile bases or in retaliation for an adversary's nuclear attack would be likely. When information about this study leaked to the media, however, Prime Minister Sato was forced to apologize. Henceforth, the SDF and government officials refrained from studying what the Japanese public considered to be the offensive use of nuclear weapons.

Nuclear nonproliferation became a higher policy priority for the Lyndon B. Johnson administration, which no longer welcomed active allied consideration of the nuclear option. It took some time for Japanese political leaders to adapt to this change. After China conducted its first nuclear weapons test in 1964, Prime Minister Sato stated in his discussion with U.S. Ambassador Edwin O. Reischauer that if an adversary had nuclear weapons, it would make common sense for Japan also to possess nuclear weapons.[31] At the Japan-U.S. summit in January 1965, Sato explicitly told President Johnson, "[If] Chicoms [Chinese Communists] had nuclear weapons, the Japanese also should have them."[32] Johnson replied that the United States would keep its promise and provide nuclear deterrence in Japan's defense. Sato said that this was exactly what he expected to hear from the U.S. president.[33]

By the mid-1960s, however, talk about a nascent Japanese nuclear capability had peaked, along with the U.S. nuclear "presence" in Japan. In 1965, Pentagon officials started removing non-nuclear bomb components from Japan.

The 1,300 U.S. nuclear weapons that were deployed to Okinawa in 1967 were returned to the United States by June 1972.[34] U.S. officials continued to believe that it was vital for the U.S. military to be able to deploy nuclear weapons to Japan at a time of crisis, but day-to-day peacetime deployments were a thing of the past by the mid-1970s.[35]

Thinking about the Nuclear Option:
The Emergence of Policy Studies circa 1970

By the early 1970s, a few informal study groups had emerged that produced assessments of Japan's nuclear options.[36] In the late 1960s, a private study group, the Research Commission on National Security (*Anzen Hoshou Chousa Kai*) was formed, which was led by Osamu Kaibara, then Director General of the National Defense Council (*Kokubou Kaigi*). The study group concluded that a plutonium-based atomic bomb could be produced more easily than a uranium-based weapon, that the graphite-moderated reactor in Tokaimura was suited for the production of weapons-grade plutonium, and that the submarine would be the most appropriate launch platform for a nuclear-tipped missile.[37] The report explained the mechanism of uranium enrichment and plutonium production, and concluded that Japan could produce 200 to 300 atomic bombs from indigenous natural uranium and that the nuclear reactor at Tokaimura could produce enough weapons-grade plutonium to make about twenty atomic bombs annually. This report also carried a list of the Japanese companies and research institutions that had the necessary technologies for producing atomic bombs. While some conclusions in this report seem questionable, it offered a comprehensive analysis of Japan's nuclear capabilities, including its ability to produce nuclear warheads and delivery vehicles, as well as the overall viability of its emerging nuclear complex.[38] The study group, however, voiced its opposition to a nuclear weapons program because of high costs and the significant political impact the program would have on neighboring countries. The group concluded that the best option for Japan was to rely upon U.S. nuclear deterrence.[39]

From 1967 until 1970, the Cabinet's Office of Research (COR) (*Naikaku Chousashitsu*) also established a project called "The Study Group on Democracy," to examine if it was possible and desirable for Japan to develop its own nuclear force.[40] At that time, many Japanese nationalists and conservatives expressed support for Japan's nuclear option, triggered by China's nuclear testing and international negotiations related to the NPT. COR analysts believed that the government should examine Japan's nuclear options to counter arguments advanced by nuclear advocates.[41] The group concluded that a nuclear weapons program was not desirable because it would be too expensive, fail to gain domestic support, and generate a security dilemma in the region.[42] It concluded that Japan could produce a small number of plutonium-based atomic bombs, but that it would find it difficult to establish a credible nuclear force.[43] The plutonium stored at the Tokaimura facilities was subject to IAEA inspection and could not be diverted for military use. Also, Japan did not at the time have a reprocessing plant to extract plutonium from spent nuclear fuel. The group noted that more than 50 percent of Japan's population and most industrial centers were concentrated in only 18.9 percent of Japan's territory, making Japan highly vulnerable to nuclear attack. The COR group concluded that an indigenous nuclear weapon would not contribute to deterrence.[44] They also stated that the possession of nuclear weapons was no longer a necessary condition for major power status.[45]

The *Gaikou Seisaku Kikaku Iinkai* (Foreign Policy Planning Committee) of the Ministry of Foreign Affairs also conducted an inquiry into Japan's nuclear future. In 1969, the Ministry of Foreign Affairs gathered "the best and the brightest" above the division-director level, and produced an internal document, "*Waga Kuni no Gaiko Seisaku Taiko* (Guidelines of Japan's Foreign Policy)." They concluded that Japan should maintain its no-nuclear-weapons policy, but that it would be prudent to develop a latent nuclear capability.[46] They also stated that it was important to educate the public that nuclear policymaking was based on pragmatic calculations of the relative merits of the nuclear option considering the developments in the international environment. It stressed that the Japanese government should avoid domestic panic or acrimony over nuclear issues, even if the United States decided to introduce tactical nuclear weapons onto Japanese soil in the event of war.[47]

In 1970, Defense Minister Yasuhiro Nakasone (who became prime minister in the 1980s) also ordered a group of experts to examine what it would take for Japan to arm itself with nuclear weapons. The group concluded that it would take a maximum of five years and an investment of 200 billion yen, which was about equal to 40 percent of the FY 1970 defense budget. According to Nakasone, the lack of a nuclear testing site in Japan was perceived as a major hurdle.[48] Eventually, the Japanese Defense White Paper commissioned by Nakasone stated: "[As] for defensive nuclear weapons, it would be possible in a legal sense to possess small-yield, tactical, purely defensive nuclear weapons without violating the Constitution. In view of the danger of inviting adverse foreign reactions and large-scale war, we will follow the policy of not acquiring nuclear weapons at present."[49]

In sum, the nuclear policy reviews and studies undertaken prior to the 1970s generally found that Japan could build a nuclear arsenal, but that the strategic benefits did not outweigh the economic and political costs of a decision to develop an indigenous nuclear deterrent. These studies highlighted the core tenets of Japan's "Four Nuclear Policies" that remain in place today. Nevertheless, Japanese officials decided to create an advanced nuclear infrastructure that is often described as a latent or "virtual" nuclear capability.

Japan as a Latent Nuclear Power

Japan's reliance upon U.S. extended deterrence was clearly articulated in Japan's defense strategy. In October 1976, the Outline of Defense Planning (*Bouei Keikaku Taikou*) stated, "Japan relies upon U.S. nuclear deterrence against nuclear threats."[50] The decision to rely on the U.S. nuclear umbrella was made in tandem with the strategic calculation to maintain a latent nuclear capability. In the 1970s, Takuya Kubo, then Bureau Director of Defense Policy of the Japan Defense Agency, wrote a famous article, "*KB Ronbun* (An Article Written by KB)," which stated: "[If] Japan prepares latent nuclear capability that would enable Japan to develop significant nuclear armament at anytime . . . the United States would hope to sustain the Japan-U.S. security system by providing a nuclear guarantee to Japan, because otherwise, the United States would be afraid of a rapid deterioration of the stability in the international relations triggered by nuclear proliferation."[51] In Kubo's view, this latent nuclear capability was expected to address any potential uncertainty surrounding the U.S. commitment to providing extended deterrence to Japan. Should the United States become reluctant about reassurance, Japan's latent nuclear capability was expected, at least theoretically, to remind the United States about Japan's indigenous nuclear option.

In the early 1980s, Ronald Reagan strengthened the Japan-U.S. alliance by deepening the U.S. presence in the Asia Pacific region. In the 1980s, Japanese officials became less concerned about the "decoupling effect" produced by the Soviet-American nuclear confrontation. As Matake Kamiya points out, during this period, Japan's defense posture was predicated on the notion that if Japan was subjected to a Soviet nuclear attack, the strike would be undertaken in the context of a global nuclear war between the United States and the Soviet Union

(U.S.S.R.).[52] Under these circumstances, the United States would probably be subjected to a nuclear attack as well. It was unlikely that Japan alone would face such a nuclear attack.

Japanese policymakers reminded U.S. officials about their latent nuclear capability as the United States began negotiations on the movement of Soviet SS-20 missiles from the European theater to the Russian Far East as part of the Intermediate Nuclear Forces Agreement.[53] Although the United States and the U.S.S.R. eventually agreed on the "zero-option," some Japanese strategic thinkers were apparently willing to remind their American counterparts about their latent nuclear options in the event that SS-20s were reintroduced into Asia.[54]

THE DEBATE ON A NUCLEAR OPTION
AFTER THE END OF THE COLD WAR

Since the 1990s, the risk of a military confrontation in Northeast Asia has been of growing concern to Japanese policymakers, especially in light of the North Korean nuclear and ballistic missile programs and the increasing tempo of Chinese military modernization aimed at developing anti-access and area denial capabilities. The potential resurgence of Russia's ambitions in the Far East is another concern. From the Japanese perspective, the Asian regional security landscape stands in contrast to the situation in Europe, where the risk of traditional military confrontation among the major powers has vastly diminished.

Reports that Japanese officials were re-examining their nuclear options again surfaced in the media in the 1990s. Driven by the development of North Korea's nuclear weapons program, several internal study groups in the Japanese Defense Agency examined whether Japan should develop a nuclear weapon. One study group concluded in 1995 that a nuclear weapons program was undesirable because of its cost and negative political effect, and that a Japanese decision to join the nuclear arms race would yield no strategic gains. The report suggested that Japan should instead maintain a posture of "a proud loser" (*Haiboku Shugi*) in the nuclear arms race.[55] These internal reviews of Japan's nuclear option were probably intended to reduce foreign concerns about Japan acquiring nuclear weapons and to demonstrate the drawbacks of any Japanese decision to launch a program to develop a nuclear arsenal. Nevertheless, the fact that North Korea may be able to strike Japan, but not the United States, with a nuclear weapon is a source of concern. Worries about decoupling have emerged in the minds of the Japanese strategic planners as North Korea's nuclear program continues to mature.

China represents the gravest strategic challenge to Japan. For Japan, a rising China creates a multifaceted situation: the largest trade relationship, military threat, diplomatic rival, and potential partner in coping with regional and global affairs.[56] The People's Liberation Army has been pursuing an anti-access and area-denial strategy and strengthening its deterrent vis-à-vis the United States. The People's Liberation Armyhas has also been strengthening its theater war-fighting capability by rapidly improving its naval and air power. So far, the United States maintains a military force second to none. But, as the United States and Russia move increasingly toward nuclear disarmament, China may find a window of opportunity to achieving strategic parity with the United States. What if China continuously strengthens its capabilities to strike the U.S. homeland with nuclear weapons? Would Washington still be willing to protect Japan even if U.S. cities were held at risk by Beijing?

These concerns have prompted some to call for Japan to reshape its contemporary strategic thinking. A small number of nongovernmental experts and politicians have become more willing to discuss Japan's nuclear option, especially in the aftermath of North Korean provocations. Government officials remain reluctant to engage publicly in speculation about Japan's nuclear options, an attitude that contrasts to past strategic assessments when officials were deeply involved in exploring potential nuclear weapons programs.

Contemporary Debates about Japan's Nuclear Option

After North Korea escalated the nuclear crisis in late 2002, debate about the nuclear option resurfaced in Japan.[57] The Japanese public tolerates this debate, although they do not support the idea that Japan should acquire a nuclear arsenal. In the February 2003 issue of *Shokun!*, a conservative opinion journal in Japan, for example, Kyorin University Professor Tadae Takubo and Mr. Nagao Hyodo, former Japanese Ambassador to Poland, argued that Japan certainly has a "nuclear card," asserting that a principle of "never say never" dominates international politics. They argued that Japanese officials should never say that Japan will never possess nuclear weapons. The August 2003 issue of *Shokun!* also featured a special section on Japan's nuclear option, with participation by forty-five experts and opinion leaders. Kyoto University Professor Terumasa Nakanishi argued that Japan should acquire a nuclear infrastructure that would allow it to build nuclear weapons on short notice because the People's

Liberation Army would continuously strengthen its power projection capabilities while U.S. extended deterrence might become unreliable. According to Nakanishi, three scenarios could materialize in the future: (1) The credibility of the U.S. commitment to the defense of Japan might erode; (2) the People's Liberation Army might acquire a blue-water navy and establish a permanent naval presence around Okinawa or the Senkaku Islands, which are the focal point of territorial disputes between Japan and China; or (3) the international community would acquiesce to North Korea's obvious interest in maintaining a nuclear arsenal.

Citing U.S. Vice President Dick Cheney's 2003 warning that North Korean nuclear threats might cause Japan to develop a nuclear arsenal, Nakanishi and other proponents of Japan's nuclear option mistakenly interpreted Cheney's statement as a signal of tacit U.S. support for Japan's acquisition of nuclear weapons.[58] U.S. support for Japan's nuclear option constitutes an important part of the argument advanced by nuclear advocates because most of them want U.S. help in construction of the Japanese arsenal. Proponents acknowledge that cooperation from other major nuclear suppliers, especially the United States, would help Japan overcome technical difficulties and legal and political constraints on Japan's use of nuclear materials for noncivilian purposes.[59]

Given the lack of strategic depth, many Japanese experts believe that Japan would have to pursue sea-based deployment of a nuclear force by acquiring a new submarine as a strategic platform. To field this capability, Japan would also need to institute a new naval doctrine and train personnel. All these initiatives would take at least a decade to complete. Some nuclear proponents suggest that nuclear-tipped cruise missiles could be deployed on existing destroyers, creating a quicker way to deploy a nuclear delivery system.[60] Others argue that surface combatants lack the requisite survivability to serve as a nuclear delivery system.[61] Some argue that Japan should develop a sea-based nuclear force under a closely coordinated arrangement with the U.S. military. According to this idea, Japan should follow the British lead in nuclear doctrine by maintaining an independent force and a coordinated command structure with the United States, rather than the French model, which adopts a more independent posture when it comes to employment doctrine.[62]

Another view holds that even if Japan could not possess a credible second-strike capability, a small nuclear arsenal would be of strategic benefit by making it more difficult for adversaries to drive a wedge between the United States and Japan by attempting to produce "decoupling effects." Kiyoshi Sugawa, former senior staff member on national security affairs of the Democratic Party of Japan, explained this view in his novel published in 2007.[63] According to this view, nuclear weapon states, such as the United Kingdom, France, Pakistan, and Israel, have decided to possess limited nuclear deterrence even though they may not necessarily possess credible second-strike capabilities. Similarly, a limited nuclear deterrent might be sufficient to bolster Japan's security because Japan's primary focus is on deterring a relatively small number of nuclear weapons launched by China or North Korea. Given Japan's significant role in the global economy, Sugawa suggested that it is doubtful that the international community could impose significant economic sanctions against Tokyo following a decision to acquire a nuclear arsenal. The international sanctions on India and Pakistan that followed their nuclear tests in 1998, for example, were sustained for only a relatively short time.

Some Japanese politicians have urged the government to create a nuclear arsenal. Others have referred to the uncertainty of Japan's future nuclear posture or the need to discuss Japan's nuclear options freely. On balance, however, it remains difficult for Japanese politicians to advocate procurement of nuclear weapons without risking their careers. Careless comments can trigger controversy, which in the past has led to the end of political careers for most elected officials.

In summary, the public still opposes policies that would lead to Japanese acquisition of a nuclear weapon. Nevertheless, it is no longer taboo to discuss nuclear strategy and the nuclear options available to Japan. Among the pragmatic thinkers who support examining (though not necessarily pursuing) Japan's nuclear options, many favor a strong Japan-U.S. alliance. In their view, the strategic challenge posed by China, together with another by North Korea, provides a real motivation for exploring openly various tools for Japan's deterrent posture, including nuclear weapons.

Technical Capabilities

Japan has sufficient technical capabilities to produce crude nuclear weapons. Japan has a nuclear fuel-cycle program to produce plutonium, although it is reactor-grade plutonium in the form of mixed oxide for civilian purposes under IAEA safeguards. It probably would take several years for Japan to turn this latent capability into a nuclear weapon.

After North Korea launched ballistic missiles in July 2006, a senior Japanese official led an internal assessment of Japan's capability to produce a small nuclear warhead.[64] This report concluded that in the absence of legal constraints it would take between three and five years for Japan to produce a prototype nuclear warhead, a budget of between 200 and 300 billion yen, and hundreds of scientific and engineering personnel. While Prime Minister Abe denied the existence of this study, Hideo Tamura, who authored this news report, said that this study might have been undertaken without informing political leaders.[65] Interestingly, while U.S. experts and officials argue that Japan can produce nuclear weapons using its stockpile of Pu 240, the report revealed that Japanese officials and experts believe that this type of nuclear weapon may not be credible because no other state employs this material in its nuclear weapons. A cultural preference for exquisite technological solutions seems to influence Japanese officials' thinking about nuclear weapons production.

The 2006 study also suggested that any Japanese effort to construct a nuclear weapon would confront several challenges. First, given that a fairly limited domestic reserve of natural uranium exists in Japan, it would be vulnerable to an embargo of fissile materials that could jeopardize any nuclear weapons program. Second, the Japanese scientific and academic communities tend to be populated by pacifists, despite the country's general shift toward becoming a "normal country." A majority of the Japanese universities and academic societies still embrace the principle of avoiding involvement in military-related research. Third, selecting the location for nuclear weapon production facilities would surely be a painstaking process for any Japanese government. The political power of local governments is expanding relative to the national government. Even the selection of a location for a radioactive waste storage site has been stalled for several decades. Local activism has been energized following the 2011 Fukushima nuclear accidents.

In terms of potential delivery system, Japan has the H-11A and H2-B rockets, which could be converted into intercontinental ballistic missiles. The H2-B launch vehicle is a two-stage rocket that uses liquid oxygen and liquid hydrogen as propellant. It also has four strap-on solid-fuel rocket boosters that can be used to extend its range or payload. The satellite launch systems employed on the rockets are based on technologies that could serve as the basis of a warhead "bus," although Japanese scientists and engineers have apparently never explored this application. Japan also has not undertaken a serious examination of a nuclear-tipped cruise missile.

The Japanese military also lacks the "intellectual" and operational infrastructure needed for a viable nuclear arsenal. It has never articulated a nuclear doctrine or a unified command and control system for nuclear operations. For its part, the government also lacks a stringent legal framework to protect classified information related to a nuclear weapons program. Additionally, no effort has been made to develop an intelligence system or information protocols to support nuclear operations.

JAPAN'S STRATEGIC POSTURE

Japan has always made every effort to ensure that U.S. extended deterrence remains credible, and will continue to do so in the future. Japan has come to place greater weight on its alliance with the United States in recent years. Japan has closely consulted the United States on extended deterrence, including discussion about U.S. nuclear doctrine and strategy. In general, Japanese officials have expressed increased confidence in U.S. extended deterrence as articulated in the 2010 U.S. Nuclear Posture Review. This increased confidence can largely be attributed to the Barak Obama administration's efforts to consult closely with Japan during the preparation phase of the Nuclear Posture Review.[66] In the Japan-U.S. Joint Statement of the Security Consultative Committee in June 2011, the U.S. government also reaffirmed its commitment to the defense of Japan utilizing "the full range of U.S. military capabilities, both nuclear and conventional."[67]

From the Japanese perspective, the credibility of deterrence is elastic because reassurance is a political phenomenon.[68] Over the past decade, Japan has developed a multifaceted national security posture that incorporates the concepts of assurance, dissuasion, deterrence, denial, defense, damage mitigation, and crisis management, which reinforces Japan's non-nuclear position.

Ballistic missile defense is at the core of Japan's denial strategy and serves as a major way to institutionalize the U.S.-Japan alliance. Japan's missile defense system consists of Aegis destroyers that can intercept ballistic missiles at the mid-course phase, Patriot PAC-3 interceptors to defeat ballistic missiles at the terminal phase, sensor systems to detect and track ballistic missiles, and the command, control, battle management, and communications systems to conduct actual missile engagements.[69] The Japanese Ministry of Defense plans to complete the entire ballistic missile defense architecture by linking four six Aegis destroyers, seventeen Patriot PAC-3 Fire Units, four FPS-5 radars, and seven FPS-3 upgraded radars, and command, control, battle management, and communications systems. Also, Japan has cooperated with the United States to improve ballistic missile defense capabilities against an adversary's use of decoys or erratic flight trajectories. Efforts are also underway to expand the areas that might potentially be protected by missile defenses.

Japan has been increasingly concerned about the shifting conventional power balance vis-à-vis China and Beijing's expanding nuclear force. As the United States and Russia pursue nuclear disarmament, there is an emerging concern in Japan that China may find an opportunity to achieve strategic parity with the United States and Russia. It could become difficult to maintain arms race and crisis stability among three nuclear weapon states if a situation of rough parity emerges among their arsenals.[70]

There are dissenting views within Japan about how to engage China in arms control. Japanese observers recognize that China the People's Liberation Army already possesses sufficient capability to target forward-deployed U.S. assets and Japanese territory, as well as some capacity to strike the U.S. homeland, with nuclear weapons. Without constraints, the People's Liberation Army may significantly improve its capabilities. If the U.S. homeland became further vulnerable to Chinese nuclear attack, Japanese observers wonder if the United States would take risks to protect Japan.

If the United States pursues an arms control agreement with China, such an agreement might officially recognize China's limited nuclear capability to strike the U.S. homeland and Japan. Under this scenario, the purpose of deterrence vis-à-vis China may differ between the United States and Japan. While Japanese officials would want to protect their country from Chinese nuclear attack, the United States might tolerate a Chinese nuclear capability to strike Japan as long as China does not fundamentally challenge the U.S. position in Asia. This would create a dilemma for the Japan-U.S. alliance. If the United States demonstrates restraint toward China, it might not necessarily be seen as reassuring to Japan. On the contrary, if China continues an arms race with the United States, it would significantly alarm Japan.[71] Future development of China's nuclear arsenals and Beijing's attitude toward arms control are factors shaping Japan's deterrence posture and Japanese confidence in U.S. extended deterrence.

CONCLUSION: CONDITIONS FOR JAPAN TO GO NUCLEAR

This survey suggests that several conditions would seem to foster a Japanese decision to develop a nuclear weapons capability. First, threat perceptions of hostile neighboring nuclear weapon states must worsen. Second, there would have to be a significant reduction in the perceived credibility of U.S. extended deterrence. Third, there would have to be a significant weakening of the international regimes for international security, arms control, and nonproliferation, including the U.N. Security Council. If Japanese officials believe that the international community can no longer enforce meaningful sanctions following a decision to acquire nuclear weapons, an important impediment to acquiring a nuclear arsenal would vanish. Fourth, anything that increases public support for Japan's nuclear option might improve the ability of those decisionmakers to start a nuclear weapons program. Fifth, a change in the balance of domestic politics whereby local governments accede to the national government's call for a nuclear weapons program would support acquisition of a nuclear weapon. Sixth, a major shift in the culture of the Japanese scientific community in favor of collaboration with the defense community would eliminate a roadblock to a nuclear program. Seventh, and most important, Washington's tacit or open approval of Japan's nuclear ambitions would increase the possibility that Tokyo would acquire a nuclear weapon.

By contrast, confidence in U.S. extended deterrence is the most important condition that fosters Japan's non-nuclear status. As the experience with the 2010 Nuclear Posture Review demonstrates, no changes in U.S. extended deterrence capabilities should be made without close consultations with America's allies and partners.[72] As the United States reduces the role of nuclear weapons in its defense strategies and increases its reliance on conventional weapons, it is increasingly important to conduct an expanded dialogue between the United States and Japan. Of particular importance in this dialogue is the role of the Japan-U.S. alliance in regional and international security, the effort to sustain credible extended deterrence, and the best way to include conventional weapons and ballistic missile defenses in protecting Japan and the United States. Since early 2010, the two governments have started a bilateral dialogue on deterrence. The United States and Japan will have to construct a joint approach toward nuclear weapon states. The creation of a trilateral dialogue with the People's Republic of China would be a good place to start this collaboration.[73] Japanese and U.S. policymakers also have to ensure that their consultations take place in the overall context of multilateral security cooperation in Asia.

NOTES

1. This article is revised and updated from Katsuhisa Furukawa, "Japan's Policy and Views on Nuclear Weapon: A Historical Perspective," *Jebat: Malaysian Journal of History, Politics, & Strategic Studies*, Vol. 37, August 2010, School of History, Politics and Strategic

Studies, University Kebangsaan Malaysia, 1-30. (http://pkukmweb.ukm.my/jebat/images/upload/Katsuhisa%20Furukawa%2037.pdf.

2. Akira Kurosaki, *Kaku Heiki to Nichibei Kankei* (Nuclear Weapons and Japan-U.S. Relations) (Tokyo: Yushisha, 2006); and Narushige Michishita, "*Kaku Mondai ni kansuru Nihon no Ugoki* (Japan's Actions regarding Nuclear Problems)," a briefing material produced for Michishita's class at the Graduate Research institute of Policy Studies in Tokyo, Japan, August 2006.

3. Hiroki Sugita, *Kenshou Hikaku no Sentaku* (Reviewing Japan's Decision to Pursue Non-Nuclear Weapon State) (Tokyo: Iwanami Shoten, 2005).

4. Ibid., 19–20.

5. Ibid., 47–48.

6. Ibid., 46–47.

7. Ibid., 47.

8. Ibid., 42–47.

9. Ibid., 46–47.

10. Ibid.

11. Ibid., 47.

12. Ibid.

13. Ibid.

14. Ibid.

15. Ibid., 53.

16. Robert S. Norris, William M. Arkin, and William Burr, "Where They Were," *Bulletin of the Atomic Scientists*, November/December 1999, 30.

17. Peter Hayes et al., *American Lake, Nuclear Peril in the Pacific* (New York: Penguin Books, 1986), 76.

18. Sugita, *Kenshou Hikaku no Sentaku*, 60–61.

19. Ibid., 61.

20. Martin E. Weinstein, *Japan's Postwar Defense Policy, 1947–1968* (New York: Columbia University Press, 1971), cited in Sugita, *Kenshou Hikaku no Sentaku*, 61.

21. Ibid.

22. Japanese translation cited in Sugita, *Kenshou Hikaku no Sentaku*, 65.

23. Ibid.

24. Ibid., 61–62.

25. National Intelligence Estimate 100-6-57, "Nuclear Weapons Production in Four Countries—Likelihood and Consequences," June 18, 1957, in the National Security Archive, "National Intelligence Estimates of the Nuclear Proliferation Problem: The First Ten Years, 1957–1967," National Security Archive Electronic Briefing Book no. 155, June 1, 2005, http://www.gwu.edu/~nsarchiv/NSAEBB/NSAEBB155/index.htm, accessed May 30, 2008.

26. Sugita, *Kenshou Hikaku no Sentaku*, 65.

27. Ibid., 64–65.

28. "U.S. Planned Atomic Attacks from Japan," *Japan Times*, May 9, 2000.

29. Memo of Conversation, Ikeda, and Rusk, November 3, 1961, FRUS 1961–1963, Vol. 22, Northeast Asia, 1996, 711, cited in Kurosaki, *Kakuheiki to Nichibei Kankei*, 42.

30. Kurosaki, *Kakuheiki to Nichibei Kankei*, 42.

31. Embtel 2067, Tokyo to SecState, December 29, 1964, NSA, no. 400; and Miki Kase, *Daitouryou ate Nihonkoku Shushou no Gokuhi Fairu* (Secret Files for the U.S. Presidents concerning the Japanese Prime Ministers) (Tokyo: Mainichi Shimbunsha, 1999), 24.

32. Central Foreign Policy Files, "Your Meeting with Prime Minister Sato," memorandum for the president from the secretary of state, secret, January 9, 1965, box 2376, RG 59, National Archives, College Park, MD, cited in Kurt M. Campbell and Tsuyoshi Sunohara, "Japan: Thinking the Unthinkable," in Kurt M. Campbell, Robert J. Einhorn, and Mitchell B. Reiss, *The Nuclear Tipping Point* (Washington, DC: Brookings Institution Press, 2004), 222.

33. "*Kaku wo Ou, Kenshou Nihon no Seisaku: Jou: Nihon 'Hikaku' ni Jirenma* (Tracking the Nukes: Reviewing Japan's Policy, Part I: Japan's Non-Nuclear Posture Faced with Dilemma)," *Asahi Shimbun*, August 1, 2007.

34. Norris, Arkin, and Burr, "Where They Were," 30–31; Ministry of Foreign Affairs, "*Iwayuru 'Mitsuyaku' Mondai ni kansuru Yuushikisha Iinkai Houkokusho* (A Report by the Expert Committee on the So-Called 'Japan-U.S. Secret Agreement')," March 9, 2010, 18.

35. For example, in 1969 during his meeting with Kazuo Aichi, the Japanese minister of foreign affairs, U. A. Johnson, then undersecretary of state, noted that the United States had to be able to locate nonstrategic nuclear weapons in Okinawa to sustain nuclear deterrence. See Ministry of Foreign Affairs, *Iwayuru 'Mitsuyaku' Mondai ni kansuru Yuushikisha Iinkai Houkokusho*, 62.

36. Michael J. Green and Katsuhisa Furukawa, "Chapter 12. Japan: New Nuclear Realism," in Muthiah Alagappa.ed., *The Long Shadow: Nuclear Weapons and Security in the 21st Century* (Stanford University Press, California 2008), pp. 347-372.

37. Research Commission on National Security (*Anzen Hoshou Chousa Kai*), *Nihon no Anzen Hoshou 1968 nenban* (Japan's National Security 1968) (Tokyo: Asagumo Shuppansha, 1968), cited in Sugita, *Kenshou Hikaku no Sentaku*, 67–70.

38. In 1981, an opposition party politician obtained a copy of the report on Japan's nuclear capabilities produced by the Research Commission on National Security (*Anzen Hoshou Chousa Kai*). Some of the contents of this report were made public during the session of the Diet's Upper House Committee on the Settlement of Account, on March 30, 1981. See *Kessan Iinkai Kaigiroku Daigogou* (The Record of the Meeting of the Committee on the Settlement of Account, no. 5), March 30, 1981.

39. Sugita, *Kenshou Hikaku no Sentaku*, 68–70.

40. "*Kakubuso Kano daga Motenu* [Nuclear Armament Technically Possible, but Not Recommendable]," *Asahi Shimbun*, November 13, 1994.

41. Sugita, *Kenshou Hikaku no Sentaku*, 70–71.

42. Ibid., 71–72.

43. Ibid.

44. Ibid.

45. Ibid.

46. Mainichi Shimbun Shakaibu, ed., *Usagi no Mimi to Hato no Yume: Nihon no Kaku to Jouhou Senryaku* (Rabbit's Ear and Dove's Dream: Japan's Nuclear and Information Strategy) (Tokyo: Liberta Shuppan, 1995); and Kurosaki, *Kaku Heiki to Nichibei Kankei*, 278.

47. Sugita, *Kenshou Hikaku no Sentaku*, 76.

48. Yasuhiro Nakasone, *Jiseiroku* (Record of Reflection) (Tokyo: Shinchosha, 2004), 224–25.

49. "Gist of White Paper on Defense," *Japan Times*, October 1970, 20, cited in Campbell and Sunohara, "Japan: Thinking the Unthinkable," 222.

50. *Asahi Shimbun*, October 29, 1976, cited in Kurosaki, *Kakuheiki to Nichibei Kankei*, 214.

51. Takuya Kubo, "Boueiryoku Seibi no Kangaekata (A Framework to Consider the Arrangement of Japan's Defense Capabilities)," February 20, 1971, http://www.ioc. u-tokyo.ac.jp/~worldjpn/documents/texts/JPSC/19710220.O1J.html, accessed April 30, 2008.

52. Remarks by Matake Kamiya at a meeting of the Japan Institute of International Affairs, May 11, 2007, Tokyo, Japan.

53. A comment by a former senior U.S. official at a conference of anonimous foundation in West Sussex, the United Kingdom, May 24, 2005. Also a comment by a former Japanese diplomat at a conference hosted by a Japanese think tank in Tokyo, September 29, 2008.

54. A comment by a former senior U.S. official at a conference of anonimous foundation in West Sussex, the United Kingdom, May 24, 2005.

55. "*Hikaku Power: Haibokushugi Tsuranuki Ginen Harae* [Non-nuclear Power: Sustain 'Defeatism' and Expel Skepticism of Other Countries]," *Asahi Shimbun*, August 4, 1999.

56. Remarks of a Japanese defense official at a meeting on May 11, 2007, Tokyo, Japan.

57. Michael J. Green and Katsuhisa Furukawa, "Chapter 12. Japan: New Nuclear Realism," in Muthiah Alagappa.ed., *The Long Shadow: Nuclear Weapons and Security in the 21st Century* (Stanford University Press, California 2008), 347-372.

58. Terumasa Nakanishi, "*Nihonkoku Kakubushou heno Ketsudan*," *Shokun!*, August 2003, pp. 22-37; and Nakanishi, ed., *'Nihon Kaku Busou' no Ronten* (Issues of Japan's Nuclear Armament) (Tokyo: PHP Publishing Co., 2006).

59. Nisohachi Hyodo, "'*Nihon Kaku Busou' no Gutaiteki Sukeju-ru* (A Concrete

Schedule of Japan's Nuclear Armament)," in Nakanishi, ed., *'Nihon Kaku Busou' no Ronten*, 174–76.

60. Kan Itoh, in Nakanishi, ed., *'Nihon Kaku Busou' no Ronten*, 137–38.

61. Hyodo, "*'Nihon Kaku Busou' no Gutaiteki Sukeju-ru*," 138.

62. Kan Itoh, "*No toha Iwanai Amerika*," *Shokun!*, August 2003, 117.

63. Kiyoshi Sugawa, *Beichou Kaisen* (Outbreak of U.S.-DPRK War) (Tokyo: Kodansha, 2007), 101–9.

64. Hideo Tamura, "*Kaku Danto Shisaku ni 3nen Ijo* (More than 3 Years Are Needed to Produce a Prototype Nuclear Warhead)," *Sankei Shimbun*, December 25, 2006.

65. Author's interview with Hideo Tamura, May 1, 2007, Tokyo, Japan.

66. A comment by a senior Japanese diplomat in a meeting in Tokyo, Japan, June 3, 2010, cited in Katsuhisa Furukawa, "Nuclear Arms Control and Disarmament: Views among Japan's National Security Community," Security Challenge, Vol. 6, No. 4, Summer 2010, 43.

67. "Joint Statement of the Security Consultative Committee---*Toward a Deeper and Broader U.S.-Japan Alliance: Building on 50 Years of Partnership*," June 21, 2011. (http://www.mofa.go.jp/region/n-america/us/security/pdfs/joint1106_01.pdf)

68. Ralph A. Cossa, "*Chairman's Report, U.S.-Japan Strategic Dialogue*," February 25-26, 2008, Maui, Hawaii, Pacific Forum CSIS.

69. Japanese Ministry of Defense, *Defense of Japan 2009*, 184, http://www.mod.go.jp/e/publ/w_paper/pdf/2009/28Part3_Chapter1_Sec2.pdf, accessed May 9, 2010.

70. Japanese National Institute for Defense Studies, *East Asian Strategic Outlook 2010* (Tokyo: Japan National Institute for Defense Studies, 2010), 240.

71. Author's email communication with Brad Roberts, Senior Fellow of the Institute of Defense Analysis, October 4, 2007.

72. U.S. Department of Defense, "Nuclear Posture Review Report," February 2010, xii.

73. Cossa, *Chairman's Report, U.S.-Japan Strategic Dialogue 2010*.

3 Will Taiwan Go Nuclear?

Arthur S. Ding

U.S. concerns about nuclear proliferation in Asia did not end with the Cold War. Instead, fears about the horizontal and vertical proliferation of nuclear weapons and associated delivery systems were reinforced by several proliferation "incidents," especially those involving North Korea. In 1994, it was revealed that North Korea was clandestinely developing nuclear weapons and medium-range ballistic missiles (the so-called Nodong missile). In 1998, North Korea tested a Taepong Dong missile that apparently possessed a 3,000 km range. The fact that this test occurred over Japanese territory made it especially alarming to those concerned about the threat of proliferation in Asia. In October 2006, North Korea tested a nuclear device, turning fears about a latent nuclear capability into reality.

Although North Korea is the primary proliferation menace faced by the international community today, other flash points in Asia have the potential for fostering proliferation. These areas of concern have not gone unnoticed by U.S. officials. Taiwan constitutes one of those flash points. Ever since 1949, when the communists established the People's Republic of China (PRC), an uneasy truce between Taiwan and China has persisted. China claims sovereignty over Taiwan and has never renounced the use of force against the island. From time to time, these tensions produce crises and even open hostilities. When officials on the mainland came to believe that Taiwan was moving closer to proclaiming its independence in the 1990s, the PRC launched a military exercise that led to the 1995–96 Taiwan Strait crisis.

Taiwanese officials thus face a challenging threat environment. The PRC's

military capability continues to grow, slowly but surely tilting the military balance in favor of the mainland. Beijing's growing diplomatic clout also can be
used to contain Taiwan on the international stage. Taiwan has few options if
relations deteriorate with the mainland. But one option remains on the table.
Given that Taiwan once had a nuclear weapons program, will officials in Taipei
opt for nuclear weapons to provide an existential deterrent?

Despite the fact that strategic logic might dictate the acquisition of a modest nuclear arsenal, Taiwan is unlikely to develop nuclear weapons for several
reasons. First, Taiwan lacks the industrial and scientific capability to produce
nuclear weapons. Second, there is a strong domestic antinuclear movement and
a national media that is likely to detect and alert the public to any change in
official policy. Third, there is an understanding that U.S. officials would vigorously oppose any effort made by Taiwan to acquire nuclear weapons. Fourth,
Taipei favors the development of ballistic missiles as a deterrent, although their
obvious role as a nuclear delivery system raises the issue of nuclear proliferation in the minds of many observers.

This chapter describes how officials in Taipei view threats to their security
and the related debate about defense policy that has occurred between 2000
and 2008. It begins by describing the security situation facing Taiwan,

THE THREAT ENVIRONMENT

According to the Republic of China's 2006 *National Security Report*, "China
poses the greatest challenges to Taiwan's national security. Other perils come
as a result of globalization and internal change."[1] The report notes that China's
military now possesses the ability to wage modern warfare across Asia. This is
a significant development. Traditionally, the People's Liberation Army (PLA)
was a mass infantry army designed to fight a protracted people's war of attri-
tion with low-tech weapons. The PLA possessed a limited ability to undertake
amphibious operations. It was relatively easy for Taiwan, with U.S. assistance,
to repel military action from the mainland. The report notes, however, that the
PLA is going "high-tech." The PLA has concentrated on developing its naval,
air, missile, information operations, electronic warfare, and aerospace capabilities.[2] China's military is attempting to integrate emerging technologies into
its modernization programs, posing a substantial and direct threat to Taiwan's
national security. The People's Liberation Army's new doctrine, fighting a high-
tech, information-based conflict, aims at enabling the PLA to fight a short-du-
ration, high-intensity conflict against high-tech adversaries.

Strategists on Taiwan believe that China might launch a "decapitation" strategy in the event of a decision to solve the Taiwan issue by force. This combined-arms offensive would involve the use of missiles to carry out precision strikes, along with operations undertaken by special operations forces and sleeper cells already in place in Taiwan. The main assault would then consist of coordinated airborne, heliborne, and amphibious attacks on Taiwan's political and economic centers of gravity. The goal of these attacks would not be to destroy Taiwan's military, but to paralyze Taiwan's government and economy, destroying the island's ability to continue to offer resistance. The U.S. Department of Defense's *Military Power of the People's Republic of China, 2006* seems to concur with this assessment: "China's strategic nuclear forces modernization, land- and sea-based access denial capabilities, and emerging precision-strike weapons have the potential to pose credible threats to modern militaries operating in the region."[3] A decapitation strategy thus holds out the prospect for China to achieve the goal of fighting a "quick war with quick results."[4]

Although the threat posed by the mainland continues to grow, Taipei has not turned to weapons of mass destruction as a response to the PLA's increasing power projection capability. The 2006 National Security Report clearly states that "Taiwan has pledged to never develop weapons of mass destruction—including nuclear and biochemical weapons—and it calls on China to openly renounce the development and use of nuclear, biochemical and other forms of weapons of mass destruction."[5]

THE NUCLEAR SHADOW

China's military modernization programs raise the issue of nuclear weapons. The *National Security Report* does not spell out the role of nuclear weapons in China's potential plans against Taiwan. The report points out that an electromagnetic pulse, created when a nuclear weapon is detonated at high altitudes, might be used to cripple Taiwan's command and control, financial, telecommunication, power, and transportation systems. Some Taiwanese analysts, however, downplay the likelihood of China's use of nuclear weapons against Taiwan. Shiang-yin Tseng, a former official in the Operations Directorate of the General Chief of Staff, notes that Beijing stated in the 2005 Anti-Secession Law (ASL) that it would not use weapons of mass destruction against Taiwan.[6]

The ASL, which was ratified on March 14, 2005, by China's National People's Congress, aims at regulating the China-Taiwan relationship from Beijing's perspective. Article 8 stipulates the conditions under which China could take "non-peaceful" actions to protect its interests in Taiwan: (1) "Taiwan independence"; the occurrence of major incidents entailing Taiwan's secession from China; or the possibilities for a peaceful reunification are completely exhausted.[7]

Article 9 of the ASL, however, requires Beijing to demonstrate restraint in using force to preserve its interests, noting that the PLA must take measures to protect the lives, property, and other legitimate rights and interests of Taiwan civilians and foreign nationals in Taiwan, and to minimize losses. Shiang-yin Tseng believes that Article 9 might preclude Beijing from using nuclear weapons against Taiwan. Instead of using nuclear, biological, and chemical warhead–tipped missiles to attack Taiwan, the PLA is more likely to use cruise missiles, which aim at economic and psychological targets, rather than short range ballistic missiles.[8]

Other analysts echo Tseng's argument by noting that it makes little military sense to respond in kind to the nuclear threat from the mainland. For example, Captain Bingyou Li notes that nuclear deterrence of Beijing is beyond Taipei's capability. Given China's size, creating a symbolic nuclear arsenal makes little military sense, while producing large numbers of nuclear weapons would exhaust Taiwan's resources. He also notes that China's first strike is likely to deprive Taiwan of the chance to launch a second strike. If Taiwan strikes first, it is likely to enrage the leadership in Beijing, leading to the total destruction of Taiwan.[9]

Nevertheless, some have advocated that Taiwan should develop nuclear weapons. But their opinions have never become mainstream in Taiwan. Dr. Holmes Liao is probably the most outspoken nuclear advocate. A computer engineer, he opines that the likelihood of China's launching a nuclear strike is high, and China's commitment to "no-first-use" of nuclear weapons should not be taken at face value.

Liao raises six reasons to support his opinion.[10] The first is that China has recently made nuclear threats related to Taiwan. Prior to the March 1996 Taiwan Strait crisis, for example, a PLA general threatened the United States, saying that Los Angeles is more important than Taipei. This implied breaking China's commitment of "no first use under any condition."[11] A second reason is that Beijing has used military force against Chinese citizens to achieve its objectives. The Chinese military brutally suppressed innocent people who were demonstrating for democracy in Tiananmen Square in June 1989. If the PLA could use tanks to crush Chinese protestors, goes this argument, why should we believe that nuclear weapons would not be used against the Taiwanese people?

A third reason relates to another Chinese commitment. If the PLA is not able to conquer Taiwan in a short period of time by conventional forces, they would break another commitment "not to use or threaten to use nuclear weapons against those without nuclear weapons," because the party leadership would be facing strong domestic pressure as a result of a prolonged war, and its regime security could be at risk.

Fourth, Liao suggests that the Taiwan scenario essentially involves basic security. He argues that in the 1960s Taiwan did attempt to develop nuclear weapons, and the United States also deployed some number of nuclear weapons on Taiwan for the purpose of deterring China from invading the island. Further, the United States has in the past threatened to launch nuclear weapons against China. At that time both Taiwan and the United States were serious about using nuclear weapons. Therefore, one should also believe that China would be willing to use nuclear weapons against Taiwan in anticipation of the fact that Beijing might not be first to introduce weapons in a conflict across the Taiwan Strait.

Related to the basic security argument, Liao suggests that national security should not rely upon other parties' good will. He is specifically worried about the potential ramifications of President William Clinton's "three-no's" policy, announced in the late 1990s,[12] and China's continuing military growth. He foresees that while the military balance in the Taiwan Strait is tilting toward China, and Taiwan becomes more and more reliant upon U.S. help, the possibility of the United States confronting China militarily for the sake of its own interests should not be excluded.

Fifth, Liao believes that peace between nuclear states can be maintained through a balance of terror provided by nuclear weapons. In a nuclear world, he argues, the size of nuclear arsenals may differ among nuclear states without having a significant impact on the efficacy of deterrent threats. As long as small powers have nuclear weapons, big powers can be deterred from invading the small powers, and peace can be maintained.

Sixth, for Liao nuclear weapons are not merely a means to accomplish a military goal; rather, they have political effects, serving to consolidate and boost morale so that Taiwan can be bailed out from serious political predicaments in the wake of a growing military imbalance in China's favor.

Some members of the former ruling party, the Democratic Progressive Party (DPP), may accept Liao's argument, but no one in the DPP has echoed his view in public. This position also might gain more adherents in the context of growing nationalism in Taiwan. Nevertheless, public debate about the nuclear issue has not emerged, despite occasional circumstances that might prompt a return to the issue (for example, the 1996 Taiwan Strait crisis that started when China test-fired short-range ballistic missiles across the Taiwan Strait).

Practical Obstacles

Several factors contribute to the absence of a nuclear debate in Taiwan. The foremost involves capability. Although Taiwan is often described as having the requisite technology to develop nuclear weapons, the country lacks the industrial capability and associated military infrastructure to field a credible nuclear arsenal. Taipei faces practical obstacles. For instance, the island lacks fissile materials. Taiwan's heavy water nuclear reactor that can enrich plutonium, which was located at the Institute for Nuclear Energy Research, has been dismantled. The Institute for Nuclear Energy Research itself has been downgraded to become a division of the civilian Atomic Energy Council of the executive branch, and its mission has been redirected toward commercial energy production. Experienced research staff also have left or retired. Waste fuel rods stored at Taipower Company, which are under the International Atomic Energy Agency's safeguard system, also are not available for use in a weapons program.[13]

Even if Taiwan managed to assemble a bomb, it lacks test facilities needed for systems integration or a full-scale test. Taiwan has no place to test a nuclear weapon, and it is impossible to test clandestinely. Simulated tests using super computers are possible; however, Taiwan has no relevant database to gauge designs tested in this way.

Many observers have described these obstacles. Chien Chung, a nuclear chemistry expert teaching at Taiwan's National Tsing Hua University, notes that although many research facilities exist on the island, today's researchers lack practical experience when it comes to designing and manufacturing nuclear weapons. He noted that it would take several billion U.S. dollars to "re-build the nuclear weapons program" given its complete disarray.[14] Another observer who is familiar with Taiwan's nuclear program also suggested that it would take eight to ten years to rebuild basic scientific and industrial capacity before any nuclear development program could be undertaken.[15]

Political Obstacles

Any effort to start a nuclear program also would encounter domestic political opposition. There is a strong antinuclear movement in Taiwan that keeps close contact with the global antinuclear movement. This opposition is also reflected in the DPP's nuclear-free homeland Taiwan program, which was endorsed in May 2003 with a pledge not to develop nuclear weapons.[16] Combined with highly competitive media, which closely watch sensational stories, it would probably be impossible to rebuild the nuclear weapons program secretly. Most Taiwanese believe that reviving the nuclear option is highly risky, with the likely costs far outweighing any potential gains.

U.S. policy on weapons of mass destruction also is likely to deter any effort to launch a nuclear program on the island. U.S. nonproliferation and counter-proliferation policy, combined with Taiwan's security dependence on Washington, would dissuade potential nuclear advocates. They know that it is counter-productive for Taiwan to advocate a nuclear option, especially in the context of an improving U.S.-China relationship.[17] Taipei also understands that a nuclear program would tarnish its international image, which would hurt ongoing efforts to gain international support and sympathy.[18]

As a Kuomintang candidate in the 2008 presidential election, President Ying-jeou Ma stated in his campaign platform that he would not pursue a nuclear option. He proposed a nuclear zone in the Taiwan Strait and in East Asia, reiterated a long-term policy of not developing weapons of mass destruction, and pledged to abide by UN Security Council Resolution 1540 by taking steps to safeguard its commercial and research facilities.[19]

Traditional considerations reinforced President Ying-jeou Ma's commitment after he assumed the presidency. The global financial meltdown and subsequent economic downturn in that began in 2007 eliminated the possibility that resources would be devoted to developing nuclear weapons–related industrial and scientific capabilities. Domestic political divisions have created incentives for closer oversight of sensitive policy. President Barak Obama's pledge to pursue a nuclear free world has also created additional nonproliferation incentives in Taipai. After taking the presidency, he reiterated the need to rebuild Taiwan's relationship with the United States, a relationship that was severely strained when his predecessor, President Shui-bian Chen, championed an independence-oriented foreign policy. Missile programs also remain the focus of defense policy in Taiwan.[20]

DETERRENCE AND THE MISSILE PROGRAM

A new strategy debate started in 2002 after the Ministry of National Defense amended its military strategy "Resolute Defense, Effective Deterrence" to "Effective Deterrence, Resolute Defense." This strategy advocated the development of an active defense posture beginning in 2002.[21] The Ministry gives a rather long "definition" to the new strategy. "'Effective deterrence' refers to the building of counterstrike and defensive capabilities with deterring effects, and actively researching and developing *long-range, precision, deep strike capabilities* (emphasis added) to effectively disintegrate or stagnate enemy forces or firepower advancements, so that enemies will forgo all military options after rational battle damage and casualty estimation." Resolute defense is defined in this manner: "The armed forces also combine all-out defense power and joint war-fighting capabilities to firmly conduct homeland defense, and to achieve repellence, deterrence, and destruction of enemy forces."[22]

The role of missiles in defense has replaced that of nuclear weapons as the focus of the deterrence debate. One side of the debate advocates the use of missiles to develop a limited punishment force.[23] Punishment advocates believe that as China continues to modernize its military, the strategic balance will shift in China's favor by 2015, making it difficult for Taiwan to withstand China's initial strike. Limited punishment advocates believe a survivable conventional missile force that holds at risk China's "valuable economic targets" could serve as a viable deterrent. Advocates of the strategy also seem to believe that other nations might put pressure on the People's Republic in a crisis to avoid economic dislocation caused by a retaliatory strike launched by Taiwan. Outside governments, "due to economic investments in China, would have significant incentive to intervene when they perceive signs of a potential conflict."[24]

Limited punishment advocates also understand that their preferred strategy is not without pitfalls. China could launch a preventive assault to wipe out Taiwan's nascent missile capability, or seek diplomatic and economic sanctions to pressure Taipei to abandon a limited punishment strategy. Despite the above consequence and constraint, this school upholds the limited punishment option as a deterrence strategy. They believe that the benefits of the strategy would outweigh the slight exacerbation of the security dilemma that would be produced by any change in defense posture.[25]

Various actions also could be undertaken to mitigate externalities, such as limiting the range of Taiwan's ballistic missiles and declaring a "no-first-use" policy. Slightly less reassuring is the notion that a preventive strike by the Chinese military could be avoided by concealing the missile program until it is fully operational.

Another approach to deterrence calls for the development of a capability to hit Chinese military targets located opposite Taiwan. That capability would be part of an active defense strategy. The goal of active defense is to thwart the adversary's initial military action. According to Chih-heng Yang and Tzu-yun Su, "An offensive defense strategy is not the same as a comprehensive attack. On the contrary, the attack is limited and confined only to military targets. For example, the enemy's nuclear forces would be singled out in the event of a nuclear war. But, in a conventional war, the focus of strikes would be the adversary's invasion force."[26] For active defense advocates, this approach offers the best way to defend Taiwan's territorial integrity and air space because it does not surrender all initiative to the mainland.[27]

Active defense advocates also are concerned about the limited barrier to invasion provided by the Taiwan Strait. At cruising speed, for instance, it takes modern combat aircraft only about twenty minutes to cross the Strait. At tactical operational speeds, that time is significantly reduced. Because Taiwan lacks strategic depth, active defense advocates believe the best option is to extend the line of defense and the line of fire as far away as possible from Taiwan to delay the enemy's onslaught.[28] The objectives behind active defense would be to delay the adversary's opening moves at the outset of the conflict. According to Chih-heng Yang and Tzu-yun Su, "In the event of a conflict in the Taiwan Strait, Taiwan's resources are not sufficient to destroy Mainland China's military capabilities. Taiwan's war objectives should therefore focus on disrupting the enemy's operational plans and disturbing his operation tempo in order to put the enemy off balance. The targets should be the enemy's airfields, ports, command and control centers, and communication nodes."[29] By giving some initiative to Taiwan, active defense would thus force China to divert resources to its own air defenses, reducing the mainland's investment in offensive systems, thereby reducing the potential threat faced by Taiwan's military.[30]

Active defense advocates believe that Taiwan is far behind China. In their opinion it is absurd to say that offensive capabilities somehow upset the military balance in the Taiwan Strait. There is no military "balance" in the Taiwan Strait, according to this perspective, only a growing gap between China's armed forces and Taiwan's increasingly obsolete military capabilities.[31]

MISSILE TECHNOLOGY

Cruise and ballistic missiles play a critical role in Taiwan's defense strategy. On April 16–20, 2007, for instance, a military exercise code-named Hanguang 23 featured a missile exchange as the central aspect of the simulation. In the war game, the Red team launched missile attacks against Blue team's command post, missile launch sites, airfields, and radars, causing major damage. In response, the Blue team launched tactical shore-based missiles for fire suppression and jet fighters to provide support for the offshore islands and to establish air superiority across the Taiwan Strait.[32] This exercise reflects emerging defense capabilities. In May 2005, for example, Defense Minister Li Jye testified to Parliament that Taiwan was developing a "strategic weapon," and this "strategic weapon" was not a short-range tactical missile; rather, it was a "strategic" and "long-range" missile.[33]

It is possible that Li Jye was referring to the HF-2E land attack cruise missile with a range of 600–800 km that is scheduled to be upgraded to a range of 1,000 km. It has reportedly passed operational testing, and some may have already been deployed.[34] This missile, which can be launched from ground, air, and sea platforms, can be equipped with high-explosive, cluster, or fuel-air explosive warheads.[35] A derivative cruise missile, the HF-3 is a supersonic antiship missile with a range of 500 km. At present, it is being tested for various functions, including compatibility with radar and fire control systems on warships. Taiwan reportedly planned to produce 120 HF-3 missiles targeting China's naval bases.[36] It has been suggested that the HF-3's range also can be extended to 1,000 km.[37]

Taiwan is currently developing two types of ballistic missiles. The first is the Tiching missile, which probably has a range of 1,000 km. There are apparently plans to produce 30 Tiching missiles, along with 120 copies of a "shorter-range" version of the weapon.[38] The second is a ballistic missile with a range of 300–600 km. Taiwan's media reported that on January 18, 2007, a two-stage rocket based on the indigenously developed Tien Kung (Sky Bow)-2 SAM missile was tested, and that it reached an altitude of 282 km. This altitude is equivalent to a range of between 300 and 600 km. The program reportedly began in 1998.[39]

CONCLUSION

Although Taiwan's missile program was revived in the late 1990s, it accelerated when the DPP became the ruling party in 2000. This reflects the DPP's "myth-thinking" when it comes to its perception of national security affairs. One fundamental tenet of this perspective is that pre-emptive and counterstrike capabilities can deter an adversary. Another belief is that offensive weapons and strategies are cost-effective on the margins, allowing Taiwan to compete with the more economically powerful People's Republic. According to Yihsiung Lai,

"In the case of the Theater Missile Defense system, it costs more than developing offensive missiles, and guaranteed defense cannot be ensured. Generally
speaking, it takes three defensive missiles to hit one attacking missile."[40]

U.S. officials are concerned about the potential impact of Taiwan's development of longer range ballistic and cruise missiles and associated deterrent strategies. U.S. officials have conveyed several reasons for their opposition: Taiwan
cannot have a credible deterrent without nuclear weapons; the United States
does not support Taiwanese nuclear capability; Taipei's acquisition of nuclear
weapons is a discernible path to a nuclear arms race; Taiwan cannot hold at risk
a militarily significant portion of China's military forces; and there would be a
general increase in crisis instability across the Taiwan Strait. According to Dennis Wilder, a member of the George W. Bush administration's National Security
Council, "We think that developing defensive capabilities is the right thing to
do. We think that offensive capabilities on either side of the Strait are destabilizing and therefore not in the interest of peace and security. So when you ask
me whether I am for offensive missiles, I am not for offensive missiles on the
Chinese side of the Strait, and I am not for offensive missiles on the Taiwan side
of the Strait. But appropriate defense capabilities are certainly the right of the
people of Taiwan."[41] From the U.S. perspective, Taiwan would be better served
by strengthening its defensive capability.[42]

U.S. officials also express lingering concerns about Taiwan's nuclear program.
Because U.S. observers generally do not believe that Taiwan's conventional
missiles alone can deter China, they believe that Taiwan might be creating a
more promising nuclear option by first developing delivery systems commonly
associated with nuclear weapons. This is probably why U.S. agencies closely
monitor Taiwan's civilian nuclear programs despite the fact that critical nuclear
research facilities have already been dismantled following U.S. demands.

Although Taipei is aware of these U.S. concerns, Taiwanese political leaders
cannot survive if they insist on adopting a purely defensive posture in response
to an attack. A missile program and associated pre-emptive strategies are politically necessary, regardless of how limited are the capabilities actually fielded.[43]
Additionally, Taiwan's concerns about the potential "defection" of the United
States during a crisis with the mainland increases the attraction of an independent retaliatory force. Similarly, Taipei has incentives never to allow its "nuclear
potential" to be forgotten, even though a "nuclear option" exists far more as an
idea than a reality.

NOTES

1. Taiwan National Security Council of the Presidential Office, *2006 National Security Report*, May 2006, 3, http://www.president.gov.tw/en/prog/news_release/appendix/2006%20National%20Security%20Report.pdf, accessed August 27, 2007.

2. Ibid., 32.

3. U.S. Department of Defense, *Military Power of the People's Republic of China, 2006*, p. I, http://www.dod.mil/pubs/pdfs/China%20Report%20202006.pdf, accessed August 28, 2007.

4. Taiwan National Security Council, *2006 National Security Report*, 41.

5. Ibid., 89–90.

6. Shiang-yin Tseng, "The Enhancement of Taiwan's Missile Defense," *Taiwan Defense Affairs*, 5, no. 3 (Spring 2005), 97.

7. The English translation of the ASL is drawn from the College of Foreign Languages, Fujian Normal University, http://www.fli.com.cn/Fli/Class1/Class82/740.html, accessed August 28, 2007.

8. Shiang-yin Tseng, "The Enhancement of Taiwan's Missile Defense," 97.

9. Bingyou Li, "Analysis of Military Conflict in the Taiwan Strait and Taiwan's Deterrence Strategy," *Navy Professional Journal*, 39, no. 8 (August 2005), http://www.mnd.gov.tw/Mp/MPPeriodical.aspx?id=8, accessed August 21, 2007.

10. Holmes Liao, "Taiwan Should Develop Nuclear Weapon," *Defense International*, no. 175 (March 1999), 18–21, cited from http://www.taiwanesevoice.net/cyber/09/19990300.htm, accessed August 18, 2007.

11. For a statement of China's nuclear weapons policy, see *China's National Defense in 2006*, http://military.people.com.cn/BIG5/1076/52984/5230074.html, accessed September 4, 2007.

12. The "Three No's" policy is that the U.S. government does not support the positions of "Taiwan independence," of "one China, one Taiwan" or "Two Chinas," nor of Taiwan's joining any international organizations of sovereign nations.

13. This section draws on Lin Jianchang, "Can Taiwan Produce a Nuclear Weapon?" *China Times*, October 26, 2006, 15.

14. Xu Shaoxuan, "Chien Chung: Taiwan's Nuclear Capability Used to Be US Leverage against China," *Liberty Times*, October 17, 2004, http://www.libertytimes.com.tw/2004/new/oct/17/today-f03.htm, accessed August 18, 2007.

15. Xu Shaoxuan, no title, *Liberty Times*, October 17, 2004, http://www.libertytimes.com.tw/2004/new/oct/17/today-f03.htm, accessed August 18, 2007.

16. Chien Chung, "Proliferation of Weapons of Mass Destruction in the Second Nuclear Age in Asia," *Taiwan Defense Affairs*, 5, no. 3, 22–23, http://www.itdss.org.tw/pub/05_03_p1.pdf, accessed August 21, 2007.

17. Xu Shaoxuan, "Chien Chung."

18. Xu Shaoxuan, "Chien Chung"; and Chien Chung, "Proliferation of Weapons of Mass Destruction in the Second Nuclear Age in Asia."

19. Candidate Ma's homepage, http://2008.ma19.net/policy4you/defence, accessed May 2, 2010.

20. *Chinese Television System*, March 29, 2010, http://news.cts.com.tw/cna/politics/201003/201003290438797.html, accessed May 2, 2010.

21. For an official version of Taiwan's military strategy development, and following explanation of the military strategy, see *2006 National Defense Report, the Republic of China*, ch. 5, http://report.mnd.gov.tw, accessed August 30, 2007.

22. Ibid.

23. Chi-hsiung Shih, "The Reality and Feasibility of Deterring China: Reexamining the Meaning of Deterrence in Taiwan's Defense," *Taiwan Defense Affairs*, 5, no. 1 (Autumn 2004), 22–50, http://www.itdss.org.tw/pub/05_01_P1.pdf, accessed August 18, 2007.

24. Ibid.

25. Ibid.

26. Chih-heng Yang and Tzu-yun Su, "Command the Air over Taiwan," *Taiwan Defense Affairs*, 3, no. 2 (Winter 2002/2003), http://www.taiwanus.net/Taiwan_Future/national_defence/2002/03_02/03_02_08_03.htm, accessed August 21, 2007.

27. Ibid.

28. Ibid.

29. Ibid.

30. Tzu-yun Su, "Taiwan's Defense and Perspective on East Asian Security," read at the Taiwan National Security Institute and Forum for Asian Security, cosponsored by the International Symposium on Taiwan's Security and Democracy, Taipei, Taiwan, January 17, 2004, http://www.wufi.org.tw/tjsf/040117g.htm, accessed August 21, 2007.

31. "Taiwan Still Needs a Good Offense," *Taipei Times*, January 14, 2006.

32. Zongming Wang, "Hanguang 23: MND Released Wargame, TSMFS Unfolded," *ET Today News*, April 24, 2007. This author would like to thank Mr. D. Y. Lu for providing this news.

33. Mingjie Wu, "Taiwan Develops Long Range Strategic Missile," *China Times*, May 3, 2005, http://news.chinatimes.com/Chinatimes/newslist/newslist-content/0,3546,110501+112005050300006,00.html, accessed September 3, 2007.

34. News media reported that 500 HF-2E missiles would be produced. Nadia Tsao and Shaoxuan Xu, "US Reportedly Opposed Taiwan Developing Surface to Surface Missiles," *Liberty Times*, June 21, 2006, http://www.libertytimes.com.tw/2006/new/jun/21/today-p13.htm, accessed September 3, 2007.

35. It was reported that President Chen Shui-bian has visited the missile development institute, Chung Shan Institute for Science and Technology, several times to inspect the HF-2E development. D. Y. Lu, "Concerned about Missile Development, Presi-

dent Chen Inspected the Program Many Times," *UDN*, June 21, 2006, and "HF-2E Tested Last Month, Able to Threaten Shanghai and Shenzhen," *UDN*, March 3, 2007.

36. Nadia Tsao and Shaoxuan Xu, "US Reportedly Opposed Taiwan Developing Surface to Surface Missiles."

37. D. Y. Lu, "HF-3 Missile Is Being Tested on Warship," *UDN*, July 31, 2006.

38. Nadia Tsao and Shaoxuan Xu, "US Reportedly Opposed Taiwan Developing Surface to Surface Missiles."

39. The purpose of this test was reportedly to test payload capability. Zhu Ming, "Technological Breakthrough in Ballistic Missile, Able to Produce Missile with a Range of 300–600 Km, Not Easily Intercepted by the Enemy," *Apple Daily*, February 13, 2006, http://www.appledaily.com.tw/News/index.cfm?Fuseaction=Article&showdate=20060213&Sec_ID=5&NewsType=twapple&loc=TP&PageType=new&Art_ID=2400328, accessed February 13, 2006.

40. This section draws from Yihsiung Lai, "On Taiwan's Strategy and Policy of Defensive Deterrence," read at the Taiwan National Security Institute and Forum for Asian Security, cosponsored by the International Symposium on Taiwan's Security and Democracy, Taipei, Taiwan, January 17, 2004, http://www.wufi.org.tw/tjsf/040117c.htm, accessed September 3, 2007.

41. Cited from AIT Director Stephen Young, May 3, 2007, press conference, http://www.ait.org.tw/en/news/officialtext/viewer.aspx?id=2007050301, accessed September 3, 2007.

42. Betty Lin, "Taiwan Deploys Special Missiles, the US Opposes Privately," *UDN*, October 21, 2006; Chunglun Kuo, "Missile Development and Taiwan's Offensive Doctrine," *China Times*, June 21, 2006; and Simon Montlake, "Next Troublesome Missile Test: Taiwan?" *Christian Science Monitor*, July 31, 2006.

43. Chunglun Kuo, "Missile Development and Taiwan's Offensive Doctrine."

4 Nuclear Proliferation and the Middle East's Security Dilemma: The Case of Saudi Arabia

James A. Russell

Between the summer of 2006 and the spring of 2007, events confirmed the worst fears of many observers who have long warned about a cascade of new nuclear proliferation throughout the Persian Gulf and the Middle East. In a region racked with open warfare, persistent interstate rivalries, powerful nonstate actors, and ominous intrastate tensions, countries throughout the Persian Gulf and Middle East now seem united on at least one issue: the need to develop their own nuclear power programs. In regional capitals such as Rabat, Algiers, Cairo, Riyadh, Abu Dhabi, Manama, Doha, Muscat, and Amman, political leaders announced their intention to start development of indigenous nuclear programs and have been beating a path to the International Atomic Energy Agency's (IAEA) door, seeking information on creating a significant nuclear research program.

These regional developments come amid growing concern that efforts to control the spread of nuclear weapons have failed and that the Nuclear Nonproliferation Treaty (NPT) is becoming irrelevant. Some believe that the international system today is perched on a nuclear "tipping point." In other words, they are concerned that states might be on the verge of abandoning normative restraints against developing nuclear weapons, resulting in a "proliferation epidemic" and a world of many nuclear powers.[1] Despite assurances by Middle Eastern leaders that their programs will represent "models" for other states seeking peaceful nuclear programs,"[2] many fear that the objective of developing commercial nuclear power represents a thinly veiled effort to acquire their own fissile material—the essential building block of nuclear weapons. Because the NPT does not deny states parties in good standing the right to undertake nuclear research, technologies to develop nuclear power are readily available to all NPT signatories regardless of the fact that it is impossible to anticipate the ultimate result of this research.

The so-called renaissance in commercial nuclear power programs represents a change in the region's nuclear posture. Most states in the region have for years espoused the goal of creating a nuclear-weapons-free zone in the Middle East, but the turn toward commercial nuclear power promises to raise the level of nuclear knowledge across the globe. Nevertheless, by emphasizing the peaceful nature of their intentions and their commitment to international oversight, Middle Eastern states have renounced the nuclear option by rejecting a nuclear "hedging" strategy as a first step toward embracing an ambiguous nuclear posture.[3] A nuclear hedging strategy means that states take full advantage of the rights afforded them under the NPT to expand their existing programs by building the physical infrastructure, developing the human capital, and acquiring the necessary technology for large-scale nuclear power programs. Once the programs mature and develop, states are then positioned to become "latent" nuclear powers, which can develop nuclear weapons on relatively short notice outside of international oversight if they choose to do so. Others refer to this phenomenon as states achieving "virtual" nuclear arsenals—another term that seeks to describe the shrinking distance between nuclear weapons programs and peaceful nuclear programs that give states the ability to build a nuclear bomb.[4]

Saudi Arabia is an important proliferation candidate and is the most likely country to move the Middle East toward an altered nuclear posture. Saudi Arabia is the leader of the Sunni-led, oil- and natural gas–rich Arab Gulf States (Kuwait, United Arab Emirates, and Qatar), which account for nearly 50 percent of all known oil reserves and currently provide 11–13 million barrels per day to world export markets. Saudi Arabia's growing economic importance is mirrored by its steadily increasing political influence in the Arab world— trends that promise to continue through 2020. As a regional political leader, the smaller regional states can be expected to increasingly look to Riyadh for leadership.

Recent statements indicate that Saudi Arabia and the Gulf States are embracing an evolving nuclear posture that departs from the region's embrace of nonproliferation norms, especially the creation of a nuclear-weapons-free zone in the Middle East. In December 2006, the Gulf Cooperation Council (GCC) announced its intention to develop nuclear energy. Saudi Foreign Minister

Saud al-Faisal told reporters at the conclusion of the summit: "This is not a se-cret and we are doing this out in the open. Our aim is to obtain the technology for peaceful purposes, no more no less. . . . We want no bombs. . . . Our policy is to have a region free from weapons of mass destruction."[5] Following the sum-mit, the Gulf States reached agreement to work with the IAEA on a nuclear power plan.

This chapter places the Saudi case in a wider regional and theoretical context to determine if there is any systemic explanation for the region's sudden inter-est in nuclear power. Political scientists offer a variety of theories to explain nuclear proliferation. Some believe that global-systemic forces are inexorably pushing states toward nuclear weapons. Others point to particular threats to security that prompt leaders to make the cost-benefit calculus to develop nu-clear capabilities. Other scholars emphasize the role of internal factors such as perceptions, behavioral norms, and domestic and organizational politics that shape the decision-making calculus of leaders in ways that both discourage them from pursuing, and encourage them to pursue, nuclear weapons. These analytical frameworks will be applied to the Gulf case to determine their rel-evance and explanatory power. The chapter will then assess which of the theo-retical frameworks or combination thereof offers the most compelling argu-ment to predict likely outcomes in Riyadh and the Gulf.

THE REGION'S EVOLVING NUCLEAR POSTURE

The December 2006 announcement by the Gulf Cooperation Council (GCC) that it was going to pursue nuclear energy must be placed in the context of preceding events. In the eighteen months before the announcement, a large number of states expressed interest in nuclear power. In September 2006, then-Egyptian President Hosni Mubarak's son, Jamal Mubarak, announced Egypt's intentions to revive its dormant nuclear program, which was abandoned in 1986. He described an ambitious plan to build three nuclear power plants by 2020 that will generate 1,800 megawatts of electricity. The first of these plants is to be located in the city of Al-Dabah. Mubarak's announcement followed sev-eral forceful statements by the regime's opponents calling for Egypt to develop its own nuclear deterrent. In July 2006, Dr. Hamdi Hassan, spokesman for the Muslim Brotherhood parliamentary caucus, stated, "We are ready to starve in order to own a nuclear weapon that will represent a real deterrent and will be decisive in the Arab-Israeli conflict." Other prominent Muslim Brotherhood leaders have called for the development of nuclear weapons, ridiculing the

Mubarak regime's policy of trying to have the Middle East declared a WMD-Free zone.[6]

Egypt operates two nuclear research reactors. Its newest reactor became operational in 1997, with construction and design assistance provided by the Argentinian company Investigación Aplicada. Egypt is an NPT signatory.

In November 2006, Algeria announced intentions to expand its own nuclear energy program—an announcement immediately followed by an offer extended by Iranian President Mahmoud Ahmadinejad to assist in Algeria's program. Tehran, however, faces stiff competition for the business. In January 2007, Russian Minister of Industry and Power Viktor Khristenko visited Algiers, where he concluded an agreement governing cooperation on developing nuclear energy. According to Khristenko, "We have agreed within the framework of the memorandum to begin contacts between experts in the two countries to study the possibilities of bilateral cooperation and to determine the areas of possible cooperation in this [nuclear] context and I hope that we can begin this work soon."[7] Algeria also approached South Korea for nuclear cooperation in mid-2006.[8]

Algeria has been operating two research reactors under IAEA supervision since the mid-1990s. Investigación Aplicada provided a 1-megawatt reactor that became operational in 1989; a second 15-megawatt reactor provided by China is located near Birine at Ain Oussera in a remote area of the Atlas Mountains about 90 miles south of Algiers. Discovery of surface-to-air missiles at the site in the early 1990s led to suspicions that Algeria was developing nuclear weapons at the Ain Oussera facility. Under pressure from the United States, Algeria acceded to the NPT and placed its facilities under IAEA safeguards in 1992.[9]

Morocco first indicated its intention to expand its nuclear power program in April 2006. These plans received a boost in September 2006 during Russian President Vladimir Putin's visit to Rabat. A Russian spokesman indicated that Russia's nuclear export agency, Atomstroiexport, would join in the bidding for Morocco's first nuclear power station, which Rabat hopes will become operational by 2016.[10] Morocco operates a small 2-megawatt reactor provided by the United States under IAEA safeguards.

Member states of the GCC announced plans to develop their own nuclear power programs under IAEA supervision.[11] In early 2007, GCC Secretary General Abderaham Al-Attiyya announced preliminary plans for the beginning of nuclear power plant construction by 2009, an ambitious timetable given the lack of a nuclear infrastructure in the Gulf. Saudi Foreign Minister Saudi al-

Faisal told reporters that Russian President Vladimir Putin's February 2007 visit to Saudi Arabia—the first ever official visit of a Russian head of state to the Kingdom—signaled that the GCC and the Saudis would find a ready supplier for all their nuclear needs in Russia. Of the GCC member countries, only Saudi Arabia is known to have an active nuclear research program, and none are believed to have nuclear reactors. All are NPT signatories.

Jordan's King Abdullah announced in the Israeli press in January 2007 that Jordan will join its Arab neighbors in pursuing a nuclear power program. Following the announcement, a spokesman for Jordan's Energy Ministry announced the formation of a committee to begin studies on the construction of a 600-megawatt reactor. Pakistani officials have offered to assist in the development of Jordan's program. The government's announcement received widespread praise from such diverse sources as the Jordanian Communist Party and the Islamic Action Party—the Jordanian arm of the Muslim Brotherhood. [12] Like other regional states, Jordan promises to observe IAEA-administered safeguards.

EXPLANATORY FRAMEWORKS

Recent developments in the Middle East offer an opportunity to assess alternative explanations as to why states initiate nuclear programs. [13] Political scientists often rely on some variant of realism to explain the phenomenon. Realism argues that states are motivated primarily by self-interest and exist in an anarchical, self-help system. [14] The modern form of realism, the so-called neorealist paradigm developed by Kenneth Waltz, holds that actions taken by states to protect and enhance their security in turn create insecurity for surrounding states that causes states to balance and counterbalance each other in a never-ending cycle. [15] This so-called security dilemma and the relative distribution of power in the international system is a driving structural dynamic that governs the interactions of states. States pursue security through a combination of arms buildups and political-military alliances. Pursuit of nuclear weapons—the ultimate guarantor of state security—or the acquisition of nuclear partners is explained under realist theory as a logical result of states' quest for security. For realists, political leaders follow a rational decision-making process to apportion available resources to meet the security needs of the state.

In 1981, Waltz suggested that underlying dynamics of the international system would inevitably result in a world of many nuclear states. He argued that nuclear proliferation would not necessarily lead to a more unstable international environment, since possession of nuclear weapons would make the costs of war high for states and would thus naturally weight the decision-making cost-benefit analysis of leaders against war. [16] Other political scientists, such as John Mearsheimer, have offered variations on Waltz's theme, noting that controlled proliferation could in certain cases stabilize international politics. [17] Scott Sagan summarized the arguments behind this explanatory framework as the "security model" for nuclear proliferation. [18]

Under neorealist theory, calculations about the relative balance of power between states form part of the explanatory logic of the paradigm as applied to nuclear proliferation. For example, Kurt Campbell argues that the hegemonic power of the United States and the nature of its security policy constitute the most important factors for states in deciding whether or not to acquire nuclear weapons. [19] Campbell draws upon the neorealist argument by emphasizing the role that U.S. hegemonic power plays in the calculations that states make regarding their security. Using his neorealist logic, it follows that states will exercise nuclear restraint as long as they believe that the distribution of power in the international system remains heavily weighted in favor of the United States. The second half of the equation is equally important—that U.S. hegemonic power must be credibly operationalized through a policy that provides security guarantees backed by a full range of military tools, including an extended nuclear deterrent. [20] Stated differently, states will exercise restraint and regard U.S. commitments as credible so long as they believe that the United States continues to exercise preponderant power relative to other actors. The opposite is also true under the argument—that is, that a structural change in the global balance of power that undermined American power would lead to a decline in the credibility of the U.S. extended deterrent posture, thereby removing a restraint to nuclear proliferation. While Campbell recognizes other variables, such as a breakdown in the NPT, the erosion of regional or global security, domestic imperatives, and the availability of technology, he sides with the neorealists by asserting that "misgivings and concerns about the long-term direction of U.S. policy on global strategy and nuclear policy are, and will continue to be, the single most decisive factor guiding the direction of would-be proliferators—both rogue and responsible." [21]

There are other variations on the neorealist theme. Like Waltz, Benjamen Frankel argued in the early 1990s that nuclear proliferation was all but inevitable, suggesting that post–Cold War structural dynamics would give added impetus to nuclear proliferation. [22] Frankel argued that Cold War nuclear guarantees extended by the United States and the Soviet Union represented a systemic and artificial restraint on the global demand for nuclear weapons. He believed that the end of the Cold War would force a reversion of the international system back to its more true anarchical form, a shift that would exacerbate the security dilemma for all states. States' pursuit of security would inevitably take place within an international framework featuring increased technology flows that would spread weapons material and know-how around the world more easily than during the Cold War. The result, Frankel argued, would be an acceleration in proliferation of nuclear and other unconventional weapons and the inevitable erosion of the NPT.[23]

An enduring critique of the realist explanation for proliferation is the short shrift the theory accords to internal factors such as domestic politics, organizational and bureaucratic dynamics, and leadership perceptions in shaping state responses to security threats. Sagan drew upon these critiques in his argument that the explanatory power of the security model is incomplete: "Nuclear weapons . . . are political objects of considerable importance in domestic debates and internal bureaucratic struggles and can also serve as international normative symbols of modernity and identity."[24] Sagan proposed an additional "Domestic Politics Model" of nuclear proliferation that explains state actions as the result of an intragovernmental bargaining process between and among civilian and military organizations.[25] In Sagan's view, domestic political actors and communities can coalesce around interests and positions that shape the policies and programs of states in ways that reinforce internal demand to acquire nuclear weapons.[26] Acknowledging that the domestic politics model is incomplete and lacks theoretical depth, he nonetheless encourages researchers to embrace an added layer of complexity introduced by these considerations into an explanatory framework of nuclear proliferation.[27]

A variant on Sagan's domestic politics theme is offered by those that draw upon neoliberal and constructivist theories. Neoliberalists reject the realist characterization of the systemic anarchy that drives the dynamics of the security dilemma. Instead, they believe that systemic anarchy can be mitigated by international regimes that constrain competition and conflict.[28] Neoliberals adopt some of the ideas of the constructivist school. They suggest that shared values and norms are the product of cooperation and their resulting normative-based regimes like the NPT can serve as useful vehicles to reduce the incentives for states to pursue nuclear weapons. Glen Chafetz articulated this point of view when he stated that "the pacifying effects of democracy and complex interdependence mean that the number of states fearful or ambitious enough to seek nuclear weapons will decline rather than increase as a result of the end of the Cold War."[29] Chafetz suggested that the development of behavioral norms within established democracies would manifest themselves in the form of political structures and ideologies that would make like-minded states less apt to fall prey to the neorealist bare-knuckled struggle for power and survival. According to Chafetz, these norms would make states less drawn to nuclear weapons.[30]

While the neoliberals argue that factors internal to the state can be important in shaping decisions by political leaders to acquire nuclear weapons, they still believe that structural dynamics in the international system are the primary force impelling states either to acquire or forgo nuclear weapons. Sagan offered up a third causative model for nuclear proliferation—"The Norms Model"— that emphasizes the role of factors internal to the state, such as shared beliefs, symbols, and identity.[31] The Norms Model suggests that state policy is determined by accepted norms and beliefs concerning legitimate and appropriate behavior in international relations.[32] Others describe this argument as the "idealist" proliferation framework. In other words, state leaders' perceptions about the usefulness of the bomb and the symbolic role that nuclear weapons can play in state identity are the key variables that determine whether states proliferate.[33] These perceptions are shaped by international and domestic forces, but the "idealist" framework generally emphasizes the role that domestic political, economic, and cultural factors play in shaping leaders' perceptions and the resulting cost-benefit calculus that frames decisions on whether and when to pursue nuclear weapons or, alternatively, to subscribe to a nuclear nonproliferation regime.[34]

REGIONAL NUCLEAR DYNAMICS

Despite being at the center of the globe's most enduring conflicts and three major regional wars, the Middle East has seen only limited nuclear proliferation.[35] Middle Eastern states have lived under the threat of nuclear weapons at least since 1968, when Israel apparently achieved a nuclear capability.[36] Other nearby states also possess nuclear weapons. India exploded a nuclear device in 1974, and Pakistan conducted a nuclear test in 1998. Nevertheless, these developments did not spur regional proliferation. While the realist paradigm might have predicted a cascade of new nuclear states, no states in or around the region responded in kind. Part of the reason that a nuclear cascade did not follow is that the security dilemma was not operating in the region, or at least not with the negative dynamics predicted by realist theory. Moreover, with the exception of Libya, none of the states ever developed significant internal bureaucratic or political constituencies (like India and Pakistan) that provided an added impetus to push governments toward robust nuclear programs.[37] This would obviate the logic of Sagan's domestic politics model throughout the region. Egypt actually abandoned its small nuclear program in 1986 following the Chernobyl disaster in the Soviet Union.

The context for regional restraint remains rooted in the outsourcing of "strategic" security by states to outside powers that resulted in a series of cross-cutting security guarantees extended by the United States and the Soviet Union beginning in the 1950s. During the Cold War, the United States and the Soviet Union carved up de facto regional alliance blocs that were glued together by nuclear guarantees. Various parts of the region have been under an implied nuclear umbrella for the last 50 years, which is one reason for the restraint in the region.[38] Restraint in developing nuclear weapons, however, did not extend to other unconventional weapons. Between 1970 and 2000, Syria, Iraq, and Iran all developed or acquired chemical and biological weapons and long-range missiles that were directed at a wide variety of regional adversaries. Yet, the existence of these programs and the actual use of unconventional weapons in the Iran-Iraq War and by Saddam against his internal opponents did not prompt states in the region to launch crash nuclear programs. In addition, while Iran's march toward nuclear weapons appears to have accelerated during the last 48 months,[39] its nuclear ambitions as manifested by the very visible development of a redundant and sophisticated nuclear infrastructure have been transparent to all regional states for the last 30 years.

IRAQ AND THE ALTERED LANDSCAPE
OF REGIONAL SECURITY

Realism combined with contributing insights from those frameworks emphasizing internal political factors offers powerful and compelling explanations for nuclear restraint in the Middle East. Due to changes in the global, regional, and intrastate environments, however, Middle Eastern states are now presented with a series of incentives that militate against a position of nuclear restraint. Ironically, these changes are forcing states to confront the logic of the realist security dilemma that had been artificially held in check by their willingness to depend on security guarantees from outside powers.[40] While these security guarantees are far from being discarded, they are now being buttressed by the very public and conscious decision to embrace a nuclear latent status.

The nature of the security dilemma faced by Middle Eastern states has been altered by the U.S. invasion of Iraq, the regional ascendance of Iran, and the radicalizing impact on domestic politics of the continued violent spiral in the Arab-Israeli dispute. These three factors have combined to create new internal political pressures on regional regimes while at the same time creating a new and disturbing regional distribution of power.[41] This changed regional distribution of power features a number of critical external and internal elements that are pressuring regional governing elites from Rabat to Muscat:

- the perceived decline in U.S. global military power and political influence;
- the decline in U.S. political influence throughout the region following the Iraq invasion;
- the U.S. failure to undertake constructive involvement in the Arab-Israeli dispute;
- the emergence of an alliance of powerful state and nonstate actors (Iran, Syria, Hizbollah, Hamas, and various Shi'ite-based militias and political organizations in Iraq);
- Iran's hitherto successful defiance of the United States and the international community in what looks like an inexorable march toward a nuclear arsenal;
- strengthened Islamist political movements that must be accommodated in various ways by regional regimes;
- regional oil producers that, while still dependent on U.S. military protection, are actively building political, economic, and military partnerships with outside powers such as India, China, Russia, and Pakistan; and,
- a public that is virulently anti-American and anti-Israeli and that increasingly sees little distinction between either actor.

These new circumstances and events have eliminated the incentives for states to show nuclear restraint and have increased the attractiveness of a more ambiguous nuclear posture.

The altered distribution of power features external and internal dynamics that have combined to force leaders to address external threats in ways that are now inexorably being shaped by internal politics. Where before these two competing priorities could be pursued independently by regional elites, it is now no longer possible for states to keep the external and internal threats separated.

This new dynamic is being shaped by a variety of forces. At the global level, there is a general perception that U.S. power and influence are on the wane. Polling data over the last five years indicates the steady erosion of popular support for the United States around the world—a critical factor limiting the ability of the United States to exert global leadership.[42] Reflecting this decline, states around the world and particularly those in the Middle East confront significant domestic political costs to maintain a supportive relationship with the United States. This phenomenon was on display in Iraq, where no regional state accepted a direct role in trying to stabilize the country. Instead of demonstrating U.S. strength and power, Iraq helped undermine it and the credibility of the security guarantees that have been relied upon by Middle Eastern states to deter external adversaries. The perceived decline in U.S. power has combined with a domestic political environment that is virulently anti-American. A 2006 Zogby/University of Maryland poll drawn from Egypt, Morocco, Saudi Arabia, Lebanon, the United Arab Emirates, and Jordan revealed that approximately 70 percent of all respondents believe that the United States and Israel represent the most serious threats to regional security.[43] Another particularly chilling finding for regional elites is that the same polling data indicated that Hizbollah leader Hassan Nasrallah has become the most popular leader in the Middle East.[44]

Shorn of the protective security umbrella provided by U.S. guarantees and facing a restive and anti-U.S./Israel public, regional regimes confront a threatening external environment that consists of an unstable Iraq, a potentially nuclear-armed Iran, and an Iranian-headed regional alliance of state- and non-state actors ranging from Baghdad to Beirut. Regional elites also see the prospect of an Iranian-allied state in Iraq after the United States withdraws from the country, and the creation of a powerful nexus of nonstate Shi'ite and Sunni militias looking for other regional climes in which to ply their destructive trade. The military prowess shown by Hizbollah against Israel in Lebanon in August 2006 and the military capabilities of various nonstate insurgent groups in Iraq provide a stark and threatening contrast to the traditional conventional military incompetence in the surrounding states.

Moving to a more ambiguous nuclear stance addresses the new regional distribution of power by signaling a variety of different messages to a variety of different actors. It reinforces the message to Tehran that regional states are not prepared to stand by and allow a nuclear-armed Iran to intimidate the region. In other words, the region's shifting nuclear posture must be seen as a hedged response to Iran. It also signals to Russia, China, and India that the era of U.S.

regional hegemony is drawing to a close and that outside powers now have an opportunity to build political, military, and economic partnerships, which include cooperation on nuclear programs.

A nascent nuclear program also sends a variety of messages to the United States. It highlights the importance of forestalling Iran's march toward nuclear weapons and the potential consequences of not stopping Iran. It also signals that it may not be possible to revert to the "business as usual" approach between Washington and regional capitals, while suggesting that Washington has time to resolve these issues because it will take nearly a decade for these nuclear programs to be established.

Additionally, nuclear programs can demonstrate to domestic political constituencies that regimes are distancing themselves from Washington and are no longer necessarily prepared either to accept a U.S. security guarantee or to exist under a threatening nuclear shadow emanating from either Tel Aviv or Tehran. Nuclear programs have the potential of becoming important symbols of national identity and prestige throughout the region. Domestic audiences also notice that a latent nuclear status communicates to Israel that states in the region will have the capability to achieve nuclear capability on short notice, effectively ending Israel's regional nuclear monopoly.

Administering their nuclear programs under IAEA supervision can allow regimes to cloak their programs in an aura of legitimacy, which means they can continue to use Israel's and Iran's noncompliance with the NPT to their political advantage with domestic and international audiences.

THE SAUDI CASE

Saudi Arabia's decision to float the idea of an enhanced nuclear posture represents a rational and measured response to its changing security environment. The House of Saud's growing uneasiness with the regional security setting has been apparent for several years. In late 2003, for instance, the press reported that the Kingdom was considering three options for ensuring its long-term security: (1) creating a WMD-free zone in the Middle East; (2) acquiring nuclear weapons; and (3) allying itself with an existing nuclear power and placing itself under that power's nuclear umbrella.[45] Additionally, a report emerged in October 2003 that Saudi Arabia and Pakistan had concluded a "secret agreement on nuclear cooperation" following a visit by Crown Prince Abdullah to Pakistan.[46] According to the report, Abudullah and Pakistani leader President Musharraf agreed to exchange Saudi oil for Pakistani nuclear "know-how and expertise."[47]

The leaders apparently discussed the possible deployment of Pakistani troops to the Kingdom, presumably to provide added assurance against external threats. Other reports suggested that an agreement was reached during these meetings to station Pakistani nuclear weapons on Saudi soil. [48]

During meetings in Islamabad on October 4, 2004, Pakistani and Saudi delegations were rumored to have discussed "ways to undertake a joint venture in the production of arms and ammunition, armored fighting vehicles, missiles and tanks." [49] This type of collaboration seems consistent with previous Saudi support for and interest in Pakistan's nuclear and missile programs, which led to reports of Saudi royal family representation at a Pakistani ballistic missile test in May 2002 and a visit by Saudi Minister of Defense and Aviation Prince Sultan in May 1999 to the Pakistani uranium enrichment facility at Kahuta. [50] Some allege that Saudi economic support to Pakistan was critical to that country's acquisition of a nuclear weapon.

What to Do with the CSS-2 Missiles

Saudi moves to embrace a new nuclear posture coincide with a looming decision on whether to replace or upgrade CSS-2/DF-2 missiles, which were purchased from the People's Republic of China in the late 1980s. The Chinese are fielding a second generation, solid propellant missile (DF-21A), which means that training and support for the liquid-fueled CSS-2 will become increasingly more complicated and expensive. [51] The Saudis thus face a decision on whether to allow the CSS-2 to lapse into obsolescence or replace it with a next-generation system. The Saudis probably have about 60 missiles with conventional warheads and about one dozen transporter erector launchers that are deployed at two sites with four to six launch pads per site. The Saudis purchased the missiles in the aftermath of the war of the cities during the Iran-Iraq conflict. The missile purchase followed a decision by the United States not to sell the Kingdom surface-to-surface missiles.

A Weakened U.S.-Saudi Partnership

The relationship with the United States has remained at the heart of Saudi Arabia's quest for security since the Kingdom's founder, Ibn Abdul Aziz al Saud, met with President Franklin Roosevelt at the Great Bitter Lake in November 1945. That meeting placed a political face on the growing commercial relationship (dating to the Standard Oil of California concession in 1932) and Saudi Arabia's gradual emergence as the dominant player in the world's oil markets. As it evolved, the U.S.-Saudi partnership reflected several critical political, economic, and military assumptions: (1) U.S. companies would exploit Saudi oil reserves and construct the Saudi energy infrastructure; (2) the United States would regard the security of the Kingdom as a "vital" political interest—a commitment conveyed to the House of Saud on a number of occasions in the post–World War II era—and would use force to defend the House of Saud; (3) the United States would develop Saudi internal and external security capabilities through sales of defense equipment, training, and program management; (4) the Saudis would use their influence as the world's dominant supplier to ensure that crude reached the market in a relatively predictable manner; (5) the Saudis would generally support U.S. interests in the region, such as the Middle East Peace process (although it would not take the lead publicly in supporting these interests); and (6) the United States would not push the Kingdom to undertake substantial internal political or economic reform.

The central elements of this partnership came under close scrutiny following the September 11, 2001, terrorist attacks against the Pentagon and the World Trade Center. The attacks unleashed a torrent of unflattering stories about the Kingdom's alleged support for terrorists around the globe, stemming partly from the fact that 15 of the 19 hijackers came from Saudi Arabia, but also due to the apparently unregulated financial support for charities suspected of links to Al Qaeda. The formulation of these stories identifies the Saudis as the source of the Wahhabi "extremist" religious ideology, which has been aggressively exported throughout the world with active Saudi political and financial support. Thus, the formulations go, the Saudis, as supporters of extremism and terrorism, are now regarded as the enemy in the global war on terror.[52] The constant battering of the Saudis in the press has taken its toll on those within the Kingdom's leadership who would continue to support a strong U.S.-Saudi strategic partnership.

The George W. Bush administration's repeated and forceful calls for the transformation of the Middle East into a series of democratic states placed additional pressures on the weakened Saudi-U.S. partnership.[53] Popular revolts in Lybia, Tehran, and Tunisia have further raised the specter of domestic unrest in the Kingdom. Indeed, one of the implicit understandings of the partnership throughout the post–World War II era was that the United States would not overtly push the House of Saud to institute political and economic reforms. This places the absolutist monarchy on a collision course with emerging trends in the region.

The Saudi Perspective in a Regional Context

As the U.S.-Saudi relationship faces increasing strains, regional developments have also taken a turn for the worse. In terms of the dispute over Palestine, there is a continuing spiral of violence in the occupied territories, while hard liners on both the Israeli and Palestinian sides appear uninterested in reconciliation and accommodation. The sway of these groups, in combination with the U.S. failure to act as an "honest broker" in the peace process, has created a seemingly permanent landscape of conflict and bloodshed that feeds a radicalizing mass anti-U.S. psychology.

The U.S. invasion of Iraq is another feature of this troubled regional landscape. The Saudis disliked Saddam, but the prospect of a Shia-led confederated pseudo democracy in Iraq can hardly be very palatable in Riyadh. The Saudis would face the prospect of a potentially powerful neighbor representing a profound political and religious threat to the Kingdom. A politically successful Iraq that will inevitably be administered by the Shia majority places the Saudi monarchy in a difficult position. They could face greater pressure to speed up their own political reform process. The emergence of a Shia-dominated Iraq also promises to play to the Saudi regime's strained relations with the Shias throughout the region, but particularly in the Kingdom's Eastern Provinces.

The potential splintering of Iraq into a series of fiefdoms defined along ethnic, tribal, and sectarian lines creates the prospect of one massive headache along Riyadh's unpoliceable northern frontier. The prospect of an Iraq consumed with ethnic, tribal, and sectarian warfare that can also provide a base of operations for Al Qaeda's infrastructure in the Kingdom is another facet of the potentially negative outcome of regime change in Baghdad. The situation in Iraq will have to improve in order to reduce Saudi Arabia's threat perception and to enhance the Kingdom's sense of security.

Iran's march toward developing its own nuclear capability represents an even more serious challenge than the situation in Iraq. Iran's intentions seem clear to most observers. It has built a redundant and hardened nuclear infrastructure that is all but impervious to an Osirak-type attack, and its hard-line religious leaders have repeatedly stated they will neither abandon their nuclear program nor place it under meaningful international oversight. When placed in the context of Iran's mature and apparently successful long-range missile program, Tehran appears positioned to become the world's next nuclear power with the ability to deliver a nuclear weapon out to a range of 1,250 miles. Iran's

August 2004 test of an enhanced Shehab-3 medium-range missile capable of carrying a 2,250-pound warhead confirmed Tehran's capability to reach targets throughout the region, including Riyadh.[54]

Saudi Domestic Politics

A complicated domestic political landscape within the Kingdom is forcing the ruling family to play to its "publics" at the same time it is waging a war against an entrenched militant infrastructure. The impact of internal politics and the battle against Al Qaeda are both factors that are difficult to gauge in the context of the House of Saud's decision-making process on how to ensure its long-term security. Western observers are often quick to dismiss the potential influence of Saudi domestic politics per se, which are indeed dominated by the House of Saud. But the House of Saud governs by consensus and has done so successfully since the inception of the Kingdom. The process of maintaining consensus—a process that is largely opaque to all but the best informed observers—has become increasingly complicated for Saudi leaders since the turn of the century. The impact of these domestic complications on security decisions is difficult to discern, but should be explored by governments that are interested in trying to forestall the Saudis from acquiring new and threatening military capabilities—be they long-range missiles or nuclear weapons.

Strategic, regional, and domestic factors are combining to highlight Saudi concerns about the security of the regime and their nation. Seen within this framework, it is not surprising that the Saudis would be giving serious thought about the way to ensure the future security of the Kingdom.

CONCLUSION

Nations of the Middle East and Saudi Arabia in particular are considering a new nuclear posture in response to a changing regional security environment that has heightened their sense of insecurity. The rise of Iranian power in conjunction with the perceived decline in U.S. influence has created incentives for these states to take the first halting steps toward a new nuclear posture. Regional elites also are confronted with domestic circumstances that militate against the continued outsourcing of their strategic security to the United States. Moving to adopt nuclear power programs represents a calculated hedging strategy that buys both the elites and the United States time to resolve the sources of regional instability. If threatening dynamics in the regimes' security dilemmas can be resolved, then the states will be less likely to operationalize a latent nuclear posture.

Should the regional environment remain unstable, however, the logic of the security dilemma suggests that states will develop a nuclear infrastructure because possessing a latent nuclear capability will become increasingly attractive.

Throughout its history, the House of Saud has exhibited a maintained track record of "realpolitik" behavior. The Kingdom's founder, Ibn Saud, cemented the U.S. relationship based on his assessment of his country's security needs and on the desirable characteristics of the provider of that security. While the U.S. partnership has been sustained by his successors, there are no guarantees that the next generation of leaders will see the U.S. relationship in the same light. Should the United States prove unable to restore its regional dominance in the aftermath of the Iraq invasion and the intervention in Afghanistan, Saudi leaders could decide to build relations with other outside powers while simultaneously building a latent nuclear capability. While Saudi Arabia possesses no substantial nuclear infrastructure, the windfall from the oil bonanza provides the Kingdom with the money to purchase at least one nuclear reactor each year, and there is no shortage of suppliers. Both Beijing and Moscow would be delighted to assist Riyadh in a nuclear program, which would fit within the growing commercial and military relationships that each state seeks to cultivate with Saudi Arabia. Moreover, as is the case in various weapons programs, the regime has shown itself to be more than willing to pay outside contractors to provide and sustain capabilities that are beyond the means of the indigenous infrastructure. Two high-profile weapons programs—the CSS-2 missile and the F-15 aircraft—are both maintained by non-nationals.

It is not inevitable that Saudi Arabia will become a nuclear power or construct a latent nuclear posture. The House of Saud would prefer to continue outsourcing its security to the United States and rely on an ambiguous extended deterrent. Nevertheless, if Iran's march toward nuclear weapons is not derailed and Tehran achieves an operational capability, Riyadh will feel compelled to respond, just as it felt compelled to respond during the Iran-Iraq War by acquiring its own missile systems. Further complicating the landscape are uncertain domestic pressures that will increasingly shape the regime's national security decision-making. Various powerful domestic constituencies remain opposed to the U.S. relationship, and it is among these constituencies that the regime needs to mitigate the internal threat posed by Al Qaeda and other Islamic extremist groups.

The House of Saud is not prone to irrational actions or other flights of fancy when it comes to ensuring the Kingdom's security and perpetuating its own hold on power. On balance, the Kingdom's national security policy reflects a calculated, realist-oriented decision-making paradigm. But if the conclusion is reached that building nuclear reactors will bolster national and regime security, the Saudis are capable of seeing that project to completion.

NOTES

1. Mitchell Reiss, "The Nuclear Tipping Point: Prospects for a World of Many Nuclear Weapons States," in *The Nuclear Tipping Point: Why States Reconsider Their Nuclear Choices*, ed. Kurt M. Campbell, Robert J. Einhorn, and Mitchell Reiss (Washington, DC: Brookings Institution Press, 2004), 3–18.

2. As asserted by Saudi Foreign Minister Saud al Faisal in Mariam Hakeem, "GCC's Nuclear Programme Will Be a Role Model," *Gulf News*, January 14, 2007, at http://archive.gulfnews.com/articles/07/01/14/10096775.html.

3. Ariel E. Levite, "Never Say Never Again: Nuclear Reversal Revisited," *International Security* 27, No. 3 (2002): 59–88.

4. Avner Cohen and Joseph Pilat, "Assessing Virtual Nuclear Arsenals," *Survival* 40, No. 1 (Spring 1998): 129–44.

5. "GCC Seeks Nuclear Energy," *Gulf News*, December 12, 2006, at http://www.gulfnews.com/region/General/10088620.html; William Broad and David Sanger, "With Eye on Iran, Rivals Also Want Nuclear Power," *New York Times*, April 15, 2007, at http://www.nytimes.com/2007/04/15/world/middleeast/15sunnis.html?ex=1334289600&en=5d61635 8682635ee&ei=5088&partner=r.

6. Sammy Salama and Gina Cabrera-Farraj, "Renewed Egyptian Ambitions for a Peaceful Nuclear Program," *WMD Insights*, November 2006; and Sammy Salama and Khalid Hilal, "Egyptian Muslim Brotherhood Presses Government for Nuclear Weapons," *WMD Insights*, November 2006.

7. "Algeria Trades Gas for Russian Nuclear Energy," January 24, 2007, World Tribune. com at http://www.worldtribune.com/worldtribune/07/front2454125.161111113.html.

8. Daniel Pinkston, "Algeria Seeks Nuclear Cooperation with South Korea as Seoul Prepares New Nuclear Plans," *WMD Insights*, June 2006.

9. "Weapons of Mass Destruction; Algeria Special Weapons," GlobalSecuirty.org at http://www.globalsecurity.org/wmd/world/algeria/index.html.

10. Sammy Salama, "Moroccan Nuclear Energy Programs Gets Boost from Russia," WMD Insights, Novembeer 2006.

11. Raid Qusti, "GCC to Develop Civilian Nuclear Energy," *Arab News*, December 11, 2006 at http://www.arabnews.com/?page=1&section=0&article=89863&d=11&m=12&y=2006.

12. Khalid Hilal and Leah Kuchinsky, "Jordan Joins List of Arab States Announcing Nuclear Energy Programs; Pakistan Promises Help," *WMD Insights*, March 2007.

13. Scott Sagan, "Why Do States Build Nuclear Weapons?" *International Security* 21, No. 3 (Winter 2006/2007), 54–86; Zachary Davis and Benjamen Frankel, eds., *The Pro-*

liferation Puzzle: Why Nuclear Weapons Spread and What Results (London: Frank Cass, 1993); Campbell, Einhorn, and Reiss, *The Nuclear Tipping Point;* John Deutch, "The New Nuclear Threat," *Foreign Affairs* 71, No. 41 (Fall 1992); and Steven M. Meyer, *The Dynamics of Nuclear Proliferation* (Chicago: University of Chicago Press, 1984).

14. E. H. Carr, *The Twenty-Years Crisis* (London: Macmillan, 1939); Hans Morgenthau, *Politics among Nations,* 6th ed., revised by Kenneth Thompson (New York: Knopf, 1985); Rienhold Niebuhr, *Moral Man and Immoral Society* (New York: Scribner's, 1947); George Kenan, *American Diplomacy,* 1900–1950 (New York: New American Library, 1951); George Kenan, *Realities of American Foreign Policy* (Princeton: Princeton University Press, 1954).

15. Kenneth Waltz, *Theory of International Politics* (New York: Random House, 1979).

16. Kenneth Waltz, "The Spread of Nuclear Weapons: Why More May Be Better," *Adelphi Papers* No. 171 (London: International Institute for Strategic Studies, 1981).

17. John J. Mearsheimer, "The Case for a Ukrainian Nuclear Deterrent," *Foreign Affairs* 72, No. 3 (Summer 1993).

18. Sagan, "Why Do States Build Nuclear Weapons?" 57.

19. Kurt M. Campbell, "Reconsidering a Nuclear Future," in Campbell, Einhorn, and Reiss, *The Nuclear Tipping Point,* 20–21.

20. James A. Russell, "Nuclear Strategy and the Modern Middle East," *Middle East Policy* 11, No. 4 (Fall 2004): 98–117; Kathleen J. McInniss, "Extended Deterrence: The U.S. Credibility Gap in the Middle East," *Washington Quarterly* 28, No. 3 (Summer 2005): 169–86.

21. Campbell, "Reconsidering a Nuclear Future."

22. Benjamen Frankel, "The Brooding Shadow: Systemic Incentives and Nuclear Weapons Proliferation," in Davis and Frankel, *The Proliferation Puzzle,* 37–78.

23. Ibid., 37, 60–61. For a similar prediction of nuclear proliferation in Europe, see John Mearsheimer, "Back to the Future: Instability in Europe after the Cold War," *International Security* 15, No. 1 (Summer 1990): 5–56.

24. Sagan, "Why Do States Build Nuclear Weapons?" 55.

25. Ibid., 63–64; Graham Allison and Philip Zelikow, *Essence of Decision: Explaining the Cuban Missile Crisis,* 2d ed. (New York: Longman, 1999); Morton Halperin, *Bureaucratic Politics and Foreign Policy* (Washington, DC: Brookings, 1974); Graham Allison and Mort Halperin, "Bureaucratic Politics: A Paradigm and Some Policy Implications," *World Politics,* 24 (Spring 1972).

26. Scott Sagan, "The Perils of Proliferation: Organization Theory, Deterrence Theory, and the Spread of Nuclear Weapons," *International Security* 18, No. 4 (Spring 1994): 66–107.

27. Sagan, "Why Do States Build Nuclear Weapons?"

28. Alexander Wendt, "Anarchy Is What States Make of It: The Social Construction

of Power Politics," *International Organization* 46, No. 2 (Spring 1992): 391–425; Robert Jervis, "Cooperation under the Security Dilemma," *World Politics* 30, No. 2 (January 1978): 167–214; Robert Powell, "Anarchy in International Relations Theory: The Neoliberal Neorealist Debate," *International Organization* 48, No. 2 (Spring 1994): 313–44; and Robert Jervis, "Realism, Neoliberalism, and Cooperation: Understanding the Debate," *International Security* 24, No. 1 (Summer 1999): 42–63.

29. Glenn Chafetz, "The End of the Cold War and the Future of Nuclear Proliferation: An Alternative to the Neorealist perspective," in Davis and Frankel, *The Proliferation Puzzle*, 128.

30. Ibid., 138.

31. Sagan, "Why Do States Build Nuclear Weapons?" 73–74.

32. Ibid.

33. Jacques E. C. Hymans, "Theories of Nuclear Proliferation: The State of the Field," *Nonproliferation Review* 13, No. 3 (November 2006): 455–65.

34. Etel Solingen, "The Political Economy of Nuclear Restraint," *International Security* 19, No. 2 (Autumn 1994): 126–69; Solingen, "The Domestic Sources of Nuclear Postures: Influencing 'Fence Sitters' in the Post Cold War Era," *Institute on Global Conflict and Cooperation Policy Paper 8* (October 1994); Solingen, "The Domestic Sources of Regional Regimes: The Evolution of Nuclear Ambiguity in the Middle East," *International Studies Quarterly* 38, No. 2 (June 1994): 305–37.

35. For background, see Shai Feldman, *Nuclear Weapons and Arms Control in the Middle East* (Cambridge, MA: MIT Press, 1997).

36. Avner Cohen, *Israel and the Bomb* (New York: Columbia University Press, 1998).

37. Wyn Bowen, "Libya and Nuclear Proliferation: Stepping Back from the Brink," *Adelphi Papers* 46, No. 380 (April 2006).

38. Russell, "Nuclear Strategy and the Modern Middle East."

39. On May 14, 2007, IAEA inspectors found that Iraq is enriching uranium on a far wider scale than had previously been realized. David Sanger, "Inspectors Cite Big Gain by Iran on Nuclear Fuel," *New York Times*, May 15, 2007 at http://www.nytimes.com/2007/05/15/world/middleeast/15iran.html.

40. Benjamen Frankel, "The Brooding Shadow," in Frankel and Davis, *The Proliferation Puzzle*.   41.   Shibley Telhami, "America in Arab Eyes," *Survival* 49, No. 1 (Spring 2007): 107–22.

42. A representative sample is polling done under the Pew Global Attitudes Project at http://pewglobal.org/reports/display.php?PageID=801.

43. Zogby International Annual Arab 2006 Public Opinion Survey at http://www.bsos.umd.edu/SADAT/2006%20Arab%20Public%20Opinion%20Survey.ppt.

44. Ibid.

45. Ewen MacAskill and Ian Traynor, "Saudis Consider Nuclear Bomb," *The Guardian*, September 18, 2003.

46. "Pakistan-Saudi Trade Nuclear Technology for Oil," United Press International, filed October 20, 2002, 7:00 p.m.

47. Ibid.

48. G. Parthasarathy, "Axis of Evidence," *Indian Express*, November 14, 2003, translation by FBIS.

49. "Pakistan, Saudi Arabia Explore Joint Ventures in Defence Production," AFP, October 11, 2004.

50. See Richard Russell, "Saudi Nukes: A Looming Intelligence Failure," *Washington Times*, January 5, 2004, 17. See also Ed Blanche, "Playing with Fire: Deepening Suspicions that Saudis Are Considering Atomic Arms," *Daily Star*, November 29, 2003, for some of the same arguments.

51. Steve McDowell, "Is Saudi Arabia a Nuclear Threat?" Naval Postgraduate School master's thesis, September 2003, at http://www.ccc.nps.navy.mil/research/theses/McDowell03.pdf.

52. As an example, see Victor Davis Hanson, "Our Enemies the Saudis," *Commentary Magazine*, July/August 2002.

53. President Bush stated on November 6, 2003, "Sixty years of Western nations excusing and accommodating the lack of freedom in the Middle East did nothing to make us safe because in the long run stability cannot be purchased at the expense of liberty." Quoted in Deb Riechmann, Associated Press, "Bush Urges Spread of Democracy in the Middle East," November 6, 2003.

54. "Analysis: Iran's Missile Capabilities," UPI, October 6, 2004.

5 Motivations and Capabilities to Acquire Nuclear, Biological, or Chemical Weapons and Missiles: South Africa?

Noel Stott

This chapter identifies four potential motivations that may lead South Africa either to modify or to radically change its approach to the threat posed by weapons of mass destruction both at the national level and in international fora. These motivations include a perceived threat posed by China's growing influence in Africa; South Africa's quest for nuclear energy, electrical power generation, and a strategic intent to develop an indigenous capacity for uranium enrichment; the lack of progress by nuclear weapon states to honor their disarmament commitments; and the loss of institutional memory among South Africa's politicians, civil servants, and diplomatic community. The chapter also describes the factors that might cause this kind of policy reversal, including South Africa's past nuclear weapons program and the country's advanced scientific, industrial, and technological infrastructure and capabilities.

I summarize South Africa's present policies, legislation, and institutional framework, and the transition to a constitutional democracy, and the consequent transformation of security institutions and redefinition of defense posture and doctrine. These policies will work against any change in South Africa's nuclear policies. I also assess the possible actions the international community could undertake to counter a potential change in South Africa's nuclear policy. This includes the utility of bilateral and multilateral treaty based nonproliferation regimes and other policy instruments such as the 1995 declaration of Africa as a nuclear-weapons-free zone.

SOUTH AFRICA AND WEAPONS OF MASS DESTRUCTION: INTERNATIONAL BODIES, AGREEMENTS, AND CONVENTIONS

Much has been written about South Africa's ascendance in January 2007 to nonpermanent membership of the UN Security Council. The Council typically deals with issues that affect global peace and security, as in the case of North Korea's nuclear tests and Iran's alleged ambitions to become a nuclear weapons state. South Africa's leadership role in other international fora that address weapons of mass destruction (WMD) has attracted less attention. Democratic South Africa has ratified or acceded to the Chemical Weapons Convention, the Convention on the Prohibition of the Development, Production and Stockpiling of Bacteriological and Toxin Weapons and Their Destruction, the Treaty on the Non-proliferation of Nuclear Weapons (NPT), the African Nuclear Weapons Free Zone Treaty, the Comprehensive Nuclear Test Ban Treaty, and the Convention on Physical Protection of Nuclear Material.

Under the African National Congress government, the country began to participate in a number of fora designed to promote multilateral approaches to arms control and disarmament, including the International Atomic Energy Agency (IAEA), the Conference on Disarmament, the Missile Technology Control Regime, the Nuclear Suppliers Group, the Zangger Committee, and the Wassenaar Arrangement. South Africa reclaimed its designated seat on the IAEA's Board of Governors in 1995. In February 2007, South Africa announced it would ratify the Convention on Physical Protection of Nuclear Material, further demonstrating its commitment to the security of nuclear materials.[1] An example of South Africa's constructive approach to policy occurred at the first session of the Preparatory Committee for the 2010 review conference of the NPT, in Vienna, Austria, in April–May 2007. Iran was not willing to accept the wording of one agenda item and stalled the meeting for three days. Abdul S. Minty, South Africa's Deputy Director-General in the Department of Foreign Affairs, proposed that rather than the chair's making a decision to modify the agenda, the meeting itself should adopt an annex to the agenda indicating that the reference in the agenda meant that the Preparatory Committee would consider it in full compliance with all provisions of the treaty. The proposal ensured that this understanding would be part and parcel of the official record of the meeting—a demand of Iran's—without opening the agenda as a whole for amendments.

South African Leadership in the Nonproliferation Community

South Africa was the initial chair of the Geneva-based Conference on Disarmament for 2007. The conference is the world's sole multilateral forum for disarmament negotiations. Since it completed negotiations for the Comprehensive Test Ban Treaty in 1996, however, its members have been unable to reach agreement on a program of work, which has prevented discussion of substantive issues. As the initial 2007 president, South Africa had the opportunity to break this ten-year deadlock. Unfortunately the conference failed to achieve much progress during the South African term: the Conference on Disarmament's second session of 2007 closed without agreement on the proposed program of work.

South Africa also served as the chair of the Nuclear Suppliers Group in 2007. This forum seeks to contribute to the nonproliferation of nuclear weapons through the implementation of guidelines governing the export of items specifically designed for nuclear use, such as nuclear materials, reactors, and equipment for the reprocessing, enrichment, and conversion of nuclear materials. A second set of guidelines governs the export of nuclear related dual-use items and technologies. The Nuclear Suppliers Group thus aims to facilitate the trade in nuclear materials while at the same time ensuring that this trade does not contribute to the proliferation of nuclear weapons.

Domestic Links to the Nonproliferation Regime

On December 5, 2006, South Africa and the IAEA signed a second five-year Country Program Framework agreement outlining the country's priorities in terms of nuclear energy. The first framework was implemented between 1999 and 2004. Between 2006 and 2009 the government implemented projects in cooperation with the International Atomic Energy Agency, which will help achieve South Africa's developmental goals. The Nuclear Energy Corporation of South Africa has been designated as the implementing agency for the Technical Co-operation Program, including assistance with the transfer of nuclear and related technologies for peaceful use.

The signing of the Program Framework makes South Africa the only African country to finalize its second country program agreement as an official IAEA member state. South Africa is currently participating in the IAEA Technical Assistance and Co-operation Program and receives almost $1 million per year in aid from the agency. South Africa also holds the only designated IAEA seat for Africa, based on the country's advanced nuclear infrastructure. Today

South Africa works closely with the IAEA to monitor international smuggling of nuclear weapons materials, after an investigation by its authorities found links between South Africans and the A. Q. Khan network.

South Africa also has established several institutions to regulate its participation in nuclear, biological, chemical, and conventional arms agreements. The National Conventional Arms Control Committee, a committee of ministers appointed by the cabinet to ensure political oversight over all arms transfers, and the Directorate of Conventional Arms Control, which administers the Armaments Development and Production Act and the Regulation of Foreign Military Assistance Act, are examples of these kinds of institutions. The South African Council for the Non-proliferation of Weapons of Mass Destruction controls the transfer of weapons of mass destruction and dual-use goods according to South Africa's responsibilities as a signatory to the International Missile Technology Control Regime. The council also administers the Non-proliferation of Weapons of Mass Destruction Act (No. 87 of 1983) and its associated amendments and regulations.

MOTIVATIONS FOR POLICY CHANGE

Several developments have reintroduced the issue of nuclear weapons into South Africa's defense debates. In particular, China's increasing involvement in Africa raises the threat of nuclear war on the continent.

China is a major investor in Africa. In 2004 it invested $900 million in the continent, up more than 300 percent over the previous year. China's trade with the continent quadrupled from 2001 to 2007 to $55 billion.[2] In 2009 alone, China's investment in 49 African countries totaled $9 billion.[3] More than 700 Chinese companies are active in Africa. China gets about a third of its oil from African countries, as well as other natural resources, which have helped fuel the country's dramatic economic transformation. The 15-page Beijing plan of action, which outlines cooperation between Africa and China up to 2009, specifies agriculture, investment and business, trade, finance, and science and technology as likely areas for future cooperation. Beijing has already written off almost $1.5 billion in debt to Africa and states it will write off a similar amount again in the future.[4]

China may be eager to capitalize upon the continent's uranium resources before Russia outmaneuvers it. A scramble for control of Africa's oil resources and China's increasing participation could lead to a concomitant increase in transaction transparency and best practice corporate governance. Given China's apparent lack of interest in African governance and human rights issues, the implementation of Beijing's Africa policy largely contradicts the New Partnership for Africa's Development initiative and the African development agenda.[5] China's actions in the Sudan, Angola, and Zimbabwe signal a new effort by Beijing to expand economic and political influence in Africa outside the confines of the "Washington Consensus." Moreover, China's engagement approach contradicts the Organization for Economic Cooperation and Development's rules for engagement of fragile states.

While much work is being done on the impact of China on African economies and development prospects, there is little overt focus on the implications for the search for improved security for Africa's people. Critics, though, see a potential for a new type of colonialism in the alliance. Human rights groups point out that the new partnership offers Africa's mostly undemocratic leaders access to generous financial assistance without any commitment to good governance or recognition of human rights. Some South Africans see an even far more ominous future. According to Renfrew Christie, a leading South African observer of diplomatic and military affairs, China's ascendancy will stress the world's system. There will be oil wars, water wars, and simple wars of greed. America, Europe, China, and perhaps India will struggle via proxies, or directly, to control Africa's wealth. Nothing promises that African wars will not be nuclear. "South Africa," in Christie's view, "must work to ensure that these wars are not nuclear wars (unless they suit our interests)."[6] China is more than simply an industrial power on the ascendant. It is a nuclear weapons power.

China's involvement in Africa apparently has raised the issue of nuclear weapons in the South African strategic debate. As Christie notes, "We cannot leave the nuclear issue to others. South Africa must be at the cutting edge of understanding changes in nuclear technology. We must know the location, readiness and deliverability of every nuclear weapon. We must quickly be able to revert to being a nuclear-weapons state if that becomes vital to our interests."[7] According to a journalist who interviewed Christie after the speech, his address was greeted with loud applause. The journalist concludes: "[O]ne wonders how long it may be before such thinking percolates through to the policy-makers, with who knows what consequences for Africa."[8]

South Africa and Nuclear Energy

South Africa's policy on nuclear weapons involves a balance between a commitment to disarmament and nonproliferation and a commitment to ensuring access to commercial nuclear technology. For example, while many countries acknowledge that it is desirable to minimize access to highly enriched uranium (HEU), reservations about international efforts to minimize the use of HEU in the civilian sphere have been voiced by South Africa. For example, Abdul Minty, Deputy Director-General of the South African Ministry of Foreign Affairs, argues that "WMD terrorism should not be a pretext for removing rights," asserting that efforts to promote HEU minimization could undermine the "inalienable right" of states parties to the NPT to peaceful nuclear use, and would amount to "disarming the disarmed." According to Minty, priority should be given to promoting nuclear weapons disarmament and peaceful nuclear use. To the extent that one seeks to minimize the use of civil HEU, it should be linked to "the HEU declared as excess in the military stockpiles of the weapons states," and should take place in tandem with the reduction of plutonium, tritium, and radioactive materials. It should be noted that for some time South Africa has emphasized the need for nuclear weapons states to declare weapons material excess and put it under International Atomic Energy Agency safeguards.[9] Among the nonaligned movement states, only South Africa retains a large amount of HEU, remnants of its former weapons program. South Africa would be the only nonaligned state directly affected by the minimization of civilian HEU stocks, use, and commerce.

SOUTH AFRICA'S ENERGY CRISIS AND RENEWED QUEST FOR NUCLEAR ENERGY

South Africa is in the process of finalizing a Nuclear Energy and Technology Strategy as well as creating a nuclear manufacturing capacity (currently being developed by the South African Nuclear Energy Corporation). South Africa is also in the process of finalizing a new Nuclear Energy Policy and Strategy, which will outline the government's principles, vision, institutional arrangements, and governance framework.[10] In July 2007, the South African cabinet released its draft policy on nuclear energy, which seeks to create a new industry around nuclear power generation to take advantage of the country's rich uranium deposits, to develop technology, and to create tens of thousands of jobs.[11] The draft presents a policy framework for the utilization of nuclear energy for peaceful purposes in South Africa. The plan, which includes promoting the recycling of spent nuclear fuel, rebuilding its uranium enrichment capacity, and producing enough nuclear fuel for its own new nuclear reactors and for the international market, was finalized in 2007.

According to the Chief Director for Nuclear Energy, Tseliso Maqubela, the policy aims to ensure that South Africa diversify its energy sources away from coal, thereby addressing security of supply and global climate change concerns. "There is no way we can have a primary energy source such as uranium which we don't use fully."[12]

South Africa is looking at 4,000 megawatts of nuclear power in the first phase of the building program utilizing the experimental pebble bed technology. The draft policy document proposes the creation of several new institutions, including a new national nuclear security agency, a national radioactive waste management agency, and a national nuclear architectural capability. The policy makes Eskom Holding Limited the only generator of nuclear power, and proposes incentive schemes to encourage the mining of uranium.[13]

South Africa intends to develop uranium conversion capabilities. Although there is no uranium enrichment infrastructure in South Africa, studies are being conducted on its feasibility. The government's strategic intent is to develop indigenous capacity in uranium enrichment as part of uranium beneficiation. South Africa also intends to develop a plan for development of its fuel fabrication capacity.

The government is aware that "beneficiation of uranium comes with its own responsibilities and sensitivities and we should pursue this beneficiation within our national and international obligations."[14] South Africa's vision for the development of an extensive nuclear energy program thus ensures that the government's use of uranium will be regulated and managed for peaceful purposes. South Africa is guided by the principle that nuclear energy shall be used only for peaceful purposes and in conformity with national and international legal obligations. Nuclear activities will take place within the internationally accepted framework of the NPT and obligations under the IAEA Comprehensive Safeguards Agreement.

South Africa will also pursue bilateral cooperation with those states that have similar nuclear programs or that have nuclear programs from which South Africa requires technology transfer, taking into account the framework of the NPT, national legislation, and other international obligations arising from legally binding treaties and instruments.[15] South African officials believe that its quest for a peaceful nuclear energy program can be undertaken within national and international nuclear nonproliferation obligations.

Relevant Legislation

South African legislation on nuclear energy dates back to 1948. Today there are two main acts, the Nuclear Energy Act of 1999 and the National Nuclear Regulator Act of 1999. Nuclear activities are also subject to other laws, including environmental impact assessment regulations in terms of the National Environmental Management Act of 1998 (and previously the Environment Conservation Act of 1989), the disclosure of information in terms of the Promotion of Access to Information Act of 2000, and the Non-proliferation of Weapons of Mass Destruction Act of 1993. In May 2000, the Department of Minerals and Energy initiated a process to develop a national policy for the management of radioactive waste. The cabinet approved a Radioactive Waste Management Policy and Strategy for South Africa in November 2005.

LACK OF PROGRESS IN THE GLOBAL
NUCLEAR NONPROLIFERATION REGIME

Despite the fact that the vast majority of its state parties continue to fully support the NPT, most commentators agree that the nuclear nonproliferation regime is in deep trouble and facing unprecedented challenges, mainly because of perceptions of the nature of the implementation and compliance challenges of the three arms of the NPT (disarmament, nonproliferation, and the transfer of nuclear technology to developing countries for peaceful purposes). South Africa is often at the forefront of voicing these perceptions or concerns.

This current debate in NPT fora regarding whether nonproliferation or disarmament should come first is a possible opportunity for South Africa to change its position on its own nuclear posture—to develop a strategy borne out by frustration at the lack of progress of nuclear weapon states toward nuclear disarmament rather than a principle or actual security need to acquire nuclear weapons. In South Africa's view, nuclear disarmament is not part of some "ultimate" objective, but a milestone to be reached on the way to the real objective of the disarmament process—namely, general and complete disarmament. The onus of effecting nuclear disarmament rests primarily on those states that possess such weapons; South Africa could not have destroyed its nuclear weapons if it did not possess them in the first place.

As a member of the Norwegian-led Seven Nation Initiative, South Africa shares the view that "the only guarantee against the use of nuclear weapons would be complete security of nuclear materials and a world free of all nuclear

weapons."[16] For South Africa, nuclear disarmament and nuclear nonproliferation are inextricably linked, and both therefore require continuous and irreversible progress. The Minister of Foreign Affairs, Nkosazana Dlamini Zuma, stated
at the opening of the Nuclear Suppliers Group Plenary meeting in Cape Town
in April 2007: "Whilst South Africa is committed to the continuous review and
strengthening of measures aimed at preventing the proliferation of weapons of
mass destruction, we believe that real progress in securing our world from the
threat of nuclear weapons can only be achieved through concomitant progress in the area of nuclear disarmament."[17] South Africa is therefore clearly in
the "disarmament first" camp together with many non-nuclear weapons states
and the nonaligned movement. In this context, one may well pose the question
whether disappointing progress on the nuclear disarmament front is not perhaps in some way linked to the nuclear proliferation threat.[18]

LOSS OF INSTITUTIONAL MEMORY IN THE DISARMAMENT COMMUNITY

Will a new breed of civil servants and diplomats who lack the institutional
memory of those who have gone before them maintain South Africa's pre-emi-
nent positions on disarmament, nonproliferation, and arms control? Whether
South Africa continues to play a leading international role and whether one
will see South Africa's progressive national and international policies and ethical positions rolled back depends to a large extent on education and memory.
Already, for example, rumors are rife that the National Conventional Arms
Control Committee will no longer make public its annual arms exports statistics—a policy change that, if true, will undermine South Africa's stated goal of
transparent governance and in particular transparency on disarmament, nonproliferation, and arms control.

At a May 22, 2007, Parliamentary Defence Portfolio Committee meeting
to discuss South Africa's "Prohibition or Restriction of Certain Conventional
Weapons Bill," disturbing statements were made by its members. These statements reflected both a lack of knowledge about South Africa's international
obligations and indeed South Africa's own domestic laws. For example, some
members argued that it was unfair to restrict the military from using antipersonnel mines, given that nothing prevented rebels from using such against
South African forces deployed on missions in Africa. A member of the ruling African National Congress Party obviously was unaware of South Africa's
law prohibiting South Africans from ever acquiring, stockpiling, transferring,

or using antipersonnel mines, and that South Africa has destroyed its entire stockpile of such mines.[19] He noted at the meeting that "it would sometimes be necessary for the [South African National Defence Forces] to use anti-personnel mines under certain circumstances."[20] Similar erroneous attitudes may arise if, and when, the committee discusses weapons of mass destruction.

SOUTH AFRICA'S NUCLEAR WEAPONS LEGACY

On April 30, 1977, the *New York Times* reported that South Africa had a secret nuclear plant that was suspected of working on a nuclear bomb. The report alleged that these bombs would be used to deter black-ruled states to the north of South Africa, which had vowed to use all means to overthrow the apartheid state. At the time, the South African government reacted by insisting that its nuclear program was for peaceful purposes and that the international inspections required under the NPT could compromise the secrecy of the South African enrichment process, which was unique and less expensive than systems elsewhere. The South African Atomic Energy Board said that the reports were absurd and that a nuclear weapon would be of little use in controlling either guerrilla warfare or urban unrest, the most likely strategies of black militants.[21]

This report turned out to be at least partially true. On March 24, 1993, State President F. W. de Klerk informed Parliament that South Africa had indeed embarked on the development of a limited nuclear deterrent in the 1970s and 1980s.[22] This put to rest years of speculation over the true status of South Africa's suspected nuclear program. The program was curtailed following South Africa's signature of a comprehensive Safeguards Agreement with the International Atomic Energy Agency on September 16, 1991. The standard explanation for the South African government's decision to develop a nuclear weapon is that of deterrence against an attack by the Soviet Union or one of its surrogates, and as an instrument to gain U.S. support should the need arise.[23] Given the technical details and managerial aspects of the program, it appears that South Africa's nuclear program was offensive, while its chemical and biological programs, which were established in 1981 and finally closed down in 1995, might have been defensive.

During the 1970s, the international security situation around South Africa deteriorated markedly as a result of South Africa's then racially based internal policies. The buildup of foreign forces in Angola from 1975 onward reinforced a strong perception within the government of international isolation, especially in the event that South African territory faced an immediate military threat. The fear of a "total onslaught" was a product of Cold War thinking that steadily embedded itself in the minds of the architects of apartheid in the 1950s and 1960s. The envisaged onslaught was Soviet-inspired and directed at all spheres of the security of the state, making use of black political movements. The effect of the notion of the "total onslaught" was a sense of mounting pressure on, and isolation of, the Republic of South Africa.

In the 1970s, a special State Security Council and a National Security Management System were established to increase the involvement of the security apparatus in the governance of the country and to manage a "total strategy" in response. The National Security Management System was a vast bureaucracy intended to coordinate a government-wide effort to counter the perceived total war against South Africa. It was here where the doctrine of the "total strategy" was embraced and expounded, and where actions—both legal and illegal—to deal with the threat were authorized.

According to Guy Lamb, South Africa's nuclear weapons program was established in 1971 by the Minister of Mines following three decades of peaceful nuclear energy research. In 1974 a non-nuclear scale model of a gun-type explosive device was constructed and tested covertly. The first nuclear device was completed in 1977, with a cold test planned in the Kalahari Desert. The test was canceled following pressure from Western governments. In 1978, the program became militarized, with ARMSCOR, the state arms manufacturer, taking control of nuclear weapons research and development. In 1982 the first deliverable nuclear explosive device was produced, and by 1989, South Africa had constructed a total of six complete nuclear weapons and one incomplete device.[24]

In April 1978, the government approved a deterrent strategy based on three phases: (1) Strategic uncertainty, in which the nuclear deterrent capability would not be acknowledged or denied; (2) Should South African territory be threatened, covert acknowledgment to certain strategic international powers would be contemplated; and (3) Should this partial disclosure of South Africa's capability not bring about international intervention to remove the threat, public acknowledgment or demonstration by an underground test of South Africa's capability would be considered. In practice, the strategy never advanced beyond the first phase. In 1985, the entire program was reviewed. The decision was made to limit the arsenal to seven fission gun-type devices and maintain the three-phase deterrent strategy. These limitations slowed the program and were possibly the first sign of an eventual turnaround in South Africa's nuclear policy.

In 1995, South Africa helped to broker an agreement establishing a nuclear-weapons-free zone on the African continent. Forty-nine of the 53 African states have pledged not to conduct research on, develop, test, or stockpile nuclear explosive devices, to prohibit the stationing of nuclear devices on their territory, to maintain the highest standards of protection of nuclear materials, facilities, and equipment, and to prohibit the dumping of radioactive waste. The Treaty of Pelindaba includes a provision allowing a member state to withdraw "if it decides that extraordinary events, related to the subject matter of this treaty, have jeopardized its supreme interests." A country that withdraws, however, would be obliged to submit a statement explaining these "extraordinary events" to the secretary general of the African Union, who serves as the depository for the treaty. Member states are to submit an annual report on nuclear activities to an African Commission on Nuclear Energy, which will monitor member states' nuclear activities.[25]

ABANDONING THE PROGRAM

Analysts have identified a host of reasons why South Africa dismantled its nuclear arsenal. By early 1990, when South Africa renounced nuclear weapons, the apartheid regime was experiencing the worst legitimacy crisis in its history. President de Klerk might have dismantled his regime's nuclear weapons to gain international recognition to prolong his hold on the apartheid power.[26] Another domestic factor was that the apartheid regime did not want an African National Congress government (and perhaps also white extremist groups) to gain access to nuclear weapons.[27] The de Klerk government also might have feared that an African National Congress government might transfer weapons grade uranium to Libya, Cuba, Iran, or the Palestinian Liberation Organization as recompense for support received during the liberation struggle. The South African government began to seriously contemplate reforming its apartheid policies that had led to its international isolation, and to look at ways to facilitate breaking out of that isolation.

There is also an external security consideration. By 1989, the South African government's perception of the likelihood of a Soviet military invasion was reduced, especially following the planned withdrawal of Cuban troops from Angola, Namibia's transition to independence, and the end of the Cold War. The termination of the program and the signing of the NPT were seen as means to reduce South Africa's international isolation, which had been brought about by its apartheid policies.[28] Military planners also came to believe that a nuclear capability was coming at the expense of military modernization.

By the end of the 1980s, significant changes occurred at the international and regional levels that started to ease the security situation around South Africa.[29] A cease-fire on the northern border of Namibia was reached in August 1988. This was followed by the signing of a tripartite agreement between South Africa, Angola, and Cuba in December 1988 ensuring a phased withdrawal of Cuban forces from Angola. In April 1989 U.N. Security Council resolution 435/1978, leading to the independence of Namibia, was also put into operation.

These events coincided with the assumption to office in September 1989 of President F. W. de Klerk, who set in motion political reforms of South Africa's domestic apartheid policies. With the removal of the external threat, it became obvious that South Africa's nuclear capability was becoming a liability. Furthermore, as the progress of domestic political reform became better understood abroad, accession to the NPT assumed distinct advantages for South Africa internationally, and especially within the African continent. Shortly after becoming State President, de Klerk therefore ordered an investigation to be carried out to dismantle the nuclear program completely, with the aim of acceding to the NPT as a state without nuclear weapons.

The first report from this investigation was submitted to him in November 1989 and was approved in principle. In the light of internal and external political factors, it was also decided that an announcement of South Africa's past nuclear deterrent capability would not take place before accession to the NPT. A steering committee of senior officials was appointed to dismantle the six completed gun-type devices at ARMSCOR under controlled and safe conditions, decontaminate the ARMSCOR facilities and return severely contaminated equipment to the South African Atomic Energy Commission, advise the government of a suitable timetable for accession to the NPT, sign a Comprehensive Safeguards Agreement with the IAEA, and provide an initial national inventory of nuclear materials and facilities, as required by the Safeguards Agreements. Although the Y Plant was actually closed down on February 1, 1990, written confirmation of these instructions was received from the President only on February 26, 1990, and that date should, therefore, stand as the official date of the termination of South Africa's nuclear program. On October 30, 1991, South Africa submitted its initial inventory of nuclear materials and facilities to the IAEA, and the first verification team from the Agency arrived on site in November 1991.

Several important lessons emerge from the South African experience. First, the perception of external threats to a state's security can influence the decision to acquire nuclear weapons. Second, nuclear disarmament is a matter of political will. Third, verification and inspections are important in the effort to restore international confidence. Fourth, the principle of irreversibility should apply to the nuclear disarmament process. And finally, the value of accurate recordkeeping considerably facilitates the verification process.[30]

CONCLUSION

There are four factors that may cause South Africa to change its policy on nuclear weapons: a perceived threat from China's growing interest and influence in Africa, a renewed quest for nuclear energy as a source of electricity, frustration at the lack of progress being made in the global nuclear nonproliferation regime, and generational change within South Africa's arms control community. A change in policy also may be facilitated by South Africa's unique nuclear weapons history as well as by its advanced scientific, industrial, and technological infrastructure. South Africa is indeed technically capable of restarting a nuclear program. It is a world leader, for instance, in the extraction of uranium from low-grade ores. The South African military, the private sector, and the scientific community have a long history of collaboration on advanced technical projects. Unlike scientists and engineers who had worked on the Soviet Union's WMD programs, South Africa's scientific community was not reemployed in internationally funded programs; they continue to work in nuclear and defense related industries.

South Africa's transition from an authoritarian state to a constitutional democracy in the 1990s and its resultant current policies, legislation, and institutional framework, however, will militate against such a change. Aspects of South Africa's nuclear history—the backdrop of apartheid and international isolation, the personalities of National Party leaders, South African "total onslaught" security strategy, and the nation's large uranium resources—still exert an influence on national strategy, but current policies are also a product of the country's democratic transformation that improved civil-military oversight, and created a new defense posture and doctrine and a responsible defense industry. A democratic South Africa also adopted several significant arms control policies, institutions, and laws that favor nuclear disarmament.

In addition, the African National Congress's approach to national and international issues is often based on moral and ethical stances. A radical change would not only entail a fundamental shift in the present government's ethical and moral stances and a redefinition of its basic political principles but would also require a rolling back of democratic gains (such as civilian oversight mechanisms), the repeal of numerous laws, and the unbundling of a variety of institutional entities established to ensure compliance with South Africa's international obligations and domestic laws.

In the unlikely event that indicators appeared to suggest that South African officials were considering a reversal in their nuclear policies, the international community could undertake six actions to counter this policy shift. First, it could provide South Africa with financial resources and educational opportunities to train new recruits into the civil service with an interest in arms control and disarmament. Second, it could provide South Africa and other African countries with economic structures and investment as a means of reducing reliance on China. Third, it could assist South Africa and other countries in the development of nuclear material energy sources and facilities. Fourth, it could ensure that significant progress is made in both the Conference on Disarmament and the NPT, allowing nuclear-weapon states to fulfill their disarmament obligations. Fifth, the international community could increase the ability of South African civil society to engage in open discussion of issues related to weapons of mass destruction. And sixth, it could convene meetings of international and African experts to discuss and explore the development of educational courses for scientists and science students on the risks, rules, and responsibilities in the prevention of the misuse of science for hostile purposes.

NOTES

1. Buyelwa Sonjica, Minister of Minerals and Energy, presentation to South Africa's Nuclear Energy and Uranium Renaissance Conference, February 14, 2007, http://www.info.gov.za/speeches/2007/07030611451004.htm.

2. Tom Robbins and Quentin Wray, "China Charms the Critics of Its Africa Business Strategy," *Business Report*, June 17, 2007.

3. "Chinese Investment in Africa Cements Friendly Ties," People's Online Daily, February 15, 2011, http://english.peopledaily.com.cn/90001/90780/91421/7288802.html.

4. "China Defends Its Role in Africa," BBC News, http://news.bbc.co.uk/2/hi/asia-pacific/6660341.stm.

5. Endorsed by all African leaders at the Organization of African Unity summit on July 11, 2001, the New Partnership for Africa's Development was launched to promote

democracy and good governance in Africa in return for increased Western investment, trade, and debt relief. The Partnership's Peace and Security Initiative focuses on building Africa's capacity to manage conflict by strengthening continental and regional institutions.

6. "Analyst Says RSA Should Consider Restarting Its Nuclear Weapons Program," *The Star*, http://www.thestar.co.za/, accessed April 26, 2007.

7. Renfrew Christie, Unclassified Seminar Paper for presentation to the South African Intelligence Community at the request of the Minister for Intelligence, August 24, 2006.

8. "Analyst Says RSA Should Consider Restarting Its Nuclear Weapons Program."

9. Abdul S. Minty, Statement to the International Symposium on Highly Enriched Uranium, Oslo, Norway, June 19–20, 2006, http://www.nrpa.no/symposium/documents/Minty%20HEU%20Oslo%20June%202006.pdf.

10. See Donald Pressly, "Nuclear Power 'Part of the Future,'" *Business Report*, May 9, 2007.

11. Hilary Joffe, "Bold State Bid to Put SA Back on Nuclear Map," *Business Day*, August 15, 2007.

12. Ibid.

13. Department of Minerals and Energy, "Nuclear Energy Policy and Strategy for the Republic of South Africa: Draft for Public Comment, July 2007," http://www.chamberofmines.org.na/uploads/media/nuclear_energy_policy_sa.pdf.

14. Buyelwa Sonjica, Minister of Minerals and Energy, presentation to South Africa's Nuclear Energy and Uranium Renaissance Conference, February 14, 2007, http://www.info.gov.za/speeches/2007/07030611451004.htm.

15. Interview with DFA official, June 5, 2007.

16. Op-ed by the foreign ministers of Australia, Chile, Indonesia, Norway, Romania, South Africa, and the United Kingdom, July 27, 2005. See also the Declaration by the Foreign Ministers of Australia, Chile, Indonesia, Norway, Romania, South Africa, and the United Kingdom on Strengthening Adherence to Nuclear Non-Proliferation and Disarmament Agreements, July 26, 2005, http://www.wagingpeace.org/articles/2005/07/26_seven-nation-declaration.htm.

17. Address by the Minister of Foreign Affairs, Dr. Nkosazana Dlamini Zuma, at the opening of the Nuclear Suppliers Group Plenary meeting, Cape Town, April 19, 2007, http://www.polity.org.za/article/dlamini-zuma-nuclear-suppliers-group-plenary-meeting-19042007-2007-04-19.

18. Interview with senior civil servant, Pretoria, June 1, 2007.

19. Convention on the Prohibition of the Use, Stockpiling, Production and Transfer of Anti-Personnel Mines and on Their Destruction, Article 1: General Obligations, http://www.info.gov.za/view/DownloadFileAction?id=68013.

20. Minutes of the Defence Portfolio Committee on the Prohibition or Restriction

of Certain Conventional Weapons Bill: Briefing, May 22, 2007, http://www.pmg.org.
za/report/20070822-prohibition-or-restriction-certain-conventional-weapons-amend-
ment-bil.

21. John F. Burns, "South Africa's Secret Atom Plant Suspected of Working on a
Bomb," *New York Times*, April 30, 1977, 1, 6.

22. Speech by State President F. W. de Klerk to Parliament, March 24, 1993.

23. Guy Lamb and Karen Peters, "The Rise and Demise of South Africa's Nuclear
Weapons Programme: Lessons for States with Nuclear Weapons Programmes?" in *Instead of Nuclear Weapons: New Views on Human, Global and National Security: Report
from an International IPPNW and Peace Researchers Seminar*, Moscow, March 25, 2002.

24. Ibid.

25. Bereng Mtimkulu, "Africa Bans the Bomb," *Bulletin of the Atomic Scientists* 52,
no. 4 (July–August 1996): 11.

26. Sung-Ju Cho, "A Diversionary Compliance Hypothesis of Nuclear Renunciation:
The Case of South Africa," Paper presented at the annual meeting of the American Po-
litical Science Association, Hilton, Chicago, and the Palmer House, Hilton, Chicago, IL,
September 5, 2004, http://www.allacademic.com/meta/p60074_index.html.

27. Ibid.

28. Lamb and Peters, "The Rise and Demise of South Africa's Nuclear Weapons Programme."

29. David Fig, "Uranium Road: Questioning South Africa's Nuclear Direction" (Jo-
hannesburg: Heinrich Boll Foundation, 2005).

30. Interview with senior civil servant, Pretoria, May 2, 2007.

6

Nuclear Energy and the Prospects for Nuclear Proliferation in Southeast Asia

Tanya Ogilvie-White and Michael S. Malley

No Southeast Asian country has nuclear weapons or plans to acquire them. To the contrary, all countries in the region have committed to the creation of a regional nuclear-weapons-free zone, and there is no obvious reason to question either their support for this initiative or their opposition to nuclear proliferation. Nevertheless, states in this part of the world share a sense of strategic insecurity stemming from actual and potential changes in the regional order. To the north and west lie nuclear weapons states and governments able to join that club in short order. In addition, bitter bilateral differences divide India from Pakistan, North from South Korea, and China from India, Japan, and Taiwan. Uncertainty over the future direction of these enduring rivalries is enhanced by rapid economic development in India and China, growing conservatism in Japan, and America's distraction from Asian affairs. Southeast Asian countries have never responded to security challenges by seeking nuclear weapons; but today, many are seeking to create domestic nuclear energy industries. Since 2005, Vietnam and Indonesia have announced separate plans to construct nuclear power generation facilities within a decade, and Indonesia and South Korea have signed a preliminary agreement to construct a nuclear power plant. In 2007 the governments of Malaysia, the Philippines, and Thailand declared their own interest in similar programs (which Thailand subsequently launched), and the Burmese military junta has struck an agreement with Russia to acquire a small research reactor. As a result, several governments are likely to develop substantial nuclear expertise and capabilities. This presents two challenges. One is the possibility that nuclear mythmakers will for the first time be able to make politically plausible claims that these countries are able to develop their own nuclear weapons capabilities. The second is that growing Southeast Asian nuclear industries may present appealing opportunities for nonstate actors to obtain know-how and materials.

Whether these emerging capabilities translate into significant proliferation threats depends on the evolution of Southeast Asia's regional security architecture. In contrast to Northeast Asia, where formal multilateral security cooperation is limited mainly to the Six Party Talks, Southeast Asian countries have committed to develop a regional security community by 2020. This initiative is part of a broader effort by the Association of Southeast Asian Nations (ASEAN) to construct an ASEAN Community. However, the association's security cooperation record is mixed. Its most notable achievement has been the creation of the ASEAN Regional Forum (ARF). Although this body has emerged as the Asia Pacific's primary apparatus for security cooperation, it has placed issues such as nuclear security and export controls in the "too hard" basket, and consequently is often accused of being nothing more than a "talk shop." Nevertheless, the Philippines and Singapore recently have suggested placing nuclear issues high on the agenda in ASEAN's own annual ministerial meetings and in ARF discussions.

This chapter focuses on Vietnam and Indonesia, the two regional states with the most advanced plans to construct nuclear energy plants. We assess their existing and planned nuclear capabilities. We also construct a nuclear mythmaking profile, and identify mythmaking scenarios that indicate how these countries are likely to treat their growing nuclear capabilities.[1] In both countries, the prospects for state-led weapons proliferation are very low. Neither faces an external threat that is likely to motivate an expensive nuclear weapons program. Both lack the capacity to develop and employ nuclear weapons, and the construction of nuclear power industries will create this capability at best very slowly. Domestic actors that control nuclear energy policy in each country are closely integrated into international networks that oppose proliferation. Consequently, the main proliferation risk posed by the development of nuclear power industries in Southeast Asia is that nonstate actors may be able to exploit weaknesses in the regulation and operation of those industries to obtain expertise and resources that are more difficult to obtain elsewhere.

VIETNAM

Vietnam has no militarily significant weapons of mass destruction (WMD) facilities, no identifiable mythmakers who favor acquiring them, and no sign of effort to engage in nuclear mythmaking, beyond the official commitment to nonproliferation and disarmament, and occasional references to the nuclear taboo. Moreover, Vietnam is an active member of the nonproliferation regime, has pursued a benign foreign policy since 1991, and is in the process of forging closer military ties with the United States, especially in the area of counterterrorism. Despite these optimistic indicators, there is a certain amount of nervousness among some Western officials and policy experts, who fear the possibility that over the longer term Vietnam could emerge as a "second North Korea" in the Asia-Pacific, challenging regional stability and unleashing a new series of proliferation threats.[2] These concerns stem from Hanoi's decision to launch a nuclear energy program, combined with historical apprehension over the ideological orientation of Vietnam's Marxist-Leninist regime, which, following the disastrous Vietnam War, successfully pursued a hegemonic agenda in Indochina. Given these concerns, what are the potential security implications of Vietnam's decision to develop nuclear energy?

Vietnam's WMD Capabilities

Besides the possible stocks of Soviet-supplied chemical weapons and toxins left over from the 1980s, there is no public information that suggests Vietnam has any biological or chemical weapons capabilities, and no evidence that it intends to develop them. Since the terrorist attacks of September 11, 2001, Vietnam's nuclear research activities have occasionally come under the spotlight in analyses of the threat of criminal or terrorist theft of WMD-related materials in Southeast Asia. This is because the Da Lat research reactor, Vietnam's only significant existing nuclear facility, used highly enriched uranium fuel, which could be used in an improvised nuclear device. However, in March 2007, Vietnam and the U.S. Department of Energy signed contracts to improve the physical protection of Vietnam's nuclear materials, to convert the Da Lat research reactor to using low enriched uranium, and to return the highly enriched uranium to Russia for safe and secure disposal.[3] The reactor now uses low enriched uranium fuel, and is scheduled to be decommissioned and replaced with a new high-power research reactor.

The world's attention is now turning to Vietnam's nuclear energy plans, and the future potential for nuclear breakout, following Hanoi's decision to develop nuclear power. Vietnam's nuclear energy strategy, which was officially signed by the Prime Minister in January 2006, calls for the development of commercial nuclear power by the year 2020 to reduce the country's dependence on hydro and fossil fuel resources.[4] According to Vuong Huu Tan, director of the Vietnam Atomic Energy Institute and a key player in terms of espousing the benefits of nuclear energy, the plan is to build three nuclear power plants by 2025, in a project that is expected to cost $16 billion and add 8,000 megawatts to the national power grid.[5]

Economic growth and associated mounting energy demands are driving Vietnam's nuclear development. The Ministry of Industry has forecast that electricity demand will double in just over four years, continuing to rise between 17 and 22 percent annually over the 2010–15 period.[6] Driving this surging energy demand is Vietnam's rapid economic expansion. In the six months between joining the World Trade Organization in January 2007 and the release of mid-year economic development figures in June 2007, Vietnam's growth accelerated by 7.9 percent and investment by 14 percent.[7] Although growth subsequently slowed following a series of anti-inflationary measures that were taken in response to global macroeconomic turbulence, it picked up again in 2009–10. At the same time, concerns over current and future energy shortages undermine confidence that this growth can be sustained, with the government particularly troubled by the country's dependence on unreliable hydropower plants (which currently generate 40 percent of Vietnam's electricity output), and the potential for outages to disrupt the economy and deter future direct foreign investment.[8] Vietnamese officials are determined to diversify their country's power industry and to develop more reliable sources of energy.

To implement its nuclear program, Vietnam depends heavily on bilateral nuclear cooperation agreements with advanced nuclear states and on technical assistance from the International Atomic Energy Agency (IAEA). Russia is Vietnam's main partner in developing its nuclear research capabilities. Since the Soviet Union supplied the Da Lat nuclear research reactor in the 1970s, commercial nuclear cooperation between the two states has accelerated.[9] Vietnam also has signed bilateral nuclear cooperation agreements with Argentina, China, France, India, Japan, South Korea, and most recently the United States, following four years of intensive energy diplomacy.[10] The IAEA Technical Assistance Program also has provided Hanoi with $1 million annually in equipment, technical support, and training since 2001.

Nuclear Decision-making in Vietnam

Nuclear policy in Vietnam is driven by a handful of officials in the government and the Communist Party of Vietnam who exercise a virtual monopoly over political discussion and policy formulation.[11] Given the closed nature of Vietnam's government and the difficult task of obtaining documentation, the only way for outsiders to identify and assess nuclear beliefs is to examine the official statements made by key representatives in relevant forums. Of course, official statements can mask actual intentions. For example, as a member of the Non-Aligned Movement Vietnam always votes in favor of disarmament resolutions sponsored by the Non-Aligned Movement; however, this is not necessarily indicative of benign nuclear intentions given the diplomatic pressure on Non-Aligned Movement members not to break ranks. More significant are the independent statements issued by Vietnam's foreign affairs officials, which stress a balanced approach to nonproliferation and disarmament, and the right of non-nuclear-weapons states to pursue peaceful nuclear energy.[12] Vietnam's disarmament officials are now outspoken on these issues, pushing states that have not done so to sign and ratify the Comprehensive Test Ban Treaty and to live up to the commitments made at the 2000 Non-proliferation Treaty (NPT) Review Conference.[13] Vietnam argues that non-nuclear-weapons states have a "legitimate right" to receive unconditional security assurances from the nuclear-weapons states. Such assurances are essential to promote the confidence of the non-nuclear-weapons and to strengthen the NPT. Perhaps most significantly, Vietnam has criticized its ASEAN partners for not going far enough to tackle proliferation threats, commenting on the complacency of some Southeast Asian states, which mistakenly believe their commitment to the Bangkok Treaty excuses them from pursuing a more proactive nonproliferation agenda.[14]

More meaningful indicators of Vietnam's current nuclear intentions, and possible future aspirations, are the steps the government has taken to boost international confidence in its ability to function responsibly in the realm of nonproliferation and counterterrorism. These actions were motivated in part by Vietnam's successful quest for a nonpermanent seat on the U.N. Security Council in 2008; but they also need to be viewed in the context of Vietnam's long-term progression toward greater international engagement and cooperation. The most relevant of these steps was Hanoi's announcement in November 2006 that it would sign the IAEA Additional Protocol, increasing the transparency of its embryonic nuclear program and accepting a relatively intrusive monitoring regime.[15] This decision was approved by the IAEA Board of Governors in March 2007 and carried out the following August. Vietnam's introduction of the Additional Protocol is an encouraging indication that Hanoi intends to abide by the word and spirit of the NPT and avoid the path taken by Iran.

Alongside this landmark decision on the Additional Protocol, Vietnam has taken an increasingly proactive stance in Track I and Track II counterterrorism initiatives. With the United States, Vietnam cochairs the Council for Security Cooperation in the Asia Pacific (CSCAP) Expert Group on the Proliferation of weapons of mass destruction, and regularly attends meetings of the subgroup on weapons of mass destruction export controls. It also has submitted relatively detailed reports (known as counterterrorism action plans) to the Asia-Pacific Economic Cooperation (APEC) Counter-Terrorism Task Force and the U.N. 1540 Committee, outlining the actions that it is taking to prevent the proliferation of weapons of mass destruction within and across its borders.[16] Despite long-standing resistance to joining ad hoc groups outside the purview of the United Nations, and despite its continuing reservations over its legal status, in March 2007 the Vietnam Ministry of Foreign Affairs spokesman, Le Dung, announced that Vietnam now "welcomes the spirit of Proliferation Security Initiative" and has agreed to consider joining. Vietnam subsequently participated in the Asia-Pacific forum of the Proliferation Security Initiative in Auckland, New Zealand, on March 29, 2007.[17]

Opportunities for proponents of a nuclear weapons option to emerge from outside government circles and trigger a change in policy are currently low, although they might increase due to the government's attempt to raise public awareness about nuclear issues and its new willingness to consult experts on key policy matters. Since the decision was taken in 2001 to explore the feasibility of developing nuclear energy, and especially after the official decision to embark on a nuclear energy program in January 2006, the government has launched education initiatives to raise awareness of nuclear energy and develop indigenous expertise. Equally significant, in terms of the mythmaking model, is the expansion of research institutions in the country, which are making a substantial contribution to foreign policy formulation in certain areas, such as trade policy.[18] Where nuclear policy is concerned, the Vietnam Atomic Energy Commission (VAEC) played a major role in persuading the Prime Minister to support a new strategy to develop nuclear energy by preparing the strategy document on which the Prime Minister's decision was based.[19] Thus, while there is no evidence of pro–nuclear weapons sentiment either inside or outside government circles, the foreign policymaking environment in Vietnam is changing and may open the way to future nuclear mythmakers emerging from the industrial sector as well as from research and academic institutions.

Future Nuclear Proliferation Scenarios in Vietnam

What factors might push the Vietnamese government to pursue a nuclear weapons capability in tandem with its nuclear energy program, following the path that Iran is widely believed to have taken, or to argue in favor of nuclear breakout, along the lines of North Korea? Three scenarios are proposed: the development of weapons of mass destruction to enhance Vietnam's power relative to its neighbors in Indochina to revive its past hegemonic agenda; the development of a nuclear capability to increase Vietnam's bargaining power in the South China Sea; and a copy-cat response to nuclear breakout by a regional power.

Vietnam is regarded as a potential regional hegemon in Southeast Asia, partly because of its military might, its geostrategic location, and its past aspirations. Any attempt to sketch out Vietnam's nuclear future must address the question of whether Vietnam's appetite for regional dominance is likely to return. If the conclusion is that Vietnam's past hegemonic ambitions are truly buried, the potential security risks posed by its nuclear energy program will be minimal. The key period in question dates back to the 1970s and 1980s, when, as part of an ambitious plan to create an Indochinese Federation under its control, Hanoi established hegemony over Cambodia (which it invaded in 1978 and occupied for 11 years), and Laos (which Vietnam reduced to a position of satellite state from 1977 to 1988).[20] Although Vietnam's hegemonic ambitions during this period relied heavily on military and financial assistance from the Soviet Union (forcing Vietnam into a hasty retreat when that assistance was terminated), the growth of Vietnam's economy may present an option to revive the old expansionist agenda. This could prompt a return to coercive policies, regional instability, and arms race dynamics.

This rise of hegemonic ambition is an improbable scenario primarily because of Vietnam's concerns over China's rising power and its long-term policy of trying to balance Beijing's influence through a policy of benign regional engagement. Vietnam has pursued this strategy for dealing with its powerful neighbor since 1991, when the Seventh National Party Congress adopted the "new outlook," a foreign policy designed to ensure that Vietnam is "friends with all countries."[21] This has led Hanoi to become increasingly embedded in a network of regional institutions, including APEC, ASEAN, and the ARF, which place strong political constraints on any future national ambitions. Significantly, this policy also has drawn Vietnam closer to the United States, including in the hard security areas of counterterrorism cooperation and military-to-military ties.[22] Many ASEAN states have long relied on tacit or formal alliances to ensure their security and balance a rising China,[23] but Vietnam's willingness to move beyond the economic realm in its relations with Washington is new and has been consolidated via a successful bilateral Political, Security and Defense Dialogue, which was held in Hanoi in 2008 and Washington, DC, in 2009.[24]

Another possible future scenario relates to political and strategic tension resulting from unresolved border disputes. There may be some concern that ongoing disagreements over competing territorial claims could lead Vietnam to decide to develop weapons of mass destruction in a bid to increase its bargaining leverage. Such a scenario might appear credible in the context of the multilateral dispute relating to the Spratly archipelago and the broader issue of the South China Sea, where overlapping sovereignty claims have created a serious conflict of interest between Vietnam and Brunei Darussalam, Cambodia, China, Indonesia, Malaysia, the Philippines, and Taiwan, resulting in a number of destabilizing incidents. Although some competing claims have been settled in recent years, serious obstacles to a permanent resolution remain, creating the potential for escalation and future conflict.[25] In particular, Vietnam's sovereignty claim to the whole Spratly archipelago could drive Hanoi to expand and flaunt its military might.

This scenario is unlikely to occur again because of Vietnam's approach to border disputes since the introduction of its new outlook in 1991 and its long-term commitment to ASEAN.[26] Hanoi's experience of the dangers of leaving border disputes unresolved has led it to pursue the peaceful, negotiated settlement of border disputes, resulting in an impressive record of bilateral and trilateral agreements since 1990.[27] Although important disagreements remain and many of the border agreements are not fully implemented, Hanoi's strategy has been to minimize tensions by downplaying its sovereignty claims, especially with China, and to support institutionalization of ASEAN and ARF preventative diplomacy.[28] Hanoi also has economic incentives not to rock the boat with Beijing, its biggest trading partner.[29]

Additional possible scenarios are based on nuclear breakout or latent proliferation in Southeast Asia or further afield. While Vietnam's response to North Korea's nuclear weapons test and Iran's nuclear defiance has been muted, it is possible to envisage future proliferation developments that could lead to exploration of a nuclear weapons option. Nuclear proliferation by Thailand, Vietnam's primary regional rival, could result in a parallel proliferation decision in Hanoi. This is hardly an "over-the-horizon" possibility, however, because Thailand is still in the early stages of launching a nuclear energy program.[30] Nuclear breakout by a nonrival in the region is a slightly more feasible scenario, though still unlikely. The development of a nuclear weapons program by Indonesia, a nation that has not posed a direct threat to Vietnam, would signal the collapse of the Bangkok Treaty and a major breakdown of the international nuclear nonproliferation regime. The loss of faith in nonproliferation norms that would accompany such a decision would no doubt spark a nuclear policy reassessment not just in Vietnam but also in virtually every nuclear-capable state in the region. Similarly, a decision by Japan or South Korea to develop nuclear weapons—a nearer-term scenario, perhaps driven by a permanent breakdown of the agreement over North Korea's nuclear disarmament or doubts over the reliability of U.S. security guarantees—would be far-reaching, possibly forcing a number of committed non-nuclear-weapons states to re-examine their commitment to nonproliferation.

Vietnam's response to regional nuclear breakout would be influenced by the faith it has in its bilateral security arrangements, the status of the emerging ASEAN Security Community, its deepening strategic partnership with India, and its closer relations with the United States. In the context of China's continuing rise and the insecurity that this generates in the region, the probability that Vietnam would be tempted to develop a nuclear weapons capability in response to further nuclear breakout would increase if the reliability of its alliances and friendships were called into question. It would not be too fanciful to imagine that, under conditions of regional breakout, plus potential future U.S. withdrawal from East Asia and an increasingly belligerent and dominant China, Vietnam would explore the creation of an independent nuclear deterrent, possibly with the assistance of India, which signed a New Strategic Partnership with Vietnam in July 2007. This is a worst-case scenario. It does not take into account the strong political and economic incentives for Vietnam to forgo nuclear weapons. Any hint of nuclear noncompliance, for instance, would jeopardize Vietnam's nuclear supplier arrangements, destroy hard won nuclear cooperation agreements, and end IAEA technical assistance programs, threatening Vietnam's energy security and economy.

A shorter-term risk associated with the development of nuclear energy in Vietnam stems from poor capacity, which creates the potential for nuclear accidents and security breaches. This problem has been recognized by IAEA officials, leading to the launch of extrabudgetary nuclear safety programs, such as the Asian Nuclear Safety Network, and the Forum for Nuclear Cooperation in Asia (FNCA), which oversee Asia's nuclear safety culture project. Although Vietnam has never signed the Nuclear Safety Convention, which sets international nuclear safety standards, it is actively engaged in the Asian Nuclear Safety Network and FNCA regional nuclear safety networks. In 2002, the Da Lat research reactor was used as a guinea pig for the first regional peer review of an Asian country's nuclear safety standards, leading the FNCA to draw up 16 recommendations for safety improvements at the facility.[31] The gradual implementation of these recommendations since 2003 has been applauded by the IAEA, which regards Vietnam as a shining example of a developing state that prioritizes the reduction of nuclear-related vulnerabilities. These developments are encouraging, but still the nuclear safety and security challenges confronting Vietnam will increase as it embarks on its nuclear energy program.

INDONESIA'S NUCLEAR CAPABILITIES AND PLANS

After Vietnam, Indonesia is the Southeast Asian country that has proceeded furthest with its plans to develop a domestic nuclear energy industry. There is little in its current plans or past practices to suggest that Indonesia's leaders have any interest in developing nuclear weapons. Concern stems instead from the context in which current plans are emerging. Over the past decade, international terrorist networks have demonstrated their capacity to operate throughout Southeast Asia. During the same era, democratization has enabled new groups to achieve influence over Indonesian foreign policy, including its approach to nonproliferation.

Like Vietnam, Indonesia's nuclear power plans are motivated by the need to expand and diversify its energy supplies in order to sustain economic growth. Its public utilities have never generated enough electricity to meet demand from households and industry, but in recent years the shortfall in production has become serious. Investment in all infrastructure types fell sharply in the late 1990s due to the deep economic crisis and subsequent collapse of the country's three-decade-old authoritarian regime. Since economic growth resumed in 2000, demand for electricity has grown by 6 percent annually. Political uncertainty has inhibited large-scale investments, and the capacity of the country's electricity system has grown only slightly. In response, about 10,000 companies maintain their own power generation capacity, relying mainly on diesel-powered generators. These captive power sources, unconnected to public power grids, produce nearly a third of the electricity consumed in the country.[32]

Rising oil prices and falling oil output have sharpened Indonesia's electricity crisis. Domestic output has fallen to its lowest level in more than three decades, and since 2003 it has been a net oil importer.[33] In 2008 Indonesia withdrew from the Organization of Petroleum Exporting States. Rising oil imports, combined with rapid oil price increases, compelled the government in 2005 to enact sharp cuts in the subsidies that previously had kept domestic fuel prices at one-third of world market prices. Immediately, the cost of diesel-generated electricity doubled. This added financial pressure to the state-owned electric utility because it relies on diesel generators to produce one-quarter of its output.[34] The rise in oil prices also drove companies that had produced their own electricity to draw from the public power grid.[35]

The government adopted a national energy policy in 2006 to diversify and expand the energy supply. This policy calls for a mixture of "new energies," such as nuclear and biomass, to contribute 5 percent of national energy consumption by 2025. In addition, the government released a "grand design" for nuclear power development that calls for the construction of four nuclear power plants starting in 2007 that are to be completed in 2016.[36] And in 2007, the House of Representatives passed, and the president signed, a new energy law that recognizes nuclear energy as a "new energy source" that should be "controlled by the state and exploited for the greatest prosperity of the people."

This policy shift has enjoyed substantial support from the International Atomic Energy Agency as well as potential foreign suppliers. In a 2003 report, the IAEA "concluded that nuclear power would become a competitive electricity generating option for Indonesia some time between 2014 and 2020."[37] Three years later, after Indonesia had established its new, comprehensive energy policy, the IAEA director general visited Jakarta, met with the president, declared that "Indonesia has been a strong and supportive partner of the IAEA," and announced that the agency would continue to support "Indonesia's preparation for its planned nuclear power plant construction."[38]

Among likely investors in Indonesia's nuclear power industry, South Korea appears to be in the lead. In 2004 the Korean government provided assistance to conduct "a three-year feasibility study on the future for nuclear power" that envisions a complex of six reactors able to generate 1,000 megawatts each.[39] Since then, Korean officials and firms lengthened their lead over other potential suppliers. In December 2006 the Korean prime minister visited Indonesia and signed an agreement "to consider jointly building nuclear power plants and exchanging fissile material and technology."[40] And in July 2007 Indonesian and South Korean companies signed a preliminary agreement to construct Indonesia's first nuclear power plant, with a capacity of 2,000 megawatts. At that time, Korean Hydro and Nuclear Power Corporation and PT Medco Energi International expected to begin the project as early as 2008 and complete it in 2016.[41] Since, then, however, public opposition in the region where the plants are most likely to be constructed has delayed these plans.

Indonesia also appears likely to rely on foreign suppliers of uranium. The previous Indonesian vice president said that he expected Australia to provide uranium for Indonesian reactors, since the security cooperation treaty they signed in 2006 calls explicitly for "strengthening bilateral nuclear cooperation for peaceful purposes."[42] The search for external sources of nuclear fuel is occurring despite the oft-mentioned claim that Indonesia possesses uranium reserves capable of providing Indonesia with enough yellowcake to satisfy domestic needs for planned reactors.[43] These sources also report that Indonesia has the capability to fabricate fuel for nuclear reactors, and that the main research complex outside Jakarta fabricates fuel for the German-built Siwabessy reactor. These claims, however, appear to be based on IAEA reports from the 1980s. They do not take countervailing evidence into account. For instance, Indonesia imports the uranium used in the Siwabessy reactor. The amount and quality of uranium discovered in Indonesia in the 1970s and 1980s also was too low to persuade France and Germany to continue exploration efforts. It was so low that Japan decided to forgo prospecting in the country. Indeed, the failure to find adequate uranium reserves "seriously undermined" the conclusions of a 1976 study by the IAEA that several nuclear reactors could be constructed on Java in the 1980s.[44]

One potential supplier of reactors is raising concern because of the type of technology it proposes to sell and the buyers it is targeting. Russian President Vladimir Putin first offered in 2003 to sell Indonesia small-scale floating nuclear reactors that can be connected to existing power grids, but Indonesia's president at the time, Megawati Sukarnoputri, apparently declined the offer. Since then, political leaders in islands that are cut off from major electricity grids have welcomed the possibility of quickly addressing their dire electricity shortages. The governor who is most eager to acquire one of these Russian power plants, a former businessman, explained his interest simply in terms of the high cost and inadequate supply of electricity from the state-owned utility in his region.[45] Although provincial governments enjoy substantial autonomy from Jakarta, it is unlikely they could acquire nuclear facilities without national government approval. It also is unlikely that such approval would come easily, but the head of the country's nuclear regulatory agency (BAPETEN) expressed his hope that this would "stimulate other regions [provinces] to use nuclear technology."[46] Nonetheless, the location of the proposed power plant is likely to raise concern: in the province of Gorontalo, just north of a long-running sectarian conflict, and facing the Celebes Sea, through which members of Southeast Asia's major terrorist networks travel between bases in the Philippines and Indonesia.

Despite high-level political backing in Indonesia and strong international support, nuclear energy plans still face domestic opposition. As Indonesia is the only country in Southeast Asia currently rated by Freedom House as "Free," Indonesian policymakers must contend with a wide array of opponents. And since the government favors the same site that the previous, authoritarian regime chose in the 1990s, activist groups are well prepared to mount campaigns today. The largest environmental group, WALHI, has designed a campaign to oppose commercial nuclear power, and the largest religious group, Nahdlatul Ulama, which has tens of millions of members and a large number in the region around the proposed site, has asked the government to reconsider its plan.[47] WALHI's head even has denounced the plan as potential "genocide."[48] They are concerned about the country's general inability to maintain high safety standards, and the threat posed by earthquakes and volcanic eruptions. These groups have found sympathy among highly placed politicians. One former president, who also led Nahdlatul Ulama, suggested that the nuclear power project be abandoned. Opposition to nuclear power peaked during the national election campaign in 2009. Early that year, the vice president announced that his party could not support a nuclear option until Indonesia had enough suitably qualified personnel, and on the last day of the campaign the president himself said that the country should pursue other sources of energy during the next 10 to 30 years.[49]

Despite this opposition, the probability that Indonesia will start a nuclear power industry is much higher than when previous governments attempted to do so. Indonesia now experiences frequent and widespread electricity shortages, and the problem is widely and popularly regarded as a crisis. And since domestic oil and gas deposits are dwindling and are no longer sufficient to meet growing energy demand, the pressure to develop alternative energy sources is mounting. Moreover, and perhaps as a result of the growing sense of crisis, the main actors in the Indonesian government appear far more unified than in earlier eras. When oil and gas were plentiful and generated large amounts of income, there was little cooperation between the nuclear energy agency, the ministry of oil and gas, and the state-owned electric utility.[50] In recent years, the minister of energy and mineral resources has supported the nuclear agency's plans, and even the House of Representatives has offered a measure of support for those plans by including references to nuclear energy in the 2007 Energy Law.

Indonesian Approaches to Nuclear Power and Weapons of Mass Destruction

Apart from the very significant allegations that the Indonesian military used chemical weapons in the 1970s, and that top political and military leaders briefly discussed plans to acquire nuclear weapons in the 1960s, there is no indication that Indonesia has ever had any capability to use weapons of mass destruction, no signs that it intends to acquire them, and only the slightest of foundations on which to construct myths that would favor the development, acquisition, or use of nuclear weapons in the future.

Allegations that Indonesia used chemical weapons are limited to its brutal counterinsurgency campaign in East Timor, the former Portuguese colony it invaded and occupied during the mid-1970s. Many Indonesian troops continued to use harsh tactics in the territory until they departed in 1999, following a U.N.-sponsored referendum in which the East Timorese overwhelmingly rejected union with Indonesia. To examine the abuses that took place under Indonesian rule, East Timor formed a Commission for Reception, Truth, and Reconciliation, which compiled testimony from eyewitnesses. The commission's report, released in 2006, claimed that in the late 1970s the Indonesian military used "chemical weapons which poisoned water supplies, killed crops and other vegetation, and resulted in the deaths by poisoning of hundreds of civilians." The commission also noted that it received reports of the use of "biological weapons."[51]

Indonesia has three nuclear research reactors—more than any other country in Southeast Asia. The largest is named after the father of the country's nuclear energy program, G. A. Siwabessy. How he came to head that program, and how he directed it for two decades, reveals a great deal about the nature of nuclear myths and policymaking in Indonesia. In the mid-1950s, the Indonesian government established a commission to study the impact in the country of radioactive fallout from U.S. nuclear tests in the Pacific Ocean. Because the commission's task was to study the effects of radiation, not to develop nuclear energy, Siwabessy, a radiologist, headed it. In the late 1950s and 1960s, the commission evolved into an agency for research and development of atomic energy, but Siwabessy remained its head. Still, it was devoted almost entirely to training technicians to employ radioisotopes in agricultural and medical fields, and in the absence of any indigenous capacity Siwabessy's organization pursued international cooperation with the IAEA, the Soviet Union, France, West Germany, and Japan. Under the Atoms for Peace program, the United States supplied Indonesia with its first operational nuclear reactor, which reached criticality in 1964 and remained Indonesia's only reactor for 15 years.[52]

During its first two decades, enduring characteristics of Indonesia's nuclear program were institutionalized. A small group of civilian experts established control over the program and adopted international standards for its management. Rather than developing a nuclear power industry or nuclear weapons, they concentrated almost entirely on applications of nuclear science and technology that could provide immediate benefits, as in agriculture and medicine. The result was a close-knit nuclear establishment that relied more on international than domestic support for access to limited resources.

Nevertheless, suspicion that Indonesia might transform its very limited, peaceful uses of nuclear energy into military capability dogged the country through the 1960s and into the 1970s.[53] In general, these observers tended to assume that Indonesian leaders aimed to attain great power status, and that they would view nuclear weapons as a means to demonstrate that status. These suspicions seemed to reflect a poorly understood episode in the mid-1960s when high-level officials expressed a desire to build or acquire nuclear weapons. Following China's detonation of a nuclear device in 1964, some political and military leaders in Jakarta claimed they would soon have the capability to do likewise, and several months later Indonesia's president, Sukarno, made the same claim.

There is little evidence to indicate their intentions were serious or that they ever took more than modest diplomatic steps to achieve their stated goals. Even the author of the sole study of Indonesia's nuclear aspirations concludes: "Indonesia did not have the indigenous capability to produce its own nuclear weapon"; there is too little evidence to conclude that the president actually made a "proliferation decision"; and there is no evidence that China intended to provide such a weapon, despite widespread speculation at the time that it might agree to detonate one in Indonesian territory.[54] Even at the time when Indonesia appeared to be moving to the left and its president had announced the formation of a "Jakarta-Phnom Penh-Hanoi-Peking-Pyongyang axis," observers of Chinese foreign policy acknowledged "no indications whatever that the Chinese had any intention of setting Indonesia up as a nuclear power by giving her the bomb" and was prepared only to provide "a very modest program of nuclear assistance to Indonesia."[55]

This historical record suggests that some high-ranking officials, with presidential support, aspired to develop or acquire nuclear weapons. They did not lay a rhetorical, diplomatic, or technical foundation for nuclear proliferation. Indeed, they had little time to do so. In 1965, less than a year after they first expressed their desire to acquire nuclear weapons, anticommunist military officers drove them from power, broke relations with China, and put an end to any discussion of nuclear weapons. Within a month, while Sukarno still remained president, the government accepted IAEA safeguards in principle in exchange for an American decision to provide $350,000 worth of funding under the Atoms for Peace program. Two years later, shortly after General Suharto replaced Sukarno as president, Indonesia signed the safeguards agreement that set the country on the course it has pursued ever since: support for peaceful use of nuclear energy and consistent opposition to nuclear proliferation.[56]

Under Suharto, Indonesia's nuclear research capabilities grew but the program remained under the control of the same community of civilian professionals. Since Siwabessy retired in the early 1970s and was replaced by a nuclear physicist, Achmad Baiquni, the nuclear agency has sought to develop a nuclear power industry. However, plentiful oil, coal, and natural gas supplies consistently undermined its claims that nuclear energy was either necessary or a cost-effective means to meet the country's needs. Although the agency failed to win government support for nuclear power in the 1970s, it did gain support in the 1980s for the construction, with German assistance, of its largest reactor, a 30-megawatt multipurpose reactor just outside the capital. This coincided with the rise of an influential German-trained aerospace engineer, B. J. Habibie, who served as minister of research and technology for two decades, beginning with his return to Indonesia in the late 1970s.

Suharto placed control of nearly all technology matters under Habibie, a trusted civilian he had known since the 1950s. These included not just research institutes such as the National Atomic Energy Agency, but also strategic industries such as shipbuilding, weapons production, and aircraft production.

That not only kept them out of military hands but also placed them beyond the control of the ministry of finance, and thereby established a separate center of power within Suharto's regime. Throughout the 1980s and 1990s, Habibie's control over defense-related industries created friction with the military leadership.[57] The nuclear establishment remained essentially under civilian direction.

After massive protests drove Suharto from power in the late 1990s, democratization broadened the range of actors that are able to influence policies on nuclear power. Some of the country's most important nongovernmental organizations are campaigning against nuclear energy. Apart from their concerns with the safety of nuclear energy, they emphasize Indonesia's general inability to manage public infrastructure safely. Their fears are well grounded. In 2006 alone, official statistics show that aircraft incidents occurred at a rate of one every nine to ten days, and two trains crashed or derailed each month.[58] In 2007, hundreds died in ferry accidents, and two fatal air crashes prompted the European Union and the United States to ban all Indonesian airlines from their skies. Adding to the public's concern are a string of natural disasters that reflect the country's precarious geology. In addition to the well-known tsunami that killed more than 160,000 Indonesians in late 2004, serious earthquakes have struck the island of Java, on which the government plans to construct its first nuclear plant. One of those quakes killed more than 5,000 people, and the other damaged an oil refinery seriously enough that it had to be shut down temporarily. An uncontrolled mudflow, caused by careless drilling for natural gas in 2006, displaced more than 15,000 people and severed road, rail, and natural gas lines running out of the country's second-largest city, Surabaya, also on Java. Worse, from the perspective of most Indonesians, has been the government's inability to muster an effective response to the disaster.[59]

Democratization also has encouraged civil society groups and elected officials to shape discussion of issues directly concerned with proliferation. Since 2005, Indonesian politicians have been drawn into the debate over the nature of Iran's nuclear program. As international pressure on Iran intensified, Indonesia initiated a diplomatic offensive designed to secure its support at the IAEA, where Indonesia holds a seat on the board of governors. Historically, the countries have not had close relations, but in the wake of Indonesia's economic crisis and political transition in the late 1990s, Tehran made pledges (largely unrealized) to invest in Indonesia, and Indonesian leaders paid visits to Tehran to demonstrate to voters at home their concern for Muslim issues in world politics.[60]

Despite Iranian pressure, Indonesia's government was reluctant to side with Tehran in its dispute with the IAEA. While the Indonesian government's plan to create a nuclear power industry inclined it to offer a vigorous defense of all countries' right to put nuclear energy to peaceful use, its long-standing support for international nuclear norms and practices and its immediate need for international support to advance its nuclear power plans discouraged it from taking steps that appeared to align it with Iran. In a speech delivered at a public seminar held by the Indonesian Academy of Sciences in April 2005 to discuss the topic of "Indonesia and Iran's Nuclear Issue," a high-ranking foreign ministry official reiterated Indonesia's positions in favor of the peaceful use of nuclear energy and against nuclear proliferation, reviewed the history of Iran's commitments to the IAEA and its failure to meet them, and described Iran's signing of the additional protocol and cooperation with the IAEA as "the only way . . . to address the doubt" that Iran's actions "may have created."[61]

In response to the resistance it met in Indonesia's executive branch, Iran sought support from Indonesian legislators and civil society leaders. Its first step was an aggressive one: it invited the speaker of Indonesia's House of Representatives and other legislative leaders to visit their counterparts in Tehran on dates in February 2006 that coincided with the meeting of the IAEA board of governors meeting that voted to refer Iran to the U.N. Security Council. Before departing, the speaker acknowledged that Iran would cover their expenses, which he considered "common practice" since Iran had "invited us."[62] Perhaps in consideration of the legislators' upcoming visit, the Indonesian foreign minister stopped in Tehran en route to the IAEA meeting in Geneva, where he chose to abstain from the resolution against Iran. During their visit, top legislators from across Indonesia's political spectrum met Iranian legislators and toured nuclear facilities in Isfahan. Afterward, according to Indonesia's official news agency, they "concluded that the Iranian nuclear power program was for peaceful purposes. There was no possibility for Iran to develop the facility into a nuclear weapon program."[63] And upon returning to Jakarta, they criticized the foreign minister for failing to join the three countries that opposed the resolution rather than the four that abstained or the 27 that supported it because, they said again, Iran's nuclear program was solely for peaceful purposes.[64]

For the next few years, senior legislative and civil society leaders continued to take positions that favored Iran and opposed their own government's position. During a summit meeting of developing countries that Indonesia hosted in May 2006, Iranian President Mahmoud Ahmedinejad failed to win support from his hosts. As if to emphasize that Jakarta did not accept Tehran's assertion that its program was devoted entirely to peaceful purposes, Indonesia's foreign minister commented that his government wanted Iran "to be more transparent in its program."[65] By contrast, the speaker of Indonesia's House of Representatives was considerably less cautious. He and his legislative colleagues offered Ahmedinejad a reception far warmer than the one extended by the president and foreign minister. And in August, while hosting an Iranian legislative delegation, he endorsed cooperation with Iran on nuclear enrichment—precisely the issue that had been at stake in the IAEA vote in February 2006.[66]

In early 2007, legislative-executive tensions again worsened over whether to support or oppose sanctions against Iran. This time the international consensus was stronger, but divisions within Indonesia were deeper and the impact on its domestic politics more serious. At the start of the year, Indonesia assumed a nonpermanent seat on the U.N. Security Council, and immediately was obliged to take a position on Iran's nuclear program. Dissatisfied with Iran's response to a previous resolution (1737) that the Council had adopted in late 2006, France, Germany, and Britain sought a new one that would widen sanctions. Ironically, this resolution was the result of the process Indonesia had tried to sidestep a year earlier when it abstained from casting a vote at the IAEA board of governors meeting. Ahead of the Security Council vote in early March, Iranian legislators visited their counterparts in Jakarta as well as the leaders of Indonesia's two largest mainstream Muslim organizations, and received sympathetic responses. The leaders of these groups were nearly unanimous in their view that Iran's nuclear program was peaceful and that Indonesia should use its position on the Security Council to resist what they saw as unfair U.S. pressure on Iran.[67]

Jakarta's effort to strike a compromise between international commitments and domestic pressures not only failed to satisfy opponents at home but also provoked a crisis that tested the constitutional authority of both the president and the House of Representatives. At the United Nations, Indonesia joined South Africa and Qatar in seeking amendments that would soften the impact of sanctions on Iran but ultimately only secured mention of "the objective of a Middle East free of weapons of mass destruction," which Indonesians viewed as an implicit endorsement of eliminating Israeli nuclear weapons. But this fell far short of satisfying most Indonesians, and the government's decision to join the unanimous vote in favor of resolution 1747 provoked criticism from all political factions. Leading political, academic, and religious figures denounced the government's vote as a sign of its weakness and willingness to align with the United States and Israel.[68] Within weeks a majority of legislators, drawn from all parties except the president's, signed a petition to employ a rarely used constitutional right to compel the government to submit to formal questioning. The leader of the movement to call the government to account explained its position by saying that the "House has to ask for a satisfactory explanation from the government. . . . Iran has not been proven to be developing its nuclear technology for military purposes. . . . The resolution was drafted by a few developed countries that have taken no measures against Israel, which has internationally admitted to using nuclear weapons."[69]

The resolution of this conflict demonstrates continuity and change in Indonesian nuclear policymaking. Over the next four months, as the two sides wrangled more over interpretations of each branch's constitutional rights than policy toward Iran, it became evident that they differed less over nuclear proliferation than over what Indonesia's main foreign policy priorities should be and who should determine them. They agreed that the government should support nuclear disarmament and oppose proliferation. But legislators with little experience in foreign policy or familiarity with international affairs, let alone the nuances of nuclear policy, sought positions they expected to be popular with voters. Since vastly more Indonesians held favorable views of Iran than the United States, it is not surprising that they would side with Iran in a conflict against Washington. Yet even in the face of enormous political pressure, Indonesia's government endeavored more to uphold its long-standing policies on nuclear energy than to satisfy public sentiment.

Future Nuclear Proliferation Scenarios in Indonesia

It is difficult to imagine Indonesian officials pushing to acquire nuclear arms. A nuclear program would require the emergence of not just a small group of people who believe Indonesia should embark on a path to nuclear proliferation but also a coalition of political leaders, nuclear scientists and engineers, and military officers who share their views. These views, or myths, would have to be based on a perception that nuclear weapons would enhance Indonesian security and on a belief that Indonesia possesses the capacity to employ them. Neither of these views has been present in the past, but the advent of a domestic nuclear power industry may provide some potential mythmakers with grounds to advance politically plausible claims that some future security need can best be addressed through the development of nuclear weapons. And a more democratic process may permit the emergence of groups that do not share the traditional views of the nuclear, military, and diplomatic establishments that nuclear proliferation should be opposed and disarmament supported.

What might motivate future Indonesian leaders to advocate nuclear weapons? The least likely motivation is a threat to the country's national security. Indonesia and its neighbors have built one of the most successful regional organizations in the Third World, the Association of Southeast Asian Nations. Its signal achievement, by most accounts, has been the avoidance of conflict among its members for the past four decades. And one of the cornerstones of ASEAN is the Southeast Asian Nuclear Weapons Free Zone treaty that has been in effect for a decade. With respect to countries outside Southeast Asia, Indonesian leaders have long sought to chart a course that avoids either conflict or alignment with any great power. The country's first president was a founder of the nonaligned movement, whose ideals retain a strong attraction among Indonesians today. Moreover, it has established a long tradition of support for nuclear disarmament and nonproliferation at the global as well as regional level. This tradition would need to be put aside to allow the pursuit of nuclear weapons. Furthermore, Indonesia's economy depends heavily on trade and investment with all the major powers, and so to assume that it would seek nuclear weapons to deter one of them requires the further assumption either that it already has lost access to that country's economy without damaging its own economy so badly that it cannot afford to develop nuclear weapons, or that one of the great powers poses such a serious threat to its own security that it is willing to risk the loss of access to that country's economy. No political party in Indonesia would find either of these assumptions plausible.

Perhaps a more likely motivation would be to secure status for Indonesia. This seems to have been one of Sukarno's motivations for talking about seeking a nuclear bomb in the 1960s. Domestic calls for the current Indonesian government to defend Iran from American pressure reflect a similar belief that Indonesia is entitled to play an important role in world affairs. Nevertheless, even those Indonesian legislators who pressed their government to defend Iran at the United Nations did not argue that Iran is entitled to develop nuclear weapons. They certainly would like Indonesia to play a greater role in world affairs, but they have proposed that Indonesia achieve that by mediating international conflicts, not arming against them.

Even if a substantial political constituency emerged in favor of nuclear weapons, major hurdles would remain. Not least would be the nuclear research establishment itself, which has a half-century tradition of adhering to and promoting international nuclear norms. And if weapons were acquired or produced, the military still would need to develop the means and ability to employ them.

Rather than trying to imagine scenarios under which Indonesia, as a government, might go nuclear, it is probably more important to focus—as many Indonesians do—on the safety and security of the nuclear facilities that the country proposes to build. Indonesia's public safety record is poor and its law enforcement institutions are weak. Small groups of terrorists slip easily across its borders. These problems reflect the turbulence of Indonesian politics during the past decade, which has undermined the strength of the state in the same way as it has weakened the country's physical infrastructure. These conditions are the ones that make another scenario more likely: that international proliferation networks may find weaknesses in Indonesia that they can exploit for their own purposes, not Indonesia's.

CONCLUSION

The likelihood of future nuclear breakout in Indonesia and Vietnam is low. Both countries are serious about their commercial nuclear energy plans, but neither wants a nuclear weapons program. A far more credible problem is posed by terrorist access to materials that could be used to manufacture crude nuclear devices. Indonesia and Vietnam, along with other states, must implement national legislation and domestic controls to ensure that sensitive materials are not vulnerable to theft and misuse. Significant progress has been made in this area since the adoption of U.N. Security Council Resolution 1540 through a series of bilateral, sub-regional, and U.N.-based initiatives, which have attempted to enhance the capacity of Southeast Asian states to secure sensitive materials.

But serious gaps remain. Regional export controls remain weak, despite the existence of major transshipment and assembly points for critical strategic dual use goods and technologies. The main reason for the low level of implementation of export controls is attitudinal. Most ASEAN members regard export controls with suspicion, viewing them as barriers to economic development at best, and, at worst, as part of a deliberate strategy of technology denial on the part of the developed world.[70] Part of the reasoning behind U.N. Security Council Resolution 1540 is that it should help ease concerns over inequitable export control regimes, raise awareness that domestic export controls need not undermine economic productivity, and build consensus on the universal requirement to apply domestic controls on the trade in and movement of sensitive technologies.[71] But in Southeast Asia attitudes are slow to change. With the possible exception of Singapore, export control systems remain unsophisticated and weak, with the most worrying gaps present in some of the region's most technically advanced states: Indonesia, Malaysia, and Thailand.

Developments over the next few years will determine if Southeast Asia's evolving security architecture will act as an effective brake on future nonstate proliferation dynamics. At present, ASEAN is divided between states that share the desire of Western states to place nonproliferation and counterterrorism high on the regional agenda (Philippines, Singapore, and, increasingly, Vietnam), and those that are reluctant to prioritize weapons of mass destruction issues within ASEAN, ARF, APEC, or other regional forums, partly because they view these issues as too closely connected with U.S. security agendas, and thus unpopular domestically (Indonesia, Malaysia, and Myanmar). The signing of the legally binding ASEAN Convention on Counter Terrorism in Cebu, Philippines, in January 2007, can be seen as a positive development in some respects, in that it signals a growing consensus around the need for a regional response to terrorism. However, the Convention says little on the subject of weapons of mass destruction terrorism prevention, merely encouraging regional readiness to deal with a weapons of mass destruction attack if it occurs.[72] Furthermore, although the Philippines took a leadership role in promoting nonproliferation and counterterrorism in ASEAN ministerial meetings and Forum discussions in 2007, Indonesia is not fully supportive of these initiatives and denies reports that agreement has been reached among ASEAN members to set up a dedicated body to deal with pressing security issues. These indicators suggest that the efforts by some states to prioritize nonproliferation and counterterrorism within ASEAN may eventually be abandoned, suspended, or watered down, in order for the ASEAN and ARF processes to move to the next stage of their institutional development. The ASEAN Security Community may well decide to focus its attention on less controversial areas of security policy. If this happens, the potential for weapons of mass destruction terrorism to occur within, or emanate from, the region could be significant.

NOTES

1. On nuclear mythmaking, see Peter R. Lavoy, "Nuclear Myths and the Causes of Nuclear Proliferation," in *The Proliferation Puzzle: Why Nuclear Weapons Spread and What Results*, ed. Zachary S. Davis and Benjamin Frankel (London: Frank Cass, 1993); and the introductory chapter to this volume.

2. "US to Help Build Vietnam's First Nuclear Plant," *Agence France-Presse*, March 20, 2007, http://www.breitbart.com/article.php?id=070320153852.sl6gfarx&show_article=1&catnum=0; Chua Hearn Yuit and Yeo Lay Hwee, "The Demise of the NPT: New Players in the Proliferation Game," *Japan Focus*, May 16, 2006, http://japanfocus.org/products/details/1820.

3. U.S. Department of Energy, "NNSA Announces Key Nuclear Non-Proliferation Projects with Vietnam," March 19, 2007, http://www.nnsa.doe.gov/docs/newsreleases/2007/PR_2007-03-19_NA-07-08.htm.

4. "Approving the Strategy for Peaceful Utilization of Atomic Energy up to 2020," Decision no. 1/2006/QT-TTg, January 3, 2006, http://www.vaec.gov.vn.

5. "Nuclear Power Exhibition Planned Tomorrow in Capital," *Viet Nam News*, May 15, 2006.

6. "Vietnam Government Approves Ambitious Power Plan," *Thanh Nien News*, September 7, 2007.

7. Asian Development Bank, Asian Development Outlook 2007 Update, September 2007, http://www.adb.org/Documents/Books/ADO/2007/Update/default.asp.

8. "ADB Ups Energy Investment in Viet Nam," *Asian Development Bank News and Events*, September 21, 2007, http://www.adb.org/media/Articles/2007/12169-vietnamese-energies-projects.

9. "Vietnam Boosts Nuclear Cooperation with Russia," *RIA Novosti*, May 17, 2005.

10. "U.S.-Vietnam Sign Nuclear Agreement," UPI, April 1, 2010, http://www.upi.com/Science_News/Resource-Wars/2010/04/01/US-Vietnam-sign-nuclear-agreement/UPI-79051270148580/.

11. Ta Minh Tuan of Vietnam's Institute of International Relations (which is part of the Ministry of Foreign Affairs) has pointed out that there is no public debate about weapons of mass destruction in his country, and that "the government is the sole actor in this field." See Chairman's Report, *Fifth Meeting of the CSCAP Study Group on Countering the Proliferation of Weapons of Mass Destruction in the Asia Pacific*, San Francisco, February 12–13, 2007.

12. Statement by Vietnam's representative, Mr. Nguyen Duy Chien, to the Third Preparatory Committee of the 2005 NPT Review Conference, April 27, 2004; Viet Nam Ministry of Foreign Affairs, "Statement of Ambassador Le Luong Minh to the 2005 NPT Review Conference," May 5, 2005, http://www.mofa.gov.vn, accessed April 12, 2007; Viet Nam Ministry of Foreign Affairs, "Vietnam Raises Concerns over Restrictions on Peaceful Use of Nuclear Energy," May 5, 2005, http://www.mofa.gov.vn, accessed April 12, 2007.

13. "Viet Nam Calls for Nuclear Disarmament at UN Meeting," *Viet Nam News*, April 11, 2007; "Vietnam Calls for End to World's Nuclear Threat," *Nhân Dân*, April 11, 2007.

14. Ta Minh Tuan, comments noted in Chairman's report, *Second Meeting of the*

CSCAP Study Group on Countering the Proliferation of Weapons of Mass Destruction in the Asia Pacific, Manila, Philippines, December 2–3, 2005.

15. "Viet Nam Calls for Nuclear Disarmament at UN Meeting," Viet Nam News, April 11, 2007.

16. U.N. Security Council, "Note Verbale," December 30, 2005, S/AC.44/2004/(02)39/Add.1; Vietnam Report to the APEC CTTF, February 26–27, 2006.

17. Roger Mitton, "Vietnam under Pressure to Join Anti-Terror Initiative," Straits Times, March 29, 2007.

18. Jorn Dosch, "Vietnam's ASEAN Membership Revisited: Golden Opportunity or Golden Cage?" Contemporary Southeast Asia 28, no. 2 (August 2006): 236–37.

19. See the VAEC announcement of Prime Minister Phan Van Khai's decision to endorse the VAEC strategy document in January 2006, available at http://www.vaec.gov.vn/News/baiviet.php?EV=0&iddomain=18&idbv=557.

20. Ralf Emmers, "Regional Hegemonies and the Exercise of Power in Southeast Asia: A Study of Indonesia and Vietnam," Asian Survey 45, no. 4 (July/August 2005): 645–65.

21. Douglas Pike, "The Turning Point: Vietnam in 1991," Asian Survey 32, no. 1 (January 1992): 74–81.

22. In December 2006 Washington made Vietnam eligible to receive nonlethal military equipment. Michael R. Gordon, "U.S. and Vietnam Agree to Broaden Military Ties," New York Times, June 6, 2006; Grant McCool, "Vietnam Plays New Anti-Terror Role," China Post, April 12, 2007.

23. Emmers, "Regional Hegemonies and the Exercise of Power in Southeast Asia," 664–65.

24. Ta Minh Tuan, "The Future of Vietnam-U.S. Relations," Brookings Institution, April 14, 2010, http://www.brookings.edu/opinions/2010/04_us_vietnam_relations_tuan.aspx.

25. Ramses Amer and Nguyen Hong Thao, "The Management of Vietnam's Border Disputes: What Impact on Its Sovereignty and Regional Integration?" Contemporary Southeast Asia 27, no. 3 (Autumn 2005): 429–53.

26. A commitment to the peaceful settlement of competing sovereignty claims in the South China Sea was signed in 1992. ASEAN Secretariat, ASEAN Declaration on the South China Sea, Manila, Philippines, July 22, 1992, http://www.aseansec.org/3634.htm.

27. One of the most far reaching settlements was the March 2005 landmark trilateral agreement between China, Vietnam, and the Philippines to jointly prospect oil and gas resources in the South China Sea. "China, Vietnam Agree on Joint Exploitation in the South China Sea," July 19, 2005, http://pk.china-embassy.org/eng/zgxw/t206783.htm.

28. Ong Keng Yong, "Enabling Effective Governance in the ASEAN Community," remarks by the Secretary General of ASEAN at the CAPAM 2006 Biennial Conference, Sydney, October 23, 2006.

29. Amer and Nguyen, "The Management of Vietnam's Border Disputes," 437; "Vietnam, China Seek to Enhance Cooperative Ties," *Vietnam Bridge Online*, March 26, 2007, http://english.vietnamnet.vn/politics/2007/03/677270/.

30. Developments in the nuclear debate and nuclear infrastructure in Thailand are closely followed in Vietnam, despite the fact that there are no bilateral nuclear links. See the VAEC news reports at http://www.vaec.gov.vn.

31. FNCA Nuclear Safety Culture Project, Summary of 2006 Workshop, September 19–21, 2006, Bangi, Selangor, Malaysia, http://www.fnca.mext.go.jp/english/nsc/e_ws_2006_m.html.

32. World Bank, *Spending for Development: Making the Most of Indonesia's New Opportunities: Indonesia Public Expenditure Review 2007* (Jakarta: World Bank, 2007), 76; Asian Development Bank, *Country Strategy and Program: Indonesia 2006–2009* (Manila: Asian Development Bank, 2006), 104.

33. Hadi Soesastro and Raymond Atje, "Survey of Recent Developments," *Bulletin of Indonesian Economic Studies* 41, no. 1 (April 2005): 27.

34. Asian Development Bank, *Country Strategy and Program*, 107; World Bank, *Spending for Development*, 76.

35. World Bank, *Electricity for All: Options for Increasing Access in Indonesia* (Jakarta: World Bank, 2005), 2.

36. "RI Exploring Possibility of Cooperating with US to Build Nuclear Power Plant," *Antara*, July 15, 2006, http://www.antara.co.id/en/seenws/?id=16372.

37. International Atomic Energy Agency, "Technical Cooperation Report for 2003: Report by the Director General," August 2004, p. 13, http://www.iaea.org/About/Policy/GC/GC48/Documents/gc48inf-6.pdf.

38. Mohamed ElBaradei, "Nuclear Power in a Changing World," Jakarta, December 8, 2006, http://www.iaea.org/NewsCenter/Statements/2006/ebsp2006n024.html.

39. Michael Richardson, "If Oil-crunched Indonesia Goes Nuclear ... ," *Straits Times*, June 4, 2004; Shawn Donnan, "Indonesia Looks at Stalled Plans for N-plant," *Financial Times*, February 11, 2004, p. 2.

40. "South Korea, Indonesia Agree to Build Reactors, Share Nuclear Fuel and Technology," Associated Press, December 7, 2006.

41. "Indonesia, South Korea Sign Preliminary Deal to Develop Nuclear Power Plant," Associated Press, July 25, 2007; "S. Korea Promotes Sale of Indigenous Nuclear Reactor to Indonesia," Yonhap, July 25, 2007.

42. Geoff Thompson, "Indonesia Wants Australia's Uranium" (interview with Indonesian Vice President Jusuf Kalla), ABC Radio, August 31, 2007, http://www.abc.net.au/am/content/2007/s2020364.htm. The text of the treaty can be viewed at http://www.dfat.gov.au/geo/indonesia/ind-aus-seco6.html; the quotation is from art. 3, para. 17.

43. Mo Bissani and Sean Tyson, "Sister Lab Program Prospective Partner Nuclear Profile: Indonesia," Lawrence Livermore National Laboratories, January 12, 2007, 2;

SIPRI, "Indonesia Country Profile," July 2004, http://www.sipri.org/contents/expcon/cnsc3ins.html; and Indonesian Embassy, Vienna, "Nuclear Facilities Profiles," http://www.kbriwina.at/indonesiapolicyissues/atomicenergy/index.php.

44. Daniel B. Poneman, *Nuclear Power in the Developing World* (London: George Allen and Unwin, 1982), 102–3; and Poneman, "Nuclear Policies in Developing Countries," *International Affairs* 57, no. 4 (Autumn 1981): 577.

45. Sulung Prasetyo, "Nuklir Mengapung: Berjudi pada Teknologi Belum Jadi," *Sinar Harapan*, April 4, 2007, http://www.sinarharapan.co.id/berita/0704/04/ipto1.html.

46. "Gorontalo, Provinsi I Bangun PLTN," *Antara*, June 17, 2007; Tom Wright and Gregory White, "Russia Floats Plan for Nuclear Plant Aboard a Boat," *Wall Street Journal*, August 21, 2001, A1; and Guy Faulconbridge, "Russia Floats Nuclear Power Plants for Export," Reuters, April 19, 2007.

47. Information about WALHI's campaign is at http://www.walhi.or.id/kampanye/energi/pltn/. On NU's opposition, see "NU Minta Pemerintah Kaji Ulang PLTN Muria," *Suara Merdeka*, July 14, 2007, http://www.suaramerdeka.com/harian/0707/14/mur06.htm.

48. "PLTN di Muria Musnahkan Etnik," *Jawa Pos*, April 5, 2007, http://www.jawapos.co.id/index.php?act=detail_c&id=279238; and Ian Mackinnon, "Javans Fired up over Reactor Next to Volcano," *The Guardian*, April 5, 2007, http://www.guardian.co.uk/indonesia/Story/0,,2050170,00.html.

49. Kurniasih Budi, "Golkar Tolak Pembangunan Reaktor Nuklir [Golkar Rejects Nuclear Reactor Construction]," *TempoInteraftif*, February 16, 2009, http://www.tempointeraktif.com/hg/nasional/2009/02/16/brk,20090216-160374,id.html; Tom Allard, "Yudhoyono Backs Down on Nuclear Power Plans," *Sydney Morning Herald*, April 6, 2009.

50. Poneman, *Nuclear Power in the Developing World*, 186–88.

51. *Chega! The Report of the Commission for Reception, Truth and Reconciliation in East Timor* (Dili: East Timor, 2006). The first quotation appears in the Executive Summary, p. 109, and in ch. 7.5, p. 47; the reference to biological weapons appears in ch. 7.5, p. 26. The Executive Summary is available at http://www.etan.org/etanpdf/2006/CAVR/Chega!-Report-Executive-Summary.pdf; ch. 7.5 is available at http://etan.org/etanpdf/2006/CAVR/07.5_Laws_of_War.pdf.

52. Poneman, *Nuclear Power in the Developing World*, 99–100.

53. Richard K. Betts, "Paranoids, Pygmies, Pariahs & Nonproliferation," *Foreign Policy* 26 (Spring 1977): 164; Lincoln P. Bloomfield and Amelia C. Leiss, "Arms Control and the Developing Countries," *World Politics* 18, no. 1 (October 1965): 15; and Ciro Zoppo, "Nuclear Technology, Weapons, and the Third World," *Annals of the American Academy of Political and Social Science* 386 (November 1969): 114.

54. Robert M. Cornejo, "When Sukarno Sought the Bomb: Indonesian Nuclear Aspirations in the Mid-1960s," *Nonproliferation Review* 7, no. 2 (Summer 2000): 31, 36, 36–38.

55. Oran R. Young, "Chinese Views on the Spread of Nuclear Weapons," *China Quarterly* 26 (April–June 1966): 163.

56. Poneman, *Nuclear Power in the Developing World*, 101; and Daniel B. Poneman, "Indonesia," in *Nuclear Power in Developing Countries: An Analysis of Nuclear Decision Making*, ed. James Everett Katz and Onkar S. Marwah (Lexington, MA: Lexington Books, 1982), 186.

57. Takashi Shiraishi, "Rewiring the Indonesian State," in *Making Indonesia*, ed. Daniel S. Lev and Ruth McVey (Ithaca, NY: Cornell University Southeast Asia Program, 1996), 164–79.

58. Lucy Williamson, "Indonesia's Public Transport Peril," BBC News, January 18, 2007, http://news.bbc.co.uk/2/hi/asia-pacific/6270797.stm; "Flying in Indonesia May Be Hazardous to Your Health," *Asia Sentinel*, July 9, 2007, http://asiasentinel.com/index.php?option=com_content&task=view&id=573&Itemid=31.

59. Heri Retnowati, "Prayers, Protests Mark One Year of Mudflow," Reuters, May 29, 2007.

60. Veeramalla Anjaiah, "RI-Iran: Will Honeymoon Become Strategic Partnership?" *Jakarta Post*, May 8, 2006.

61. Sudjanan Parnohadiningrat, "Indonesia and Iran's Nuclear Issue," in *Indonesia and Iran's Nuclear Issue*, ed. Indriana Kartini (Jakarta: LIPI Press, 2005), 6.

62. "DPR ke Iran Akhir Januari," *Tempo Interaktif*, January 28, 2006, http://www.tempointeraktif.com/hg/nasional/2006/01/28/brk,20060128-73090,id.html.

63. "Indonesian Legislators Observe Iranian Nuclear Power Plant," *Antara*, February 9, 2006, http://www.antara.co.id/en/seenws/index.php?id=8794.

64. "MPs Regret Indonesia's Abstain [sic] on Iranian Nuclear Issue," *Antara*, February 15, 2006, http://www.antara.co.id/en/seenws/index.php?id=8939.

65. "Officials Set Agenda for Weekend D-8 Summit on Bali," *Jakarta Post*, May 10, 2006; Tomi Soetjipto and Muklis Ali, "Iran President Says West Nuclear Concern a 'Big Lie,'" *Reuters*, May 10, 2006. The foreign minister is quoted in Shawn Donnan and Gareth Smyth, "Tehran Searches for Allies in Muslim World," *Financial Times*, May10, 2006, 7.

66. "RI Should Cooperate with Iran on Nuclear Projects: House Speaker," *Jakarta Post*, August 28, 2006; and "Indonesia Bisa Bekerja Sama dengan Iran," *Kompas*, August 28, 2006.

67. Abdul Khalik, "Muhammadiyah Backs Iran's Nuclear Program," *Jakarta Post*, February 9, 2007; Abdillah Toha, "No Real Evidence of Iran's Launch of Nuclear Weapons Development," *Jakarta Post*, March 6, 2007.

68. "Sikap RI Atas Iran Menuai Kecaman," *Pikiran Rakyat*, March 27, 2007; "Hassan Wirajuda Dicecar DPR," *Koran Tempo*, March 30, 2007.

69. Ridwan Max Sijabat, "House to Question Government over UN Sanctions on Iran," *Jakarta Post*, May 16, 2007.

70. CSCAP, Summary of Key Findings, Report of the Third Meeting of the CSCAP Export Controls Experts Group, Tokyo, Japan, February 9–10, 2007.

71. Peter Burian, "Keynote Speech," U.N. Department for Disarmament Affairs, *United Nations Seminar on Implementing Security Council Resolution 1540 in Asia and the Pacific*, DDA Occasional Papers, no. 11, November 2006, http://disarmament.un.org/ddapublications/OP1106-64948web.pdf.

72. ASEAN Convention on Counter Terrorism, Cebu, Philippines, January 13, 2007, http://www.aseansec.org/19250.htm.

7 Burma and Nuclear Proliferation

Andrew Selth

Before 2000, the idea that Burma might become a nuclear power was considered fanciful. Indeed, it was seen as so unlikely that major military institutions in two Western countries used such a scenario as the basis for classroom training exercises. These institutions asked their students to consider what would happen if Burma, supplied with nuclear weapons and ballistic missiles by another pariah state, precipitated an international crisis. In one case, the threat was immediate, with the notional nuclear-armed missiles aimed at a neighboring country allied with the United States. In the other case, the threat was less direct, and formed the basis of an attempt by Burma's military government to exercise leverage over other countries, mainly through the United Nations.

After 2000, these fictional scenarios seemed to be coming true. That year, Burma announced that it planned to purchase a nuclear reactor from Russia. Given Burma's political instability and low level of technical development, this was itself a cause for concern. When the Russian deal appeared to break down in 2003, there were fears that Burma had turned to North Korea to acquire nuclear technology, and possibly nuclear weapons. There was also speculation that even if Burma did not want its own nuclear weapons, it could be enlisted to support North Korea's nuclear program and perhaps even to hide a few North Korean weapons from the United States and international monitoring agencies. These stories, which were given wide circulation in the news media, followed reports that Rangoon was trying to purchase ballistic missiles from Pyongyang.

The Burmese government strongly denied that it was seeking to acquire strategic weapon systems, but suspicions remained. These fears were strengthened by the restoration of diplomatic relations between Burma and North Korea in

April 2007, and the signing of a new nuclear cooperation agreement between Burma and Russia the following month.

As with so many issues relating to Burma's security, the real situation is difficult to discern. There is little verifiable information available to put rumors and sensationalist press reporting into a clear perspective. The highly charged atmosphere surrounding most issues concerning Burma compounds this problem. The public debate tends to be dominated by Burmese expatriates, foreign activists, and specialist academics, many of whom have strong personal views and specific policy agendas. Yet, Burma's approach to global disarmament, its plans for a research reactor, and its possible interest in acquiring nuclear weapons (and the missiles to deliver them) all demand careful analysis. If the news reports are true and Burma indeed poses a nuclear proliferation risk, there would appear to be little that the international community can do to dissuade Burma's military leaders from their present course.

BURMA'S NUCLEAR RESEARCH PROGRAM

Ever since Burma regained its independence in 1948, successive governments have sought to enhance the country's security by opposing the manufacture, deployment, and use of nuclear weapons by any state, anywhere in the world. This policy has also been followed by the State Law and Order Restoration Council (SLORC) and the State Peace and Development Council (SPDC), which have ruled Burma since 1988. In 1992, for example, Burma became a State Party to the 1968 Nuclear Non-proliferation Treaty, and in 1995 it signed the Treaty on the Southeast Asia Nuclear Weapon-Free Zone. In 1996, Burma signed the Comprehensive Nuclear Test Ban Treaty. Publicly at least, Burma's military government has abided by its obligations under these international agreements.

While opposed to the manufacture, storage, and use of nuclear weapons, Burma has not been averse to exploiting the peaceful uses of nuclear technology, as far as its limited resources have allowed. In 1956, a "nuclear power department" was formed within the Union of Burma Applied Research Institute. The department handled matters relating to radioactive materials, usually in the form of isotopes, required by the country's health, education, and agriculture sectors. Some of these functions were later devolved to individual ministries, but they were given renewed attention following the creation of a Ministry of Science and Technology in 1996.[1] Some Burmese scientists may have dreamed of their own nuclear reactor but, until the advent of the SPDC, no serious consideration was given to building one.

Burma's reactor project dates back at least to 2000, when the Minister for Science and Technology, U Thaung, paid an official visit to Moscow and held discussions with the Russian Minister of Atomic Energy. U Thaung expressed interest in the construction of a nuclear reactor in Burma "with the capacity of ten megawatts for peaceful research."[2] He spent four days in Russia visiting institutes that specialized in the training of nuclear scientists. He reportedly told his hosts that he wanted to send Burmese technicians to Russia to learn how to operate nuclear reactors. There also were press reports around the same time that the Burmese had approached China and India, making their interest in a nuclear reactor known to potential vendors.[3] U Thaung created a Department of Atomic Energy in his Ministry, which appears to have been made responsible for pursuing this project, including the maintenance of contacts with the International Atomic Energy Agency (IAEA) in Vienna.

In 2001, it was revealed that the SPDC had formally approached the Director General of the IAEA for assistance in obtaining a nuclear research reactor.[4] According to *Nucleonics Week*, the Agency initially decided to ignore this request because it had no "confidence that Burma either needs a reactor or has the infrastructure and funding required to support such a project."[5] The IAEA's concerns about Burma were broadly similar to those raised in connection with other less-developed countries, where there was a worrying absence of adequate safety standards and physical protection for research reactors. Agency officials apparently believed that Burma's low economic status, its poor technological base, and the virtual collapse of its public education system under the SLORC and SPDC made it a poor candidate for a nuclear research reactor. Despite these reservations, an IAEA inspection team was sent to Burma in June 2001. The team's assessment, however, simply confirmed the agency's original views.

By the beginning of 2002 there were rumors that, without the IAEA's help, Burma could not afford the reactor project.[6] The Russian ambassador, however, had signaled his country's willingness to receive at least part of the payment for a Russian reactor in primary goods such as teak, fish, and rice, and a deal was eventually struck.[7] In May, it was announced in Moscow that Russia's Atomic Energy Ministry (Minatom) had agreed with the SPDC to "cooperate in designing and building a nuclear studies centre that will include a research nuclear reactor with a thermal capacity of 10 megawatts and two laboratories."[8] According to the Russian statement, Minatom had undertaken to design the center, help choose the site, deliver the nuclear fuel, and supply all essential equipment and materials. Russian experts would assemble, install, and help operate the center's main technical equipment. The agreement included structures for the disposal of nuclear waste and a waste burial site. Russia would also train Burmese technicians to help build and operate the reactor.

In July 2002, Foreign Minister U Win Aung, accompanied by the ministers for defense, energy, industry, and railways, traveled to Moscow to finalize the deal. Russian Foreign Minister Igor Ivanov described Burma as a "promising partner in Asia and the Pacific region."[9]

There was initially some speculation that the nuclear facility would be built in Rangoon. A ground-breaking ceremony, however, was apparently scheduled to take place at a secret location near the town of Magwe, in central Burma, in January 2003.[10] The reactor and associated equipment were to be delivered later that year. The regime said that it expected the facility to be built "within a few years."[11] In late 2002, however, the deal with Russia was shelved, apparently because the SPDC could not reach agreement with Moscow regarding payments. By late 2005, the SPDC had found the necessary funds, and discussions resumed.[12] In April 2006 it was reported that a new agreement had been signed with the Kurchatov nuclear research center, opening the way for a revival of the controversial project.[13] Despite news stories referring to construction of the reactor, the British government revealed that "there is no evidence that this matter has progressed beyond the signing of a memorandum of understanding."[14]

This statement was confirmed on May 15, 2007, when it was unexpectedly announced that Russia and Burma had signed a new agreement in Moscow on the establishment of a nuclear research center in Myanmar. The signatories were U Thaung and the head of Russia's Nuclear Power Agency (Rosatom), Sergey Kiriyenko. According to the agency's press release:

> The sides have agreed to cooperate on the establishment of a centre for nuclear studies in the territory of Myanmar (the general contractor will be Atomstroyexport). The centre will comprise a 10MW light water reactor working on 20%-enriched uranium, an activation analysis laboratory, a medical isotope production laboratory, silicon doping system, nuclear waste treatment and burial facilities.[15]

It was also announced that the center would be "controlled by the IAEA," and that Russian universities were supposed to train 300 to 350 specialists for the center.[16] The agreement was expected to promote mutually beneficial economic and scientific ties between the two countries, a possible reference to Russian interest in Burma's natural gas reserves and the SPDC's interest in Russian arms.

Burma's Deputy Foreign Minister claimed at the time that Burma had been planning to build a nuclear reactor ever since it joined the IAEA in 1957.[17] Yet, the reasons behind Burma's interest in such an installation have never been made clear. Several official statements have emphasized that the reactor was to be used for "peaceful medical purposes," and the 2007 press release refers to the production of radioisotopes, which were in short supply in Southeast Asia.[18] In 2002, however, the Foreign Minister apparently said that the reactor could be used "possibly to generate nuclear power," adding that Burma was interested in studying "the different uses of nuclear energy."[19] Burma's official Ministry of Energy website refers to nuclear energy "only as an option" for the future, and states that it is only initiating study into nuclear power as a possible alternative source of energy.[20] Even so, in 2003 a Ministry official stated that "nuclear power production [is] desirable for [the] long term" and suggested that Burma could consider the construction of several additional reactors in the 100–400 megawatt range that would be introduced around 2025.[21]

Yet, the construction of even one of these expensive, highly specialized and technically advanced facilities seemed an illogical thing to do. Burma was still on the U.N. list of least developed countries and could barely maintain its civil infrastructure. Its level of technological development was generally low. Isotopes could be produced far more economically and reliably elsewhere. While it suffered from electricity shortages, Burma had abundant natural gas reserves and was constructing several new hydroelectric power stations. The main impetus behind the nuclear reactor project was apparently status and prestige, driven by the enthusiasm of the Minister for Science and Technology, who believed that nuclear research was necessary for a modern nation.[22] Senior officials also have drawn attention to the large number of countries, including several of Burma's regional neighbors, that already had nuclear reactors. One was reported as saying that "it was imperative for developing countries like Burma to seek to narrow the development gap and avoid their being marginalized."[23]

When it was first revealed, and again after the 2007 announcement, news of Burma's nuclear reactor project prompted a strong international response. A number of concerns were expressed, relating largely to the safety and security of any reactor built in Burma. With the 1986 Chernobyl disaster in mind, the Thais were worried about Russia's involvement in the project, and the nature of the facility to be built. Also, there were fears in Thailand and other neighboring countries that the Burmese would be unable to operate the reactor properly.[24] The IAEA team that visited Burma in 2001 to assess the country's preparedness to use and maintain a nuclear reactor safely did nothing to dispel these fears. Its report was highly critical of the country's general standards, which were "well below the minimum the body would regard as acceptable," even for conventional power plants.[25] Burma's record of earthquakes also was raised. In 1975, for example, Burma experienced several major tremors less than 100 kilometers from the area that was apparently chosen for construction of the nuclear reactor.

There also were security concerns. By 2000, most of Burma's major insurgent groups had negotiated ceasefire agreements with Rangoon, but some were still fighting the regime and posed a threat to a nuclear reactor. The National Council of the Union of Burma, an alliance of opposition forces, condemned the project, describing it as a serious security, environmental, and health risk.[26] Extensive measures will be taken to protect any facility built, but it would still remain an attractive target. Despite the crushing of widespread prodemocracy demonstrations in 1988 and 2007, and the imposition of tight controls over popular protest, there was also the danger of civil unrest, arising from decades of repression by the military government and its inept handling of Burma's economy. A nuclear reactor would represent a potent symbol of the regime's penchant for costly high-status projects, pursued at the expense of basic services such as health and education. With the international terrorist threat in mind, the U.S. State Department has already sought assurances from the SPDC that it could secure such sensitive facilities and materials.

Since the initial announcement of the project, few details have been made available about the reactor, its location, or the safeguards being put in place to ensure that it is built and operated according to international standards. This information gap has given rise to additional concerns about the project. For example, there have been a number of unconfirmed reports that the reactor is no longer going to be built near Magwe. In April 2003, the expatriate *Democratic Voice of Burma* reported that the reactor was going to be built on Kalagok Island, north of Ye in Mon State.[27] It is unlikely, however, that a nuclear reactor would be built in such an isolated, undeveloped, and potentially vulnerable location. Claims of another construction site, in a protected defense complex near Maymyo in central Burma, are more plausible but remain unconfirmed.[28]

There have been several stories that large numbers of Burmese have gone to Russia for training in nuclear technology. Between 200 and 300 were reported to have undertaken studies there in 2002, and an additional 328 officers were said to have departed for Moscow in 2003.[29] A report in the expatriate press claimed that 1,000 Burmese, including army officers and civil engineers, were receiving nuclear training in Russia.[30] Training was always part of the deal negotiated with Moscow, but, even if these figures are accurate, it does not follow that all these students have been sent for nuclear-related courses. For example, Burma's armed forces have acquired a range of arms and equipment from Russia over the past decade. Such contracts usually include training packages in the source country.[31] Russia also is in a position to offer Burma other types of advanced technical training. In 2005, the Russian Foreign Ministry stated that "the approximately 1,000 [Burmese] students are studying in Russia on a commercial basis and are in no way related to agreements in the nuclear sphere."[32] The British government, however, has revealed that some of these students were studying nuclear technology.[33]

Given Burma's status as an international pariah, the military regime's failure to explain its nuclear ambitions, and the climate of ill-informed speculation that usually surrounds security developments in Burma, it is not surprising that some unlikely scenarios have been canvassed in the news media. Even so, it is a leap to interpret Rangoon's ill-conceived plans for a small research reactor as cover for a clandestine nuclear weapons program.

NUCLEAR WEAPONS AND BALLISTIC MISSILES

Following the announcement of Burma's nuclear reactor project, a few commentators and expatriate groups expressed fears that Burma would become a "rogue terrorism state" and try to develop a nuclear weapon.[34] They suggested that the notorious Pakistani scientist A. Q. Khan had been to Burma and met senior military officers.[35] One Indian publication hinted darkly that Burmese officials had attended meetings in Singapore and Malaysia that were related to nuclear weapons.[36] No target was specified, but Burma's MiG-29 fighter aircraft were identified as a likely delivery system. Even if a nuclear weapons option was not available, it was argued, the presence of a nuclear reactor would at least give the Rangoon regime the capability to develop a dirty bomb, which could spread radioactive material using a conventional explosion.

At first, these suggestions were dismissed as rather far-fetched and self-serving. An attempt to develop a nuclear weapon seemed out of character for a country that had actively participated in global disarmament initiatives since 1948. Although the SPDC expected increased revenues from natural gas sales, there would be enormous practical difficulties to overcome, and serious political risks to manage. Also, many of the claims made in the news media were clearly based on speculation and unsubstantiated rumors. A number seemed to be aimed at winning support for the anti-Rangoon cause from the George W. Bush administration, which had invaded Iraq on the premise that it was developing weapons of mass destruction. A few Burmese exiles and defectors said that they could reveal details of the SPDC's nuclear weapons and uranium enrichment programs, but none of their claims could be proven and some were incredible.

Nevertheless, the possibility of Burma's acquiring a nuclear weapons capability attracted attention. Reports began to appear in the media that, after the Russian deal was shelved, the regime had asked North Korea to help build several secret nuclear facilities. North Korea's reputation as a state that provided nuclear technology for cash raised the specter of a Burmese nuclear weapons program.

Fears of a North Korean connection were given greater substance by the news that, after a lengthy hiatus, Pyongyang was developing closer links with Rangoon. Contacts between Burma and North Korea had been restricted since 1983, when three North Korean terrorists attempted to assassinate South Korean President Chun Doo Hwan during a state visit to Burma.[37] Not only was it a grave violation of Burma's sovereignty, but General Ne Win considered the incident a personal betrayal by President Kim Il-sung. Diplomatic ties between the two countries were severed. In the years that followed, Rangoon rejected several attempts by Pyongyang to restore relations. The sanctions imposed on Burma after 1988, however, forced the regime to look for new sources of arms and technical assistance, including from North Korea.[38]

Given the closed nature of the Rangoon and Pyongyang governments, details of bilateral contacts are difficult to obtain. During the 1990s, Burma apparently purchased some small arms ammunition and field guns from North Korea.[39] In 2002, the SPDC reportedly held discussions with Pyongyang on the possible purchase of one or two small submarines.[40] The frequent visits of North Korean freighters to Rangoon since then, and the secrecy surrounding their cargoes, suggest that other conventional arms and military equipment have been delivered. These suspicions have been strengthened by evidence that North Korean technical experts have visited Burmese military bases. In 2003, for example, it was reported that about 20 North Korean technicians had been seen at the regime's main naval facility in Rangoon.[41] North Korea has also constructed numerous underground facilities for the Burmese armed forces.[42]

The SPDC also has shown interest in purchasing some Hwasong (Scud-type) short-range ballistic missiles from North Korea. A secret meeting to discuss such a deal was reportedly held in Rangoon in August 2003, while another was supposedly held in Phuket, Thailand, that October.[43] In 2004 the U.S. government said that it had reason to believe North Korea had offered Burma short-range ballistic missiles, prompting Washington to register its concerns with the SPDC in unambiguous language.[44] Despite claims by some activists that Burma has already acquired up to a dozen short-range ballistic missiles, missile shipments to Burma have yet to be detected.[45] The ability of these delivery systems to carry weapons of mass destruction, however, makes them of continuing interest to analysts.

In November 2003, the *Far Eastern Economic Review* published an article suggesting that North Korea had taken over from Russia as the primary source of Burma's nuclear technology.[46] North Korean technicians were reportedly seen unloading large crates and heavy construction equipment from trains at Myothit, "the closest station to the central Burmese town of Natmauk, near where the junta hopes to build a nuclear research reactor."[47] In addition, aircraft from North Korea's national airline, Air Koryo, were reportedly seen landing at military airfields in central Burma. These reports suggest that Pyongyang was providing equipment and materials to help build a nuclear reactor. These developments apparently coincided with the arrival in Rangoon of representatives of the Daesong Economic Group.[48] There have also been reliable reports that the Namchongang Trading Company has been active in Burma. Both North Korean organizations have been involved in proliferating sensitive nuclear and ballistic missile technologies. The small research reactor Burma was getting from Russia was said to be unsuited for the manufacture of fissile material, but Pyongyang had the expertise to provide Rangoon with other options.[49]

The *Far Eastern Economic Review* story triggered a spate of other reports on Burma's supposed nuclear weapons ambitions, ranging from the plausible to the highly imaginative.

In 2003, the *Democratic Voice of Burma* stated that 80 Burmese military officers had gone to North Korea to study "nuclear and atomic energy technology," and one activist group has claimed that North Korea is training 25 Burmese nuclear physicists.[50] In 2004, an Indian commentator claimed that North Korea had signed an agreement to build a nuclear reactor in Burma. The value of the deal was said to exceed $200 million.[51] There also were claims that Burma had purchased uranium from Pakistan and North Korea.[52] Around the same time, stories appeared alleging that Burma was exporting uranium (and even heroin) to North Korea as part of a barter deal, in return for ballistic missiles and nuclear weapons expertise. Before shipment, the uranium was reportedly being processed into yellow cake at secret facilities in Thabeikkyin, north of Mandalay, and at Ongyaw, near Kyaukse.[53] Another report stated that the Burma Army's "Nuclear Battalion" was testing high-explosive nuclear triggers at a research complex southwest of Maymyo. It was even claimed that North Korea had already provided Burma with several nuclear weapons.[54]

There is no evidence to support any of these stories. Given the arms sales that have occurred, it is possible that a few Burmese servicemen have attended training courses in North Korea, but it does not follow that they studied nuclear technologies, peaceful or otherwise. The SPDC has denied that Pyongyang has provided instruction to Burmese officials, while the British government has stated that it has "no specific information" on the matter.[55] Burma's Ministry of Energy has identified five uranium deposits, but they appear to be small and none are being commercially exploited.[56] In 2005 and 2006, the British government stated that no uranium was being processed in Burma, nor did it have any operational enrichment facilities. London was not aware of any Burmese uranium exports.[57] Washington has dismissed suggestions of heroin being used in barter deals.[58] Since 1988, the regime has expanded Burma's defense industries, but there is no reliable evidence of any secret nuclear weapons–related plants. Nor are there any grounds to believe that North Korea has given, or would ever give, Burma nuclear weapons, either to use or to hide on its behalf.

In their efforts in 2005 and 2006 to have Burma cited by the U.N. Security Council as "a threat to international peace and security," the United States and the United Kingdom did not at any time refer to Burma's supposed nuclear weapons program. On one occasion, the U.S. Permanent Representative mentioned Burma's attempts to acquire "nuclear power capabilities," but even then he based his public comments on press reports of Burmese plans for a reactor.[59] No U.S. intelligence agency has publicly referred to a Burmese nuclear weapons program in its periodic appearances before congressional committees. Suggestions that the U.S.-led initiative in the U.N. Security Council was based on attempts by the SPDC to buy nuclear weapons technology from Pyongyang are incorrect.[60] When questioned about this subject in parliament, the British government stated that it was not able to corroborate reports about the alleged transfer of nuclear technology from North Korea to Burma.[61]

For its part, the SPDC has repeatedly denied that it has any plans to acquire weapons of mass destruction.[62] In 2002, the Myanmar Information Committee stated that Burma had no desire to develop nuclear weapons, but had the right to develop nuclear facilities for peaceful purposes.[63] In 2003, a spokesman for the military government stated:

> There has been speculation going on for quite some time regarding Myanmar and North Korea military-to-military exchanges. . . . Logically, why would Myanmar want to develop WMDs [sic] . . . when the country needs all her strength and resources in pursuing a peaceful, stable and smooth transition to a multi-party democracy and an open-market economy?[64]

Burma's nuclear reactor was said to be for peaceful research purposes.[65] The spokesman further stated that the country had no ambition to acquire nuclear weapons, rejecting the idea that Burma would ever threaten its neighbors.[66]

The thought of Burma acquiring nuclear weapons and delivery systems is the stuff of nightmares in the Asia-Pacific region. Such a scenario remains unlikely, but it is made more credible by the regime's political isolation, its continuing fears of external intervention, and its preparedness to do almost anything to survive.

BURMA'S THREAT PERCEPTIONS

Over the last 20 years, Burma's strategic environment has changed significantly. During the Cold War, the Rangoon government was recognized as a thinly disguised military dictatorship, but it was accepted in world councils and given considerable assistance by the international community. The regime saw its greatest threats as civil unrest, local insurgencies, pressure from Burma's larger and more powerful neighbors, and entanglement in the strategic competition between the superpowers.[67] As a result, Burma's armed forces were geared mainly to fight guerrilla wars. China and India were managed through tactful diplomacy, while a strictly neutral foreign policy, reliance on the United Nations, and a focus on global disarmament helped Burma avoid Cold War rivalries. Internal challenges still worry the SPDC, but, since 1988, Burma's external threat perceptions have been turned on their head. China, India, and Russia have become the regime's closest supporters. The United States and the United Kingdom, once seen as friends, if not potential allies, are considered threats to Burma's sovereignty and the continued existence of the military government. Even the United Nations is now regarded with suspicion.

Fear of Regime Change

These changes have profoundly affected the regime's strategic calculations and prompted new thinking about Burma's security policies. They have encouraged the growth of the armed forces and highlighted the need for a cred-ible deterrent capability. The regime has made a concerted effort to expand and modernize Burma's armed forces, consistently devoting 30 to 40 percent of the national budget to defense. After decades of being a small, lightly armed infantry force geared to regime protection and counterinsurgency, Burma now boasts a large, reasonably well integrated and well armed, triservice defense force. These enhanced capabilities raise the stakes faced by a hostile neighbor and help act as a deterrent against invasion. Despite all the improvements in Burma's armed forces over the past 20 years, however, defense analysts in Burma are increasingly concerned about trends in modern warfare.[68] Even with a new command structure, fresh recruits and more modern weapon systems, Burma's armed forces are unlikely to withstand a major assault by the United States or a multinational coalition.

After the 1988 military takeover, there were real fears in Burma of external intervention. Among the SLORC's first arms purchases were search radars and antiaircraft guns, hardly the kinds of weapons needed to counter rural guerril-las or urban dissidents.[69] SLORC Chairman Senior General Saw Maung referred to a U.S. fleet off Burma's coast as a potential invasion force.[70] Since then, the regime has repeatedly expressed fears that the United States and its allies might attempt forcibly to restore democracy to Burma. These concerns were perhaps greatest after the regime ignored the results of the 1990 general elections, which, being surprisingly free and fair, were won easily by the opposition parties. Since 2000, the military government seems to have become more confident of its ability to resist international pressures, but it is still highly sensitive to calls for regime change, and to other perceived threats to Burma's independence and sovereignty. As late as October 2005, Burma's Ministry of Defense was studying ways of resisting U.S. attempts to overthrow the regime, including through a direct invasion of the country.[71]

To most observers, the idea that Burma might be invaded by the United States or a U.N. multinational force seems bizarre. Such a dramatic step has never been seriously contemplated. From the point of view of the country's military leadership, however, it is not difficult to see how the SPDC might feel threatened, or why it is at least nervous about the possibility of external inter-vention.

The regime has long been subject to harsh criticism from Western leaders. Implicit in most of these comments has been a demand for regime change. In 2003, for example, U.S. Secretary of State Colin Powell referred to "the thugs who now rule Burma," and his successor labeled Burma "an outpost of tyranny" to which the United States must help bring freedom.[72] In President Bush's 2006 State of the Union speech, Burma was ranked alongside Syria, Iran, and North Korea as places where "the demands of justice, and the peace of the world, require their freedom."[73] Also, senior members of Congress have characterized the SPDC as repressive and illegitimate.[74] In the United Kingdom, Prime Minister Blair was reported as saying that the SPDC was a "loathsome regime" that he would "love to destroy."[75] After the regime crushed prodemocracy demonstrations in 2007, it was the target of another round of criticism from the international community.

In stark contrast, public comments about the Burmese democracy movement and opposition figures like Aung San Suu Kyi have been uniformly complimentary and supportive. To an isolated, insecure, and fearful group of military officers in Burma, the way the regime and its opponents are depicted could be interpreted as evidence of an intention to impose political change on Burma.

The Need for an Existential Deterrent

Global developments have sharpened Burma's concerns that it might fall victim to a more powerful state. In the past, this fear was focused on China, but today there is concern that the Western democracies will be able to impose their liberal, democratic and humanitarian agenda on Burma. Since 2002, there have been numerous calls for Burma to be included in President Bush's "axis of evil."[76] The armed interventions in Haiti, Panama, Somalia, Kosovo, Bosnia, Afghanistan, and Iraq (twice) are all viewed as examples of U.S. willingness to intervene in the affairs of other states and overthrow regimes whose policies are inimical to Washington. The 1999 multinational operation in East Timor, where a separatist movement was able to win independence from its parent state, is cited by members of Burma's military hierarchy as another example of the way in which the United States and its allies are forcibly reshaping the world order. The United Nations is seen as unwilling or unable to defend the interests of its smaller and weaker members.

Under these circumstances, acquiring a nuclear deterrent might be appealing to Burma's leaders. The SPDC may have already drawn this conclusion from the 2003 Iraq War and will seek to acquire a nuclear weapon as a bargaining chip to protect itself against the United States and its allies. According to one report, some Burmese generals "admire the North Koreans for standing up to the

United States and wish they could do the same."[77] The SPDC could argue that North Korea's possession of a nuclear weapon has been the main reason why the United States has not taken tougher action against Pyongyang, despite its provocative behavior. Viewed from this perspective, the possession of nuclear weapons has given North Korea a higher international profile, a stronger position at the negotiating table, and the proven ability to win concessions from the international community. Iran's nuclear weapons program may have a different outcome, but there are reportedly a few generals in Burma who believe that the SPDC should at least consider the benefits of acquiring a nuclear weapon.[78]

Possession of nuclear weapons and ballistic missiles would be more than symbolic. If Burma's military government ever felt seriously threatened, it might actually consider using them. For example, faced with an imminent invasion, ballistic missiles could be aimed at Thailand, a U.S. ally and Burma's "nearest enemy."[79] This might help dissuade the Thai government from allowing its territory to be used to launch a major ground and air assault against its western neighbor. Short-range missiles launched from a Burmese site near the Thai border could easily reach Bangkok, a city of nearly 9 million people. An attack with conventional warheads would cause unprecedented disruption within the Thai capital, while an attack with a nuclear weapon clearly creates the threat of visiting unprecedented destruction upon its neighbor.[80]

Although the strategic logic behind acquiring nuclear weapons can be easily identified, the news reports and public comments describing this thinking need to be kept in proper perspective. There is little verifiable information about Burma's interest in acquiring short-range ballistic missiles.[81] There have been several official statements about Burma's nuclear reactor, but circumstances change. Pronouncements by the military government, however, are often unreliable as guides to actual policy and future initiatives. Nor is there much hard evidence regarding Burma's developing bilateral relationship with North Korea, an obvious source of missile and weapons technology. There also is no evidence confirming reports of the SPDC's reported aim of acquiring a nuclear weapon.

Even if some of the open source reports are accurate, it is likely to be several years before Burma can take delivery of any strategic weapons, integrate them into its existing order of battle, and make them operational. Similarly, if the nuclear reactor project goes ahead, it would take about three years to build and bring on line, even if the entire facility was imported from abroad.[82] Development of a nuclear weapon would take at least ten years after the reactor came fully online, assuming that the political will, technical expertise, and financial resources were available. For Burma, these requirements would constitute formidable obstacles, even if no attempts were made by the international community to halt the program.

In international affairs, however, perceptions often become reality. Countries make national policy on what they believe to be the case, or fear might happen, as much as on the objective truth. Already, concerns have been expressed about Burma's potentially dangerous relationship with North Korea and the destabilizing policies the SPDC has adopted. Given the regime's record to date, however, there is little reason to believe that it will take any notice of these representations and change its current policies.

BURMA AND THE INTERNATIONAL COMMUNITY

Since 1988, Burma's military government has been the target of harsh criticism from powerful members of the international community, including in the United Nations. It has been denied assistance from international financial institutions and has suffered economic sanctions, travel bans, restrictions on arms sales, and other forms of diplomatic pressure. These measures have been insufficient to dissuade Burma's leaders from pursuing their core policy, the maintenance of a strong central government dominated by the armed forces. Repeated accusations of widespread human rights violations, forced labor, and involvement in narcotics trafficking all appear to have fallen on deaf ears. The regime has shown that it is prepared to pay a high price to protect Burma's sovereignty and independence. The uncompromising stance taken by the United States, United Kingdom, and other countries over the past 20 years has probably strengthened the regime's nationalist tendencies and hardened its resolve to resist external pressures.[83]

In an attempt to draw Burma out of its isolation, and win political and economic reforms from the regime, some countries and multinational groupings like the Association of Southeast Asian Nations have tried a policy of constructive engagement. Yet this approach, too, has proven unsuccessful. The regime has usually pocketed any inducements offered and then failed to make any significant concessions. When it has made tentative moves toward dialogue, by releasing a few political prisoners or agreeing to discuss the question of forced labor with the International Labour Organization, for example, it has invariably been criticized for giving too little and imposing too many conditions on policy changes. Feeling betrayed, the regime has retreated even further into isolation and refused to acknowledge the concerns of the international community. While there are clearly exceptions, many in the armed forces now seem to believe that Burma is better off trusting to its own resources and having as little as possible to do with the outside world.

This isolationism is encouraged by the fact that the military government is stronger now than at any time in the past 20 years. It is more firmly entrenched in power and faces a much weaker domestic opposition. Most major insurgent groups have negotiated ceasefire agreements, while the others have been significantly weakened. With its growing military capability, Association of Southeast Asian Nations membership, and expanded bilateral ties, the regime is militarily more powerful, diplomatically better connected, and strategically more influential than ever before. Burma's economy has fluctuated since 1988, but the discovery of large natural gas deposits over the past few years promises to give the SPDC a useful buffer against hard times, and an important bargaining chip in relations with its energy hungry neighbors. The general population continues to suffer, but the armed forces constitute a virtual state within the state, and are protected from the hardships faced by average Burmese.

The SPDC's fears of an invasion seem to have diminished in recent years, as Burma has become stronger and as more countries seem to have accepted that there is little they can do to change the political situation there. Despite their strong criticisms of the regime for its brutal handling of the 2007 demonstrations, most political leaders in the Asia-Pacific region still seem prepared to do business with Burma. With some notable exceptions, there also are signs that the regime's other critics have lost the influence they once enjoyed. Even before the 2007 crisis, however, there was little doubt that the SPDC still believed that it faced a hostile strategic environment, dominated by powerful countries seeking its downfall. It has created a circle of friendly states prepared to assist it in international fora, but it remains convinced that it can only rely on its own resources to survive. With this belief in mind, the SPDC has expanded its military capabilities, increased its stockpiles of strategic materials, and attempted to become more self-reliant in critical areas such as food, fuel, and arms production.

Under these circumstances, there is little that the international community can do to persuade the Burmese government to alter its current strategic trajectory. As long as the regime feels threatened by external forces, it is unlikely to rule out any option to protect itself. At present, this does not appear to include any serious attempt to acquire weapons of mass destruction, but if circumstances change, the few senior military officers who advocate a nuclear deterrent may receive more attention. Given his rather idiosyncratic view of the world, there also remains the possibility that Burma's paramount leader may simply decide to acquire nuclear weapons and set the wheels in motion.

CONCLUSION

There is a tension between Burma's publicly stated and clearly demonstrated policy of global nuclear disarmament, and popular perceptions that it maintains a clandestine nuclear weapons program. These perceptions have little factual basis, but they have been encouraged by unsubstantiated rumors, inaccurate and often alarmist news reports, and some questionable strategic analysis. These news reports also contain an element of deliberate misinformation, designed to fuel concerns that Burma has become a proliferation risk. These stories, however, are made more credible by the military government's history of provocative and seemingly irrational behavior, including an apparent disdain for international opinion and norms of conduct. They are also supported by Burma's renewed relationship with North Korea, another pariah state with a history of clandestine nuclear weapons production and a key player in the proliferation of nuclear and missile technologies.

Since 1988, the major Western countries have expressed their interest in peaceful political change in Burma, and have sought to sway the regime through dialogue and diplomatic pressure. Aggressive rhetoric, open support for opposition figures, funding for expatriate groups, and military intervention in other undemocratic countries, however, have led Burma's leaders to believe that the United States and its allies are bent on forcible regime change. This has created a climate of uncertainty, if not fear, leading to Burma's leaders themselves calling for military preparations against external intervention, including a possible invasion of the country. A few military officers have reportedly claimed that Burma needs a nuclear deterrent to combat these threats. Whether or not the Burmese government ever acts to acquire nuclear weapons will depend on a number of factors, but key will be its perceptions regarding regime survival in the face of possible external intervention.[84]

NOTES

1. Interview with Burmese official, Canberra, February 27, 2007.

2. Veronika Voskoboinikova, "Myanmar Shows Interest in Russian Research Reactor," *Tass*, December 22, 2000.

3. "IAEA Will Ignore Burmese Request for Research Reactor Assistance," *Nucleonics Week*, October 25, 2001, 14; and Arun Bhattacharjee, "India Frets over Yangon-Pyongyang Deal," *Asia Times*, June 4, 2004.

4. "IAEA Will Ignore Burmese Request for Research Reactor Assistance," 14; and "Launch of Research Reactor Project," *Nuclear Engineering International*, February 2002, 6. The Burmese delegation to the IAEA first raised this issue with the Director General in September 2000. "Regular Press Conference Held," *New Light of Myanmar*, January 22, 2002.

5. "IAEA Will Ignore Burmese Request for Research Reactor Assistance," 14.

6. Thomas Crampton, "Burma Seeks Nuclear Research Plant," *International Herald Tribune*, July 14, 2001; and Julian Moe, "US Findings on Burma: An Overview," *Irrawaddy*, November 7, 2003.

7. Crampton, "Burma Seeks Nuclear Research Plant."

8. "Myanmar Reactor," *Moscow Times*, May 17, 2002. Elsewhere, the plant is described as a "10 MW pool-type light-water nuclear reactor using low-enriched uranium fuel." "Myanmar to Construct Nuclear Reactor with Russian Supervision," *International Export Control Observer*, Issue 3, December 2005/January 2006, 34.

9. Bertil Lintner, "Burma Joins the Nuclear Club," *Far Eastern Economic Review*, December 27, 2001–January 3, 2002, 26.

10. Bertil Lintner, "Myanmar Gets a Russian Nuclear Reactor," *Wall Street Journal*, January 3, 2002; and Richard Stone, "Planned Reactor Ruffles Global Feathers," *Science* 295, No. 5556 (February 1, 2002): 782.

11. A. C. LoBaido, "Nuclear Politics in Burma," *WorldNet Daily*, February 8, 2002, at http://www.worldnetdaily.com/news/article.asp?ARTICLE_ID=26375.

12. Alison Hunter, "Talks on Burma Nuclear Facility Resume," *Mizzima News*, September 30, 2005; and Hunter, "Burma's Nuclear Ambitions: Progression or Threat?" *Mizzima News*, October 26, 2005.

13. Sergei Blagov, "From Myanmar to Russia with Love," *Asia Times*, April 12, 2006.

14. The United Kingdom Parliament, "Burma," Answer from Mr. Ian Pearson to Mr. Clegg, *Hansard*, January 16, 2006. See also "Developments in Burma," Testimony of Matthew P. Daley, Deputy Assistant Secretary, Bureau of East Asian and Pacific Affairs, U.S. Department of State, before the House International Relations Committee, Subcommittee on Asia and the Pacific, March 25, 2004, at http://www.state.gov/p/eap/rls/rm/2004/30789.htm.

15. "Russia and Myanmar Sign Inter-governmental Cooperation Agreement," Press Service of the Federal Agency for Nuclear Energy, May 15, 2007. See also "Russia to Build Nuclear Centre for Myanmar with 20% U-235," *RIA-Novosti*, May 15, 2007.

16. Ibid.

17. "Russia to Build Nuclear Reactor in Myanmar," *New Scientist*/Reuters, May 15, 2007.

18. Larry Jagan, "Yangon's Nuclear Ambitions Alarm Asia and Europe," *Straits Times*, January 18, 2002.

19. LoBaido, "Nuclear Politics in Burma"; and Larry Jagan, "Burma Announces Nuclear Plans," *BBC News*, January 11, 2002.

20. Ministry of Energy, "Nuclear Energy," at http://www.energy.gov.mm.

21. Paul Kerr, "US Accuses Burma of Seeking Weapons Technology," *Arms Control Today*, May 2004.

22. Lintner, "Burma Joins the Nuclear Club," 26.

23. "Burma to Build Nuclear Reactor," *BBC News*, January 21, 2002; and Lintner, "Burma Joins the Nuclear Club," 26.

24. Interview, Bangkok, October 2001. See also Jagan, "Yangon's Nuclear Ambitions Alarm Asia and Europe."

25. "Burma's Nuclear Plans Worry IAEA," *Far Eastern Economic Review*, February 21, 2002, 11; and "Launch of Research Reactor Project."

26. Phil Thornton, "Burma the Next Chernobyl," *Reportage*, September 2002, http://www.reportage.uts.edu.au/stories/2002/international/burma3.html.

27. "Freighters Carrying 'Nuclear Reactor' Equipment Arrive at Naval Base," *Democratic Voice of Burma*, April 3, 2003.

28. "Nuke Plant: From the Plains to the Hills," *Shan Herald Agency for News*, August 31, 2005, http://www.shanland.org/war/2005/Nuke-plant/.

29. "Burma Goes Nuclear," *Burma News Update*, No. 148, February 21, 2002; and "Junta Officers Secretly Depart for Pyongyang to Study Advanced Technology," *Democratic Voice of Burma*, November 25, 2003.

30. Moe, "US Findings on Burma."

31. Andrew Selth, *Burma's Armed Forces: Power without Glory* (Norwalk: EastBridge, 2002), 215–16.

32. "Myanmar Reactor Research Talks Halted."

33. The United Kingdom Parliament, "Burma," Answer from Dr. Howells to Mr. Clifton-Brown, *Hansard*, July 10, 2006.

34. Kanbawza Win, "The Burmese Regime Has Nuclear Weapons," *Kao Wao News Group*, October 3, 2004.

35. Ibid.; and Esther Pan, "Nonproliferation: The Pakistan Network," Council on Foreign Relations, *Backgrounder*, February 12, 2004, at http://www.cfr.org/publication/7751/.

36. "Neighbours' Envy." *News Insight.net*, 27 December 2003, found on the internet at http://www.indiareacts.com/fulldebate2.asp?recno=742.

37. *The Bomb Attack at the Martyr's Mausoleum in Rangoon: Report on the Findings by the Enquiry Committee and the Measures Taken by the Burmese Government* (Rangoon, 1983).

38. Andrew Selth, *Burma's North Korean Gambit: A Challenge to Regional Security?*

Canberra Paper No. 154 (Strategic and Defence Studies Centre, Australian National University, Canberra, 2004). See also "DPRK Restores Ties with Myanmar," *Agence France Presse*, April 11, 2006; and Clifford McCoy, "Rogues of the World Unite," *Asia Times*, April 28, 2007.

39. "Burma Buys AK-47 Rounds," *Jane's Defence Weekly*, February 2, 1991, 139; and Bruce Hawke, "Rice Buys Artillery for Myanmar," *Jane's Defence Weekly*, August 5, 1998, 8.

40. Rangoon opted to purchase one Sang-O class boat, but was later forced to abandon the deal. Robert Karniol, "Myanmar Ditches Submarine Deal," *Jane's Defence Weekly*, June 11, 2003, 12.

41. "North Koreans Return to Burma," *Far Eastern Economic Review*, July 10, 2003, 8; and Bertil Lintner and S. W. Crispin, "Dangerous Bedfellows," *Far Eastern Economic Review*, November 20, 2003, 22–24.

42. Bertil Lintner, "Myanmar and North Korea Share a Tunnel Vision," *Asian Age*, July 19, 2006.

43. "Neighbours' Envy"; and "N. Korea Ballistic Missiles for Burma Likely," *News Insight.net*, October 14, 2003.

44. Daley, "Developments in Burma," March 25, 2004.

45. Roland Watson, "Analysis of Burma's Nuclear Program," *Dictator Watch*, January 2007, http://www.dictatorwatch.org/articles/burmanuclear2.html.

46. Lintner and Crispin, "Dangerous Bedfellows," 22–24.

47. Ibid. 22.

48. Ibid., 22–24.

49. "Specialists to Make Nuclear Reactor for Burma," *RIA-Novosti*, January 23, 2002, cited in *Rangoon Suspense: Report Card, Burma, 1 December 2001–31 March 2002* (ALT-SEAN Burma, Bangkok, 2002), 23.

50. "Junta Officers Secretly Depart for Pyongyang to Study Advanced Technology"; and Watson, "Analysis of Burma's Nuclear Program."

51. Bhattacharjee, "India Frets over Yangon-Pyongyang Deal."

52. "We Want Justice," *Burma Digest*, April 9, 2006, http:// www.burmadigest.word-press.com/2006/04/09/we-want-justice/; and "Uranium Search in Burma Intensifies," *Irrawaddy*, October 2006.

53. Roland Watson, "Nuclear Proliferation and Burma: The Hidden Connection," *Dictator Watch*, http://www.dictatorwatch.org/articles/burmanuclear.html; and "Images of Suspected Uranium Mine and Refinery in Burma," *Dictator Watch*, March 2007, http://www.dictatorwatch.org/phshows/burmafacility.html.

54. Watson, "Nuclear Proliferation and Burma"; and Bhattacharjee, "India Frets over Yangon-Pyongyang Deal."

55. Interview with Burmese official, Washington, March 2004; and The United Kingdom Parliament, "Burma," Answer from Dr. Howells to Mr. Clifton-Brown, *Hansard*, July 10, 2005.

56. The IAEA's database of world uranium deposits lists no entries for Burma. On its website, the Ministry of Energy cites deposits at Magway (Magwe), Taungdwingyi, Kyaukphygon, Kyauksin, and Paongpyin. See www.energy.gov.mm. The total quantity of uranium in Burma is unknown, but it is believed to be relatively small.

57. The United Kingdom Parliament, "Burma," Answer from Dr. Howells to Miss McIntosh, *Hansard*, July 18, 2005; and The United Kingdom Parliament, "Burma," Answer from Dr. Howells to Mr. Clifton-Brown, *Hansard*, July 5, 2006.

58. Daley, "Developments in Burma." In 2006, however, these claims were still appearing. See "Financing Nuclear Projects with Drug Money," *Burma Digest*, April 2, 2006.

59. "US Accuses Burma of Nuclear Goal," *Sydney Morning Herald*, November 30, 2005; and "Burma Denies Nuclear Ambition after UN Move," *Australian*, December 5, 2005.

60. Greg Sheridan, "Burma Seeks Nuclear Weapons Alliance with N Korea," *Australian*, July 5, 2006.

61. The United Kingdom Parliament, "Burma," Answer from Ms. Margaret Beckett to Mr. Hague, *Hansard*, June 5, 2006.

62. "Burma Rejects Magazine Report of Missile, Nuclear Links with DPRK," *Agence France Presse*, November 17, 2003.

63. Myanmar Information Committee, February 13, 2002, cited in Kerr, "US Accuses Burma of Seeking Weapons Technology."

64. "Myanmar Rejects Report of Military, Nuclear Ties with North Korea," *Associated Press*, November 14, 2003, reproduced in *BurmaNet News*, November 14, 2003.

65. Ibid.

66. "No Weapons of Mass Destruction (WMD) for Myanmar, Only the Weapons of Mass Development (WMD) for Myanmar," Myanmar Information Committee, Information Sheet No. C-2839 (I/L), Yangon, November 17, 2003.

67. Andrew Selth, *Burma: A Strategic Perspective*, Working Paper No. 13 (Asia Foundation, San Francisco, 2001).

68. See, for example, Andrew Selth, "Burma in a Changing World: Through a Glass Darkly," *AQ: Journal of Contemporary Analysis* 75, No. 4 (July–August 2003): 15–21.

69. Bertil Lintner, "Myanmar's Chinese Connection," *International Defense Review* 27, No. 11 (November 1994): 12; and Andrew Selth, *Burma's Arms Procurement Programme*, Working Paper No. 289 (Strategic and Defence Studies Centre, Australian National University, Canberra, 1995).

70. Tin Maung Maung Than, "Myanmar: Preoccupation with Regime Survival, National Unity, and Stability," in Muthiah Alagappa, ed., *Asian Security Practice: Material and Ideational Influences* (Stanford: Stanford University Press, 1998), 730, n. 27.

71. Special Correspondent, "Myanmar (Burma's) Junta Fears US Invasion," *Asia Times*, April 27, 2006.

72. "Time to Turn Up the Pressure on the Burma Regime, Powell Says," *Wall Street*

Journal, June 12, 2003; and "Rice Names 'Outposts of Tyranny,'" *BBC News*, January 19, 2005.

73. Address before a Joint Session of the Congress on the State of the Union, January 31, 2006, at http://www.c-span.org/executive/transcript.asp?cat=current_event&code=bush_admin&year=2006.

74. "McConnell Says Burma's Ambassador to US Should Be Sent Home: Senator's Remarks at Press Briefing, 18 June 2003," http://www.usinfo.state.gov/eap/Archive/2004/Jun/30-782132.html.

75. Geoffrey Wheatcroft, "Saddam Was a Despot. True. This Justifies the War. False," *Guardian*, April 22, 2003.

76. Andrew Chang, "Access to Evil? Burma: A Potential, but Unlikely, Partner for Iran, Iraq and North Korea," *abcNews.com*, October 22, 2002, http:// www.abcnews. go.com/sections/world/DailyNews/burma021022.html; and Joshua Kurlantzick, "Rangoons: Why Isn't Burma on Bush's 'Axis of Evil?'" *Washington Monthly Online*, April 2002, at http://www.washingtonmonthly.com/features/2001/0204.kurlantzick.html.

77. Lintner, quoting a Bangkok-based Western diplomat, in "Myanmar and North Korea Share a Tunnel Vision."

78. Interview with a senior Rangoon-based diplomat, Singapore, July 2006.

79. "Myanmar (Burma's) Junta Fears US Invasion."

80. Burma began a clandestine chemical weapons program in the early 1980s, but that pilot project was probably shut down a few years later, after protests from the United States. Reports in the media over the past decade that Burma has used chemical and biological weapons have never been confirmed. See Selth, *Burma's Armed Forces*, 233–52.

81. Carefully worded statements on this issue made by senior U.S. officials, such as Senator Richard Lugar, probably reflect a greater awareness of developments than is possible to gain only from open sources. See R. G. Lugar, "Seeds of Trouble from Burma," Statement issued in Washington, DC, on September 28, 2003.

82. Jagan, "Yangon's Nuclear Ambitions Alarm Asia and Europe."

83. David Steinberg, "Minimizing the Miasma in Myanmar," *Spero News*, January 24, 2007. For two contrasting views on the sanctions debate, see John Badgley, ed., "Reconciling Burma/Myanmar: Essays on US Relations with Burma," *NBR Analysis* 15, No. 1 (March 2004); and *The European Union and Burma: The Case for Targeted Sanctions* (London: Burma Campaign UK, 2004).

84. "Myanmar," in *Preventing Nuclear Dangers in Southeast Asia and Australasia* (London: International Institute for Strategic Studies, 2009), 101–18; and David Allbright, Paul Brannan, Robert Kelley, and Andrea Scheel Stricker, "Burma: A Nuclear Wannabe, Suspicious Links to North Korea and High-Tech Procurements to Enigmatic Facilities," (Institute for Science and International Security, January 28, 2010), at http:// www.isis-online.org/uploads/isis-reports/documents/BurmaReport_28January2010. pdf.

8 Hindsight and Foresight in South American Nonproliferation Trends in Argentina, Brazil, and Venezuela

Etel Solingen

Argentina and Brazil were considered potential nuclear proliferators for many years when they acquired capabilities in the entire nuclear fuel cycle and refrained from joining the Non-proliferation Treaty (NPT).[1] In the 1990s they joined the NPT regime, and despite residual concerns (particularly with Brazil), few today envisage a return to the pre-1990s era. Venezuela was never included in the "problem countries" list until recently, when Hugo Chávez became suspect of dubious nuclear collaborations, particularly with Iran.[2] South America thus includes two Southern Cone countries—Argentina and Brazil—with high capabilities and arguably low incentives to pursue nuclear weapons, and one Northern Rim country—Venezuela—with low capabilities and *potentially* high incentives. Budding cooperation between Southern Cone states and Venezuela have raised concerns about a prospective marrying of capabilities and intentions over the horizon, although there is no evidence of any agreements to that effect.

Different theories can explain decisions to acquire, or refrain from acquiring, nuclear weapons. The next section relies on a theoretical framework designed to explain tendencies in either direction, based on the history of various nuclear programs. This framework suggests that dominant approaches to the global economy adopted by leaders and ruling coalitions have implications for nuclear decisions. The chapter then applies the framework to explain the nuclear trajectories of Argentina and Brazil, and examines a complementary hypothesis linking democratic institutions to nuclear behavior. The political-economy framework and the erosion of democracy also shed light on why Venezuela under Chávez has become a source of concern. The chapter concludes by highlighting evolving relations among these three countries.

THE THEORETICAL FRAMEWORK

Domestic models of political survival and their orientations to the global political economy have important implications for nuclear trajectories.[3] Leaders or ruling coalitions advocating economic growth through integration in the global economy ("internationalizers") have incentives to avoid the costs of nuclearization because the existence of a nuclear program impairs domestic economic and political reforms favoring internationalization, including macroeconomic and political stability, economic reforms, and efforts to enhance exports, economic competitiveness, and global access. These are all requirements for implementing models leaning on economic performance, export-led industrialization, the expansion of private economic activities and foreign investment, the contraction of military expenditures, progressive reduction of barriers to trade, and compliance with international institutions that validate and promote these choices. A cooperative regional environment and restrained and transparent nuclear policies serve these objectives well, maintaining macroeconomic and political stability, and facilitating domestic and foreign investment, export markets, technology transfer, foreign aid, and other financial and political benefits. These benefits also broaden domestic political support for more open economies and strengthen domestic institutions favoring related reforms. Internationalizing models thus have synergistic effects across the domestic, regional, and global arenas, and are averse to ambiguous nuclear programs that impair those objectives.

By contrast, nuclearization implies fewer costs for "inward-looking" leaders and constituencies less dependent on international markets, investment, technology, and institutions. Such leaders can rely on nuclear weapons programs to reinforce nationalist platforms of political survival. These programs contribute to the expansion of state power, the maintenance of unproductive and infla-tion-inducing military investments, and the perpetuation of economic rents to state and private actors opposed to internationalization. Inward-looking models resist global integration through extensive trade protection and im-port-substitution, shielding favored constituencies, which often include protected industries, sprawling state enterprises, bureaucracies, and ancillary mili-tary-industrial and nuclear complexes. Reforms required by the International Monetary Fund (IMF), the World Bank, and other institutions are portrayed as Western creations curtailing national sovereignty.

Ambiguous nuclear programs entail fewer costs for leaders who scorn international markets, investment, technology, and international institutions. They also provide ideal technological and political allies because such programs develop protected scientific, technological, industrial, military, and bureaucratic complexes, attracting new constituencies with vested interests in those complexes. The latter often operate beyond formal budgetary oversight, sometimes even under democratic rule, as in Argentina and Brazil in an earlier era. Furthermore, the actual or imaginary output ("the bomb") of these complexes is a powerful source of myths ripe for exploitation by inward-oriented leaders as much for domestic as external purposes.[4] Inward-looking leaders from Juan D. Perón to Gamal Abdel Nasser, Zulfikar Ali Bhutto, Saddam Hussein, Mua'mar Qadhafi, Kim Jong-Il, and Mahmoud Ahmadinejad have explicitly wielded nuclear myths of invincibility and modernity to boost domestic appeal.

Nuclear aspirants are thus more likely to emerge from domestic political landscapes dominated by inward-oriented leaders and ruling coalitions than from those where leaders and ruling coalitions favor internationalization. These models are not merely about "domestic politics" but also embody leaders' orientations to global politics and economics. Such orientations filter external threats and opportunities, and shape positions vis-à-vis nuclear policies and international regimes such as the NPT. Classical studies of nuclear proliferation have largely overlooked this particular influence on the calculus of potential proliferators. Yet preliminary findings led to greater attention to this variable in subsequent studies.[5] More recently, quantitative studies found support for the propositions that "economic liberalization is associated with a reduced likelihood of exploring nuclear weapons"; that "economic openness has a statistically significant negative effect across all three levels of proliferation" (that is, exploring, pursuing, or acquiring nuclear weapons); that "economic liberalization dampened the risk" of states deciding "to explore seriously the nuclear option"; and that economic liberalization had a positive and statistically significant effect on nuclear-weapons-free zone treaty ratification.[6] Another recent study refers to the connection between increasing trade openness and reduced incentives to develop nuclear weapons as a "general law."[7]

The association between models and nuclear choices is evident from several observations. Of all nuclear aspirants in the last three decades, not one endorsed denuclearization fully under domestic regimes that shunned integration in the global political economy. Only leaders and ruling coalitions advancing their political survival with an eye on export-led industrialization undertook effective commitments to denuclearize (Japan, Taiwan, South Korea, Sadat's Egypt, South Africa, and Brazil and Argentina, among others). Nuclear decisions were nested in a broader shift toward internationalization in economics and security. Where internationalizing leaders and coalitions became stronger politically, as in Japan, South Korea, and Taiwan, the departure from nuclear claims was maintained even as their security context deteriorated (as in the Korean peninsula and the Taiwan Straits). The relationship between politically stronger internationalizers and the timing of rolling back nuclear ambitions was also evident in Argentina under Carlos S. Menem, Brazil under Fernando H. Cardoso, Spain's accession to the NPT preceding European Union membership, South Africa, Libya, Algeria, and others. Where leaders and coalitions favoring internationalization were weaker, as in Argentina and Brazil until the early 1990s, the more politically constrained they were in curbing nuclear programs, as seems the case in contemporary Iran. Defiant nuclear courses have been unmistakably embraced by autarkic or inward-oriented models from Perón to Getulio Vargas, Nasser and others. And even internationalizers sometimes have to contend with dangerous regions where neighbors endorse alternative economic and nuclear policies. This problem is more severe in the Middle East than in East Asia, where export-led industrialization developed strong roots (except in North Korea).

ARGENTINA AND BRAZIL: THE DECADES
OF INWARD-LOOKING NUCLEAR AMBIGUITY

The Southern Cone has largely been at peace for most of the twentieth century, excluding internal repression.[8] Argentina and Brazil have not fought a war since 1828 but have been involved in a nuclear competition under inward-looking regimes since the early 1950s, when Argentina's Perón launched a statist, nationalist, populist movement supported by small- and medium-size import-substituting national firms, state firms in infrastructural industries, and Peronist-controlled trade union organizations. Perón's national-populist movement rejected free trade, unpredictable international markets, foreign investment and borrowing, and membership in the IMF, World Bank, and other institutions assailed as instruments of U.S. power, and enhanced the popular appeal of "self-reliance" by pursuing nuclear capabilities. In 1953 he announced, on the basis of a false claim by Austrian physicist Ronald Richter, who managed Argentina's nuclear program, that Argentina had mastered fusion technology. The origins of a well-funded nuclear program in Argentina are thus deeply rooted in Perón's inward-looking national-populism, which survived for decades in different guises.

Following the 1955 navy-led coup that deposed Perón, a tripartite division of industrial sectors among Argentina's armed services allowed the navy to shelter the nuclear program under an unstable succession of military and civilian regimes. Arturo Frondizi's acceptance of an IMF-stabilization plan and foreign exploitation of Argentina's oil reserves coincided with attempts in the 1960s to curtail the nuclear program and reduce its autonomy. Jorge R. Videla's military administration and his attempted turn to orthodox economic policies challenged the bloated and inefficient state sector, protectionist private firms, and the costly nationalist-self-reliant nuclear program. These constituencies were politically resilient, however, and the navy continued to protect the nuclear program from budgetary cuts.

A parallel process took place in Brazil in the early 1950s, when President Vargas organized a similar inward-looking, statist coalition restricting foreign investment (which led the World Bank to refuse to finance populist programs until 1964) and seeking independent nuclear capabilities. Vargas's policy of "specific compensations" aimed at obtaining nuclear know-how in exchange for uranium or thorium sales to the United States. National Research Council Director Admiral Alvaro Alberto attempted to purchase ultracentrifuge enrichment technology from Bonn in 1954. President Café Filho dismissed Alberto and granted the United States a monopoly over uranium research and extraction for two years, as policy shifted toward attracting foreign investment. Café Filho's brief interlude ended with the pro-Vargas coalition's return in 1955 under Juscelino Kubitschek, who resisted IMF stabilization programs and appointed a parliamentary commission to investigate alleged "improper" U.S. influences on Café Filho's nuclear policies. The commission urged Brazil's development of independent nuclear capabilities and the establishment of a National Atomic Energy Commission (CNEN) accountable to Brazil's president. President Jânio Quadros's national-populist team took over in 1961, reaffirming a "self-reliant" nuclear policy based on natural uranium that would grant Brazil fuel independence, reflecting a broader inward-looking industrialization policy that Quadros's successor, Joào Goulart, maintained until his ousting by a military coup in 1964.

The Brazilian and Argentine military regimes in the 1960s and 1970s were hybrids insofar as they initially tried to discontinue some of their predecessors' foreign investment and industrial export policies. However, they fundamentally maintained statism, protectionism, nationalism, and military-industrial complexes, of which nuclear programs were an important part despite the availability of alternative sources of energy. These regimes also upheld ambiguous nuclear policies, rejected the NPT as a discriminatory tool, and refused to apply Latin America's 1967 Tlatelolco Nuclear Weapons Free Zone. Chile and Cuba remained outside Tlatelolco for decades as well. Brazil and Chile signed and ratified Tlatelolco but did not waive the conditions required for its entry into force on their territories.[9] Argentina later signed but did not ratify Tlatelolco, and Cuba took no action until the mid-1990s.

Argentina and Brazil acquired the foundations of complete nuclear fuel cycles, including enrichment and reprocessing technologies. Generals Videla and Joào B. Figueiredo reached modest nuclear agreements, a far cry from a transparent, NPT-bound process of denuclearization. Indeed, Brazil's military reportedly intended to test a nuclear device in Cachimbo.[10] A congressional inquiry revealed that Brazil's military intended to build a nuclear weapon.[11] President Fernando Collor de Mello's science minister, José Goldemberg, reported that a nuclear test under Figueiredo was expected to enhance national pride and support for the military.[12] José Luiz Santana disclosed in 2005 that Brazil's military had acquired enriched uranium "from a foreign source" hoping to test a nuclear device in September 1990 until—as CNEN president—Santana managed to gain control over the enriched uranium in August 1990.[13] A successor, Odair Gonçalves, disputed that Brazil ever possessed weapons-grade material, arguing that the imported uranium was only about 20 percent enriched and, although it was unclear where it came from, the material was known to the International Atomic Energy Agency (IAEA) and under safeguards. Former President José Sarney stated that he had terminated a secret nuclear bomb program—the first confirmation from such a high-level source—but Santana insisted the program was not definitively canceled until 1990.

The newly installed democratic regimes retained basic features of inward-looking economic models throughout the 1980s, although they labeled some of their reforms "heterodox" (in contrast to economic orthodoxy).[14] Sarney endorsed populist anti-IMF policies leading to Brazil's 1987 debt moratorium. Raul Alfonsín's structural adjustment policies sought cooperation with international creditors, business, and labor. Argentine-Brazilian relations improved, but there were no breakthroughs either in internationalizing the economy or in nuclear cooperation. Despite his efforts to assert civilian control over the nuclear energy program, Alfonsín was pressured to retain Argentina's long-standing independent nuclear (and economic) policy. Brazil's military expanded its ambiguous "parallel program," resisting attempts to place nuclear activities under democratic control. The "parallel program" included the navy's gas centrifuge enrichment program, ostensibly geared for nuclear powered submarines, which succeeded in enriching uranium in 1986 and led to further centrifuge work at Aramar.[15]

The joint renewal of democracy in Argentina and Brazil thus retained ambiguous nuclear programs until the early 1990s. Mutual presidential visits to sensitive facilities and joint declarations of peaceful intentions had symbolic value, but unsafeguarded facilities with military potential remained in place. Cooperative rhetoric was not matched by effective mutual inspections, ratification of Tlatelolco and the NPT, abstention from peaceful nuclear explosions or development of delivery systems. Alfonsín rejected international commitments on ballistic missiles as his Air Force nurtured the Condor II project. Explicit commitments materialized only with the inception of internationalizing models in both countries.

Economic Internationalization and Nuclear Restraint: The 1990s

As pressures for IMF-style stabilization mounted in the early 1990s, Argentina finally abandoned classical Peronism, ironically under Peronist president Menem, whose internationalizing revolution dramatically reduced a Weimar-style inflation, balanced budgets, privatized many public services, and attracted sizable foreign investment. This unprecedented embrace of liberal trade rules was matched by the abandonment of Argentina's historical nationalist foreign and nuclear policy. With strong support from finance ministers and business interests, Menem neutralized sensitive nuclear facilities (shutting down a reprocessing plant); deepened privatization of nuclear activities; ended decades of navy control over the nuclear program, a chronic budgetary black hole; suspended two (of three) nuclear cooperation agreements with Iran; joined international regimes previously challenged, such as the Missile Technology Control Regime; distanced Argentina from the nonaligned movement; and sent a naval contingent to the U.S.-led multilateral force in the first Gulf War.

Upon winning presidential elections with significant support from Brazil's unorganized poor but not unions or other beneficiaries of import-substitution, Collor de Mello (1990–92) announced major trade reform and stabilization measures, replaced quantitative restrictions with tariffs, lowered average tariffs, rescinded protectionist measures, downsized the state bureaucracy, eliminated budget deficits, and privatized 22 of 26 state enterprises. Congress and the military opposed those reforms. Collor slashed the military's share of the budget from 6 to 2.2 percent (between 1989 and 1990), denied raises to 320,000 military personnel, purged important officers, and shut down presumed nuclear test sites in Cachimbo.[16]

During this internationalizing period, Collor and Menem ushered in explicit agreements renouncing nuclear weapons and establishing mutual verification and inspection procedures (Declaration on the Common Nuclear Policy of Brazil and Argentina, 1990). The 1991 Common Accounting and Control System was followed by another agreement on the Exclusively Peaceful Use of Nuclear Energy. The latter created an *Agência Brasileiro-Argentina de Contabilidade e Controle de Materiais Nucleares* or Agency for Accounting and Control of Nuclear Materials (ABAAC) to oversee a joint inspection regime and deter diversion of nuclear materials. A Quadripartite Agreement for the Application of Safeguards signed in 1991 by the IAEA, ABAAC, Argentina, and Brazil, applied full-scope safeguards to all their nuclear facilities, entering into effect in 1994. Menem ratified the NPT unilaterally (without reciprocal Brazilian commitment) in 1994.

Brazil, Argentina, and Chile also agreed to amendments facilitating adherence to Tlatelolco and joined regional and international agreements banning chemical and biological weapons, creating a zone free of all weapons of mass destruction. Whereas nuclear exports had been part of its nationalist diplomatic kit in the 1980s (supplying low-enriched uranium and other services to Iran, for instance), Argentina now joined the Nuclear Suppliers Group and canceled the (internationally legal) sale of an experimental nuclear reactor to Syria. With Collor's demise in 1992 and the return of inward-looking policies under Itamar Franco, who courted nationalist and military constituencies, Brazil stalled on bilateral nuclear agreements, attacked international financial institutions and their domestic "allies," and endorsed statements on Brazil's sovereignty in nuclear matters. Under heavy pressure from its Foreign and Economic Ministries, however, Brazil's House of Deputies in 1993 approved agreements signed with Argentina. Opposition to NPT ratification remained as a side-payment to nationalist and military constituencies. Following the inception of Cardoso's internationalizing economic model in 1994, Brazil assumed comprehensive safeguard commitments through ABAAC; joined the NPT in 1998 after decades of challenging its legitimacy; shelved the navy's nuclear submarine program; and joined the MTCR, which had been strongly resisted by the Ministry of Aeronautics.[17]

This account makes clear that the two countries' approaches to the global economy had a conspicuous impact on the choice between maintaining ambiguous nuclear status over decades and undertaking momentous steps toward nuclear restraint in the 1990s. Foreign ministries became key bureaucratic actors attuned to the organic links between internationalizing models and nuclear postures.[18] Democratization in the 1980s dislodged the military from power, but a new regional order and the implementation of bilateral and multilateral nuclear commitments (including full accession to the NPT) came about only with the rise of internationalizing ruling coalitions in the 1990s and their unprecedented reforms embedding Argentina and Brazil more deeply in the global economy. These steps were "primarily a result of an indigenous bilateral process, rather than a direct response to external pressure . . . . External pressure exerted by nuclear supplier states and the IAEA influenced the process, but only at the margins: it was never the determining factor."[19] Nor can balance of power models explain these shifts in nuclear policy. The rise of Brazil in the last two decades would have led neorealists to predict nuclear balancing by Argentina, which did not happen.

Maintaining Nuclear Commitments: The 2000s

Leaders invoking rhetoric critical of global integration were elected in both countries in the last decade, but they pursued policies relatively open to the global economy, accommodating the interests of internationalizing constituencies that have grown stronger since the 1990s, with some exceptions. Argentina's 2001 economic collapse led to greater instability and domestic turmoil, but its democratic consolidation had resulted in strong civilian control over the military. By contrast, Brazil's military, perceived as a more effective agent of modernization, retained more leverage.[20] Luis Inácio da Silva (Lula), who campaigned as a Workers' Party critic of both the global economy and the NPT, remained closer to the military's nationalist themes than his Argentine counterparts, reflected in support for nuclear energy and space programs, and demands for permanent U.N. Security Council status. While he initially resisted funding the navy's nuclear submarine project, he later approved budgets to complete it by 2015.[21]

Lula's first Science and Technology Minister, Roberto Amaral, argued that Brazil should not "renounce any type of scientific knowledge," including that needed to build atomic bombs.[22] Amaral's replacement, Eduardo Campos, wielded the Resende enrichment plant as a special technological achievement—"100 percent Brazilian"—a characterization that others disputed.[23] Lula's accommodation with the military may explain Brazil's resistance to sign the IAEA Additional Protocol. In 2004 there was a six-month standoff when IAEA inspectors were precluded from inspecting centrifuge components. Brazil allowed monitoring the entrance and exit of uranium to prevent potential "industrial espionage," which Brazil wielded as a justification for abstaining from the Additional Protocol.[24] The IAEA's mandate was to verify low levels of enrichment suitable for civilian reactors only. Brazil dismissed rumors that it might have tried to hide unlawful purchases of enriched uranium that it would have been compelled to report had it signed the Additional Protocol. Brazil demanded acknowledgment of its "special situation" as once having had a nuclear weapons program but having ended it; that the Additional Protocol should not be a "one-size-fits-all agreement"; and that Brazil had no desire to obtain nuclear weapons.[25]

U.S. Secretary of State Colin Powell expressed confidence in the peaceful nature of Brazil's nuclear program. Foreign Minister Celso Amorim reiterated that "Brazil has nothing to hide . . . except for the technology that Brazil has acquired, and . . . naturally wishes to protect," adding that while Brazil had accepted "the package deal" when acceding to the NPT, IAEA agreement to limited access to Resende would pave the way for Brazil to approve the Additional Protocol. A 2004 confidential agreement reportedly increased IAEA access to Resende short of total and unrestricted inspections.[26] These events were of special concern because of their implications for Iran and North Korea. Brazil defended its right to peaceful enrichment at the 2004 IAEA General Conference, with Iran under discussion. Brazil was also active in the New Agenda Coalition of eight non-nuclear weapons states pressuring for implementing NPT disarmament obligations. In January 2006 Brazil temporarily suspended Resende's official start as the IAEA Board of Governors called upon Iran to suspend enrichment activities.

Brazil's gesture was an effort to avoid comparisons between Iran and Brazil. In 2006 Brazil voted in favor of IAEA transfer of Iran's dossier to the U.N. Security Council and followed with a ban on nuclear technology or equipment transfers to Iran and the freezing of financial assets related to Iran's program. Amorim stated that "[Iran] will have to provide guarantees that it is using nuclear technology for peaceful purposes."[27] A Defense Ministry undersecretary, however, declared that Brazil should develop the technology necessary for building an atomic weapon.[28]

Vice President José Alencar declared in 2009 that Brazil should have the right to have nuclear weapons to endow his country with greater "dissuasive" power and more "respectability" in world affairs.[29] Both Lula and his Defense Minister immediately clarified that Alencar did not represent the government's position. Lula's Strategic Affairs Minister, Roberto Mangabeira Unger, declared: "Brazil may well be the least powerful of the four nations [Brazil, Russia, India, China] because it is the only one that has renounced nuclear weapons."[30]

The internal tension between Lula's advisors was evident as his Science and Technology Minister announced plans to build several nuclear plants while Lula and his Finance Minister favored hydroelectricity. By 2007, however, while restating hydroelectricity as a priority because of lower costs, Lula also endorsed the construction of as many nuclear power plants as needed, and expansion into enriched uranium exports. Industrias Nucleares do Brasil was to supply 60 percent of enriched uranium for the Angra 1 and 2 power plants and a wide range of fuel cycle products and services. Brazil is home to the world's sixth-largest natural uranium reserve.

Argentina's ruling coalitions since 2003 also returned to selected populist rhetoric critical of global integration, but their policies, on the whole, sought to remain open to the global economy. Similar compromises characterized the nuclear arena. President Néstor Kirchner grasped the double-edged features of the nuclear issue: enhancing populist appeal and satisfying some military elements but also the potential for a creeping military role in domestic politics and for reviving strategic threats. Hence, on the one hand Kirchner declared he would revive Argentina's nuclear program as embedded in Perón's 1950 principles; complete Argentina's third power plant (Atucha II), under construction for 25 years; conduct feasibility studies for a fourth power plant to be completed by 2012; reopen the Pilcaniyeu enrichment facility shut down in 1983; restart the Arroyito heavy water plant; and advance the small nuclear reactor CAREM developed by the state-owned firm INVAP.[31] On the other hand, Kirchner also aligned Argentina's nuclear policy with the principles of the NPT, endorsing more transparent positions than Brazil by joining the Proliferation Security Initiative and in statements regarding the Additional Protocol. Argentina's Deputy Minister of Foreign Affairs stated at the 2005 NPT Review Conference that Argentina had participated in the drafting of the IAEA's Model Additional Protocol and favored the universalization of the latter, which enhances the regime and provides confidence-building regarding countries suspected of violations. He added that the voluntary nature of this instrument should not be forgotten, but Argentina's intention is "to move forward to . . . ratification of the Protocol." Brazil's reluctance has been cited as a main reason for Argentina's abstention from signing the Additional Protocol thus far. A third Latin American country that has failed to sign it is Venezuela.

CHÁVEZ AND VENEZUELA'S INWARD-LOOKING TURN

Hugo Chávez's regime emulated 1950s-style Peronism as an inward-looking model of political control based on populist rhetoric, economic self-sufficiency, and rejection of the global economy. Were Chávez to embrace an ambiguous nuclear program, such developments would be compatible with expectations from the framework described earlier. His regime's questionable statements and actions defying the nonproliferation regime have attracted international attention, but it remains unclear whether Venezuela's nonproliferation commitments have been compromised thus far.

Chávez became President in 1999, launching his "Bolivarian Movement" or Chavismo, designed to fulfill Simón Bolívar's objectives of an independent Latin America. Attacks on the "failed neoliberal economic model" espoused by the United States are at the core of Chavismo's self-described socialist alternative emphasizing *desarrollo endógeno* (endogenous development).[32] The model proclaims principles of social inclusion, political mobilization, rejection of imports that can be domestically produced, and using Venezuela's oil reserves to advance self-sufficiency.[33] Chávez nationalized Venezuela's economy, including the largest iron and steel company, banks, electricity, communications, coffee, and the media. He approved the Hydrocarbons Law and the Land Law through decrees, enabling him to nationalize the oil industry in 2007. Chávez also severed ties with the World Bank and the International Monetary Fund. The 1999 "Plan Cívico-Militar Bolívar 2000" used self-sufficiency to attract populist support through investments in infrastructure, housing, education, welfare, and health care. The plan mobilized targeted constituencies but, as with 1950s Peronism, also increased corruption among loyal local administrators and the military. A currency reform deepened Chávez's inward-looking nationalist agenda and aggravated inflation.

The centralization and nationalization of the economy accompanied the concentration of political power. Chávez suspended Congress and allowed a committee of judges to approve constitutional changes increasing presidential terms, changing the legislature to a unicameral institution, and officially changing Venezuela's name to *República Bolivariana de Venezuela*.[34] Chávez also removed 600 judges and eviscerated the Supreme Court, once a barrier to Chávez's accumulation of power, by packing it with twelve loyal justices.[35] He also purged the military, turning it into his pivotal ally while allowing no dissent and asking it "to raise the flag and chant from the bottom of their hearts our slogan 'fatherland, socialism or death,' without any ambiguity or complex."[36] Several billion dollars went to military purchases, particularly from Russia but also aircraft from China. Chávez thanked "socialist . . . revolutionary China" for selling it planes after Brazil refused, arguably due to U.S. pressures.

Alleged U.S. involvement in a 2002 aborted coup allowed Chávez to militarize Venezuelan society to preempt challenges to his rule, creating a civilian militia designed to "persecute political dissidence."[37] Political opponents, including former allies and many journalists, have been attacked, persecuted, and illegally prosecuted in military courts. The military has raided media stations. The regime has ignored warnings about severe violations from the Inter-American Commission on Human Rights and the Inter-American Court on Human Rights.[38] In 2007 Chávez lost a referendum that would have broadened his powers, but in 2009 he won another allowing him to govern indefinitely.

Whereas oil windfalls under high oil prices allowed Chávez to distribute political patronage for social and military projects, subvention of regional allies, and subversion of others—a pattern reminiscent of Qadhafi's Libya in the 1970s—Venezuela's economy suffered a pronounced decline. Even according to Venezuela's Central Bank, inequality measured by Gini coefficients has increased under Chávez, and the results of his social programs were not better than those of his predecessors.[39] Imports of luxury goods have grown more rapidly than other imports, while shortages of basic foodstuffs and rising inflation have further eroded support for Chavismo. Despite the country's vast oil and natural gas deposits and waterways, Venezuelans have been forced to endure electricity and water shortages, leading Chávez to declare a state of emergency in February 2010. Murder rates are among the highest in the world, and dependency on oil is as high as ever. In the words of an independent observer, "[It] is undoubtedly true that the pre-1999 political and social system was deeply flawed. Many of its least attractive aspects, however, have worsened under Chávez: in particular, the concentration of power and the corrupt and politically -biased administration of justice." Upon completing 12 years in power, Chávez declared that he was ready to govern Venezuela until 2031 even after being diagnosed and treated for cancer in Cuba.

NUCLEAR OVERTURES: IRAN

Venezuela reportedly has large deposits of uranium ore, especially in the south. In the 1950s it built South America's first nuclear reactor, subsequently dismantled. Chávez expressed great interest in a "peaceful" nuclear program to produce nuclear fuel, labeling press speculation on his nuclear designs a "rotten pot."[40] Like other inward-looking rulers, Chávez accuses Western countries of keeping Venezuela dependent in nuclear technologies. Although insisting that Venezuela supports nuclear disarmament, he has repeatedly expressed support for Iran's development of nuclear arms, offered to negotiate on behalf of Iran with Western countries, and supported Iran against UNSC resolutions (unlike his Southern Cone counterparts).[41] While visiting Venezuela, Iranian President Ahmadinejad expressed firm commitment to help Venezuela develop nuclear fuel and build its atomic program, promises reiterated in subsequent visits by Iran's Minister of Foreign Affairs and Parliamentary President Ali Jaddad Adel.[42] Chávez thanked Ahmadinejad for technology transfer for Venezuela's "nuclear village."[43] He also agreed to export 20,000 barrels of refined oil daily and use the proceeds to finance machinery and technology purchases from Iran. Despite Venezuela's dire economic crisis, Chávez ordered additional funds for an allegedly secret nuclear program.[44]

Venezuelan sources reported that Iran intends to reward Venezuela with nuclear missiles, a claim that Iran has denied.[45] Chávez favored seeking missile systems from Iran, but Vice President José Vicente Rangel accused the U.S. Central Intelligence Agency of "concocting" such stories. Chávez also denied rumors of interest in uranium enrichment, calling it "the fruit of (Colombian) author and Literature Nobel Award winner Gabriel García Márquez's imagination."[46] Yet Chávez insists that a nuclear program is the "sacred" right of any country and that the United States only wants hegemonic control of the world.[47] Iran's investments in Venezuela have increased to nearly 200 bilateral agreements involving at least $9 billion, and Venezuela invested in petrochemical facilities in Iran.[48] A new Venezuelan bank with an all-Iranian cast of directors is owned by Iran's Saderat, a bank under U.N. Security Council sanctions for involvement in nuclear and terrorist activities. The two countries have defined themselves as an "axis of unity" and have reportedly deepened ties with terrorist groups as Iran trains Venezuelans in intelligence and crowd control techniques.[49]

CHÁVEZ BETWEEN THE SOUTHERN CONE
AND THE NORTHERN RIM

Chávez criticized Colombia and Perú for "selling out" through free trade agreements with Washington and promoted close relations with "Bolivarian" leaders in Ecuador and Bolivia, promising to purchase $500 million of Ecuador's debt to free it from IMF dependence. Neighboring countries are concerned with Venezuela's $5 billion military buildup, including 100,000 Kalashnikov rifles for a national militia, 30 Russian SU fighters, 35 helicopters, and 9 submarines that would endow Venezuela with one of the largest submarine fleets in Latin America.[50] Colombia denounced Chávez for initiating an arms race and the arming of Colombian antigovernment guerrillas (FARC). A 2008 Colombian raid into Ecuador resulted in the assassination of a leading Colombian FARC leader and the capture of computer-based data suggesting Venezuelan support for those groups.[51] Venezuela mobilized its military along the Colombian border. The crisis brought the region close to military conflagration. Perú expressed concerns with Venezuela's meddling in support of Ollanta Humala, a presidential candidate defeated in the 2006 Peruvian elections who later distanced himself from Chávez and won the presidency in 2011. Mexico and other neighboring states have also expressed concern with the Chávez-Castro and other collaborations in the region.

Chávez cast the revival of Venezuela's nuclear program as a step in regional integration, reaching out to Brazil and Argentina, using a mix of economic carrots from oil windfalls, coercive diplomacy, intervention in internal politics, and veiled or direct attacks against would-be Latin American opponents of stronger relations with Venezuela. His overtures to Argentina and Brazil are particularly important because of their capabilities in the nuclear field. While pushing Venezuela into Mercosur, Chávez strongly pressured Argentina and Brazil to reject U.S. influence and share nuclear technology with Venezuela. The internal tension within Brazil's ruling coalition between inward-looking and internationalizing forces carried over into Brazil's relations with Venezuela (and Iran). Lula's national security adviser Marco Aurélio Garcia reacted with enthusiasm to Chávez's initial expression of interest to acquire reactors from Brazil, though Foreign Minister Amorim was more cautious. Vice President José Alencar minimized Chávez's remarks as simply another attempt to annoy Washington, stating that "there is no [nuclear] agreement whatsoever with Venezuela or Iran" and that "Brazil has an accord for developing energy for peaceful ends with Argentina and the United States. There is no accord with Iran or Venezuela."[52] Another Brazilian official argued that Iran's participation, as suggested by Chávez, "would be risky for Brazil . . . . Brazil is not interested in cooperating with countries that do not follow international treaties and whose nuclear programs are not monitored by competent authorities."[53] CNEN Chief Odair Gonçalves noted that, in the context of nuclear cooperation with Venezuela, "transferring uranium enrichment technology is unthinkable."[54] Brazil's Congress, labeled "a U.S. parrot" by Chávez, pressured for reviewing Venezuela's Mercosur membership. Lula opposed revisiting that decision and expressed willingness to help Venezuela gain peaceful nuclear technology under IAEA supervision.[55]

Chávez skillfully exacerbated competition between Brazil and Argentina as potential suppliers of nuclear technology. Argentina's Foreign Minister Rafael Bielsa confirmed reports that Chávez was interested in purchasing a nuclear reactor from Argentina, affirming Argentina's commitment to IAEA monitoring and export controls.[56] Head of Cabinet Alberto Fernández also acknowledged discussions between state-run Petróleos de Venezuela (PDVSA) and Argentina's INVAP (which had also won a contract for Libya's Tajoura reactor). Defense Minister Orlando Maniglia claimed to have no information on this issue, and Energy and Petroleum Minister Rafael Ramírez denied claims that Venezuela would purchase a nuclear reactor but acknowledged that Venezuelan scientists would study peaceful uses of atomic energy in Argentina. Chávez acknowledged that Venezuela had approached Argentina and Brazil to reach nuclear cooperation agreements.[57] According to Argentina's Atomic Energy Commission, Venezuela reportedly sought a Carem-type nuclear reactor from INVAP, ostensibly for oil prospecting in the Orinoco Oil Belt. Other official Argentine sources reported that if Venezuela proposed any kind of nuclear partnership with Iran, Argentina would refrain from participating.

Argentina's relations with Iran were tense after Argentina requested Interpol assistance to search for Iranians indicted for connections to terrorist attacks in Buenos Aires. Iran then backed Brazil in various statements meant to undermine Argentina. At the same time, Iran (and Syria) reportedly approached Argentina repeatedly in recent years for technology and uranium dioxide transfers, recruitment of nuclear scientists, and offers to fund the resumption of Argentina's nuclear program.[58] Argentina has also revealed strong interest in deepening economic relations with Iran. Chávez mentioned the purchase of a nuclear power plant from Argentina again in April 2007, suggesting to Colombian President Uribe, jokingly, that the plant could be built near Venezuela's border with Colombia.[59] Argentina's own gas and power shortages made it more vulnerable to Venezuela's overtures. Of all bilateral agreements signed under Néstor Kirchner, Venezuela was the second largest partner after Chile. Chávez's initial promise to build a 3,700-mile-long natural gas pipeline from Venezuela to Argentina was replaced by an agreement to build a regasification plant in Argentina that would begin receiving shipments of liquefied natural gas from Venezuela by 2009.

Chávez also purchased Argentine bonds to enable Argentina to pay off its IMF debt, and offered to buy $500 million in Argentine bonds, and another $500 million later, following previous purchases totaling well over $4 billion. There was little Bolivarian solidarity here: the bonds paid Venezuela 11 percent interest and were sold at a discounted price to favored Venezuelan banks.[60] Furthermore, Argentina paid PDVSA about 20 percent over and beyond prices for fuel oil charged by competitors, while well-connected Argentine firms enjoyed lucrative discretionary contracts from the PDVSA trust fund that purchases Argentine products. The links between the Kirchners and Chávez were strong indeed, and both governments sought to cover up a scandal involving the alleged transfer of $800,000 by Chávez for presidential candidate Cristina Fernandez de Kirchner, who said that "the Latin American energy equation won't be solved without the presence of Venezuela and Bolivia . . . . Latin America needs Chávez like Europe needs Putin." And Chávez declared: "[E]ven the stones in Argentina and Venezuela shout out that Cristina Kirchner will be president." This marriage of convenience between nuclear-capable Argentina and nuclear-aspiring Venezuela was not universally sanctioned in Argentina. The Kirchners' political competitors and sectors seeking closer ties to the United States and Europe were particularly suspicious of Chávez's designs for a deepening strategic alliance with Argentina. As in Brazil, Argentine responses varied largely along internationalizing versus inward-looking cleavages. The President, Planning Ministry (under Julio De Vido), and segments of the Foreign Ministry were more favorable to Chávez than competing sectors in the Foreign Ministry and the Economy Ministry.[61] The Kirchner- Chávez alliance suffered when Venezuela announced its suspension of the proposed $1.5 billion Southern Bond, leaving Kirchner scrambling for alternative sources. During Venezuela's bicentennial celebrations in 2010, however, Kirchner was the only foreign leader to address Venezuela's National Assembly.

Chávez sent an ultimatum to Mercosur members, threatening to withdraw support unless Venezuela was granted full membership. His abuse of coercive diplomacy backed by energy windfalls led to some backlash, even among South America's left-leaning leaders in Uruguay, Chile, and Brazil.[62] Chávez also has advocated a regional alternative to the World Bank and Inter-American Development Bank, in the form of the Bank of the South. However, Lula's government advanced an entirely different design, particularly since Brazil's development bank was already a leader in the region.[63] Lula's energy solutions also collided with Chávez's grand plan. In 2008 Russia's Atomstroy-export, which built Iran's Bushehr reactor, agreed to help Venezuela build its first nuclear power plant. Russia also committed to develop Venezuela's space industry. Chávez met Ahmadinejad over a dozen times and has been, as Presidents Lula and Cristina Kirchner, a strong supporter of Libya's Qadhafi and Syria's "humanist...brother" Bashar el-Assad. Brazil's new president Dilma Rousseff initially tried to distance herself from those repressive regimes on human rights grounds but Brazil's policy remained, for the most part, unchanged.

CONCLUSION

This account suggests that balance of power theories are unhelpful in explaining the evolution of nuclear programs in Argentina, Brazil, and Venezuela. Bilateral Argentine-Brazilian relations, including in the nuclear field, remain friendly despite Brazil's dramatic rise as the region's hegemon and its recent investments in five submarines (including a nuclear one) and 36 fighter jets, in what has been deemed the largest purchase of military equipment in 50 years ($14 billion). The trajectory of these countries' nuclear programs was highly influenced by their models of political survival and approaches to the global economy. Leaders relying on inward-looking constituencies, extensive state entrepreneurship, and economic autarky had stronger incentives to develop ambiguous nuclear programs, from the Middle East to North Korea and the Southern Cone. Such tendency does not bode well for Venezuela. By contrast, leaders embracing economic growth via global integration were averse to ambiguous programs that strengthened domestic opponents of economic reform, lowered their country's appeal to foreign investors, and upset regional stability and access to international markets for exports, capital, technology, and raw materials. This pattern has characterized East Asian countries in recent decades (except for North Korea). Whereas inward-looking models tend to regard nuclear weapons as assets in the arsenal of building regime legitimacy, outward-oriented ones tend to gain legitimacy through sustained economic growth.

Grave setbacks to internationalization in Argentina after its 2001 default, enormous social disparities, legacies of statist-protectionist policies, and bungled and corrupt reforms have accentuated the ambiguity of Cristina Kirchner's program, which some describe as "Chávez light." Brazil, by contrast, has derived gargantuan benefits from staying its internationalizing course under Lula and Rousseff, which has turned Brazil into an undisputed regional power. Social tensions remain both countries' Achilles heel, even though Brazil has invested heavily in poverty reduction as well as military purchases. The two countries remain democratic (despite Kirchner's assaults on the independent media), and thus far apparently committed to peaceful nuclear programs while abstaining from endorsing the Additional Protocol. Venezuela, in turn, has progressed along a path reminiscent of 1950s-style Peronism, which could foster ambiguous nuclear ambitions. Alternative paths are possible over the horizon given Chávez's illness and scheduled presidential elections in 2012, which would have implications for Venezuela's relations with Argentina, Brazil, and the rest of the continent.

NOTES

1. I would like to thank participants at the conferences in Paris and Singapore and Matias Spektor for helpful comments, and Lee Ballesteros and Wilfred Wan for research assistantship.

2. While Venezuela's mining minister declared that Iran is helping Venezuela detect uranium deposits, the science and technology minister denied it. "Iran Not Helping Venezuela Find Uranium," *Buenos Aires Herald* (April 12, 2010); Cynthia Arnson, Haleh Esfandiari, and Adam Stubits, eds., *Iran in Latin America: Threat or "Axis of Annoyance"?* Woodrow Wilson Center Reports on the Americas, 23 (n.d.), http://www.wilsoncenter. org/topics/pubs/Iran_in_LA.pdf.

3. Etel Solingen, *Nuclear Logics: Contrasting Paths in East Asia and the Middle East* (Princeton: Princeton University Press, 2007); Solingen, *Regional Orders at Century's Dawn* (Princeton: Princeton University Press, 1998); and Solingen, "Mapping Internationalization: Domestic and Regional Impacts," *International Studies Quarterly* 45, no. 4 (December 2001): 517–56.

4. Peter R. Lavoy, "Nuclear Myths and the Causes of Nuclear Proliferation," in *The Proliferation Puzzle: Why Nuclear Weapons Spread and What Results*, ed. Zachary S. Davis and Benjamin Frankel (London: Frank Cass, 1993); and the introductory chapter to this volume.

5. Etel Solingen, "The Political Economy of Nuclear Restraint," *International Security* 19, no. 2 (Fall 1994): 126–69, and "The New Multilateralism and Nonproliferation: Bringing in Domestic Politics," *Global Governance* 1, no. 2 (May–August 1995): 205–27; and Peter Liberman, "The Rise and Fall of the South African Bomb," *International Security* 26, no. 2 (Fall 2001): 45–86.

6. Sonali Singh and Christopher R. Way, "The Correlates of Nuclear Proliferation: A Quantitative Test," *Journal of Conflict Resolution* 48, no. 6 (December 2004): 876, 878; and Matthew Fuhrmann and Xiaojun Li, "Legalizing Nuclear Abandonment: The Determinants of Nuclear Weapon Free Zone Treaty Ratification," Managing the Atom Project, Harvard University, March 14, 2008, available at http://belfercenter.ksg.harvard.edu.

7. Scott D. Sagan, "Introduction: Inside Nuclear South Asia," in *Inside Nuclear South Asia*, ed. Scott D. Sagan (Stanford: Stanford University Press, 2009), 6.

8. Bolivia and Paraguay fought the Chaco War between 1932 and 1935. There also was a military confrontation between Argentina and Chile in 1984 and the Malvinas/Falklands War in 1982. For an in-depth discussion of Argentina and Brazil's nuclear programs since the 1950s, see Etel Solingen, *Industrial Policy, Technology, and International Bargaining: Designing Nuclear Industries in Argentina and Brazil* (Stanford, Stanford University Press, 1996).

9. According to Article 28, certain conditions need to be met for the treaty to enter into force, including ratification by all Latin American states, by countries with possessions in Latin America, and by all nuclear weapons states. Most Latin American signatories of Tlatelolco waived these requirements at ratification.

10. Daniel Poneman, "Nuclear Proliferation Prospects for Argentina," *Orbis* 27, no. 4 (Winter 1984): 853–80; "Brazil Nearly Built Bomb in 1990's, Scientist Says," *Associated Press, August* 30, 2005; David Albright, "Bomb Potential for South America," *Bulletin of Atomic Scientists* 6, no. 4 (May 1989): 16–18; "Ex-Leader Says Brazil Pursued A-Bomb," *Associated Press, August* 8, 2005.

11. "Brazil Probe Finds a Bomb-Plan," *Los Angeles Times*, December 7, 1990, 2.

12. Eugene Robinson, "South America Steps Back from Atomic Brink: Brazil, Argentina Stand Down after Decades of Racing to Obtain Nuclear Arms," *Washington Post*, January 26, 1992, A24.

13. William Huntington, "Brazilian Regulator Denies Uranium Claims," *Arms Control Today* 35, no. 9 (November 2005).

14. Karen L. Remmer, "Does Democracy Promote Interstate Cooperation? Lessons from the Mercosur Region?" *International Studies Quarterly* 42, no. 1 (March 1998): 25–51; Andrew Hurrell, "Security in Latin America," *International Affairs* 74, no. 3 (July 1998): 529–46.

15. Some scientists involved in this program reportedly assisted Iraq in its enrichment efforts. See Jack Boureston, "Brazilian Nuclear Debate Highlights Parallels and Contrasts with Iran," *WMD Insights* 7 (July–August 2006), at http://www.wmdinsights.

com; John R. Redick, Julio C. Carasales, and Paulo S. Wrobel, "Nuclear Rapprochement: Argentina, Brazil, and the Nonproliferation Regime," *Washington Quarterly* 18, no. 1 (Winter 1995): 107–22; and José Goldemberg and Harold A. Feiveson, "Denuclearization in Argentina and Brazil," *Arms Control Today*, 24, no. 2 (March 1994): 10–14.

16. James Brooke, "Brazil's President Makes the Military Toe the Line," *New York Times*, September 9, 1990; Redick et al., "Nuclear Rapprochement."

17. Paulo S. Wrobel, "Brazil and the NPT: Resistance to Change?" *Security Dialogue* 27, no. 3 (September 1996): 337–47.

18. David Pion-Berlin, "From Confrontation to Cooperation: Democratic Governance and Argentine Foreign Relations," in *Civil-Military Relations: Building Democracy and Regional Security in Latin America, Southern Asia, and Central Europe*, ed. David R. Mares (Boulder, CO: Westview, 1998): 79–100.

19. Redick et al., "Nuclear Rapprochement"; Tom Zamora Collina and Fernando de Souza Barros, "Transplanting Brazil and Argentina's Success," *ISIS Report* 2, no. 2 (February 1995): 1–11.

20. Arturo C. Sotomayor Velazquez, "Civil Military Affairs and Security Institutions in the Southern Cone: The Sources of Argentine-Brazilian Nuclear Cooperation," *Latin American Politics and Society* 46, no. 4 (Winter 2004): 29–60.

21. Admiral Othon Luiz Pinheiro da Silva, who spearheaded the naval nuclear program, criticized the decision to postpone construction, arguing that completing the nuclear submarine was "a gesture of independence." "Submarino Nuclear é gesto de independência, afirma almirante," *Brasilia InfoRel, Relações Internacionais* (December 5, 2006); and "Ministro quer fortalecer Forças Armadas e Lula defende Programa Nuclear," December 6, 2007, at http://www.inforel.org.

22. *O Estado de São Paulo*, October 1, 2003.

23. Larry Rohter, "If Brazil Wants to Scare the World, It's Succeeding," *New York Times*, October 31, 2004, 3.

24. Claire Applegarth, "Brazil, IAEA Reach Inspection Agreement," *Arms Control Today* 35, no. 1 (January–February 2005).

25. Brazil's Ambassador to the United States, Roberto Abdenur, quoted in Gabrielle Kohlmeier, "Brazil May Permit Broader Inspections," *Arms Control Today* 34, no. 5 (June 2004).

26. "Brazil Reaches Tentative Inspections Agreement with IAEA," *Global Security Newswire*, November 29, 2004.

27. *O Estado de Sao Paulo*, February 6, 2006.

28. José Benedito Pereira, quoted in http://movv.org/2007/12/02.

29. Andres Oppenheimer, "Brazil a Nuclear Power? Probably Not," *Miami Herald*, October 18, 2009.

30. Juan Landaburu, "Interview," *La Nación*, November 24, 2009.

31. CAREM was described as the first nuclear power plant "made in Argentina," but is only a prototype scheduled to operate in 2012, with plans to market it to developing

countries. "Lanzó el Gobierno un plan de impulso a la energía nuclear," *La Nación*, August 24, 2006.

32. "Chávez Advocates Mercosur Free from Neoliberalism," *El Universal*, April 19, 2007; April 23, 2006 (all references to this source retrieved in May 2007 from http://buscador.eluniversal.com).

33. Simon Romero, "Chávez Rattles Takeover Saber at Steel Company and Banks," *New York Times*, May 5, 2007, A6.

34. T. Hernandez, "Cesa la Asamblea Nacional constituyente," *El Universal*, January 30, 2000; "National Assembly Resumes Sessions," *El Universal*, September 16, 2004.

35. "HRW Accuses Chávez of Undermining Independence of Courts, Press," *El Universal*, January 11, 2007; J. Alonso, "Courts and Attorney General Office Accused of Leading Attacks on Freedoms," *El Universal*, May 3, 2007.

36. V. Castillo, "Chávez Urges the Military to Embrace Socialism without 'Ambiguity,'" *El Universal*, April 13, 2007.

37. "Military Expert: Chávez Is Creating a Parallel Army," *El Universal*, March 21, 2005, April 17, 2006.

38. "International Federation of Journalists Warns against Media Closure Threat in Venezuela," *El Universal*, April 26, 2007.

39. Francisco Rodríguez, "An Empty Revolution: The Unfulfilled Promises of Hugo Chávez," *Foreign Affairs* 87, no. 2 (March–April 2008).

40. "President Chávez Insists on Nuclear Energy Plans," *El Universal*, October 18, 2005.

41. "Chávez Backs Iranian Nuclear Program," *El Universal*, March 11, 2005; "Venezuela Backs Iran in Nuclear Dispute," *El Universal*, January 30, 2006; "Iran Thanks Venezuelan Support," *El Universal*, February 14, 2006.

42. "Iranian, Venezuelan FMs Meet in Caracas," *El Universal*, April 20, 2007; *Noticiero Digital*, February 22, 2010, http://www.noticierodigital.com.

43. "Chávez tendrá energía nuclear," September 10, 2009, http://www.hoy.com.ec/noticias-ecuador/chavez-tendra-energia-nuclear-367141.html.

44. According to a document provided by a source in Venezuela to Roger Noriega, cited in "Time to Confront the Tehran-Caracas Axis," *Wall Street Journal*, April 9, 2010.

45. "Iran Not Sending Nuke Missiles to Venezuela, Official Says," *El Universal*, April 18, 2006; "Iran Willing to Support Venezuelan Nuke Program," *El Universal*, February 15, 2006; "Iran, Venezuela Voice Full Agreement on Nuke Issues," *El Universal*, September 19, 2006.

46. "VP Rangle Dismisses Rumors on Uranium Enrichment," *El Universal*, March 20, 2006.

47. "Rhetorical Exchange between Venezuela and the U.S. Continues," *El Universal*, April 23, 2006.

48. "Brazil: Venezuela, Iran Tighten Economic Ties, Relationship Criticized," *Folha de Sao Paulo*, August 5, 2007.

49. On Venezuela's ties to Hezbollah, the FARC, and ETA, see Arnson, Esfandiari, and Stubits, *Iran in Latin America*; and *New York Times*, September 6, 2008, A23. Prominent Venezuelan officials with presumed links to radical Middle East groups include Tarek Zaidan El Aissami Maddah (Minister of Interior and Justice); Tarek William Saab Halabi (Governor of Anzoategui Province); George Kabboul Abdelnour (Head of Bariven, purchasing arm of PDVSA); Imaad Saab (Venezuela's Ambassador to Syria); Radwan Sabbagh (President of a mining company in Orinoco); Brigadier General Aref Richany Jiménez (Director of PDVSA); Fadi Kabboul Abdelnour (PDVSA's Director of Planning); and the Minister of Interior's sister, Amin Obayda El Aissami Maddah (PDVSA executive). See Roger F. Noriega, "Hugo Chávez's Criminal Nuclear Network: A Grave and Growing Threat," American Enterprise Institute, *Latin American Outlook*, no. 3 (October 2009), http://www.aei.org/docLib/No.3-LAOg.pdf.

50. "The List: The World's Biggest Military Buildups," *Foreign Policy*, November 25, 2007.

51. On FARC's reported interest in acquiring 110 pounds of uranium, see Simon Romero, "Crisis at Colombia Border Spills into Diplomatic Realm," *New York Times*, March 4, 2008, A3.

52. Larry Rohter and Juan Forero, "Venezuela's Leader Covets a Nuclear Energy Program," *New York Times*, November 27, 2005, 8; "Brazil Downplays Alleged Venezuelan Nuclear Plans," *El Universal*, May 24, 2005.

53. Brazil accounts for 72 percent of South America's trade with Iran. "Brazil Shuns Nuclear Cooperation with Venezuela," *Global Security Newswire*, May 24, 2005.

54. Rohter and Forero, "Venezuela's Leader Covets a Nuclear Energy Program."

55. "Lula Backs Cooperation with Venezuela in the Nuclear Area," *El Universal*, September 7, 2006.

56. Argentina sold nuclear reactors to Egypt, Australia, Algeria, and Perú. Quotations from M. Leon and M. Parraga, "Negotiations to Purchase Nuclear Reactors from Argentina Confirmed," *El Universal*, October 11, 2005.

57. "Venezuela to Seek Nuclear Deal with Argentina and Brazil," *El Universal*, October 19, 2005.

58. Bruno Lima, "Teerã oferece apoio nuclear à Argentina," Ministério das Relações Exteriores, http://www.mre.gov.br/portugues. José Cárdenas, "State snubs House request to examine Argentina-Iran ties," August 10th, 2011, http://interamericansecuritywatch.com.

59. Kirchner was reportedly not amused and was first to leave this meeting of South American presidents to create UNASUR (Union of South American Nations). "Chávez Raises Nuclear Power Plant Idea," *Associated Press*, April 17, 2007.

60. "An Alternative Dracula Makes a Buck," *Economist*, August 11, 2007, 41. The bonds' value is at the official dollar rate for Venezuelan banks, which, in turn, resell them in secondary U.S. markets, reaping about 30 percent profit.

61. Natasha Niebieskikwiat, "Venezuela quiere comprarle un reactor nuclear a la Argentina," *Clarín*, October 9, 2005.

62. Patrick J. McDonnell, "Chávez Brings Oil Diplomacy to Neighbors," *Los Angeles Times*, August 8, 2007, A3

63. Simon Romero and Alexei Barrionuevo, "Brazil's Objections Slow Chávez's Plan for Regional Bank," *New York Times*, July 22, 2007, A12.

9 Ukraine: The Case of a "Nuclear Inheritor"

Isabelle Facon

Immediately before and after Ukraine's independence in 1991, Ukrainian political leaders declared they would not retain the many Soviet nuclear weapons deployed on their territory, but would transfer them all to Russia and join the Nuclear Non-proliferation Treaty (NPT) as a non-nuclear-weapons state. The following year, Kiev reconsidered its policy after realizing that the only way it could gain international assistance for its emerging economy and support to counter Russian political pressure was by negotiating denuclearization. Ukraine ultimately joined the NPT in November 1994 when the government concluded that maintaining its nuclear inheritance would be technically daunting, politically isolate the country, jeopardize its economic growth, and heighten rather than deter the Russian threat. Domestically, no prominent nuclear mythmaker emerged, as both the nationalist and liberal political camps agreed that Ukraine was better off without nuclear arms.[1] Domestic Ukrainian political support for some sort of hedging approach to nuclear weapons could emerge only if Ukraine were to become isolated from the West and seriously threatened by Russia, a worst-case scenario in which the West would have to reinforce the credibility of security assurances it offered Ukraine when it joined the NPT.

UKRAINE'S NUCLEAR INHERITANCE

When Ukraine gained its independence in 1991, it possessed the world's third largest nuclear arsenal. The breakup of the Soviet Union left Ukraine with several thousand strategic and tactical nuclear weapons. About 1,200 warheads were deployed on intercontinental ballistic missiles (ICBMs), including 130 SS-19s (each armed with six warheads) and 46 SS-24s (each with ten warheads).

Ukraine also possessed 44 Bear (Tu-95) and Blackjack (Tu-160) heavy bomb-ers (armed with air-launched cruise missiles and gravity bombs).[2] In the early 1990s, some Western observers considered it "unlikely that Ukraine [would] transfer its remaining nuclear weapons to Russia, the state it fears most," and believed a Ukrainian nuclear deterrent was "inevitable."[3] However, Kiev never obtained operational control of these weapons from Moscow.

When the Ukrainian Soviet Socialist Republic declared its independence in August 1991 and adopted a resolution subordinating all military units deployed on Ukrainian territory to the Republic's Parliament, the international commu-nity reacted with alarm. U.S. President George H. W. Bush first had to contend with the fact that these weapons still were targeted at the United States. In addi-tion, U.S. officials believed that a decision by Kiev to seize operational control of its nuclear arsenal would upset Russia, Poland, and Germany, which could only complicate the European security situation. The Bush administration also doubted Ukraine's ability to secure nuclear weapons and other sensitive mate-rials and technologies.[4]

European governments agreed that a non-nuclear Ukraine would be best for stability in Europe. Moscow, for its part, made it clear that Russia should be the sole nuclear successor to the Soviet Union. The Russians feared that if Ukraine retained its nuclear arsenal, then other states, in particular Kazakhstan, might be tempted to follow suit. The Kremlin stated that it would not carry out its Strategic Arms Reduction Talks (START) I obligations unless Ukraine ratified the treaty and acceded to the NPT as a non-nuclear-weapons state. While it initially resented Washington's efforts to keep Ukrainian nuclear intentions in check, Moscow soon saw the wisdom of joining forces with the United States to compel Kiev to respect its "non-nuclear pledge."[5]

Early on, Ukrainian officials had declared that they would not retain control of the nuclear weapons deployed on their soil, but rather would transfer all of these weapons to Russia and join the NPT as a non-nuclear state. This was the Ukrainian leadership's official line even before its declaration of independence in August 1991. After the collapse of the Soviet Union, Kiev reiterated this non-nuclear commitment in various Commonwealth of Independent States (CIS) military-related agreements. By that time, nuclear weapons were perceived as standing in the way of Kiev's key foreign policy objectives: to demonstrate that an independent Ukraine could act as a responsible state, to attract political and financial support from the West, and to appease Russia.[6]

Ukraine soon reconsidered its nuclear options. With foreign support slow in coming, officials in Kiev realized that negotiating denuclearization might be a good way to be taken seriously by the international community and get its support. Government officials began to suggest that their earlier non-nuclear commitments were not binding. In March 1992, the first president of post-Soviet Ukraine, Leonid Kravchuk, suspended the withdrawal of tactical nuclear weapons from Ukrainian territory, which had been stipulated in agreements signed with Russia just a few months before,[7] and Kiev proposed to build a dismantlement plant on its soil.[8] In the fall of 1992, Ukrainian authorities listed several conditions they wanted fulfilled before they sent their nuclear weapons to Russia: the international community had to guarantee Ukraine's security and contribute financially and technically to the dismantlement of Ukrainian weapons; Ukraine should receive compensation for the value of the nuclear materials derived from weapons on its territory; and it should be given assistance to deal with the environmental problems connected with nuclear disarmament.[9]

In October 1993, just five days before U.S. Secretary of State Warren Christopher's visit to Kiev, President Kravchuk said that Ukraine might keep its 46 SS-24s.[10] While the Ukrainian Parliament ratified START I on November 18, 1993, the ratification resolution contained 13 reservations conditioning the treaty's entry into force. The resolution stated that Ukraine was not bound by article V of the Lisbon protocol, under which it committed to accede to the NPT as a non-nuclear state "in the shortest possible time," declared ownership of the weapons on its territory, and asserted that only 36 percent of the delivery vehicles and 42 percent of the nuclear warheads deployed in Ukraine were subject to elimination. While some Ukrainian experts ex ante argued that Ukraine was not seeking nuclear weapons status but appropriate legal mechanisms and economic compensation to make the best of its nuclear inheritance,[11] the resolution alarmed the international community. A vicious circle had arisen: Ukraine's vacillation about its nuclear future stemmed mostly from the perception that Ukraine's independence was not welcomed by the international community and that playing the "nuclear card" was the only way to make the world pay it due attention; but this further deteriorated Ukraine's international image.

Following two years of negotiations, Kiev joined the NPT as a nuclear-free state on November 16, 1994. In exchange for abandoning its nuclear weapons, the permanent members of the U.N. Security Council offered Kiev security assurances as well as financial and economic aid. Since then, some Ukrainian politicians have expressed regrets concerning the decision to forgo a nuclear option. How widespread and serious are such opinions in today's Ukraine? How far should Kiev be viewed as a "disaffected disarmer"—that is, one of those countries that "feel they have been unfairly forced out of the nuclear weapons game"?[12] Could Ukraine's nuclear and ballistic missile capabilities be reactivated for a nuclear weapons program? What is left of the motives that in the 1990s led Kiev to question its non-nuclear pledge, and of those that finally led it to choose the denuclearization option?

UKRAINE AS A POTENTIAL NUCLEAR STATE: CAPABILITIES

By May 1992 Russia had taken possession of all tactical nuclear warheads that were deployed in Ukraine. In early June 1996 the last strategic nuclear warhead was sent to Russia. In late October 2001, following the destruction of the SS-19 ICBMs and silos, the last of the 46 silos for the SS-24 ICBMs was destroyed.[13] In January 2006 Ukraine completed the dismantlement of all its strategic bombers (some of them were transferred to Russia as part of payment for the huge gas debt). These actions were undertaken under full compliance with International Atomic Energy Agency guarantees.

Ukraine never established full operational control of its Soviet nuclear inheritance, and never was able to detonate the warheads.[14] According to former President Leonid Kuchma, Ukraine was not able to independently maintain these weapons, nor did it have the required infrastructure, technology, and economic resources needed to build them. In his view, lack of resources was the key factor influencing the decision of Ukraine's leaders to give up their nuclear weapons.[15] Nevertheless, Ukraine inherited significant nuclear and missile industrial capabilities that could encourage a government interested in developing an independent bomb program. Reflecting on "why states want nuclear weapons and why they don't," Joseph Cirincione argues that states generally refrain from nuclear weapons ambitions when "the technological and economic barriers are too significant to overcome."[16] For Ukraine, the technological barrier, though high, may not be insuperable. Former Prime Minister Yuriy Yekhanurov once asserted that Ukraine would encounter "no technical problems" if it decided to build nuclear weapons.[17] According to Anatoliy Shevtsov, the head of the Dnipropetrovsk branch of the National Institute for Strategic Studies, it would take only six months, $1 billion, and political will to restore Ukraine's nuclear status.

Ukraine never had a manufacturing facility for nuclear bombs nor the capacity to produce bomb-making quantities of weapons-grade plutonium or uranium. By relinquishing its nuclear weapons, it also deprived itself of materials needed to manufacture new nuclear warheads. According to the State Export Control Service of Ukraine, however, about 50 Ukrainian enterprises could contribute to a nuclear weapons program.[18] Ukraine's technical and scientific capabilities in the nuclear field prompted the United States to initiate several Cooperative Threat Reduction projects there.[19] Washington has long urged Ukraine to give away the almost 70 kilograms of highly enriched uranium stored in several research facilities to make sure they will not fall into the hands of rogue states or nonstate actors. Furthermore, Ukraine has approximately 11 percent of the natural uranium reserves of the former Soviet Union in 21 identified uranium deposits.[20] It has fourteen reactors (mostly pressurized water VVER-type reactors) at four nuclear power plants, which generate half of its electricity; and it intends to increase nuclear power generation by extending existing reactors and building new ones. In 2004 Ukraine commissioned two large new reactors, and the government plans to build up to eleven new reactors by 2030 to more than double nuclear capacity.[21] Ukraine also intends to increase its uranium production, and build a factory for nuclear fuel production. It also possesses mining and milling facilities for uranium. It inherited a major heavy-water production plant as well as the Pridneprovsky Chemical Factory, which produces nuclear-related dual-use commodities such as zirconium, hafnium, and ion exchange resins.[22]

The most "optimistic" experts believe that with this capability Ukraine would require five to seven years and an annual investment of about $300 million to create the infrastructure needed to build nuclear weapons.[23] Some experts believe that Ukraine is able to use either enriched uranium or plutonium to make weapons, although, in their view, the plutonium option is the simplest path.[24] Ukraine officially has given up plans to enrich uranium but could build an enrichment plant if it decided to expend the economic and scientific resources.[25]

Ukraine also inherited major ICBM design and production capabilities. A substantial portion of the Soviet missile industry was located in Ukraine, giving it the ability to design, develop, and manufacture liquid- and solid-fueled ICBMs. In fact, most of the strategic missile systems developed by the Soviet Union were produced in the Ukrainian Dnepropetrovsk facilities, especially the Yuzhnoe design bureau and the scientific and production unit Yuzhmash. Similarly, the Pavlograd facilities and the Khartron Production association played an important part in supplying the Soviet missile force with guidance systems.

Yuri Alekseyev, then general director of Yuzhmash, noted in 2001 that there was no plan for Ukraine to resume ICBM production in light of Ukraine's non-nuclear status and the inherent technical obstacles. Ukraine's missile industry has suffered from the loss of a substantial part of its state funding. Nevertheless, Ukraine's development of a space program and the help it still provides Russia to maintain its SS-18 ICBMs suggest that Ukraine retains some missile expertise.[26] The fact that former missile industry employees have occupied prominent political positions has probably helped the industry survive.[27]

Both foreign and Ukrainian experts consider that Ukraine would be able to become a nuclear and ballistic power much more easily and quickly than, for instance, did India or Pakistan. Ukrainian security specialists believe that "de facto Ukraine remains a threshold state in the international nuclear hierarchy" in the sense that its "economic and scientific and technical potential . . . is fully sufficient to develop nuclear weapons."[28]

Could Ukraine become a victim of technological determinism? According to Cirincione, "[S]ome experts contend that if a state has the technological ability to develop nuclear weapons, then it will do so," if only because this is perceived as a source of prestige based on the demonstration of economic and technological capacities.[29] Ukrainian leaders treat their missile and nuclear industries as jewels of the national economy and symbols of the country's technological maturity and ability to compete on foreign markets. Ukraine has tried more or less successfully to consolidate its domestic nuclear industry and protect it from Russia's controlling attempts.[30] The government also has tried to support its domestic industry for missile research, development, and production. It is developing new short-range missiles for the army and the navy. These plans also open up commercial opportunities. Among the most publicized projects is the conventional surface-to-surface missile system (Hrom), which is intended, according to former Ukrainian Defense Minister Hrytsenko, to "deter other states from aggressive actions against" Ukraine.[31] But Hrytsenko also insisted: "[T]he establishment of missile forces equipped with nuclear warheads, which existed in the Soviet period, is out of the question." He added that Kiev would abide by international agreements to control missiles and missile technologies.[32]

The optimistic assessment of Ukraine's nuclear capability has limits. In Soviet times, Ukraine never controlled all the technologies needed to master the whole cycle of nuclear weapons production. Despite its extensive technical and industrial assets, it would struggle to obtain the technologies it needs to manage the full cycle. One of the reasons why Ukraine relinquished nuclear weapons was that a decision to become a nuclear weapons state would have compelled Ukraine to create fissile material production facilities and nuclear test sites. The government could not afford the financial outlays needed to create such capabilities, if it ever thought of the possibility to do so.

A decision to start a national nuclear weapons program would be costly in economic and political capital, which Ukraine is probably neither able nor prepared to pay. There are no indications that Ukrainian politicians have a strong political motivation to act on any latent nuclear ambitions. However, members of the political elite periodically revisit the issue, saying that Ukraine might have been better served by a different nuclear choice.

THE NUCLEAR ISSUE: A STAKE IN TIMES OF TENSION

In the early 1990s nationalist political forces used the "nuclear card" against President Kravchuk, whom they accused of having sold nuclear weapons to Russia for nothing in return. Since then the issue has periodically re-emerged. In the spring of 1999, the Communist-dominated Parliament, unhappy with the North Atlantic Treaty Organization's (NATO) Allied Force operation in the former Yugoslavia, adopted a resolution stating that "the Cabinet of Ministers of Ukraine shall submit to the Supreme Council a draft law on canceling the decisions and renouncing Ukraine's obligations concerning its non-nuclear status." The decision was approved by nearly two-thirds of the deputies.

The debate on the nuclear weapons decision resumed when a dispute erupted in the autumn of 2003 over the border between Ukraine and Russia in the area of the Sea of Azov. The Azov seabed is reputedly rich in oil reserves, while the Kerch Strait, which permits access to the Black Sea, is of strategic military importance. Russian authorities unilaterally started building a dam across the Kerch Strait toward the Ukrainian island of Tuzla. Ukraine warned that it would not allow the construction to proceed to its side of the waterway and implied it would use force by deploying troops to Tuzla. As the dispute unfolded, the Ukrainians perceived that nobody was prepared to aid them despite the security assurances they had received when they gave up the nuclear option. Two prominent Ukrainian security experts commented: "[P]oliticians have again started thinking about the question of whether a rebirth of nuclear status for the state would help provide a restraint shield that would force even the strongest players on the international scene to reckon with Ukraine." They highlighted several questions that often re-emerge as security threats become salient: "Can

Ukraine protect itself from external threats and territorial claims by the re-creation of a nuclear shield? How much does it cost and what are nuclear weapons for Ukraine—a man-made Pandora's box or a tempting panacea?"[33] They also noted that "a few politicians and representatives of the authorities" believe that holding a serious discussion about resuming Ukraine's nuclear status might revive the nonfunctioning security guarantees that Ukraine received when it relinquished its nuclear arsenal.

In 2004, just before the "Orange Revolution," President Leonid Kuchma noted that the international community had not delivered on these guarantees. He wondered whether the world realized "the importance of this difficult step" that Kiev took in the 1990s.[34] On another occasion, he said, "[If] we had the world's third biggest nuclear potential today, we would be treated differently."[35] A Ukrainian political scientist speaking after the Orange Revolution expressed the same idea differently: "[If] we had the bomb, then there would have been no 'colored revolutions' here, because the West would have understood that instability here is dangerous. Russia would not have backed the separatists' feelings in the east of the country, and some countries in the West would not have done the same in West Ukraine."[36] Although these arguments appear emotional, they demonstrate that some Ukrainians believe the decision to adopt a non-nuclear status resulted in a loss of status and security. The nuclear status debate also resumed briefly in the aftermath of North Korea's 2006 nuclear test.

THE RUSSIA FACTOR

Russia's assertiveness was a major factor in Ukraine's initial hesitation in its nuclear posture. Independent Ukraine resented Moscow's heavy-handed effort to re-create a unified military space under its leadership. President Kravchuk's March 1992 decision to suspend the withdrawal of tactical nuclear arms occurred just a few days before a CIS summit that was to be held in Kiev. The Ukrainian government may have hoped that this would give it some bargaining leverage in the ongoing disputes with Russia over the Black Sea fleet and energy supplies. This tactic was seen in Kiev as a way to affirm Ukraine's sovereignty in relations with Russia just as the regional landscape was being redefined.

Ukrainian strategists fear that Russia could threaten the existence of Ukraine as a state. The Tuzla episode revived Ukrainian worries on this regard, together with Russia's reaction to President Yushenko's speeding up Ukraine's rapprochement with NATO by all kinds of pressures.[37] In 2008 President Putin stated that Russia would have no choice but to target its missiles at Ukrainian territory should Ukraine join NATO. The fact that Ukrainian officials some-times publicly regret that the country has given up its tactical nuclear weapons is a reflection of the concern that Russia's attitude creates.[38]

Following the election of Viktor Yanukovich in February 2010, Russian-Ukrainian relations have improved considerably. While this may result in Ukraine's de facto reduced sovereignty, it will lessen, at least for a while, the country's feeling of insecurity, and thus a major source of frustration about giving up nuclear weapons. Ukraine's political volatility may change the situation again in the future. In any case, Ukrainians' perception that the security assurances Ukraine received when it accepted denuclearization in 1994 never were credible is here to stay.[39] Many Ukrainian officials continue to believe that Russia's repeated assaults on Ukraine's sovereignty did not generate an ade-quate international reaction. This judgment was confirmed during the Tuzla crisis when President Leonid Kuchma asked the Foreign Ministry to identify the mechanism that would trigger the guarantees given by the international community when Ukraine abandoned its nuclear status. To many Ukrainians, this crisis confirmed that there are no such mechanisms.[40]

IN SEARCH OF INTERNATIONAL STANDING: THE PARADOXES OF THE NUCLEAR OPTION

States often decide to obtain nuclear weapons when they believe that nu-clear weapons will enhance their international prestige. This factor no longer seems prevalent in Ukraine, where experience has led to doubts that nuclear weapons confer status. Looking back, Ukrainian leaders see that they may not have received credible security guarantees. However, they also know they re-ceived financial compensation and assistance to cover the dismantlement cost of nuclear weapons in volumes above what the United States had initially of-fered. The negotiations between Ukrainian and U.S. officials on the fate of the Ukrainian nuclear arsenal enabled Kiev to operate outside of the unfavorable tete-a-tete with Russia. And it forced Russia, not without difficulties, to com-pensate Ukraine for the fissile material contained in the nuclear weapons with-drawn from its territory.

Ukraine has put itself in the category of states that "forgo nuclear weapons because of the international norm against the weapons."[41] The lessons from the past are very much alive in the minds of Ukrainian leaders, who are aware of how much the country's equivocation on its nuclear status harmed its po-litical standing, creating a perception that the Ukrainian elite was incompetent or immature. Kiev wants to appear as a responsible actor on the world stage, which would not have been served by harming the nonproliferation regime. To strengthen its international reputation, Ukraine has preferred to contribute troops to international peacekeeping and to join international arms trade and military technology transfers regimes.[42]

Ukraine lacks the "nuclear motivation" that some states derive from their position "on the periphery of the international system."[43] Its leaders believe that the smooth integration of Ukraine into the international community would be compromised by a decision to pursue a nuclear arsenal. Its geographical situation and ethnic composition have encouraged Ukraine to try to find a delicate balance between Russia and the West. Although relations with NATO will slow down under Yanukovich, Ukraine will continue to try to move closer to the West, as signaled by Yanukovich's announcement in April 2010 that Ukraine would get rid of its 68 kilograms of weapons-grade uranium by 2012 and convert its civil nuclear research facilities to operate with low enriched uranium fuel.[44]

Ukraine is increasingly economically integrated with Europe and the non-CIS world. A decision to seek a nuclear program would expose Ukraine to Western trade sanctions that would jeopardize its economy. In any case, if Ukraine opted for nuclear weapons, it would risk complete isolation, as the United States, Europe, and Russia would likely join forces again to pressure Kiev, including through trade sanctions. A move by Ukraine to obtain nuclear arms probably would cause the Russians to suspend projects (for example, the provision of nuclear fuel rods to commercial reactors) of critical importance to the Ukrainian economy.[45]

DOMESTICALLY: WEAK NUCLEAR ASPIRATIONS

Ukraine lacks a domestic nuclear constituency, or set of nuclear mythmakers, that wants to reverse its nuclear policy. In the early 1990s, nationalist, pro-independence parties were quite active, and, openly questioning the government's ability to handle security issues properly, they cited the nuclear issue as an example of its presumed incompetence. Today, however, Ukrainian factions and political parties are more likely to fight over economic issues than military and security ones. Russian-oriented groups do not advocate nuclear reversal, and Western-oriented political forces do not want to limit the support they seek from the United States and Europe.

In addition, the trauma caused by the Chernobyl nuclear power plant explosion in April 1986 has had lasting effects.[46] The subsequent nuclear allergy is probably the top reason why Ukrainian officials are not willing to host U.S. nuclear weapons on their territory if the country joined NATO.[47] This popular nuclear aversion is backed up by polling data: in March 2003, according to an opinion poll conducted by the Razumkov Centre, only 19 percent of respondents believed that Ukraine needed nuclear, chemical, or bacteriological weapons.[48]

CONCLUSION

Ukrainian officials frequently stress that their decision to forswear nuclear weapons and accede to the NPT has enhanced the international nonprolifera- tion regime and global security. Nevertheless, resentment lingers about the way the West welcomed Ukraine as an independent state and the fact that denucle- arization was not accompanied by a real commitment to ensure Ukraine's secu- rity. Some observers believe that Ukraine might have gained more by asserting itself as a responsible nuclear state, claiming a status as a "nuclear inheritor, and hence a special case."[49] They argue that Ukraine should have held out for a better offer from the international community in exchange for denucleariza- tion. Although under Yanukovich Ukraine has become more cooperative with Moscow, some politicians believe that Russia still poses an existential threat, and that things would have been quite different had Kiev preserved its nuclear option.

Today this option looks still less desirable. A nuclear arsenal is unlikely to generate tangible economic, security, or status benefits, and international and domestic opposition is sure to be high. According to former Ukrainian Defense Minister Konstyantyn Morozov, it is "absolutely impossible to create nuclear weapons today from the economic point of view, and from the defense point of view it is not advisable."[50] This statement reinforces Ukraine's non-nuclear com- mitment because in the early 1990s Morozov had questioned Ukraine's initial non-nuclear pledge.[51] Even during the dark days of the Tuzla crisis, President Kuchma made it clear that he would not seek to reverse Ukraine's non-nuclear status: "What is gone is gone. Ukraine decided on its nuclear-free status, so let us stick to that."[52]

The nuclear issue arises periodically in Ukrainian politics during interna- tional or domestic crises, not as a matter of considered debate. Arguments for nuclear reversal reflect a variety of opinions about the potential benefits of nu- clear arms and their possible targets. For some politicians, reviving the nuclear option would help to break up the undesirable West-Ukraine connection; for others, it could be used to deter Russia. Today, Ukraine stands between Russia and NATO; it does not fall under the protection of any nuclear umbrella; and it has no formal alliance. Depending on political and geopolitical conditions, a worst-case scenario could see Ukraine confronted with an increasingly aggressive Russia and isolation from the West. In such circumstances, Ukraine could adopt some sort of nuclear hedging policy. If this worst-case scenario actually were to materialize, the West would have to reinforce the credibility of security assurances it offered Ukraine when it closed the nuclear weapons file.

NOTES

1. Peter R. Lavoy, "Nuclear Proliferation over the Next Decade: Causes, Warning Signs, and Policy Responses," *Nonproliferation Review*, 13, no. 3 (November 2006): 433–54.

2. Nuclear Threat Initiative (NTI), Ukraine Profile, http://www.nti.org/e_research/profiles/Ukraine/index.html. According to some sources, an additional 14 SS-24 ICBMs were present in Ukraine but not operationally deployed with warheads. *Ukraine: Army, National Security and Defense Policy Handbook* (Washington, DC: International Business Publications, 2005), 59.

3. John J. Mearsheimer, "The Case for a Ukrainian Nuclear Deterrent," *Foreign Affairs*, 72, no. 3 (Summer 1993): 50–66; see also Martin J. De Wing, "The Ukrainian Nuclear Arsenal: Problems of Command, Control and Maintenance," Working Paper no. 3, Program for Nonproliferation Studies, Monterey Institute of International Studies, October 1993.

4. Mitchell Reiss, *Bridled Ambition: Why Countries Constrain Their Nuclear Capabilities* (Washington, DC, Woodrow Wilson Center Press, 1995), 92, 155.

5. Yuri Dubinin, "Yadernyy dreyf Ukrainy" [Ukraine's Nuclear Drift], *Rossiya v global'noy politike*, no. 2 (March–April 2004), www.globalaffairs.ru.

6. Serguiy Galaka, "La coopération entre l'Ukraine et l'Occident: le cas de la non-prolifération nucléaire," in *L'Ukraine, nouvel acteur du jeu international*, ed. Anne de Tinguy (Brussels: Emile Bruylant, 2000), 154.

7. According to the Alma-Ata Declaration of December 21, 1991, "Until their destruction in full, nuclear weapons located on the territory of the Republic of Ukraine shall be under the control of the Combined Strategic Forces Command, with the aim that they not be used and be dismantled by the end of 1994, including tactical nuclear weapons by 1 July 1992." The Minsk agreement on Strategic Forces repeated the same wording (December 30, 1991).

8. By March 1992, the Ukrainian Parliament had not ratified the Alma-Ata and Minsk agreements; hence they were not binding. To justify its decision, Kiev argued that the weapons transferred to Russia might not be destroyed and instead might be used against Ukraine in the future. Ukrainian officials complained that they had no informa-

tion about the status of the tactical nuclear weapons that had been removed from their soil, which motivated their request for an international monitoring mechanism for the dismantlement process.

9. Galaka, "La coopération entre l'Ukraine et l'Occident," 158.

10. "Ukraine Now Says It May Keep Nuclear Weapons," *New York Times*, October 20, 1993.

11. Lesya Gak, "Denuclearization and Ukraine: Lessons for the Future," *Nonproliferation Review*, 11, no. 1 (Spring 2004): 106–35.

12. Peter R. Lavoy and Robin Walker, "Conference Report: Nuclear Weapons Proliferation: 2016," Naval Postgraduate School, Monterey, CA, August 2006, http://www.nps.edu/academics/sigs/ccc/conferences/recent/NuclearWeaponsProliferation2016Jul06_rpt.pdf, 4.

13. "Ukraine Eliminates All Its Nuclear Weapons," *Interfax-Ukraine*, October 30, 2001, available at http://www.nti.org/db/nisprofs/ukraine/weapons/mslsilo.htm.

14. Bruno Tertrais, "Nuclear Proliferation in Europe. Could It Still Happen?" *Nonproliferation Review*, 13, no. 3 (November 2006): 569.

15. UNIAN, March 29, 1999, cited in NTI Ukraine Profile, http://www.nti.org/e_research/profiles/Ukraine/nuclear_weapons_agreements.html.

16. Joseph Cirincione, *Bomb Scare: The History and Future of Nuclear Weapons* (New York: Columbia University Press, 2007), 224.

17. "MP Says Ukraine Can Resume Nuclear Arms Production if Necessary," BBC Monitoring International Reports, October 29, 2003 [translation from an interview in *Stolichnye Novosti*, October 28, 2003].

18. Oleksandr Hryshutkin, Deputy Head of the State Export Control Service of Ukraine, quoted by UNIAN News Agency (BBC Monitoring International Reports, April 27, 1999).

19. Galaka, "La coopération entre l'Ukraine et l'Occident," 163.

20. NTI, Ukraine, Uranium Mining and Milling, http://www.nti.org/e_research/profiles/Ukraine/Nuclear/facilities.html.

21. Uranium Information Center, Melbourne, Australia, "Nuclear Power in Ukraine," Briefing Paper 63 (May 2007); Stephen Mulvey, "Ukraine's Strange Love for Nuclear Power," BBC News Website, April 26, 2006, http://news.bbc.co.uk/2/hi/europe/4948976.stm.

22. William C. Potter, *The Politics of Nuclear Renunciation: The Cases of Belarus, Kazakhstan, and Ukraine* (Washington, DC, Henry L. Stimson Center, 1995), 9.

23. Sergeï Zgurets and Valentin Badrak, "Yadernyi khod. Za i protiv" [Going Nuclear. Pros and Cons], *Zerkalo Nedeli*, no. 45 (470), November 22–28, 2003.

24. Ibid.

25. Ibid.

26. Ukraine has made a substantial effort to develop its space launch programs.

Ukrainian missile enterprises are involved in a variety of space projects, including converting ICBMs to space launch vehicles in cooperation with Russian firms (*Kosmostras* is a Russian-Ukrainian joint venture that converts SS-18 missiles into *Dnepr* space launch vehicles), participating in the Sea Launch program, and working with Russian enterprises on new SLV designs.

27. The most prominent example is that of Leonid Kuchma who, before becoming the President of Ukraine, worked as a missile engineer. He was the Director General of *Yuzhmash*.

28. Zgurets and Badrak, "Yadernyi khod. Za i protiv."

29. Cirincione, *Bomb Scare*, 70.

30. Nikolay Sokov, "Ukraine Considers Uranium Enrichment," *WMD Insights*, March 2006, http://www.wmdinsights.com/I3/R2_Ukraine_Considering.htm.

31. Cited in Tor Bukkvoll, "Effective Deterrent: Ukraine Begins Work on New Missile System," *Jane's Intelligence Review*, 19, no. 1 (January 1, 2007): 55–57. Viktor Yanukovich, now Ukraine's President, is thought to be in favor of a Europe-wide approach to the issue of missile defense so that the Ukrainian missile industry could compete for lucrative contracts. Nikolai Sokov and Jacob Quamme, "No Consensus in Ukraine over Missile Defense," *WMD Insights*, June 2007, http://www.wmdinsights.com/I16/I16_RU2_NoConsensus.htm.

32. "Ukraine: Defense Minister Says No Plans to Restore Nuclear Missile Potential," *Interfax*, March 16, 2006.

33. Zgurets and Badrak, "Yadernyi khod. Za i protiv."

34. "Kuchma: World Community Not Meeting Obligations after Ukraine's Nuclear Disarmament," *World News Connection*, July 22, 2004.

35. "Ukraine Won't Change Its Nuclear-Free Status: President," *Interfax*, November 12, 2003.

36. Vitaliy Kulik, cited in "Ukraine Can Create Its Own Nuclear Bomb in Three Years but Has No Reason To," *BBC Monitoring International Reports*, October 11, 2006.

37. Interestingly, Kiev made references to the memorandum on security guarantees in the framework of the NPT (Budapest memorandum) in connection with its 2006 gas dispute with Russia. "Ukraine's Reference to Non-Proliferation Treaty Ungrounded: Foreign Ministry," *RIA Novosti*, December 28, 2005. It has to be recalled that when in November 1994 the Ukrainian Parliament agreed to Ukraine's joining the NPT, it emphasized that any threat to use force or any use of force against Ukraine's territorial integrity, or political independence by a nuclear power, or the use of economic pressures aimed at limiting Ukraine's sovereignty, would be considered as "extraordinary events endangering its supreme interests." This means that Ukraine considers such events as legitimate reasons to withdraw from the NPT, in conformity with Article 10 of the treaty. Galaka, "La coopération entre l'Ukraine et l'Occident," 159.

38. Given that Ukraine is more likely to be involved in a regional military conflict than

a major war, tactical weapons could be viewed as more appropriate than strategic systems. Oleksandr Kuzmuk, former Ukrainian Defense Minister, stated that the decision to abandon tactical weapons was a mistake, as, contrary to strategic nuclear weapons, there was, to his knowledge, a possibility to ensure their maintenance. "Ukraine's Abandoning Tactical Nukes Was a Mistake," *Interfax-AVN*, January 25, 2006.

39. In the trilateral declaration issued in January 1994 by the presidents of Ukraine, the United States, and Russia, Washington and Moscow pledged to respect the independence and sovereignty of Ukraine as well as to refrain from using force or the threat of force against it, including a commitment not to use nuclear weapons. The United States, the United Kingdom, France, Russia, and China offered security assurances (not guarantees) to Ukraine in December 1994, which provide for the territorial integrity, sovereignty, and inviolability of Ukraine's borders (Budapest Memorandum).

40. "The MFA must study the situation to elaborate mechanisms that would make it possible to obtain the guarantees. . . . I am glad that the event occurred. We all got an opportunity to estimate the level of the treaty on the territorial integrity. Now you can see if they want to protect us." *Ukraine News*, December 19, 2003.

41. Cirincione, *Bomb Scare*, 49.

42. In 1996 Ukraine joined the Nuclear Suppliers Group; in 1998 it became a member of the Missile Technology Control Regime; and it joined the Hague Code of Conduct against ballistic missile proliferation in March 2004.

43. Cirincione, *Bomb Scare*, 53.

44. "Fact Sheet on Ukraine's Non-Proliferation Efforts," the White House, Washington, DC, April 12, 2010, http://www.whitehouse.gov/sites/default/files/Fact%20Sheet%20on%20Ukraine%20HEU%20announcement_FINAL%20(4-12-10).pdf.

45. When it agreed to transfer strategic nuclear weapons to Russia, Ukraine received fuel rods for nuclear power stations. Russia provides all of Ukraine's nuclear fuel requirements, but President Yanukovich said Ukraine would try to "return 50 percent to itself." Nikolay Sokov, "Ukraine to Develop Nuclear Fuel Production Capability but without Uranium Enrichment," *WMD Insights*, November 2006, http://www.wmdinsights.com/I10/I10_R2_UkraineToDevelop.htm. Ukraine has struggled to diversify nuclear fuel sources for its reactors. In 2005 fuel supplied by Westinghouse Electric Company, a U.S.-based subsidiary of British Nuclear Fuels, Ltd., was used for the first time at the South-Ukrainian nuclear power plant. But the U.S. fuel is 40 percent more expensive than that supplied by Russia, which keeps the upper hand on the Ukrainian market. Sokov, "Ukraine Considers Uranium Enrichment." In spring 2010, as relations between Moscow and Kiev were improving, a large-scale nuclear cooperation deal was discussed.

46. The non-nuclear commitment pronounced in the 1990 Declaration of Sovereignty was a direct reference to the way the Soviet leaders had mishandled the Chernobyl disaster. See Reiss, *Bridled Ambition*, 93.

47. "Ukraine Will Not House Nuclear Weapons if It Joins NATO: Minister," *AFP* (Kiev), June 30, 2005, quoting former Defense Minister Anatoliy Hrytsenko.

48. Zgurets and Badrak, "Yadernyi khod. Za i protiv."

49. Mearsheimer, "The Case for a Ukrainian Nuclear Deterrent," 61.

50. Zgurets and Badrak, "Yadernyi khod. Za i protiv."

51. In 1993 Morozov told his NATO counterparts he thought the West would "take heed of what the Ukraine says only as long as there are nuclear weapons on its soil." Quoted in Gregory J. Rattray, "Explaining Weapons Proliferation: Going Beyond the Security Dilemma," *INSS Occasional Papers*, USAF Institute for National Security Studies, July 1994.

52. "Ukraine Won't Change Its Nuclear-Free Status: President," *Interfax*, November 12, 2003.

PART II:
FOSTERING NONPROLIFERATION

10 The NPT Regime and the Challenge of Shaping Proliferation Behavior

Christopher A. Ford

This chapter focuses on the role that the nonproliferation regime, especially the Treaty on the Non-proliferation of Nuclear Weapons (NPT), can play in influencing the survival and persuasiveness of proliferation-inducing and proliferation-disfavoring nuclear "myths."[1] National decisions regarding nuclear weapons development occur within the context of an international system containing rules, institutions, and practices for dealing with proliferation threats—as well as participants who have particular views, policy priorities, and capabilities that they are able to bring to bear on such matters if they wish. This context influences the cost-benefit calculus of would-be proliferators, providing elites with data that can affect the persuasiveness of nuclear myths or countermyths.

A treaty regime can affect the behavior of potential proliferators in several ways. First, it can help set norms and prioritize policy agendas for States Party to the treaty. When this works, a regime can establish a "mainstream" baseline from which debates between mythmakers and counter-mythmakers are undertaken so that deviation from the baseline will require special justification to be persuasive. A strong nonproliferation norm-set provides a ready-made cluster of arguments, an international constituency, and a source of support, favoring courses of action that shift opinion and policy against the "nuclear option." A weak or confused norm-set, on the other hand, levels the playing field between competing pro- and antiproliferation myths, or may even provide ammunition for those who offer proliferation arguments. A regime also can shape the cost-benefit calculations of would-be proliferators, influencing perceptions of risk and opportunity costs.

A treaty regime that sets clear and powerful norms, enables the early detection of violations, facilitates effective political mobilization against violators, and makes both violation and nonparticipation seem unattractive will help shape would-be proliferators' behavior in ways that slow or prevent proliferation. A "good" regime will not in itself suffice to prevent every instance of proliferation, because fighting proliferation is a complex, iterated game of shaping participants' perceptions and internal debates regarding their degree of commitment to the regime. Nevertheless, the regime's structure and operation help determine its effectiveness.

The first part of this chapter discusses the strengths and weaknesses of the NPT regime. The second describes how the emergence of alternative futures will depend upon how NPT Parties handle today's challenges. The treaty has played an important role in supporting international peace and security. The NPT regime nonetheless needs to be understood as an imperfect one with real problems. To paraphrase what the philosopher Leo Strauss wrote of democracy, the real friend of the NPT cannot be its flatterer.[2] We must on occasion tell it hard truths precisely *because* we truly support it.

THE NPT REGIME'S INFLUENCE UPON
WOULD-BE PROLIFERATORS

Multilateral treaty regimes perform an international norm- and agenda-setting function, which can help influence behavior by shaping states' understandings of their environment, their prioritization of issues, and their willingness to bear burdens in pursuit of collective objectives. To the extent that such values are internalized by elites or those to whom elites are accountable, they may act relatively directly upon policymaking. Regime norms also may affect choices by shaping the behavior of those with whom states interact in the international community (for example, in prompting mobilization against noncompliance).

NPT Norm-Articulation

The NPT articulates a reasonably clear norm against the proliferation of nuclear weapons. The first sections of its preamble emphasize that "the proliferation of nuclear weapons would seriously enhance the danger of nuclear war," and that such a conflict would visit "devastation . . . upon all mankind." It also describes States Party as acting in conformity with U.N. General Assembly resolutions on "the prevention of wider dissemination of nuclear weapons."[3] The so-called "Irish Resolution" of 1961, for instance, said proliferation would "intensify the arms race and . . . increase the difficulties of avoiding war and of establishing international peace and security based on the rule of law."[4] Acting upon this conviction, it called upon all states to conclude an agreement

> under which the nuclear States would undertake to refrain from relinquishing control of nuclear weapons and from transmitting the information necessary for their manufacture to States not possessing such weapons, and . . . States not possessing nuclear weapons would undertake not to manufacture or otherwise acquire control of such weapons.[5]

This resolution was the conceptual fountainhead of the NPT, and this phrasing developed into the first two articles of the final NPT text,[6] the provisions that Canadian officials rightly called "the core of the Treaty."[7]

In the course of the NPT negotiations, the theme that the fundamental goal of preventing nuclear weapons proliferation was in the interest of all states was frequently repeated. Representatives of the United States,[8] which introduced the first draft treaty, the Soviet Union,[9] India,[10] the United Arab Republic,[11] and the so-called Non-Aligned Eight members of the U.N.'s Eighteen-Nation Disarmament Committee[12] all spoke out generally along such lines. A panel of experts appointed by the U.N. Secretary General concluded that global security required preventing "the further spread and elaboration of nuclear weapons."[13] Indeed, the general view at the time was that nonproliferation was a vital goal that served the interests of all states.[14] A case was even made that the treaty provided *more* security benefit to non-nuclear-weapons states than to those possessing such weapons.[15]

The basic norm-setting function of the NPT might thus seem quite clear: nuclear weapons proliferation is a threat to everyone, and must be prevented. As the Canadian negotiators put it, "[P]reventing States other than the existing nuclear Powers from acquiring nuclear weapons . . . is the main purpose of the treaty."[16] Such clarity, however, has not persisted over time.

Historical Revisionism

The loss of clarity with respect to the NPT's norm-setting function is due to the fact that, in the four decades since the NPT was opened for signature, battles lost in the negotiation of the treaty's text have been revisited by their losers in efforts to read back into the document elements that had failed initially to win support and codification. The most obvious example involves Article VI, which addresses nuclear disarmament.

Article VI was understood not to impose specific disarmament obligations upon the nuclear weapons states (NWS) recognized by the treaty.[17] Instead, the preamble only expressed the desire of all States Party to bring about disarmament,[18] while Article VI obliged everyone merely to "pursue negotiations in good faith" toward that end.[19]

This failure to impose concrete disarmament requirements, however, was not for lack of trying. Some nonaligned nations proposed that nonproliferation be linked to concrete disarmament requirements.[20] U.S. and Soviet negotiators, however, insisted that such a connection could jeopardize the negotiations,[21] and most participants agreed to give special priority to nonproliferation.[22] Some still pushed for formal linkage between nonproliferation and disarmament,[23] but that did not win support. All that was secured was the insertion of phrasing reflecting the intention of the NWS to move toward nuclear disarmament.[24] In a last-ditch effort, Mexico proposed obliging Parties to "pursue negotiations in good faith" toward particular disarmament objectives,[25] but this phrasing was adopted without any reference to such specific objectives.[26]

Despite this clear negotiating record, NPT diplomacy has since seen repeated attempts to rewrite history by reading back into Article VI just the sort of concrete disarmament requirements that were considered and rejected in its drafting. Today, for instance, it often is suggested that the lack of total nuclear disarmament is an NPT compliance problem—and even that such purported noncompliance with Article VI somehow excuses the noncompliance of others with the NPT's nonproliferation rules.

To be sure, there was broad agreement during the negotiations that disarmament was desirable, and some warned that the treaty might not last unless it were followed by nuclear disarmament measures.[27] To assert that the lack of complete nuclear disarmament is a violation of the treaty, however, is to misread the text and ignore its negotiating history. Such revisionism has been aided by a poorly reasoned dictum rendered by the International Court of Justice (ICJ) that Article VI requires not merely pursuing disarmament negotiations (as Article VI specified) but also concluding them (which it did not).[28]

The campaign to resurrect disarmament obligations rejected by the treaty's drafters does not always ignore the negotiating history. Instead, it is sometimes asserted that whatever Article VI was written to say, its meaning has changed. Some suggest the ICJ's comment accomplished this change in the NPT's objectives,[29] while others claim that the 1995 and 2000 NPT Review Conferences created new obligations.[30] Neither argument, however, holds up.

The view that the comment contained in the Court's 1996 advisory opinion changed Article VI seems to rest on a misunderstanding of the ICJ's role.[31] The ICJ's jurisdiction does not extend to making or changing the law; its decisions do not form case precedents in the way that domestic court cases can, except insofar as they are binding on the specific parties to a case submitted to the Court—a qualification that does not apply to advisory opinions anyway. Technically, ICJ cases are only "subsidiary means" for understanding legal rules.[32] Most advocates of the rereading of Article VI seem to ignore the fact that the ICJ case upon which they rely was merely an advisory opinion without binding effect on states.[33] Moreover, the meaning of Article VI of the NPT was not a legal question "upon which the advisory opinion of the Court" was requested and was therefore outside the scope of the question posed to the Court by the General Assembly. (It had been asked, instead, to consider the legality of the threat or use of nuclear weapons.)[34] Accordingly, the Court's pronouncements on this matter were mere dicta.

As for alleged impact of Review Conference decisions on Article VI obligations, it may be that such a conference could reach an "agreement between the parties regarding the interpretation of the treaty or the application of its provisions" that could aid in interpreting Article VI.[35] No Review Conference, however, has yet done this. They have sometimes articulated states' views about what measures would help implement Article VI,[36] but no conference has yet claimed to change or add to its meaning by making such desirable steps into legal obligations. The strongest case made by disarmament advocates is not a legal one, but one that assumes that concrete steps toward disarmament were promised as part of a *political* bargain at the time of decision in 1995 to extend the NPT indefinitely. Debates over the extent to which this is true—and what that would mean anyway—may say much about current NPT politics, but essentially nothing about the meaning of Article VI.

Despite the clarity of Article VI, at least some diplomatic support appears to exist for the idea that purported NWS disarmament "noncompliance" somehow excuses noncompliance by the non-nuclear-weapons states (NNWS) with the nonproliferation rules of Article II. Others seem to suggest, for example, that it is "unfair" for the NWS to criticize Iran for its violations because the NWS are also noncompliant for not having already abandoned nuclear weapons. Such arguments are flawed as matters of law and logic, but they have had enough political impact to undermine the regime's norm-setting clarity and effectiveness.

Today, we are far indeed from the original understanding that nonproliferation "is the main purpose of the Treaty." Instead, the dominant view now seems to be that it has "three pillars"—nonproliferation, disarmament, and the promotion of peaceful uses—all of which are presumptively *coequal* priorities and must perforce be traded off against each other. According to diplomatic veterans of the period, this "three pillars" phrasing was itself largely an invention of U.S. officials in the 1980s, who coined the phrase to persuade other parties to focus less upon disarmament. Today, the ahistorical mantra of tripartite "balance" has become the conventional wisdom, but it seems no longer to help the cause of nonproliferation, for its main contemporary purpose is to provide rhetorical sustenance for those who do not wish NPT diplomacy to spend too much time insisting upon nonproliferation in this era of Iranian and North Korean provocations.

Timely Detection

The likelihood that violations of the provisions of a treaty regime will be detected will affect the decision calculus of would-be proliferators, because few violators will wish to be caught trying to develop nuclear weapons. (It is at that stage, when their arsenal is not yet deployed, that they are perhaps most vulnerable: exposed as dangerous scofflaws, but not yet able to take refuge in any "deterrent" that weapons might provide.) The ability to provide timely detection—early enough to permit action to return the violator to compliance or to counter the threat—is thus a key variable affecting regime success.

In this regard, the NPT has a bifurcated structure. The International Atomic Energy Agency (IAEA) plays a critical role in verifying compliance with the nuclear safeguards agreements required by Article III,[37] but there exists no multilateral mechanism for verifying compliance with NPT provisions. Instead, the treaty leaves such determinations to States Party. The United States has explained its approach to compliance under Article II,[38] noting that judgments informed by an analysis of all available information "as to the purpose of a Party's nuclear activities . . . lie at the core of Article II compliance assessments."[39] Activities related to the acquisition or testing of components involved in the nuclear explosion itself would provide a fairly direct indicator of a program's weapons purpose. Dual-use technologies or activities—ones that could serve both legitimate (for example, power generation) or illegitimate (nuclear weapons) ends—can be indicators of a weapons program when evaluated in light of all available information. For example, if the country using such dual-use technologies has engaged in a pattern of willful safeguards violation or if it has engaged in deception and denial efforts aimed at concealing its nuclear activities, one might reasonably suspect nefarious intent.

Treaty verification is a tougher challenge than safeguards verification. IAEA officials have occasionally suggested that they can assess whether a country's nuclear "intent" is peaceful or otherwise.[40] For the most part, however, they eschew such phrasing, and it is not hard to see why. Drawing conclusions about the intentions behind some activity that has been declared or discovered demands skills more akin to those of an intelligence service than an inspectorate made up of international civil servants responsible to a diverse and largely consensus-driven body of multinational overseers and dependent upon host government permission to operate. A verification authority must also be able to reach decisions on the basis of ambiguous or incomplete information, while operating in a highly charged political environment. It must even sometimes make determinations, in the midst of such contestation, about the meaning of the law itself. The IAEA is not responsible for determining NPT compliance, and would have a difficult time doing so.

The situation is different, however, with respect to safeguards. Most observers think that the IAEA does a good job of monitoring declared facilities to prevent the diversion of a significant quantity of fissile material.[41] With the gradual adoption of the Additional Protocol, inspectors increasingly are able to look for undeclared facilities. As more states accept and implement the Additional Protocol and it becomes the new safeguards standard[42]—and as inspectors direct effort and resources against the highest proliferation risks—the regime will be better able to deter misbehavior.[43]

Nevertheless, even in the comparatively institutionalized safeguards realm, the regime's ability to handle denial and deception by a determined proliferator is limited. For all the good work that IAEA inspectors did in gathering information about Iran's nuclear program once it was exposed, it still remains difficult to discover a clandestine program. The Iranian program began in the mid-1980s, but IAEA inspectors were only sent to investigate it after the underground enrichment facility at Natanz—then under construction—was revealed in August 2002 by an antigovernment group. Based upon this tip, the inspectors documented many of Iran's nuclear activities and exposed some of Iran's denial and deception techniques. The Agency is working to improve its capabilities,[44] but will likely rely on outside sources of information. It will remain better at following up on leads than in developing them in the first place. It would thus be a mistake to view a treaty regime's verification challenges as addressable by international institutions alone. The Iran example demonstrates that national governments should understand that they have a role to play in how a regime shapes behavior by increasing the likelihood of timely detection.

Another lesson of the NPT regime's experience is that a determined violator may require more inspection tools than even the Additional Protocol supplies. The previous IAEA Director General, for instance, conceded that "[g]iven Iran's past concealment efforts over many years . . . transparency measures [by Iran] should extend beyond the formal requirements of the Safeguards Agreement and Additional Protocol."[45] Highlighting the point, the IAEA has been stone-walled by authorities in Damascus in trying to investigate evidence of North Korea's construction of a plutonium-production reactor in Syria, which was subsequently bombed by Israel in 2007.[46] Verification authorities exist in a long-running, iterated game of "cat and mouse" with proliferators, and successfully shaping the behavior of would-be future proliferators may require adaptation over time. The Iran and Syrian cases suggest that the safeguards verification system has had some success in creating the perception that inspections are to be feared by those who wish to conceal nuclear activity. This system, therefore, seems to have some deterrent effect upon would-be proliferators. Nevertheless, deterrence will rest not merely upon the perceived likelihood of detection but, rather, what follows once detection occurs.[47] Few violators are likely to be de-terred by the prospect of shame alone.

In the safeguards system, the notion of timely detection has an explicit em-bodiment in INFCIRC/153, the model for comprehensive safeguards agreements with member governments, which declares that "the objective of safeguards is the timely detection of diversion . . . and deterrence of such diversion by the risk of early detection."[48] As one former IAEA official explained, the Agency has "timeliness detection goals" for facility reinspection that are designed to corre-spond to conversion times—that is, to the time needed to convert safeguarded material into a weapons-usable form.[49]

The IAEA, however, has admitted that conversion time can be "very short."[50] If, indeed, the objective is to make detection timely enough to permit an effec-tive response, one might wonder whether it is adequate to rely upon a system that can give only limited warning of potential conversion to weapons uses.[51] According to Australian government figures, there is reason to doubt that safe-guards on fuel-cycle facilities can provide any real advance warning at all.[52] One senior Iranian official has even offered the conclusion that "you just have to trust us that we want to produce fuel, not a bomb."[53]

The situation might actually be worse than such technical assessments suggest because the integrity of the regime requires viewing "timeliness" not simply from the perspective of a would-be proliferator's conversion time, but with an eye to the international community's response time. After all, the point is not just to *document* proliferation, but to permit it to be *stopped*. To the extent that a safeguards violation is the result of error, unauthorized action, or a lack of capability to comply, the fact of detection itself may tend to ensure a return to compliance. Where a violation is deliberate, however, the regime must rely upon multilateral response mechanisms involving complex dynamics of political mobilization to bring compliance pressure to bear. Unlike some forms of unilateral reaction, multilateral reactions take time, but it is this time that safeguards seem increasingly hard pressed to provide. Given the need for political mobilization, providing timely detection can become challenging indeed.[54]

The example of Iran is instructive. The first public revelations about its secret program occurred in August 2002, and IAEA inspectors quickly developed a mass of data documenting Iran's safeguards violations. In November 2003, the IAEA Board of Governors found Iran to have committed "failures and breaches of its obligation to comply with the provisions of its Safeguards Agreement."[55] Only in February 2006, however, did the Board manage to comply with the IAEA Statute,[56] by deciding to report Iran to the U.N. Security Council.[57] Not until December 2006 did the Council itself begin to impose sanctions upon Iran for its continued defiance.[58] The Natanz facility was still under construction when it was first revealed publicly. By the time the first sanctions were applied against Iran, however, the facility had been completed, and Iran had begun enriching small quantities of uranium.[59]

Timely detection is difficult when groups of countries must coalesce in support of nonproliferation norms in order to mount a response to a safeguards violation. This illustrates the interrelationship among compliance enforcement, detection, and norm-setting: timely detection is harder where compliance enforcement requires multilateral activity, and compliance mobilization—the process of building diplomatic coalitions to bring compliance pressure to bear upon a violator—is more difficult (and slower) where the norm-setting clarity of the regime has been eroded.

Compliance Mobilization

Treaty regime dynamics can affect how easy it is to mobilize other regime participants in collective efforts to impose costs upon a violator.[60] As a multilateral system, the NPT regime faces more formidable compliance policy challenges than those that confronted policymakers in Cold War–style bilateral arms control. In bilateral state or alliance bloc relationships, the principal problem seemed to be detection: if one discovered that the adversary was cheating, compliance policy became a question of taking action to counter the threat or pressure a return to compliance. Collective action dynamics are minimized where the principal protagonists are individual arms race opponents or rival alliance blocs each led by a dominant partner. The situation is different, however, in today's multilateral nonproliferation regimes because compliance action involves complex coalition building and maintenance. For multilateral regimes, detection is only part of the problem, which often begins with a political battle over what constitutes an NPT violation.

Erosion of the NPT's norm-setting function is highly problematic because confusion about the fundamental purposes of the regime impedes collective action against a violator. Such erosion can make compliance promotion measures difficult to implement early in a developing crisis, when the violator may be most susceptible to dissuasive steps. By the time a modest measure becomes saleable in a contentious and norm-ambiguous political environment, it may be too late for that measure to be effective.

Such too-little-too-late dynamics have plagued efforts to respond to Iran's safeguards violations and destabilizing enrichment program. With respect to safeguards, it proved difficult to persuade the Agency even to follow its own rules in the Iranian case. The IAEA's Statute has some provisions potentially useful for safeguards compliance pressure, permitting the suspension of IAEA assistance, allowing for the return of materials and equipment provided to the violator, and, if need be, providing for noncompliance to be reported to the U.N. Security Council for more dramatic action.[61] Given the sweeping authorities that could be invoked by the Security Council, and given that many countries depend upon the IAEA's Technical Cooperation program for assistance,[62] these provisions potentially offer the Agency significant influence.[63]

Early efforts to report Iran to the Security Council, however, were superseded by negotiated compromises with Iran that occurred outside IAEA mechanisms. These compromises did not persuade it to change its course.[64] Even after Tehran's continued intransigence had provoked a return to such mechanisms, pressures have emerged slowly, even at the Security Council. Several rounds of mild sanctions have elicited nothing but continued Iranian defiance, and agreement from Russia and China even to only slightly tougher measures remains elusive despite Iran's decision to begin enriching uranium to levels much higher than needed for power reactor fuel.[65] Threats of "crippling sanctions" are proving quite empty.[66]

Nevertheless, the Iran case suggests that public-domain information produced by the IAEA inspectorate can contribute to compliance enforcement mobilization. The record developed by IAEA inspectors, even in the face of Iranian gamesmanship, has helped build diplomatic coalitions against Iran's nuclear program. Reaching multilateral noncompliance conclusions is difficult even in the best of times. The United States has been warning publicly about Iran's nuclear weapons ambitions since at least 1993.[67] Although these warnings have clearly turned out to be correct, they were based in large part on information from intelligence sources not available to other NPT Parties. Compiled by an international source widely considered to be objective, the IAEA's data is in the public domain and has proven hard to second-guess. As inadequate as the international compliance enforcement response has been to Iran, it is hard to imagine that even this reaction would been possible without IAEA-developed open-source information.

Participation Incentives

Treaty regimes can affect proliferator behavior according to how attractive participation in such regimes appears to be. States in a regime will make decisions based on their anticipation of the costs of noncompliance, the benefits of continuing to play by the rules, and the costs associated with withdrawal.

The second factor—the benefits from playing by the rules—illustrates why international nuclear cooperation can be important to the NPT regime. For parties not faced with the immediate danger that a neighbor will acquire nuclear weapons, the security benefits of the treaty are somewhat abstract. By contrast, shared benefits from peaceful uses can be tangible fruits of regime participation. Accordingly, international cooperation in nuclear technology is valuable not merely in its own right, but also for its role in encouraging countries to remain good-faith regime participants.[68]

With respect to the costs associated with withdrawal, the regime also can affect the behavior of would-be proliferators. To the extent that they perceive withdrawal from the treaty to be costly, they will be more inclined to remain subject to its strictures. Whether the NPT regime can create this perception will depend on what happens with North Korea, which in 2003 announced its withdrawal from the NPT.[69] Whether or not North Korea's actions are seen as successful will help shape how future would-be proliferators view their own choices. Already, there seems to be increasing concern that measures are needed to enhance the regime's ability to deter withdrawal by a violator before Iran follows North Korea's course.[70] Since 2005, the NPT review process has included discussion of such withdrawal issues, albeit with no tangible result.[71]

Yet, treaty violators moving out of the NPT regime are not the only danger. In some respects, Iran presents an even more corrosive possibility: continued unremedied violation within the regime. Iran appears to be trying to continue a nuclear weapons program while remaining a Party to the NPT, perhaps aiming to emulate Israel's presumed policy of nonannounced nuclear weapons possession—but from inside the NPT. This presents a troubling challenge: if a state can develop nuclear weapons while still a Party to the NPT, the most fundamental rules of the treaty will have become essentially meaningless.

NPT FUTURES . . . TEN YEARS HENCE

The next ten years will offer some watershed developments related to proliferation and the NPT. Even confining ourselves to "known unknowns,"[72] the list of factors and alternative possibilities that will shape the NPT environment over the next decade is breathtaking. Given this array of variables, how might the NPT regime affect proliferation decision-making?

Norm-Setting

The erosion of the NPT's norm-setting function for the international community is unlikely directly to affect any country's decision to seek nuclear weapons. None of the countries studied in this volume seem to be in any danger of developing nuclear weapons specifically as a result of some weakening of the normative force of nonproliferation rules.

Nonetheless, the erosion of political commitment to the NPT regime is likely to affect proliferation behavior in at least three ways. First, the progressive undermining of the treaty's central nonproliferation ethic may shape "nuclear myth" debates by depriving counter-mythmakers sources of political support. Through the ostensibly zero-sum prism of "three pillars" NPT interest-balancing, such erosion helps pro-proliferation mythmakers, allowing them to turn complaints about the pace of disarmament and nuclear benefit-sharing into arguments against enforcing nonproliferation rules.

Second, confusion surrounding the "peaceful use rights" issue of the NPT's Article IV—specifically, the degree to which States Party give credibility to the regime-erosive notion that efforts to prevent the spread of technology that increases proliferation risks are somehow a violation of the Non-proliferation Treaty[73]—may undermine support for responsible nuclear cooperation, undercut interest in fuel supply programs, and encourage the spread of sensitive fuel-cycle capabilities. The proliferation of fissile material production technology also could make the pursuit of nuclear weapons less costly and more quickly realizable, affecting internal debates between "pro" and "anti" proliferation myths. Technology proliferation will put more countries in the position of being able—by virtue of their possession of a nuclear "option"—to have debates between myth-spinning factions in the first place, and it will affect how easy it will be for weapons-seekers to win them by making weaponization easier, quicker, and less costly.

Third, norm-erosion would undermine compliance mobilization. The less compelling the nonproliferation norm, the harder it will be to persuade governments to bear meaningful burdens in support of it, and the less receptive they will be to calls for vigorous action against a violator. The resulting erosion of the regime's ability to rally against noncompliance would make proliferation harder to stop and more common. It would, for instance, affect debates between nuclear mythmakers and counter-mythmakers within would-be proliferator governments. Nuclear weapons proponents who can demonstrate that the international community does not care whether that country undertakes a nuclear weapons program—or who can show that the NPT regime cannot respond to stop such a program—will find it easier to win their internal arguments against opponents who urge restraint on account of the risks associated with proliferation.

This could create dangerous feedback loops. The more proliferation occurs, the more pressure there may be upon additional states—for example, those confronted by the emergence of a nuclear-armed rival or adversary—to board the weapons bandwagon. Furthermore, the more that the nonproliferation regime seems unable to prevent such proliferation, the harder it will be to persuade otherwise responsible governments to stick their necks out to resist the inevitable.

Supporters of the nonproliferation regime should seek to short-circuit such a cycle of erosion quickly. This is more easily said than done. Embracing the "three pillars" ideology of NPT interest-balancing, the Barak Obama administration has sought to turn the political tide against nonproliferation by adopting a more ostentatious and forward-leaning disarmament posture—in the hopes thereby of purchasing improved nonproliferation cooperation. The new, more restrictive nuclear declaratory policy articulated in its 2010 *Nuclear Posture Review*, for instance, was "intended . . . to persuade non-nuclear weapon states party to the Treaty to . . . adopt effective measures to strengthen the nonproliferation regime."[74]

Nevertheless, it is far from clear that this will have a positive result. There are reasons to be skeptical that the currency of disarmament "progress" can purchase meaningful nonproliferation cooperation in the first place.[75] Even if it can, today's open U.S. endorsement of the notion of "three pillars" balancing might worsen things by creating a market for nonproliferation cooperation, transforming what was once believed to be in the security interest of all States Party into a saleable commodity whose price would skyrocket as proliferation progresses. A time of multiple proliferation crises, moreover, would be a seller's market. Potential cooperators against proliferation would have an incentive to hold out for the highest possible disarmament "price": the longer enforcement is delayed, the more dramatic and costly are the measures that would be needed to stop it, and thus the higher their price would need to be. An explicit U.S. willingness to start "buying" nonproliferation cooperation with disarmament or other concessions could end up undermining nonproliferation by encouraging rent-seeking foot-dragging by those from whom assistance is needed. Since demands for disarmament "progress" sometimes seem to shift as quickly as they are met,[76] the price to be exacted could be dramatic indeed, if in fact it is ultimately "payable" at all.

So far, there are few signs that the new U.S. approach is affecting other countries' willingness to support vigorous nonproliferation, or their purported belief that sufficient disarmament progress is being made. In the first week of the 2010 NPT Review Conference, the Non-Aligned Movement issued a statement expressing disappointment with the new Russo-American strategic arms treaty ("New START")—which it described as being "below the international community's expectations"[77]—and insisting upon the implementation of a notably unrealistic disarmament plan of action that includes calls for adherence to defunct or nonexistent treaties.[78] Implementing this agenda, the Non-Aligned Movement made clear, was "crucial to the credibility of the Treaty."[79]

Detection: Challenges of Verification and Compliance Assessment

The NPT regime's lack of an institutional framework for verifying treaty compliance need not leave the regime entirely defenseless. Individual parties can apply their own energy and resources to detection and assessment, collecting information through what has traditionally been called "national technical means" and applying independent judgment to available data.

The IAEA verification system certainly deserves strong support. In this regard, the next ten years will be crucial. The additional protocol has been described as already being the de facto safeguards standard,[80] but it is still some ways from universal application. Repeated calls have been made in NPT fora for Additional Protocol universalization, but this remains controversial—in part because norm-erosion has helped lead some countries to see the Protocol as an unfair imposition. Additional Protocol universality, however, remains an important objective if the safeguards regime is to have success in deterring undeclared nuclear activity. The safeguards system also might be strengthened if IAEA inspectors were given the ability to act upon authorities beyond traditional safeguards and the Additional Protocol in situations of special compliance difficulty.

Safeguards will face significant challenges during the next decade because of the nuclear energy "renaissance" needed to meet electric power requirements. The Additional Protocol's focus on searching for undeclared activity is a welcome addition to IAEA authorities but, while it is supposed to be revenue-neutral over the long term, implementing the Additional Protocol probably will increase IAEA costs. If worldwide nuclear power generation increases to help cope with rising energy needs, the cost of traditional IAEA safeguards will grow as the Agency is asked to keep track of more and more nuclear activities in more and more countries.

The persuasiveness of "nuclear myths" advocating the overt pursuit of nuclear weapons also will be affected by safeguards-related developments. Internal debates between nuclear mythmakers and counter-mythmakers may be affected by the international community's understanding of safeguards' effectiveness in providing timely warning of diversion of nuclear material from peaceful uses to nuclear weapons, and by the extent to which the nonproliferation regime succeeds in preventing the spread of enrichment and reprocessing. If safeguards cannot provide significant warning of diversion sufficient to permit an effective international response, or if fuel-cycle technology becomes more widespread, proweapons mythmakers may have an easier time winning internal debates. After all, an inexpensive fait accompli using existing or easily acquired technology is easier to "sell" to one's colleagues than a costly and risky technological gamble.

Apart from grappling with such issues of basic detection, the NPT regime can improve its ability to handle compliance assessment. There needs to be more honesty and seriousness in international discussions of verification and compliance issues, particularly when it comes to compliance assessment. Such assessment frequently requires drawing inferences from incomplete or ambiguous information. Approaches that await "smoking-gun" levels of "proof" before undertaking even the most basic compliance enforcement measures will likely lead to action only when it is too late. Friends of the NPT therefore must understand that waiting for absolute certainty is a luxury good that international peace and security cannot afford. Particularly when what is at issue is pressuring an apparent violator to abandon a course of technological development or to permit extensive transparency into a questionable program, "false positives" are less dangerous than "false negatives."[81]

Compliance Mobilization

Perhaps the most important lesson from compliance mobilization is that "precedent" matters. Future would-be proliferators will learn lessons from today's events about the costs and benefits of proliferation. Other regime participants also will learn lessons about whether it is worthwhile for them to stick their necks out in support of compliance enforcement.

Compliance mobilization is thus a game of virtuous—or vicious—circles: nothing succeeds like success, and nothing fails quite like failure. This logic suggests that every proliferation challenge must be met resolutely, lest each successive instance prove both harder to deter and harder to handle from a compliance mobilization perspective.[82] The international community must ensure that any attempt at proliferation will be extremely costly, for the anticipation of such costs will help affect which nuclear myth survives and replicates in internal policy debates.

Measures that make other States Party better able to resist nuclear threats, cope with nuclear attacks, and be less militarily "deterred" by a proliferator's possession of nuclear weapons may also reduce the anticipated strategic benefits of actually acquiring nuclear weapons, thereby affecting "nuclear myth-making" debates.

Each compliance mobilization failure can have a doubly bad, "vicious circle" impact. It is not merely that such a failure might lead other would-be proliferators to conclude that the regime is toothless. Failures also might lead otherwise good-faith participants to conclude that the regime can no longer meet their security needs—perhaps turning the more capable among these good citizens into reluctant proliferators themselves. The NPT's ability to guarantee that others do not obtain nuclear weapons helps ensure that each non-nuclear-weapon state feels less desire to seek them. But each failure to contain proliferation increases the incentive for defections from the regime.

Lewis Dunn identifies one way out of some of these dynamics, suggesting that policymakers need to be prepared to take advantage of proliferation setbacks to improve the regime. To some extent, this dynamic is already at work with North Korea; the shocks of its nuclear weapons test have sparked interest— though apparently not yet sufficient interest to drive real changes in policy—in taking concrete steps to increase the costs associated with NPT withdrawal by a country in violation of the treaty's provisions. Similarly, the shock produced by the world's discovery of how close Saddam Hussein had come to developing a nuclear weapon before the Gulf War of 1991, notwithstanding IAEA inspections, led directly to the development of the Additional Protocol. Dunn's approach would elevate this ad hoc response to unpleasant circumstances into a principle of strategy: leveraging "proliferation shocks" into improvements in the regime.

From all of these perspectives, the next ten years will be critical. It is certain that the way the international community deals with Iran and North Korea in the coming years will be an important determinant of how would-be future proliferators view their own prospects.

So what can we do today to strengthen both the regime's ability to enlist participants in compliance enforcement and the anticipated costs facing potential proliferators? The most obvious answer is to resolve the Iran and North Korea situations so as to ensure that proliferation remains unattractive to others, although this is admittedly more easily said than done. Regime participants also should be more willing to employ existing tools to help shape proliferator behavior, such as the provisions of the IAEA Statute pertaining to safeguards compliance, or, as appropriate, the Chapter VII authority of the Security Council. The instinct to seek more and better ways to shape proliferator cost-benefit calculations is the right one.

Participation Incentives

One key variable over the next decade will be the degree to which non-nuclear-weapon states can be made to understand that the participation benefits that many of them have come to expect from the NPT regime are dependent upon the regime's ability to ensure the continued efficacy of safeguards and to prevent further proliferation.[83] The degree to which non-nuclear-weapons states' decision-makers internalize this truth is important. A real understanding of the link between international cooperation and ensuring nonproliferation compliance, and thus an appreciation for developing countries' powerful stake in the latter, can help not only in influencing nuclear myth-making debates within potential proliferator governments, but also in helping improve compliance mobilization against any country in which proweapon mythmakers "win."

To the extent that countries prize the disarmament of nuclear weapons states as a goal of the NPT, it must be made clearer than ever that the surest way to ensure that weapons possessors are never willing to give up their last nuclear weapons is to demonstrate that the NPT regime is unable to prevent new arrivals in the atomic weapons business. Nonproliferation compliance enforcement, in other words, is the inescapable predicate for and sine qua non of nuclear disarmament. To the extent that weapons states' disarmament is desired by political elites within a would-be proliferator country, this simple truth may also help tilt the tables against nuclear mythmakers.

CONCLUSION

The NPT regime can affect decision-making within would-be proliferator governments, and it is possible to improve the regime's influence. Friends of the NPT should help ensure that by the time the next state considering the development of nuclear weapons surveys its environment, it will see a world in which the mores, institutions, and precedents of the treaty regime all make such a weapons route seem unwise—even if, and perhaps *especially* if, Iranian nuclear weaponization is not stopped and North Korea's is not reversed. The path of NPT good citizenship should appear to be irresistibly attractive, and the path of violation—even if rewarded with nuclear weaponry—enormously painful and costly in myriad ways. It is the job of responsible citizens of the NPT regime to make life as difficult as possible for future nuclear weapons mythmakers.

NOTES

1. Treaty on the Non-Proliferation of Nuclear Weapons [hereinafter NPT], available at http://www.state.gov/t/isn/trty/16281.htm.

2. Leo Strauss, *The Rebirth of Classical Political Rationalism* (Chicago: University of Chicago Press, 1989), 6.

3. NPT, Preamble.

4. U.N. General Assembly Resolution 1665 (XVI): Prevention of the Wider Dissemination of Nuclear Weapons (December 4, 1961), from the first preambular paragraph.

5. Ibid., para. 1.

6. NPT, at Article I (prohibiting transfer of nuclear weapons or assistance in their manufacture or acquisition); see also Art. II (prohibiting receipt and their manufacture or acquisition).

7. U.S. Arms Control and Disarmament Agency, *International Negotiations on the Treaty on the Nonproliferation of Nuclear Weapons* (Washington, DC, 1969) [hereinafter *ACDA Negotiating History*], at 81 (quoting General Burns, in ENDC/PV.338, at 5–6); see also Conference of the Eighteen-Nation Committee on Disarmament, *process verbal,* ENDC/PV.378 (March 13, 1968), at 11.

8. *ACDA Negotiating History*, at 29 (citing comments by Secretary of State Rusk); see also 21 (quoting ACDA Director William Foster).

9. Ibid., at 96, 116.

10. Ibid., at 58 (quoting Ambassador Trivedi).

11. Ibid., at 123.

12. See ibid., at xiii, 53 (quoting joint memorandum by Non-Aligned Eight).

13. See ibid., at 98–99.

14. U.N. General Assembly Resolution 1664 (XVI): Prevention of Further Spread of Nuclear Weapons (December 4, 1961), at preambular ¶¶ 1–2; Resolution 2028 (XX): Nonproliferation of Nuclear Weapons (November 19, 1965), at preambular ¶ 6; Resolution 2149 (XXI): Renunciation by States of Actions Hampering the Conclusion of an Agreement on the Nonproliferation of Nuclear Weapons (November 4, 1966), at preambular ¶ 2; Resolution 2153 (XXI): Nonproliferation of Nuclear Weapons (November 17, 1966), at Part B, at preambular ¶ 1.

15. *ACDA Negotiating History*, at 24 (quoting ACDA Director Foster); see also 45 (same), and 106 (quoting U.S. Ambassador De Palma); see also 115 (quoting U.S. Ambassador Goldberg), and 58 (quoting Goldberg).

16. Conference of the Eighteen-Nation Committee on Disarmament, ENDC/PV.378 (March 13, 1968), at 11 (remarks of General Burns).

17. Christopher A. Ford, "Nuclear Disarmament and the 'Legalization' of Policy Discourse in the NPT Regime," remarks to the James Martin Center for Nonproliferation Studies, Washington, DC (November 29, 2007), available at http://cns.miis.edu/cns/activity/071129_nprbriefing/media/071129_nprbriefing_ford_comments.pdf; Ford, "Debating Disarmament: Interpreting Article VI of the Treaty on the Non-Proliferation of Nuclear Weapons," *Nonproliferation Review*, 14, no. 3 (November 2007), available at http://cns.miis.edu/pubs/npr/vol14/143/143ford.pdf.

18. NPT, from the Preamble.

19. NPT, at Art. VI.

20. *ACDA Negotiating History*, at x, 15 (discussing efforts by India, Sweden, and Nigeria).

21. Ibid., at x, 15–16, 23, 24.

22. Ibid., at x.

23. Ibid., at 20 (recounting efforts by India, Sweden, and UAR); see also 44 (discussing efforts by Sweden, Brazil, Ethiopia, Mexico, and UAR), and 44–45, 106–8 (discussing efforts of UAR, Burma, Spain, Romania, Brazil, and India).

24. Ibid., at 86; see also 75 (quoting Canadian representative).

25. Ibid., at 87.

26. Ibid., at 88, 96, 106.

27. *ACDA Negotiating History*, at 76 (discussing comments by U.K., Canada, and Sweden), 118 (comment by Japan).

28. Advisory Opinion of the International Court of Justice on the "Legality of the Threat or Use of Nuclear Weapons" (July 8, 1996) [hereinafter *ICJ Weapons Case*], available at http://www.icj-cij.org/icjwww/icases/iunan/iunanframe.htm.

29. Ernie Regehr, "Washington Parses a Foundational Disarmament Text" (May 3, 2007), available at http://www.igloo.org/disarmingconflict/ttt.

30. John Burroughs, "Legal Requirements to Achieve Non-Proliferation and Disarmament," remarks to the Article VI Forum, Park Hotel, The Hague (March 2, 2006), available at http://gsinstitute.org/mpi/docs/BurroughsSpeechA6F.pdf, at text accompanying n. 10.

31. Ford, "Debating Disarmament," at 401, 402–11.

32. Statute of the International Court of Justice [hereinafter *ICJ Statute*], at Art. 38(1).

33. "Contrary to judgments, and except in rare cases where it is stipulated beforehand that they shall have binding effect . . . the Court's advisory opinions have no binding effect." See http://www.icj-cij.org/jurisdiction/index.php?p1=5&p2=2.

34. Request for Advisory Opinion (December 15, 1994), at 2, 6, available at http://www.icj-cij.org/icjwww/icases/iunan/iunan_iorders/iunan_iapplication_19941215_requestopinion.pdf; *ICJ Weapons Case*, at text following ¶ 105; *ICJ Statute*, at Art. 65.

35. Vienna Convention on the Law of Treaties (May 23, 1969), *United Nations Treaty Series*, 1155, at 331, at Art. 31(3)(a) (providing rules for interpreting treaties).

36. 2000 NPT Review Conference, "Article VI and preambular paragraphs 8 through 12," *Final Document* (May 20, 2000), available at http://www.fas.org/nuke/control/npt/docs/finaldoc.htm, at ¶¶ 1–15; 1995 NPT Review Conference, "Principles and Objectives for Nuclear Non-Proliferation and Disarmament," NPT/CONF.1995/32 (Part I), Annex, at Decision 2, available at http://disarmament2.un.org/wmd/npt/1995dec2.htm.

37. NPT, at Art. III(1).

38. The United States is apparently the only Party to have articulated Article II com-

pliance standards. No one has ever publicly set forth a standard for assessing Article I compliance.

39. U.S. Department of State, Bureau of Verification and Compliance, *Adherence to and Compliance with Arms Control, Nonproliferation, and Disarmament Agreements and Commitments* (August 30, 2005) [hereinafter *2005 Noncompliance Report*], available at http://www.state.gov/t/vci/rls/rpt/51977.htm, at 64–65.

40. See, for example, IAEA, *IAEA Safeguards: Stemming the Spread of Nuclear Weapons* (undated fact sheet), available at http://www.iaea.org/Publications/Factsheets/English/S1_Safeguards.pdf , at 1, 4 (quoting IAEA Director General describing inspectors as needing the ability to provide "verification of the exclusively peaceful intent of a State's nuclear programmes"); IAEA, *IAEA Safeguards: Staying Ahead of the Game* (August 2007), at 6 (describing the purpose of IAEA verification in language tracking that of Article II).

41. A "significant quantity" is defined as "the approximate amount of nuclear material for which the possibility of manufacturing a nuclear explosive device cannot be excluded." *IAEA Safeguards Glossary, 2001 Edition*, IAEA/NV/S/3 (June 2002), available at http://www-pub.iaea.org/MTCD/publications/PDF/nvs-3-cd/PDF/NVS3_prn.pdf, at § 3.14. The IAEA gives these figures as being 8 kilograms of plutonium and 25 kilograms of uranium (U^{235}). Ibid., Table II.

42. See, for example, U.S. State Department, "Safeguards and Nuclear Security" (April 18, 2007), available at http://www.state.gov/t/isn/rls/other/83397.htm.

43. The IAEA's Standing Advisory Group on Safeguards Implementation (SAGSI) has played an important role in articulating a new concept of "information-driven safeguards" whereby inspectors could consider "state-specific factors" in determining where to focus activity. See John Carlson, "SAGSI: Its Role and Contribution to Safeguards Development," paper presented by Jim Casterton (on Carlson's behalf) to the 48th Annual Meeting of the Institute for Nuclear Materials Management, Tucson, Arizona (July 9, 2007), at 1.

44. The IAEA has been trying to improve its ability to analyze open source information and commercial satellite imagery to generate leads. IAEA, *Verification and Security*, Annual Report 2002, available at http://www.iaea.org/Publications/Reports/Anrep2002/safeguards.pdf, at 70.

45. IAEA, Implementation of the NPT Safeguards Agreement in the Islamic Republic of Iran, Report of the Director General, GOV/2005/67 (September 2, 2005), at ¶ 50.

46. IAEA, *Implementation of the NPT Safeguards Agreement in the Syrian Arab Republic*, GOV/2010/11 (February 18, 2010), available at http://isis-online.org/uploads/isis-reports/documents/IAEA_Report_Syria_18Feb2010.pdf.

47. Fred C. Iklé, "After Detection, What?" *Foreign Affairs* (January 1961), 208.

48. IAEA, *The Structure and Content of Agreements between the Agency and States Required in Connection with the Treaty on the Non-Proliferation of Nuclear Weapons*, IN-

FCIRC/153 (Corrected) (June 1972), available at http://www.iaea.org/Publications/Documents/Infcircs/Others/infcirc153.pdf, at 9, ¶ 28.

49. Richard Hooper, "The Changing Nature of Safeguards," *IAEA Bulletin*, no. 45/1 (June 2003), at 11, available at http://www.iaea.org/Publications/Magazines/Bulletin/Bull451/article2.pdf.

50. IAEA Director General Mohammed ElBaradei, "Addressing Verification Challenges," remarks to the Symposium on International Safeguards (October 16, 2006), available at http://www.iaea.org/NewsCenter/Statements/2006/ebsp2006n018.html. Most of the so-called separative work units (SWUs) required to enrich uranium to weapons-usable levels are expended in enriching it to low-enriched uranium (LEU) form. The amount of work required to turn LEU into weapons-usable, highly enriched uranium (HEU) is much less. Compare *IAEA Safeguards Glossary, 2001 Edition*, at § 3.13, and Table 1 (defining "conversion time" and giving estimates for various types of nuclear material).

51. Nonproliferation Policy Education Center [NPEC], "Falling Behind: International Scrutiny of the Peaceful Atom" (n.d.).

52. According to John Carlson, "[t]imely warning from safeguards inspections alone [is] not really possible" see John Carlson, "Addressing Proliferation Challenges," PowerPoint presentation delivered to the 48th Annual Meeting of the Institute for Nuclear Materials Management, Tuscon, Arizona (July 8-12, 2007).

53. Mehdi Mohammadi, "Nuclear Case from Beginning to End in Interview with Dr. Hasan Rowhani," *Tehran Keyhan* (July 23, 2005) [translation from Farsi by FBIS, #IAP20050726008002], at 12ff (quoting Rowhani).

54. Christopher A. Ford, "Why Not Nuclear Disarmament?" *New Atlantis* (Spring 2010), 3, 14–15.

55. IAEA Board of Governors, *Implementation of the NPT Safeguards Agreement in the Islamic Republic of Iran*, GOV/2003/81 (November 26, 2003), available at http://www.iaea.org/Publications/Documents/Board/2003/gov2003-81.pdf, at operative para. 2 ("[s]trongly deplor[ing]" Iran's failures and breaches). The Board actually used the word "noncompliance" in September 2005. IAEA Board of Governors, *Implementation of the NPT Safeguards Agreement in the Islamic Republic of Iran*, GOV/2005/77 (September 24, 2005), available at http://www.iaea.org/Publications/Documents/Board/2005/gov2005-77.pdf.

56. Statute of the IAEA, available at http://www.iaea.org/About/statute_text.html#A1.12, at Art. 12.C ("The inspectors *shall* report any non-compliance to the Director General who *shall* thereupon transmit the report to the Board of Governors. . . . The Board *shall* report the non-compliance to all members and to the Security Council and General Assembly of the United Nations") (emphasis added).

57. IAEA Board of Governors, *Implementation of the NPT Safeguards Agreement in the Islamic Republic of Iran*, GOV/2006/14 (February 4, 2006), available at http://www.

iaea.org/Publications/Documents/Board/2006/gov2006-14.pdf. In fact, the reporting did not occur until March.

58. U.N. Security Council Resolution 1737, S/RES/1737 (December 27, 2006), available at http://daccessdds.un.org/doc/UNDOC/GEN/N06/681/42/PDF/N0668142. pdf?OpenElement; see also Resolution 1747, S/RES/1747 (March 24, 2007), available at http:// daccessdds.un.org/doc/UNDOC/GEN/N07/281/40/PDF/N0728140.pdf?OpenElement.

59. "Iran Declares Key Nuclear Advance," *BBC News* (April 11, 2006), available at http://news.bbc.co.uk/2/hi/middle_east/4900260.stm; U.N. Security Council Resolution 1696, S/RES/1696 (July 31, 2006), available at http://daccessdds.un.org/doc/UNDOC/ GEN/N06/450/22/PDF/N0645022.pdf?OpenElement.

60. U.S. Special Representative for Nuclear Nonproliferation Christopher Ford, "Strengthening the Nonproliferation Regime," remarks at Wilton Park (December 21, 2006), available at http://www.state.gov/t/isn/rls/rm/78454.htm.

61. Statute of the IAEA, at XII.C; see also Art. XIX.B.

62. See, for example, IAEA, "TC Programme Recipient Countries or Territories," at http://www-tc.iaea.org/tcweb/tcprogramme/recipients/default.asp.

63. In early 2007, the IAEA Board partially or complete froze nearly half of its 55 Technical Cooperation projects with Iran. See, for example, Radio Free Europe, "IAEA Cuts Technical Aid to Iran" (March 8, 2007), available at http://www.rferl.org/ featuresarticle/2007/03/66aaced3-c509-4233-ac46-ee1e61911f8b.html; IAEA, "Cooperation between the Islamic Republic of Iran and the Agency in the Light of United Nations Security Council Resolution 1737 (2006)," GOV/2007/7 (February 9, 2007), available at http://www.isis-online.org/publications/iran/TechnicalCooperationFeb2007.pdf.

64. In late 2003, as momentum was building for referring Iran to the Security Council as required by Article XII.C of the IAEA Statute, France, Germany, and the United Kingdom (the so-called EU-3) reached a deal with Iran whereby Tehran would suspend its enrichment program temporarily, in return for which the Europeans would apparently derail U.S. efforts to take the issue to the Security Council. See "Statement by the Iranian Government and Visiting EU Foreign Ministers" (October 21, 2003), available at http://www.iaea.org/NewsCenter/Focus/IaeaIran/statement_iran21102003.shtml; GOV/2003/75, at ¶ 19 & n.2; GOV/2004/1, at ¶ 58; Supreme National Security Council Secretary Hassan Rohani [Hasan Rowhani], "Beyond the Challenges Facing Iran and the IAEA concerning the Nuclear Dossier," *Tehran Rahbord* (September 30, 2005), at 7–38 (translation from Farsi by FBIS, #IAP20060113336001) (recounting EU-3's quid pro quo). This agreement, and a written successor arrangement in 2004 (the "Paris Agreement"), were not honored by Iran, but the Security Council push was successfully delayed for several years. See GOV/2004/34, at ¶ 40; GOV/2004/60, at ¶¶ 7, 19, 51–53; IAEA Information Circular, "Communication dated 26 November 2004 received from the Permanent Representatives of France, Germany, the Islamic Republic of Iran, and the United Kingdom concerning the agreement signed in Paris on 15 November 2004,"

INFCIRC/637 (November 26, 2004); Hasan Rowhani, quoted by Mohammadi (bragging about success of Iranian tactics with EU-3).

65. "Iran Seen Improving Higher Atom Enrichment," *Reuters* (May 14, 2010), available at http://uk.reuters.com/article/idUKTRE64D19P20100514.

66. Tim Reid, "Hillary Clinton: US Will Organize 'Crippling' Iran Sanctions if Diplomacy Fails," *Times Online* (April 22, 2009), available at http://www.timesonline.co.uk/tol/news/world/us_and_americas/article6149692.ece.

67. U.S. Arms Control and Disarmament Agency, *Adherence to and Compliance with Arms Control Agreements and the President's Report to Congress on Soviet Noncompliance with Arms Control Agreements* (January 14, 1993), at 17.

68. U.S. State Department, *Challenges of Nonproliferation Noncompliance* (April 18, 2007), *available at* http://www.state.gov/t/isn/rls/other/83398.htm.

69. *2005 Noncompliance Report*, at 89.

70. U.S. State Department, *Article X of the Nuclear Nonproliferation Treaty: Deterring and Responding to Withdrawal by Treaty Violators* (February 2, 2007), available at http://www.state.gov/t/isn/rls/other/80518.htm; U.S. Special Representative for Nuclear Nonproliferation Christopher Ford, "Implementing Provisions of the NPT Relating to the Nonproliferation of Nuclear Weapons," remarks to the 2007 NPT Preparatory Committee (May 9, 2007), available at http://www.state.gov/t/isn/rls/rm/85167.htm.

71. *Article X of the Nuclear Nonproliferation Treaty: Deterring and Responding to Withdrawal by Treaty Violators*; U.S. Special Representative for Nuclear Nonproliferation Christopher Ford, "Other Provisions of the Nuclear Nonproliferation Treaty, Including Article X," remarks at the 2007 NPT Preparatory Committee meeting (May 11, 2007), available at http://www.state.gov/t/isn/rls/rm/85182.htm; Government of Luxembourg, *Withdrawal from the Treaty on the Non-Proliferation of Nuclear Weapons*, NPT/CONF2005/WP.32, working paper submitted on behalf of the European Union (May 10, 2005), available at http://www.reachingcriticalwill.org/legal/npt/RevCon05/wp/wp32.pdf; *Working Paper on Article X (NPT Withdrawal) Submitted by Australia and New Zealand*, NPT/CONF.2005/WP.16 (April 28, 2005), available at http://www.reachingcriticalwill.org/legal/npt/RevCon05/wp/WP16.pdf?OpenElement; Senior Advisor to the U.S. Bureau of Verification and Compliance Sally Horn, "NPT Article X," remarks to Main Committee III of the 2005 NPT Review Conference (May 23, 2005), available at http://www.state.gov/t/vci/rls/rm/46644.htm.

72. Compare, for example, CBS News, *Public Eye*, blog posting (November 9, 2006) (quoting former U.S. Defense Secretary Donald Rumsfeld), available at http://www.cbsnews.com/blogs/2006/2006/11/09/publiceye/entry2165872.shtml.

73. Cuba, "Peaceful Uses of Nuclear Energy," working document submitted at the 2005 NPT Review Conference, NPT/CONF.2005/WP.25 (May 4, 2005) http://nuclearfiles.org/menu/key-issues/nuclear-weapons/issues/proliferation/fuel-cycle/un_N0533353.pdf, at ¶ 7 (claiming that technology transfer restrictions "put in place by some States Parties [*sic*] to the Treaty . . . are a violation of the Treaty"); see also People's Republic

of China, "Peaceful Uses of Nuclear Energy," working paper submitted to the 2005 NPT Review Conference, NPT/CONF.2005/WP.6 (April 26, 2005) http://www.reachingcriticalwill.org/legal/npt/RevCon05/wp/6.pdf, at ¶ 1 ("Non-proliferation efforts should not undermine the legitimate rights of countries, especially the developing countries, to the peaceful uses of nuclear energy").

74. U.S.DepartmentofDefense,*NuclearPostureReviewReport*(April2010),at15,available at http://www.defense.gov/npr/docs/2010%20Nuclear%20Posture%20Review%20Report. pdf. .

75. Christopher A. Ford, *Nuclear Disarmament, Nonproliferation, and the "Credibility Thesis"* (Hudson Institute, September 2009), available at http://02e18f7.netsolhost. com/New_Paradigms_Forum/Documents_and_Links_files/Ford%20Hudson%20Pape r%20on%20Credibility.pdf.

76. Christopher A. Ford, "The NPT Review Cycle So Far: A View from the United States of America," remarks presented at Wilton Park, United Kingdom (December 20, 2007), available at http://merln.ndu.edu/archivepdf/wmd/State/98382.pdf.

77. Foreign Minister R. M. Marty M. Natalegawa (of Indonesia), remarks presented on behalf of the Non-Aligned States Party to the 2010 Review Conference of the Treaty on the Non-Proliferation of Nuclear Weapons (May 3, 2010), at 2, available at http:// www.reachingcriticalwill.org/legal/npt/revcon2010/statements/3May_NAM.pdf.

78. Ibid. (calling for "full implementation of the 13 practical steps"); compare *Final Document of the 2000 Review Conference of the Parties to the Treaty on the Non-Proliferation of Nuclear Weapons*, NPT/Conf.2000/28 (Parts I and II), at 14–15 (setting forth 13 "practical steps for the systematic and progressive efforts to implement Article VI," including "early entry into force and full implementation of START II and the conclusion of START III as soon as possible while continuing and strengthening the Treaty on the Limitation of Anti-Ballistic Missile Systems"), available at http://www.un.org/disarmament/WMD/Nuclear/2000-NPT/pdf/FD-Part1and2.pdf.

79. Natalegawa remarks to the 2010 Review Conference of the Treaty on the Non-Proliferation of Nuclear Weapons, at 2.

80. As of mid-2007, at least 45 of the 64 NNWS under the Treaty that have significant nuclear activities had APs in force, and a further 12 have signed protocols or had them approved by the IAEA Board of Governors. John Carlson, "Five Decades of Safeguards, and Directors for the Future: An Australian Perspective," paper presented by Russell Leslie (on Carlson's behalf) to the 48th Annual Meeting of the Institute for Nuclear Materials Management, Tucson, Arizona (July 9, 2007), from PowerPoint slide 8. One country with significant nuclear activities that has *not* agreed to the AP, of course, is Iran. Brazil is also a laggard—though, it is to be hoped, for different reasons.

81. Cf. Robert Zarate, "The NPT, IAEA Safeguards and Peaceful Nuclear Energy: An 'Inalienable Right,' But Precisely to What?" (September 2007), available at http://128.177.28.81/files/20070301-Zarate-NPT-IAEA-PeacefulNuclear.pdf, at 35–39.

82. Christopher Ford, "Compliance Assessment and Compliance Enforcement: The

Challenge of Nuclear Noncompliance," *ILSA Journal of International and Comparative Law*, 12, no. 2 (Spring 2006), at 583.

83. Christopher Ford, "Nuclear Proliferation: Some Context and Consequences" remarks to NATO Seminar on Proliferation Issues, Vilnius, Lithuania (April 18, 2007), *available at* http://www.nti.org/e_research/source_docs/us/department_state/briefings_speeches_testimony/35.pdf; Christopher A. Ford, "A Work Plan for the 2010 Review Cycle: Coping with Challenges Facing the Nuclear Nonproliferation Treaty" opening remarks to the 2007 Prepatory Committee Meeting of the Treaty on the Non-Proliferation of Nuclear Weapons," Vienna, Austria (April 30, 2007) *available at* http://www.nti.org/e_research/source_docs/us/department_state/briefings_speeches_testimony/34.pdf.

11 Leveraging Proliferation Shocks

Lewis A. Dunn

Today's nonproliferation regime took shape over many decades. From the creation of the International Atomic Energy Agency in 1957 to the passage of U.N. Security Council Resolution 1540 in 2004, the regime has broadened and deepened. Partly as a result of the successful incorporation of the tenets of this regime into international law and diplomacy, both the scope and pace of proliferation have proven to be far less than once was feared.

The nonproliferation regime has been the result of many developments—the thinking of official practitioners and outside experts about how to meet tough nonproliferation challenges, policymaking decisions often at the seniormost levels of many governments, and the slow building of a global norm against proliferation. Past proliferation shocks also have had a fundamental impact. By way of example, Table 11.1 lists a series of past proliferation shocks that shaped today's nonproliferation institutions, practices, and norms. Many of the most important elements of today's global nonproliferation regime can be linked to such shocks. Proliferation shocks directly galvanized action—whether triggering new thinking, generating internal bureaucratic support within a particular government, or stimulating the political will for action needed globally. The nature of the response to these past shocks by the United States and other countries was one of the drivers of the eventual scope and pace of proliferation. More often than not, the response to these shocks has served as a "proliferation decelerator."

Many factors will shape future proliferation dynamics and the characteristics, elements, vitality, and effectiveness of the future global nonproliferation regime. Such key factors range from the outcome of today's continuing nonproliferation crises involving the Democratic People's Republic of North Korea

TABLE 11.1

Regime Impacts of Proliferation Shocks—Some Examples

Nonproliferation advance	Linked proliferation shock
Nuclear Non-Proliferation Treaty (NPT)	China's 1964 nuclear test
Zangger Committee agreement on nuclear supply regulations	India's 1974 nuclear test
Nuclear Suppliers Group	India's 1974 nuclear test
Australia Group CB controls	Iraq use of chemical weapons in Iran-Iraq
Extension of the Missile Technology Control Regime (MTCR)	War
	Use of missiles in the Iran-Iraq War
Chemical Weapons Convention	UNSCOM inspections post Gulf War
Enhanced IAEA safeguards	Iraq's undetected mini-Manhattan Project
UNSC Res. 1540	Uncovering A. Q. Khan nuclear supply network

(DPRK) and Iran to the continuing vitality of American security guarantees and alliances. "Internal" political, social, and other developments in many different countries also will be critical. The extent to which countries' leaders seek their futures in economic transformation and openness to the global economy can affect interest in acquiring weapons of mass destruction, which is a point highlighted by Etel Solingen in this volume. Other possible internal factors range from a rising demand for energy (with its implications for the use of nuclear power and the spread of sensitive enrichment and reprocessing technologies) to a perception among non-nuclear-weapons State Parties to the Nuclear Non-proliferation Treaty (NPT) of a global nonproliferation double standard between nuclear haves and nuclear have-nots that could reinforce other motivations to seek nuclear weapons.

As in the past, future proliferation shocks—and even more important, how the world's nations respond to those shocks—will decisively impact future proliferation trends and shape the vitality of the global nonproliferation regime. Such shocks could result in the erosion or rapid unraveling of today's global nonproliferation regime; conversely, future proliferation shocks will provide the United States and other countries with an opportunity to strengthen global nonproliferation institutions, practices, and norms.

This chapter explores that latter proposition—that the all but inevitable future proliferation shocks are not simply a danger, but more importantly provide a critical opportunity to shape the proliferation future. To do so, it first describes a variety of potential proliferation shocks. The chapter then explores how to leverage some of these possible future proliferation shocks to strengthen global nonproliferation institutions, practices, and norms.

FUTURE PROLIFERATION SHOCKS

Many future proliferation shocks are conceivable. Table 11.2 offers one such list. Both state and nonstate shocks are included. Shocks entailing not only nuclear weapons but also chemical, biological weapons, or radiological dispersal devices are listed. These shocks also fall into a number of possible "baskets" relating to several aspects of the overall proliferation process and threat today: inspections and verification; withdrawal from a treaty or violation of treaty obligations; nuclear or missile testing or deployments; theft or other breakdowns of nuclear control; transfers of nuclear materials or weapons from a state to another state, or from a state to a terrorist group (authorized or unauthorized); accidents with chemical, biological, radiological, and nuclear materials and devices; aborted or successful terrorist attacks; and state nuclear weapon use. Some of these shocks are more likely than others, and several contributors to this volume address these shocks from different national perspectives. Some readers may question how "shocking" a given development would be or even

TABLE 11.2

Some Illustrative Potential Future Proliferation Shocks

Iran "throws out" IAEA inspectors
Iran detected producing 90% HEU
Iran tests a longer-range ballistic missile
Iran withdraws from NPT
Iran tests a nuclear weapon
Saudi Arabia announces plans for "dual-key" deployment of Chinese nuclear warheads
Saudi Arabia and Egypt announce intention to withdraw from NPT unless Iran stops
    pursuit of nuclear weapons
Saudi Arabia, Egypt, Gulf States launch biological weapons programs in response to Iran
Unexplained anthrax or other highly lethal bio agent incident in an Arab neighbor of Iran
Israel openly deploys nuclear weapons
Israel openly tests a nuclear weapon
Multiple cross-regional NPT withdrawals—including by countries that had renounced
    nuclear weapons such as Brazil, Argentina, South Africa
IAEA detects significant discrepancy in Japan's nuclear materials accounting—ambiguous
Taiwan declares independence on eve of 2008 Olympics, China responds militarily, U.S.-
    China nuclear confrontation ensues
Failed terrorist attack on a nuclear weapons storage site
Failed terrorist theft of nuclear materials
Aborted transfer of CBRN weapon or materials from a state to a nonstate entity—
    intentional, unauthorized
Successful terrorist seizure of a nuclear weapon or nuclear weapon materials
Successful interdiction of a nuclear weapon being smuggled into the United States
Successful or unsuccessful terrorist nuclear, biological, chemical, or RDD attack
Nuclear, biological, or chemical weapon accident—state or nonstate
Terrorist CBRN attack—successful or unsuccessful

---

whether it is plausible. Yet, none of these shocks should be dismissed out of hand, particularly in light of past proliferation. Taken together, this list highlights the extent to which the occurrence of future proliferation shocks is likely to be a dominant feature of the emerging proliferation landscape.

LEVERAGING PROLIFERATION SHOCKS

How the United States and other countries respond to proliferation shocks will reflect many considerations. Responses will be shaped by the character and experience of leaders around the world. The U.S. president will have an especially important role to play. Limiting the damage done by a proliferation shock clearly will be at the forefront of many officials' thinking. Depending on the specifics, officials could be animated by any or all of the following concerns: protection of immediate political and security interests, containing regional and global spillovers, assuaging domestic political pressures, and limiting damage to nonproliferation institutions and procedures. In the most extreme cases of a terrorist attack with chemical, biological, nuclear, or radiological weapons on the American homeland, policymakers will become preoccupied with the need to limit loss of life and destruction, managing the immediate consequences of the attack, ensuring against a follow-on attack, and reassuring the American public.

If the past serves as a guide to the future, proliferation shocks will provide an opportunity to attempt to strengthen global nonproliferation cooperation and to shape the future nonproliferation regime. In some instances, a proliferation shock may provide the right climate to bring to fruition incremental if important changes that already are being pursued. In other cases, some shocks may be so compelling as to make possible more fundamental transformations of existing states' policies. In between the extremes of incremental and revolutionary change, future proliferation shocks may create opportunities for policy innovation that go beyond today's proposals but stop short of fundamental transformation of the nonproliferation regime.

With these broad possibilities in mind, the remainder of this chapter speculates about how several of the future proliferation shocks listed in Table 11.2 could be leveraged to strengthen global nonproliferation cooperation and the overall nonproliferation regime. Some of the specific proposals may be thought too far-reaching; others may be considered perhaps not far-reaching enough. Some of the proposals need to be refined and developed further; some of them might even be set aside following further analysis. Whether or not there would be sufficient political will to pursue and enforce even the more modest initiatives outlined in this chapter also can be debated. What matters most is that the nonproliferation community should buy into the overall concept set out here: proliferation shocks are not only a danger, but also an opportunity. Those who champion the nonproliferation regime need to be planning for them.

Iran Withdraws from the Nuclear Non-proliferation Treaty

Iran's leadership could ultimately decide that its pursuit of nuclear weapons would be served best by withdrawal from the NPT because of the greater freedom of action that withdrawal would provide for achieving their strategic objectives. If Iran withdraws from the NPT, several immediate challenges would quickly emerge. U.S. policymakers would have to decide whether or not to seek Iran's return to the NPT, what type of response to make if Iran fails to return, or how to respond to all but certain Iranian claims that withdrawal is fully justified. Policymakers also would have to recognize that their response would influence efforts to contain the broader regional and global spillovers that would follow an abrupt shift in Tehran's policy. Particular attention likely would be paid to how to build a proliferation firebreak to contain a cascade of regional proliferation. U.S. security assurances to countries threatened by Iran could be an important first step in stopping a proliferation cascade.

In the aftermath of this shock, it might become possible to unite all of the great powers, including the P-5 nuclear powers, to pledge to Iran's neighbors and other countries in the region that they are prepared to act together to ensure that Iran will not gain from its apparent decision to obtain nuclear weapons. This joint commitment could enhance the perceived value of any assurances offered individually by the United States or one or more other countries. A joint pledge would build on the specific relationships between individual great powers and countries in the region and could well have greater political acceptability than unilateral commitments. It also would signal a unified front to possible efforts by Iran to leverage its nuclear weapons for regional political gain. Specific actions could be taken to reinforce this pledge. The great powers, for example, might offer to engage in consultations about the types of responses that might be considered in the face of Iranian provocations, describe the forces available to counter a nuclear-armed Iran, or highlight ongoing contingency planning activities.

Another option that might be considered after the shock of an Iranian withdrawal from the NPT would be to institutionalize the Permanent Five (P-5) and the U.N. Security Council's role in preventing proliferation. In varying degrees, both the P-5 and the Security Council already are involved in proliferation prevention. Their record, however, is mixed. Nonetheless, the shock of Iranian NPT withdrawal could be used to institutionalize that involvement, reinforce habits of cooperation, and drive home the importance of working together to bolster each country's security. Biannual foreign and defense ministerial meetings of all the P-5 countries would be one way to create a nascent institution. In the U.N. Security Council, an annual State of Proliferation Prevention Exchange could be established.

Policymakers also might consider exercise of a so-called right of return of nuclear supplies. In recent years, there has been considerable discussion of the principle that a country that violates its NPT obligations and then withdraws from the treaty should not gain from its prior NPT membership. The concept that any such country should be required—within the limits of technical feasibility—to return items previously supplied to its "peaceful" nuclear program has gained support. The shock of an Iranian NPT withdrawal to pursue nuclear weapons could be leveraged to set a precedent of requiring such a return of material supplied for what were originally described as commercial purposes.

Another option would be to set a precedent by forcing the target state to pay a price for withdrawal from the NPT. Other countries will be watching whether Iran can withdraw from the NPT, pursue nuclear weapons, and not pay a price for doing so. The answer could well affect not only their own proliferation calculations but also the overall effectiveness of the nonproliferation regime, an assessment echoed in Chris Ford's contribution to this volume. In the immediate aftermath of withdrawal as a step to nuclear weapons, other countries (including Russia and China) might be more willing to impose stiffer sanctions on Iran. In so doing, this would set a precedent that NPT withdrawal is not cost-free.

Saudi Arabia Announces Plans for Dual-Key Deployment of Pakistani Nuclear Warheads and Medium-Range Ballistic Missiles

Fearful of a nuclear-armed Iran, Saudi Arabia is assessing its security options. One such option would be to obtain a nuclear guarantee from an outside power. The United States is one possibility; some type of broader great power security guarantee could be another. But there also is speculation that the Saudi royal family is thinking about acquiring nuclear weapons "on loan" from Pakistan. The transfer of those weapons could be modeled on North Atlantic Treaty

Organization nuclear-sharing arrangements, with some type of dual-key arrangement and day-to-day Pakistan control.

The shock of a Saudi announcement of its intention to borrow a small nuclear arsenal could be leveraged to strengthen habits of great power cooperation to prevent proliferation, as well as to institutionalize the P-5 U.N. Security Council roles in the effort to slow proliferation. The goal would be to provide a credible alternative to Saudi acquisition of nuclear weapons "on loan."

This shock could provide an opportunity for the United States to encourage Middle East countries to pursue a new regional security and nuclear restraint regime. The purpose of such a regime would be to provide an alternative to Arab pursuit of nuclear weapons by alleviating short-term political-military concerns about Iran and longer-term concerns about other neighbors. It also would seek to bring Iran into a wider process of security and confidence-building in and beyond the region, thereby strengthening regional stability. Possible insights might be drawn from the Helsinki process in Europe, the Conference on Security and Cooperation in Europe, the Association of South East Asian Nations, and Latin American nuclear confidence-building efforts. As part of this effort to avoid a Middle East proliferation cascade, the United States and the other great powers could encourage each of the key protagonists to take some step showing nuclear restraint. Specific examples might include an Iranian freeze on those activities of most concern at the time, deferral of Saudi plans to acquire dual-key nuclear warheads, and some symbolic restraint on Israel's part.

Unexplained Major Anthrax Outbreak in an Arab Neighbor of Iran

One of the Arab countries neighboring Iran might pursue acquisition of biological weapons as its "matching" weapon of mass destruction to deter Iranian nuclear blackmail or threats. Limited technical capabilities, the possibly more rapid pursuit of a highly lethal biological agent, greater ease of concealment, and the fact that outsiders already are focused on the dangers of nuclear spillovers from Iran's program all would provide a motivation for acquiring a biological weapon. One way that such a program could be publicly revealed would involve a major anthrax outbreak, with significant loss of life and no natural explanation, such as the Sverdlovsk anthrax outbreak that occurred in the Soviet Union in the late 1970s. After this bio-shock, there again could be a readiness among the great powers to think anew about how to address the security concerns that would be driving more widespread proliferation—and perhaps to take some of the security-related actions already discussed.

In addition, the shock of a major unexplained anthrax outbreak could be used to energize the now-mothballed U.N. capability to carry out a range of fact-finding, inspection, and monitoring missions to investigate activities related to chemical and biological weapons proliferation. International fact-finding could be one way to deal with the specific situation posited here, providing a more acceptable basis for bringing pressure to bear on the country in question to shut down activities of concern. The precedent set also could be useful in other cases by providing an element of deterrence to other countries' pursuit of biological weaponry.

The great powers also could consider pursuing regional or global bio–confidence building measures. An unexplained anthrax outbreak in a Persian Gulf state almost certainly would generate concerns in other countries about the possible existence of clandestine biological weapons programs around the Middle East. Those concerns could become a self-fulfilling prophecy, heightening domestic arguments for launching biological or even nuclear weapons programs. Full implementation of the types of confidence building and transparency measures identified by the Biological and Toxin Weapon Convention Review process could help to lessen those concerns. More specific transparency actions—including reciprocal visits of experts, dialogue on uncertain activities, and even invitations for U.N. Security Council fact-finding—might be pursued on a bilateral or regional basis. These actions then could set a precedent for moving forward at a global level.

After the shock of a major unexplained anthrax outbreak, it might be possible to generate international support for accelerated implementation of U.N. Security Council Resolution 1540 (UNSCR 1540). This resolution obligates all states to put in place effective controls to ensure that their firms and other entities do not contribute to proliferation. Other countries' readiness to accelerate implementation would be greatest if the unexplained anthrax outbreak could be linked not only to questionable national activities but also to the transfer of equipment, components, materials, or know-how from a third country's firms or individuals. Involvement of a biological weapons entrepreneur that attempted to sell weapons-related material and technology could also help generate support for more stringent controls on activities that involve dangerous biological agents.

Using this shock to encourage accelerated implementation of UNSC 1540 could entail a variety of specific actions: statements by national leaders, either on their own or in joint declarations, calling on all nations to meet their UNSC 1540 obligations; offers of greater assistance in buttressing controls; a follow-up Security Council resolution; and greater outside support to countries in implementing the resolution's mandates. The model of the Proliferation Security Initiative or of the new Global Initiative to Combat Nuclear Terrorism—in effect, building habits and channels of cooperation by *doing*—might be followed. Potential aiders and recipients could come together to put in place a network of cooperation in upgrading national controls under one of these existing cooperative initiatives or in a new "1540 Implementation Initiative."

Israel Openly Tests a Nuclear Weapon

At some point, Iran's pursuit of nuclear weapons could result in an Israeli decision to test one or more nuclear weapons. Political, technical, strategic, and domestic factors would drive that decision. Among the set of potential future proliferation shocks set out here, an open Israeli test of a nuclear weapon is one of the most difficult to leverage to strengthen the global nonproliferation cooperation. For U.S. officials, past precedents suggest that top priority would probably be placed on limiting damage to U.S. political-security interests in the region, protecting U.S. economic (that is, oil) interests in the Middle East, and almost certainly containing pressures for political-economic action against Israel. For the countries in the region, pressures would be intensified greatly to seek their own nuclear weapons. Here, too, however, some possible ways to attempt to leverage this shock might emerge.

For example, in the crisis atmosphere, new actions could become possible to reinvigorate the Middle East peace process. Such efforts might be widely seen as a last resort to head off a Middle East slide into nuclear competition, confrontation, and possible conflict. Assuming that a U.S. Middle East special envoy already was in place, that envoy could seek to leverage the shock to bring the parties together to address underlying political-military conflicts. Some type of global "Camp David–type" meeting, with leaders from both regional countries and great power, might be considered.

After the shock of an Israeli nuclear test, U.S. cost-benefit calculations could dramatically shift. U.S. policymakers might come to believe that it is a priority to ensure that any new nuclear forces in the region are as stable, secure, and accident-proofed as possible. Specifically, the limits placed by U.S. treaty obligations under the NPT, U.S. regional political interests, and classification restrictions all could be reassessed in the interest of greater regional nuclear stability. From one perspective, a flexible interpretation of the NPT could be seen as undermining the global nonproliferation regime. But from a different perspective, engagement with new nuclear powers could be important to preserving the nuclear taboo, itself arguably one of the most critical elements of today's restraints on runaway nuclear proliferation. Specific topics of these exchanges could range from a broad, nontechnical discussion of nuclear surety best practices, to more specific technical discussions of the fundamentals of negative command and control.

Policymakers also might consider how to leverage this shock of an Israeli nuclear test to press forward toward entry into force of the Comprehensive Test Ban Treaty (CTBT). At first glance, the prospects for success would appear very poor for advancing the CTBT in the aftermath of a proliferation shock. Once having paid the political price for nuclear testing, Israel would have little incentive not to continue with a test series until it had satisfied whatever political-technical-military rationales had led to the decision to test a nuclear weapon in the first place. For their part, both India and Pakistan—if not also China and Russia—might seek to take advantage of Israel's action to resume testing on their own. Within the United States, there is little reason to believe that a CTBT would be any less controversial than in 1999, when the Senate failed to ratify it in the first place, especially if other states took advantage of the Israeli test by undertaking their own nuclear testing.

Nonetheless, over time, should the prospects of an accelerating Middle East nuclear arms race prove sufficiently unnerving to the region's elites and to concerned outsiders, the CTBT could offer Israel, Iran, and Arab countries a vehicle for signaling a desire for nuclear restraint. There is a partial precedent for this type of action. At least one of the roots of rapid and successful U.S.-Soviet negotiation of the 1963 Limited Nuclear Test Ban Treaty was the mutual desire of Washington and Moscow to transform their strategic relationship after the shock of the Cuban Missile Crisis in October 1962. U.S. opinion also could be shaped by a comparable belief that bringing CTBT into force would be an important political step toward Middle East regional restraint.

Terrorist Attack on a Nuclear Storage Site

A terrorist attack on a nuclear weapons storage site could take place in any of the acknowledged, unacknowledged, or future nuclear weapon states. This variant of that shock assumes that the attack is a failure in the sense that the terrorists fail to steal or detonate a nuclear weapon or release radioactive material. There are several different ways that the shock of a failed terrorist nuclear attack could be leveraged.

The existing nuclear weapon states could decide to pursue a Nuclear Powers Code of Conduct. Specifically, under such a code, the nuclear powers all would commit themselves to a number of undertakings: (1) to ensure the safe, secure, and stable maintenance of their nuclear forces; (2) to put in place best practices for nuclear surety and control; and (3) to avoid provocative doctrine, operations, or other actions. As part of this type of Code of Conduct, the nuclear powers party to this code could agree to exchange information designed to help realize the code's security and stability objectives—consistent with their national situations, technical experience, and legal constraints.

Another initiative might involve the creation of an international nuclear response team. Within the United States, for instance, the Nuclear Emergency Support Team was created to ensure prompt response to terrorist and other possible nuclear threats. The mission of the Nuclear Emergency Support Team is to determine if the threat is a hoax or real, to search for a nuclear device, and to provide technical support in assessing and disabling any nuclear device. Over the years, it has evolved as the threat of a terrorist nuclear incident has evolved. Designated U.S. military units bring to bear other capabilities for rendering-safe a terrorist nuclear device. Presumably, some if not all of the other nuclear powers have some types of emergency nuclear response capabilities.

As an initial step in developing an international nuclear response team, the United States could undertake exchanges with all of the other nuclear weapon states concerning the types of capabilities each country could bring to bear to respond to a terrorist nuclear emergency, especially one that transcends any one country's borders. Lessons learned and best practices could be shared. Possibilities for bilateral, trilateral, or wider cooperation to respond to a nuclear terrorist emergency might be discussed.

With regard to specific types of cooperation, subject matter experts could discuss how these countries could cooperate if a third party that was not a nuclear power called for assistance in dealing with a nuclear terrorist incident. As appropriate, specific bilateral or multipower agreements to provide assistance might be developed, as well as channels and mechanisms of cooperation to permit real-time exchanges of technical information to assess or render-safe a terrorist nuclear device. Exercises also could be undertaken among nuclear powers—and perhaps with others—to test political and technical communication channels as well as to build habits of cooperation that would come in handy during a nuclear terrorist emergency. Ultimately, a multinational Nuclear Emergency Support Team could be created. An international team might remain on call, procedures and channels for cooperation could be created, an exercise program could be undertaken, and communications could be practiced before the crisis disrupts normal diplomatic channels. The highest level of political support for an international nuclear response team could be secured in advance.

The shock of an actual attempt to breach the security at a nuclear weapons storage site could be leveraged to create the depth of support globally that may well be needed to achieve the Barak Obama administration's goal of a "lock-down" of all nuclear materials within four years. Such a shock also could be leveraged to establish a virtual global Manhattan Project to ensure effective security and controls over all proliferation sensitive materials around the globe. This type of Manhattan Project approach would build on existing programs and cooperation to secure nuclear, biological, and chemical weapons and materials in the former Soviet Union and elsewhere. A global Manhattan Project could begin with agreement to a "date certain" by which the full range of needed controls on all materials would be put in place. It could include creation of a steering committee with an executive secretary to monitor progress. The steering committee also could be empowered to identify possible sources of assistance to fill existing gaps in materials controls as well as in regulation of know-how and technology.

In the immediate shock of an unsuccessful terrorist nuclear seizure it also could become possible to convince some key holdout countries to join the Proliferation Security Initiative (PSI). Adherence by China, for instance, could expand PSI's geographical coverage and potential effectiveness in stopping future shipments of proliferation concern. Monitoring of key ports also could force clandestine trade to use unusual and inefficient transportation networks, which make it easier for governments to detect and interdict unusual activity.

Aborted Transfer of Chemical, Biological, Radiological and Nuclear Weapons or Materials from a State to a Nonstate Group

One of the major sources of concern about more widespread proliferation is that it will increase the likelihood of witting or unwitting transfer of chemical, biological, radiological, or even nuclear weapons or materials from a state to a nonstate group. Assuming successful interdiction of such a transfer, how

the United States and other countries respond will be shaped by many considerations: the specific transferring state, the degree of state leadership complic-
ity in a nonstate actor's access to materials or a weapon, how the transfer was
prevented (including by which states), the consequences averted, the risks of
response (including the state's deterrent capabilities and other capacities to fo-
ment instability or impose costs), the feasibility of given responses, the international context, and the psychology of individual leaders.

In addition to consultations among the great powers on how to prevent a
future witting or unwitting transfer by any state to a nonstate actor, the shock
of a transfer of a weapon or dangerous materials to a nonstate actor could be
leveraged to buttress global habits of cooperation and nonproliferation norms.
For instance, both on their own and as part of a united front in the Security
Council, the P-5 could affirm that any future intentional transfers would not
be tolerated—and that they would act in concert to block such transfers (if detected) or to track any such transfers back to the source and to hold the transferring state accountable. With regard to the immediate case at hand, Security
Council actions could include authorization of controls on shipments from the
country-in-question (if not a blockade) as well as imposition of more specific
political-economic penalties. Looking forward, Council action could authorize
a right of "hot pursuit" to prevent and block a future transfer—in effect, sup-
planting more traditional international legal obligations and providing a legal
basis for action to interdict chemical, biological, and nuclear weapons and materials in transit.

Terrorist Attack Employing a Weapon of Mass Destruction

After a terrorist attack employing a weapon of mass destruction, top priority will be on the immediate response: managing the physical, political, and
psychological consequences; attributing the attack (including identifying the
persons behind the attack and any state involvement); determining whether
a follow-on attack is in train and if so, preventing it; and responding against
those persons, states, or entities responsible. In addition, the shock of a terrorist chemical, biological, radiological, or nuclear attack would provide an even
more compelling opportunity to press forward many of the possible initiatives
already suggested, especially creating a Nuclear Powers Code of Conduct, a
global Manhattan Project for all proliferation sensitive materials, a multipower
nuclear response team; and buttressing habits and norms of global cooperation.

The shock of such an attack almost certainly would make possible other actions to reinforce the global legal obligation on states to cooperate to prevent, attribute, and manage the consequences of a terrorist attack involving chemical, biological, or nuclear weapons. In particular, the 2005 International Convention for the Suppression of Acts of Nuclear Terrorism already obligates its parties to cooperate to prevent a terrorist nuclear attack. In the aftermath of a successful or unsuccessful terrorist attack, Security Council action would be one way to press countries to join that Convention. The Council might also independently state that all countries have a legal obligation to cooperate to prevent any type of terrorist attack involving weapons of mass destruction. Cooperation could include sharing information and early warning of a planned or imminent attack, cooperation in interdicting such an attack, cooperation in attributing the source of the attack and responding against those entities responsible, and cooperation in consequence management.

Simultaneously, the shock of a terrorist attack involving nuclear weapons could be leveraged to enhance and expand ongoing cooperation through the U.S.-Russia Global Initiative to Combat Nuclear Terrorism. Depending on the nature of the attack, one step would be to expand the Global Initiative to cover other types of attack—especially with biological weapons or with attacks on industrial chemical facilities. The Global Initiative's membership also could be expanded, using the opportunity to win over important holdouts. The Initiative could provide a forum for discussion of lessons learned as well as steps to be taken to prevent any recurrence.

State Use of a Nuclear Weapon

State nuclear weapon use would be the most dramatic and possibly far-reaching future proliferation shock. Suffice it to suggest that there are quite a few conceivable pathways to a future state use of one or more nuclear weapons, and these pathways would shape the international response to the use of a nuclear weapon in war. Key dimensions of any such use would include whether such use was by intention, by accident, or involved unauthorized action by a subordinate command, the objective of use, the targets attacked, the magnitude of the damage, and whether such use succeeds in achieving the attacker's objectives. Two other critical elements would be the extent to which the nuclear taboo is eroded and proliferation incentives are enhanced. Many of the initiatives already discussed to respond to either state or terrorist threats might be pursued in the wake of the state use of a nuclear weapon. Four other possible actions, all of which entail fundamental transformation of the nuclear doctrines and policies of the United States and other nuclear weapon states, might also gain traction in the aftermath of a nuclear detonation. All of these actions stretch credulity today. But after the shock of a highly damaging and destructive use of nuclear weapons, they might become reality.

The shock of the first nuclear use in over six decades could provide an opportunity as well as the political necessity to restructure today's global nuclear order. This could entail the initiation of negotiations among some or all of the nuclear powers not only on the type of Nuclear Code of Conduct to be adopted but also on the need for radical changes in their nuclear force postures. Drastically reduced force numbers, agreed steps to ensure against loss of control or accident, moves to maintain those forces only on a nonalert status, and doctrinal changes to circumscribe the role of nuclear weapons all could follow in the wake of a nuclear detonation. Such actions could be taken in different ways, from unilateral steps by sets of countries to more formal arrangements among all or most of the nuclear powers.

The shock of a nuclear next use also could provide an impetus for putting in place a global missile defense system. Such a system would hark back to the U.S. Global Protection against Accidental Launch, first explored by the United States and Soviet Union in the late 1980s and early 1990s. More recently, both U.S. and Russian leaders have talked about possible joint missile defenses. The shock of nuclear next use could well provide the needed impetus in both Washington and Moscow to make such talk of joint missile defenses a reality. The goal would be to deploy cooperatively a global system to offer defense against ballistic missile attack to any threatened country. One purpose would be to constrain pressures for further nuclear missile proliferation. Another purpose would be to provide protection against unauthorized or accidental launch against any country.

Policymakers also could use the shock created by the next nuclear use to pursue an enforceable global ban on any first use of chemical, biological, radiological, or nuclear weapons. This ban could be reflected in appropriate action by the U.N. Security Council or less formally in an agreement among the P-5 nuclear powers. Its purpose would be to deter any additional use of these weapons. Enforcement could take different forms, including a readiness to use military force preemptively, to leverage missile defenses to prevent successful use (involving a ballistic missile), or to respond militarily up to the tit-for-tat use of a nuclear weapon. Enforcement would be the responsibility of the great powers, not least the five NPT nuclear weapon states. These states would declare that regardless of any other political-security interests that they might have at stake in a confrontation that could lead to chemical, biological, or nuclear weapons use, their interest in preventing a world in which the use of chemical, biological, or nuclear weapons becomes commonplace requires their cooperation.

Even more far reaching, the shock of next use of a nuclear weapon could provide the trigger needed for the great powers to agree that henceforth they would block further proliferation—whether to states or nonstate actors. In particular, they could reach agreement to use whatever means necessary to stop proliferation—from political-military leverage and coercion through conventional military power to coordinated actions to bring about regime changes where needed. Again, the driver for taking this step would be both the shock of a dramatic next use of a nuclear weapon and the resulting belief that life in a proliferating world had become intolerable for their own security.

CONCLUSION

A number of different types of proliferation shocks could occur in the future. In the past, proliferation shocks have been the catalyst for action to strengthen global nonproliferation cooperation. In good measure, today's global nonproliferation regime is the result of creative efforts by U.S. and other officials to leverage those shocks to gain support for new nonproliferation institutions, procedures, and norms. Looking ahead, the global nonproliferation regime will be shaped by how the United States and other countries respond to future proliferation shocks. Prudent proliferation contingency planning would begin now to identify possible proliferation shocks and to think about how those shocks might be leveraged to enhance global nonproliferation cooperation. In so doing, it is important to think broadly and to stretch the definition of what might become possible to accomplish after a shock. Indeed, for the most extreme shocks entailing a next use of a nuclear weapon (or perhaps a highly lethal biological weapon), such proliferation shock response planning should not be afraid to contemplate far-reaching and now virtually unthinkable transformations of the global security order.

12 Intelligence, Interdiction, and Dissuasion: Lessons from the Campaign against Libyan Proliferation

Wyn Q. Bowen

The U.S.-U.K. campaign to dissuade Libya from developing nuclear and other unconventional weapons demonstrates how proactive intelligence and interdiction can be applied to dissuade other states from developing nuclear, biological, or chemical (NBC) weapons capabilities.[1] The U.S. Weapons of Mass Destruction (WMD) Commission described intelligence and interdiction in the Libya context as "a critical factor in Tripoli's decision to open up its weapons programs to international scrutiny." The Commission also noted that "the Intelligence Community should be commended for its contributions to forcing Tripoli to openly declare its nuclear and chemical materials and abandon development efforts, as well as hand over parts of its missile force and cancel its long-range missile projects. Such renunciation is, we believe, the real measure of a WMD-related intelligence success."[2] Similarly, the Butler review commented that British involvement in Libya's rollback decision amounted to "a major intelligence success."[3] It would appear then that much can be learned from the Libya experience in terms of how intelligence and associated interdiction efforts could potentially be used to apply pressure to dissuade other states from pursuing WMD.

When it comes to the proliferation of WMD, national and international efforts at dissuasion can encompass many types of activity. Dissuasion can embody diplomatic, intelligence, military, and economic elements of national power and influence that could potentially be applied as part of a strategy to convince a state actor to cease the pursuit of NBC weapons. A dissuasion strategy would involve formulating a specific plan of action, drawing on all available instruments of national influence and power to dissuade a specific target country from pursuing a nuclear weapons capability.[4] The target of such a strategy could be an actual or potential adversary, as in the Libya case prior to 2003, but dissuasion also could be directed toward an allied or friendly country. Indeed, it appears that many future nuclear nonproliferation challenges may well involve the United States and its allies seeking to dissuade allied or friendly states from venturing down the nuclear path in response to perceived security threats. In the Middle East there are concerns about several Arab states hedging their nuclear bets in the context of a nuclearizing Iran. Saudi Arabia, Turkey, and Egypt have been the cause of most anxiety to date, all of which have friendly or allied relations with the United States. Similarly, in Northeast Asia, there is concern about the long-term nuclear status of South Korea, Japan, and Taiwan in the face of security challenges posed by North Korea and China. Again, all three states have friendly or allied relations with the United States. As an international strategy, dissuasion policies can and might have to be targeted against more than just the traditional "states of proliferation concern" typified by the likes of Iran and North Korea.

A dissuasion strategy could also encompass the goal of dissuading a target state from proliferating nuclear weapons–relevant technology, materials, and technical expertise to further centers of control, whether these are constituted by state or nonstate actors. While a specific strategy would focus on individual state actors, there would appear to be scope for developing more general strategies to dissuade more than one state actor. Since the Qadhafi regime made its unilateral decision to give up the development of nuclear and other WMD capabilities in December 2003, following secret negotiations with the American and British governments, several officials in Washington and London have touted the so-called Libya model for rolling back state-level programs. The Libya experience certainly offers a solid illustration of how dissuasion can work in practice. It is also what can be described as a positive example of dissuasion. As a long-term state of proliferation concern, Libya was given the room to reach a decision that its core interests were best served by negotiating the elimination of its weapons programs, albeit with significant encouragement and prodding from outside and assurances that regime change was not a Western objective. This case study stands in stark contrast to the Saddam Hussein regime in Iraq, which was toppled for its perceived failure to comply with its disarmament obligations as spelled out by the U.N. Security Council. In this respect, Iraq can be painted as a negative example of what could potentially happen to actual and potential proliferators if they are unresponsive to external pressure.

There has been some debate over the potentially coercive effect of the Iraq War on the Qadhafi regime. Libya's decision was accelerated and cemented by the fate of the regime in Baghdad. For future dissuasion to be credible, and therefore effective, it might require both positive and negative options for dissuasion to be available in order to illustrate where different paths may lead a proliferator. This argument has certainly been made by Richard Perle, who, in response to a question on changing the behavior of rogue states during a February 2004 interview, noted with regard to Syria that Damascus "should be invited to choose between two models: Iraq and Libya. Qadhafi got the message and responded, appropriately, with a white flag. Saddam didn't and he now sits in jail, awaiting trial."[5]

Foreign intelligence plays an important role in efforts at dissuasion. Intelligence generally refers to the process of collecting and analyzing information and the dissemination of related findings, the so-called product, which is often referred to as finished intelligence, in support of governmental decision-making. It encompasses the organizations and individuals that compose a government's intelligence machinery, and includes covert action overseas designed to support government objectives.[6] Intelligence thus supports dissuasion and interdiction efforts by keeping government officials apprised of the threats they face and the opportunities that may present themselves to mitigate those threats.

Interdiction is often used to refer to actions taken to divert, disrupt, delay, or destroy another state's or nonstate actor's military potential.[7] In the context of WMD proliferation, interdiction generally is used to describe the disruption of the clandestine transfer of weapons, dual-use technologies, or associated delivery systems and their components. While the concept is often applied purely in the context of military action, a broader approach is adopted here to include the full gamut of national power. For example, the activities of intelligence, law enforcement, customs, and other government agencies can be included in an assessment of national and international efforts at interdiction. The National Military Strategy to Combat WMD, published by the Joint Chiefs of Staff in February 2006, offers a similar definition of interdiction operations. According to the U.S. Joint Chiefs, they are defined as being "designed to stop the proliferation of WMD, delivery systems, associated and dual-use technologies, materials, and expertise from transiting between States of concern and between State and non-State actors, whether undertaken by the military or by other agencies of government (e.g. law enforcement)."[8]

This chapter explores the role that proactive intelligence and interdiction—typified by the efforts of the United States and the United Kingdom to roll back Libya's nuclear program—could play as part of national or international strategies to head off other nuclear weapons programs in the future. It lays out the three steps that counterproliferation planners must consider when developing a specific dissuasion strategy: (1) determining the susceptibility of target states to dissuasion; (2) assessing the advantages offered by dissuasion; and (3) assessing the drawbacks produced by the effort to curtail a WMD program. The Libya case is used to illustrate how these considerations were addressed in practice. The aim is not to provide an exhaustive analysis of Libya's rollback, as this has been done elsewhere. The goal is to illustrate key points relevant to current and future efforts to apply intelligence and interdiction in the context of dissuasion campaigns by drawing on some examples drawn from the Libya experience. Nevertheless, the specific combination of factors that resulted in successful dissuasion in this case are unlikely to be completely replicated elsewhere.[9] Hence, it is important that policymakers benefit from detailed intelligence pictures of all potential proliferation cases that may become the target of a dissuasion campaign.

STEP 1: GAUGING THE SUSCEPTIBILITY OF TARGET STATES

Several issues should be considered when evaluating the potential contribution and value of intelligence and interdiction to a dissuasion strategy in any given scenario. Considering these issues generates an understanding of the potential susceptibility of different states to dissuasion. It also begins to cast light on the role that proactive intelligence and interdiction might play as part of a dissuasion strategy. Indeed, gauging the susceptibility of potential target states should be an important focus of intelligence analysts from the very outset of any effort at dissuasion.

The best place to begin is probably with an assessment of the likely responsiveness of the target state to external influence (See Table 12.1). Is the target a long-term adversary or a traditional ally? In the case of Libya's efforts to acquire nuclear weapons, the United States and the United Kingdom were confronted by a situation where they were dealing with a long-term adversary, although their relations with Tripoli, particularly the British relationship, improved between 1998 and 2003 as a result of movement toward resolving the Lockerbie issue. Movement on the issue of the Lockerbie bombing allowed other negotiations—in this case weapons proliferation issues—to be possible. So, despite the

TABLE 12.1

Evaluating the Susceptibility of Target Countries

Key factors	Types of questions		
Responsiveness to external pressure	Is the target a long-term adversary?	Is the target a traditional ally?	Is the target neither an ally nor an adversary?
Willingness or reluctance to roll-back capability	Has the target demonstrated willingness or reluctance to consider roll-back either publicly or in private?	Is there an open or semi-open door to push on?	Is the door double-bolted from the inside?
Accurately understanding the drivers of nuclear ambitions	To what extent is the pursuit of nuclear weapons influenced by security concerns?	To what extent is the pursuit of nuclear weapons influenced by the quest for regional influence?	To what extent is the pursuit of nuclear weapons influenced by domestic politics?
Political system	Is the target a democratic or authoritarian country, or more of a hybrid?	Is there a single political entity to influence?	Is there more than one domestic political faction to influence?
Technical capability	How much would the target have to give up?	How close is the target to developing a nuclear weapon?	Has the target yet to physically initiate a weapons project?
Development of new military capabilities	Is the development of new military capabilities such as missile defense likely to have a dissuasive effect?	Will the development of such capabilities undermine the incentives to seek nuclear weapons?	Can proliferators be convinced that NBC weapons may not be effective asymmetric capabilities?

history of antagonism in Tripoli's relations with Washington and London, the Qadhafi regime was increasingly responsive from the late 1990s to negotiating overtures quietly offered by the United States and the United Kingdom.[10]

Another issue that policymakers and analysts must consider is how much the target state would have to give up in order to comply with their demands. Has the target been pursuing nuclear weapons for several years? How close is it to developing a nuclear weapons capability? Has it recently embarked down this route? Or, has the target state yet to physically, as opposed to politically, initiate such a course of action? In terms of sunk costs and public commitment, the Libyans had only made a modest commitment to their nuclear program. The Qadhafi regime had been pursuing nuclear weapons for three decades and, despite acquiring a great deal of nuclear equipment and material via the A.

Q. Khan network and other sources, Libya had not made much progress. A dearth of local expertise, poor management, and the international embargo had slowed the pace of their efforts.[11] Consequently, Libya was not being asked to abandon a weapons program in its advanced stages, and the dissuasion effort did not have to overcome deeply entrenched bureaucratic interests, the tyranny of sunk costs, or public expectations of success. Moreover, the regime may have thought that trading off the program as part of its broader strategy of reengaging the United States and the international community to address the country's domestic economic and political problems was good value, given its overall lack of technical achievements.[12]

Officials also should consider whether or not the target state has already demonstrated any willingness to contemplate rolling back its nuclear capability or ambitions. By the time the United States and the United Kingdom had started secret weapons negotiations in early 2003, for instance, the Qadhafi regime had already demonstrated some willingness to give up its weapons programs, although they had yet to come clean on their exact nature and extent of their efforts. But when intelligence and interdiction operations subsequently uncovered the clandestine effort to acquire nuclear weapons, Libyan officials apparently saw this as a good excuse to get the best deal possible for abandoning their program.[13]

Policymakers and intelligence analysts also should consider whether the drivers of the target state's nuclear weapon ambitions, and therefore its susceptibility to dissuasion, are accurately understood. To what extent is the target's pursuit or contemplation of a nuclear weapons program driven by security concerns, the quest for regional influence, or domestic politics? The Libyan program, for example, was driven by external security concerns, but it also was influenced by visions of Arab leadership and regional influence. Domestic politics were always a strong motivation for embarking on the quest to obtain nuclear weapons in the sense that the Qadhafi regime's foremost priority was retaining power in the face of external and internal threats. Any decision to renounce the nuclear weapons program could not have jeopardized the regime's perceived prospects for survival over the long term.[14]

Identifying the motivations behind a program to acquire weapons of mass destruction should also be linked to an effort to identify the political factions and domestic institutions that favor acquisition of a nuclear, chemical, or biological arsenal. Is the target a democratic or an authoritarian country, or is it more of a hybrid? Is the scientific community fully behind weapons acquisition, or is it largely favored by a specific service within the armed forces? For example, in terms of domestic governance Libya was on the right of the democratic-authoritarian continuum. Qadhafi was able to make and implement far-reaching decisions because of his preponderant role in the political process. The Libyan leader was in a position, therefore, to deliver on the weapons front—as he had already done on the Lockerbie and wider terrorism issue—regardless of any internal opposition. In terms of Libya, the focal point of dissuasion efforts was on influencing a "supreme leader," or at least the small cadre of trusted officials and ideological supporters who might have had some say on major military and foreign policy issues.

A further factor in gauging susceptibility revolves around the question of whether the development of new military capabilities designed to negate the effects of NBC weapons, notably missile defenses and passive chemical and biological defenses, will have a dissuasive effect on proliferators. This question is based on the view that the acquisition of NBC weapons can potentially provide less developed states and nonstate actors with the basis for asymmetric strategies when confronted by opponents such as the United States that have a significant technological advantage in the conventional military sphere. In other words, will the development of military capabilities specifically designed to negate the effects of NBC weapons undermine the incentives for target states to continue pursuing or possessing such capabilities? This issue focuses on calculations of the utility of NBC weapons, including perceptions of whether or not their use can be credibly threatened when faced by an opponent with an increasingly decisive conventional military advantage.

Although attempts to assess the potential susceptibility of particular target states to dissuasion is no simple matter, this brief overview suggests that it is not beyond the capacity of most governments or even loosely organized international coalitions. Once this sort of assessment is offered, however, policymakers have to devise appropriate diplomatic, economic, and even military campaigns to dissuade target states from acquiring nuclear weapons. As the Libyan case suggests, these plans have to remain flexible so that they can adapt to information and opportunities created by ongoing intelligence and interdiction campaigns that are an integral part of any effort at dissuasion.

STEP 2: ASSESSING THE ADVANTAGES

Rollback decisions are influenced by a mix of political, security, and economic factors. The key to applying external influence is in estimating when the context is ripe for applying pressure to derail ongoing or nascent programs. One of the central roles for intelligence analysts is to identify points of convergence where the political decision-making context in a target country appears ripe for dissuasion, and where accurate and sufficient knowledge exists about the technical progress of a weapons program. For example, analysts must consider whether the target state is actively looking for a way to abandon a fledgling program. Alternatively, it would be productive to determine if the target is fully committed to the pursuit of nuclear weapons.

Technical intelligence also can help identify the status of the program to assess how urgent it may be to engage the target in negotiations. Policymakers will want to know whether the program is at a crossroads. If enthusiasm for the program is waning because of a lack of progress, then policymakers can tailor their initiatives to exploit potential opposition. If analysts suspect that an impending breakthrough is about to occur, policymakers will want to act quickly to prevent a fait accompli. Several indicators might suggest that a weapons program has reached a critical juncture. The program might be encountering technical or financial difficulties that are about to force leaders in the target to reassess their priorities and programs. The program also might be about to receive significant infusions of technology and knowledge from abroad, creating new options for target states.

Although it was the Qadhafi regime that initiated the weapons negotiations by first approaching the United Kingdom in early 2003, the Libya case provides a useful illustration of the importance of timing when it comes to derailing a weapons program. The U.S.-U.K. campaign to dissuade Libya capitalized on Tripoli's desire to end its international isolation. This desire to reengage with the outside world, especially with the United States, was evident from as early as 1992. A discernible change in Libya-U.S.-U.K. relations came in April 1999, following the hand-over of the Lockerbie suspects, which coincided with the growing availability of intelligence about the country's nuclear procurement efforts via the A. Q. Khan network. The increased availability of intelligence between 1999 and 2003 paralleled a shifting domestic context inside Libya to create a situation that was ripe for external influence to bear fruit.[15]

By 2002, the Qadhafi regime was relatively susceptible to outside influence on the weapons front. Indeed, during the secret negotiations in 2003, the Americans and British revealed to the Libyans that they possessed significant and current knowledge about the nuclear program, including information derived from the interdiction of the cargo ship *BBC China* in October 2003.[16] The coercive effect of the Iraq conflict also appeared to increase the Qadhafi regime's desire to resolve the weapons issue, creating increased political incentives to move forward rapidly.[17] The presence of a nuclear weapons program now seemed to threaten, rather than guarantee, the survival of the regime.

Validation of Intelligence

Information gathered as a direct result of interdiction operations could be used to validate or invalidate either previously gathered information on the target, or the intelligence assessments that are used to identify programs as posing a serious threat. Validation could increase confidence in intelligence collection vis-à-vis the target, while information deemed to be inconsistent or misleading could be used to reassess the collection process and methods. Libya, for instance, was long suspected of posing a proliferation threat; U.K. and U.S. intelligence knew that Libya was "already in receipt of nuclear-related materiel," and it was known to be "a prime customer of the A. Q. Khan network by 2002–3".[18] The interception of nuclear equipment on board the *BBC China* en route to Libya in October 2003 validated the U.S.-U.K. intelligence estimate that the regime possessed a gas centrifuge enrichment program, supplied via the A. Q. Khan network. The interdiction of the *BBC China* validated U.S.-U.K. intelligence on the A. Q. Khan network, increasing confidence in the reliability of reporting from existing intelligence sources, which in this case involved "a variety of innovative collection efforts."[19] In turn, the validation of intelligence increased U.S.-U.K. confidence about the significance and timeliness of continuing with and completing their dissuasion effort in the Libya context.

Indications and Warning

Information uncovered as a result of interdiction activities also could be used to provide indications and warning related to pending technical developments associated with a particular program. "Indications" can be defined as activities related to a threat that generates signatures that can be observed and fed into a warning system. Paradoxically, these warnings also can involve the absence of "expected" activities and data that suggest that normal operations have been suspended as a state or nonstate actor generates its forces or operatives to launch a major operation.[20] These warning systems are generally part of a deliberate planning process.[21] According to Mary McCarthy, warning is "a process of communicating judgments about threats . . . to decisionmakers wherein such communications must be received and understood in order for leaders to take action."[22] Warnings of a significant change in a weapons program based on interdiction-generated indicators, and communicated to decision-makers in a timely fashion, could be used to influence the urgency accorded to the implementation of a dissuasion strategy, particularly whether negotiations should be initiated or accelerated. Indeed, an effective indications and warning system based in part on interdiction activities could potentially generate confidence in an international response to a weapons program, including the avoidance of overreaction to suspected proliferation activities.[23]

Signals and Negotiations

Information derived from interdictions also could be used to send signals to target states and to apply pressure during discussions or negotiations. By revealing information generated as a result of interdiction activities, signals could potentially be sent that a particular program or activity has been discovered and has been placed under surveillance. Such revelations could pressure the target state into being more open about its capabilities and ambitions by constraining its room for maneuver during negotiations, thereby increasing the chances of successful dissuasion.

The fact that proliferation activities had been detected by the intelligence services of potential adversaries apparently played a major role in the Libyan officials' decision to reassess their nascent nuclear program. Intelligence on Libya's procurement activities, including information generated as a result of the *BBC China* interdiction, was used by the American and British governments to pressure the Qadhafi regime during the secret negotiations over the status of Libya's weapons programs. During October and December 2003, Libya was provided with reports that demonstrated that the American and British governments had detailed and current information on Tripoli's efforts to acquire weapons of mass destruction, including its active uranium enrichment project.[24] According to the Butler review, the two governments were able "to confront Libyan officials with this evidence of their nuclear-related procurement at a time when Libya was still considering whether to proceed to full admission of its programs." Qadhafi, according to the WMD Commission, "may well have thought that he could achieve rapprochement with the West while retaining nuclear, chemical and ballistic missile programs."[25] The WMD Commission also highlighted this dimension of the dissuasion campaign, noting that "the Community collected significant intelligence on Libya's nuclear and missile

TABLE 12.2

Assessing the Advantages

Existing intelligence and related assessments can be validated or invalidated;	Interdiction derived 'indicators and warnings' can generate knowledge and understanding related to pending technical developments associated with a particular programme	Interdiction and intelligence can feed directly and significantly into communicating signals to actual and potential proliferators as well as suppliers;
Third party facilitation	In the event that a rollback breakthrough is achieved, previous interdiction and intelligence gathering activities can increase confidence in the process of verifying and monitoring dismantlement commitments.	Intelligence officers can play a covert diplomatic role in initiating or facilitating negotiations with proliferators

programs, providing a vital lever used by policymakers to pressure Tripoli to openly declare its nuclear and chemical materials and disavow its WMD and long-range missile programs."[26]

Covert Diplomacy and Third-Party Facilitation

The work of intelligence agencies is not confined to the collection and analysis of information. Intelligence organizations in many countries also undertake covert actions in pursuit of national objectives. Intelligence officers working in the field can provide an important means to establish and nurture secret lines of communication ("covert diplomacy") in the event that a political decision is taken to initiate a dialogue with a government that is posing a proliferation challenge. Dissuasion campaigns can be facilitated by clandestine efforts at communication, particularly when relations are strained between the dissuasion target and the state or international coalition that seeks to halt proliferation activity. Allied intelligence services also can play pivotal roles as third-party facilitators in dissuasion strategies.

The interaction among Libyan officials and intelligence operatives provides an interesting example of the role clandestine communication and negotiations can play in overcoming an absence of formal diplomatic activity. A report by Britain's Intelligence and Security Committee in June 2004 noted that Libya's decision to dismantle its weapons programs was the result of months of work by the Secret Intelligence Service, the Foreign and Commonwealth Office, and Central Intelligence Agency.[27] Although this statement is short on detail, it highlights the central role played by British intelligence officers in facilitating the secret weapons talks and not just in the collection and analysis of information on the programs themselves.

The Libyans approached Secret Intelligence Service operatives in mid-March 2003 with a proposal to initiate talks aimed at dismantling their weapons programs in exchange for the removal of sanctions and normalizing relations.[28] The Libyan approach took place immediately before the outbreak of the Iraq conflict. Secret Intelligence Service officers apparently met Qadhafi's son Saef al-Islam during the initial stage of the campaign to unseat Saddam Hussein.[29] British intelligence officials subsequently began meeting and negotiating secretly with Musa Kusa, then head of Qadhafi's external intelligence agency, and other Libyans in London and at other locations.

The involvement of British and U.S. intelligence officers helped to keep the negotiations a closely held secret; only a handful of officials in the three countries involved were aware of the talks. Following Britain's resumption of formal diplomatic relations in 1999, London provided Tripoli with a vital back channel to approach Washington.[30]

Verification and Monitoring

If a dissuasion strategy is successful in influencing a target state to give up a clandestine weapons program, then intelligence collected previously on that program, including any information gathered through interdiction activity, should assist the verification process and increase confidence that it actually has been terminated. The continued collection and analysis of proliferation-related intelligence also would contribute to monitoring a country's ongoing compliance with agreements to abandon the nuclear weapons business.[31] In terms of monitoring the behavior of Libyan scientists and officials, the collection and analysis of intelligence prior to December 2003 assisted in the verification of Tripoli's declarations that were made in 2004 about the scope and nature of its clandestine weapons program. The process of verification actually began when American and British officials informed their Libyan counterparts about what was generally already known about their weapons programs, which encouraged the Qadhafi regime to be fully cooperative in the dismantlement process.[32]

STEP 3: ASSESSING THE DRAWBACKS

Using proactive intelligence and interdiction as part of a dissuasion campaign is not without drawbacks. Indeed, there are some significant shortcomings, particularly if the proactive use of intelligence and interdiction are to be applied as part of an ongoing dissuasion campaign. In such circumstances the broader political-strategic context will be of central importance to the overall success of a dissuasion initiative. Three potential drawbacks—interdiction might be taken as evidence of bad faith, interdiction could create a backlash, and intelligence itself may be fundamentally flawed—should be considered by officials before they undertake a dissuasion campaign.

Interdictions as Evidence of Bad Faith

As Andrew Winner notes, "States bargaining about their WMD programs may see interdictions as evidence of bad faith on the part of their negotiating partners."[33] Interdictions also may reveal to the target government what is known about its activities before it is politically ready to renounce its weapons program, thereby complicating negotiations. Paradoxically, successful interdiction operations can jeopardize the overall success of a dissuasion campaign by causing embarrassment among members of the targeted regime, stiffening resolve to pursue increasingly controversial and counterproductive programs. While the *BBC China* was being monitored en route to Libya, for instance, there were debates within the U.S. and British governments about whether interdicting the shipment would accelerate the ongoing negotiations or knock them off track.[34]

Proliferation Backlash

Because intelligence agencies were able to shed light on the A. Q. Khan network and Libya, proliferators might become increasingly careful about protecting their information and activities to evade detection and interdiction. While proliferators will probably seek greater flexibility in their operating procedures—for example, by opting for air versus maritime transportation of illicit materials—the onus will be on governments to keep track of such tactical and operational developments through targeted intelligence collection and analysis. The requisite legal and procedural mechanisms need to be put in place to facilitate interdictions when policymakers believe that they are necessary. Although a great deal of this type of activity is already being coordinated under the Proliferation Security Initiative, the international community should be alert to other opportunities to police the global commons.[35]

Potential Sources of Error in Intelligence

There are several main sources of error regarding indications and warning in the intelligence field. Flagging these is useful when it comes to thinking about the risks and drawbacks of utilizing proactive intelligence as a central tool of dissuasion strategies. The intelligence studies literature highlights several potential sources of error that focus on the target country, the intelligence analyst, the policymaker as a consumer of intelligence, and the intelligence system itself. Errors emanating from these sources could potentially result in flawed intelligence assessments. They also could cause policymakers and analysts to disregard information when it does not conform to preconceived ideas or positions. Intelligence biases and faulty estimates are probably the most important hurdle that faces dissuasion campaigns.

Target states often could implement deception measures to deceive intelligence gathering, analysis, and prediction. Deception can involve creating false fronts and misleading signals to lull opposing intelligence analysts into a false sense of security or to misdirect collection efforts toward unrewarding targets. Operational security also could occur to hide programs behind a cloak of secrecy, muting the signals produced by clandestine activity until they were no longer detectible by opposing intelligence organizations. Another challenge involves the susceptibility of intelligence analysts to mirror-imaging, received opinion, "intelligence to please," or the "not-invented-here" syndrome. Mirror-imaging involves a tendency to project one's own logic, value hierarchy, and mindset onto that of the opponent, thereby not allowing for differences based on divergent cultures, value systems, and frames of reference. Given the cultural diversity of actual and potential proliferators, mirror-imaging could be a significant problem in terms of dissuasion strategies because it can cause analysts to be slow to detect accurate signals of clandestine activity or to construct dissuasion strategies that have little impact on the targeted audience. Received opinion can lead to a resistance to change in the face of contradictory evidence, which can result in the exclusion of information that does not fit the conventional wisdom. This can make the analyst susceptible to deception, whether this is self-induced or induced by the enemy. Another source of error can involve the policymaker in situations where there is a desire for intelligence to be supportive of a particular policy priority, which can result in the disregarding of information or assessments that are not supportive. Systemic deficiencies stemming from "the inertial force of habit" that is endemic in large bureaucratic organizations can create errors of omission and commission.[36] The "not-invented-here" syndrome also could cause analysts to fail to recognize novel solutions to weapons engineering or production issues. Programs that embody designs and production processes that are novel or inefficient are often difficult to detect when analysts and policymakers suffer from an inflated sense of technical prowess and hubris.

Several of these issues emerged in the effort to estimate weapons production activity in Libya. Intelligence proved to be generally accurate. Nevertheless, U.S. intelligence analysts overestimated certain capabilities and developmental timelines.[37] The original source of this analytical error appears to have been the increase in intelligence on Libya's active procurement efforts via the A. Q. Khan network. From 1999 to 2000, U.S. analysts began to re-examine their past assumptions and launched formal efforts to explore alternative scenarios. In 2001 and 2002, analysts at the Central Intelligence Agency set up simulation workshops to assess the implications of suspected changes in Libya's nuclear and missile programs.[38] One outcome of this reassessment was that technical analysts began to alter their assessments concerning the capability of the Libyans to integrate technologies into weapons. This resulted in the adoption of what has been described as a worst case approach to the analysis of intelligence on Libya. A National Intelligence Estimate in 2001, for example, stated that Libya could have a nuclear weapons capability as early as 2007 with foreign help.[39] By contrast, an estimate produced in 1999 estimated that the earliest date that Libya could develop a nuclear weapon was 2015.[40] Following Libya's decision to forgo nuclear, biological, and chemical weapons, information revealed during the dismantlement process in 2004 led analysts to conclude that the 2007 projection was "unrealistic."[41]

The overestimation of Libya's weapons potential has been attributed to various factors, not least the disproportionately large volume of procurement-related intelligence that may have caused intelligence analysts to overemphasize the importance of the program to Libyan officials and the progress that was being made. In the United States, this overestimation has been attributed to an insufficient depth of information, knowledge, and training when it comes to analysts incorporating "the systems integration capabilities of a would-be nuclear power into their assessments." As a result, analysts seemed automatically to equate procurement activity with a weapons capability, while giving short shrift to broader economic, industrial, and scientific issues that shape the pace of a weapons development program. While there is insufficient material available in open sources to determine exactly the source of this overestimation, it does seem to bear the hallmarks of mirror-imaging.[42]

Ironically, prior to the growth in procurement-related intelligence in 1999–2000, U.S. intelligence analysts had been skeptical regarding Libya's ability to make significant progress in the nuclear area because of the country's dearth of personnel with the requisite technical expertise, the absence of a sophisticated industrial infrastructure, and the constraining effect of the international embargo.[43] It is important, therefore, not to automatically and uncritically equate increased procurement activity with progress in the development of weapons capabilities. The problem with such inferences is that proliferation problems may be made to appear worse than they actually are, at any given point, which in turn could have detrimental effects for political and diplomatic efforts aimed at negotiating rollback or a cessation of activities.

CONCLUSION

Using the Libya experience to illustrate key points, this chapter has examined the role that proactive intelligence and interdiction can play as elements of broader strategies designed to head off new nuclear weapons programs. Numerous factors were highlighted for consideration by counterproliferation planners if security arrangements break down in the Middle East and Northeast Asia, and dissuasion plans need to be developed in an effort to prevent nuclear proliferation.

The first step for counterproliferation planners will be to gauge the susceptibility of potential target states to being influenced by identifying plausible dissuasion targets as well as those states that are potentially nondissuadable. This task will involve taking into account the broader political, security, and economic context of the specific country concerned. Given the diversity of the countries examined in this book, intelligence agencies might begin in advance to collect information on an ongoing basis to fine tune their dissuasion estimates.

The second step is to assess the advantages that proactive intelligence and interdiction might offer to the development of a dissuasion plan targeted at a specific country. Several potential advantages have been highlighted, but it is important to balance these against potential drawbacks. The wider political context will have a direct bearing on the potential costs that are perceived to be involved relative to the potential gains. For example, in some instances it will probably make sense to forgo interdiction opportunities if there is a strong risk of pushing off course a specifically targeted dissuasion effort. Indeed, getting a dissuasion plan wrong or misjudging a state's susceptibility could make the proliferation problem in question more difficult to address in the longer term.

In the end, any dissuasion plan will always carry a significant amount of risk because it is not possible to acquire perfect knowledge of target states, even in the case of democratic governments and open societies. Nevertheless, if security arrangements break down in key regions such as the Middle East and Northeast Asia, then the risks of dissuasion would certainly appear to be worth taking—particularly if the alternative is doing nothing in the face of unconstrained proliferation and arms races.

NOTES

1. In addition to thanking the other project participants and editors for their comments on earlier drafts of this paper, I thank Brad Roberts and Joe Hogler for their observations and recommendations on how to improve the final version.

2. "Chapter Two Case Study: Libya," *Commission on the Intelligence Capabilities of the United States Regarding Weapons of Mass Destruction* (subsequently referred to as the WMD Commission), Report to the President, 31 March 2005, 258, 263, http://www.wmd. gov/report/wmd_report.pdf.

3. This was one of the conclusions on Libya from the Butler Report. *Review of Intelligence on Weapons of Mass Destruction* (subsequently referred to as the Butler Report), Report of a Committee of Privy Counsellors, Chairman: The Rt Hon The Lord Butler of Brockwell KG GCB CVO, HC 898 (London: The Stationery Office, 14 July 2004), 22.

4. Strategy can be defined in this way: "A prudent idea or set of ideas for employing the instruments of national power in a synchronized and integrated fashion to achieve theater, national, or multinational objectives." "Strategy," DOD Dictionary of Military Terms, Defense Technical Information Center, http://www.dtic.mil/doctrine/jel/doddict/data/s/05190.html.

5. Jamie Glazov, "An End to Evil," FrontPageMagazine.com, Wednesday, 18 February 2004, http://www.frontpagemag.com, accessed 10 March 2008.

6. This description of intelligence was derived in part from Greg Hannah, Kevin A. O'Brien, and Andrew Rathmell, *Intelligence and Security Legislation for Security Sector Reform* (Santa Monica, CA, and Cambridge: RAND Europe, 2005), 1–7.

7. See Joint Operations Execution, Joint Warfare Publication 3-00, Second Edition, March 2004, Promulgated as Directed by the Chiefs of Staff, Director General Joint Doctrine and Concepts, 2E1–7, http://www.mod.uk/DefenceInternet/AboutDefence/CorporatePublications/DoctrineOperationsandDiplomacyPublications/JWP/Jwp300Jo intOperationsExecution.ht; "Interdiction," DOD Dictionary of Military Terms, Defense Technical Information Center (DTIC), http://ww.dtic.mil/doctrine/jel/doddict/data/i/02760.html.

8. Chairman of the Joint Chiefs of Staff, *National Military Strategy to Combat Weapons of Mass Destruction*, Washington, DC, 13 February 2006, 7, http://www.defenselink. mil/pdf/NMS-CWMD2006.pdf.

9. See Wyn Q. Bowen, *Libya and Nuclear Proliferation: Stepping Back from the Brink* (IISS Adelphi Paper, May 2006); Målfrid Braut-Hegghammer, "Libya's Nuclear Turnaround: Perspectives from Tripoli," *Middle East Journal*, 62, no. 1 (Winter 2008), 55–72; Robert Litwak, *Regime Change: U.S. Strategy through the Prism of 9/11* (Washington, DC: Woodrow Wilson Centre Press, 2007); Bruce W. Jentleson and Christopher A. Whytock, "Who 'Won' Libya? The Force-Diplomacy Debate and Its Implications for Theory and Policy," *International Security*, 30, no. 3 (Winter 2005/6); Gordon Corera, *Shopping for Bombs: Nuclear Proliferation, Global Insecurity and the Rise and Fall of the A. Q. Khan Network* (London: Hurst, 2006).

10. Bowen, *Libya and Nuclear Proliferation*, 47–69.

11. Ibid., 25–45.

12. Ibid., 67.

13. Ibid., 47–69.

14. Ibid., 11–23.

15. Ibid., 58–69.

16. Ibid., 65–66.

17. Ibid., 63–64.

18. Butler Report, 20.

19. WMD Commission, 258.

20. James J. Wirtz, "Hiding in Plain Sight: Denial, Deception, and the Non-State Actor," *SAIS Review of International Affairs*, 27, no. 1 (Winter–Spring 2008), 55–63.

21. See, for example, Dr. Joshua Sinai, ANSER, Red Teaming the Terrorist Threat to Preempt the Next Waves of Catastrophic Terrorism, 14th Annual NDIA So/LIC Symposium & Exhibition, 12 February 2003.

22. Mary McCarthy, "The National Warning System: Striving for an Elusive Goal," *Defense Intelligence Journal*, 3, no. 1 (Spring 1994), 5.

23. Fritz W. Ermarth, "Signs and Portents: The 'I & W' Paradigm Post-9/11," *In the National Interest*, 2 October 2002, http://www.inthenationalinterest.com/Articles/Vol1Issue4/vol1issue4Ermarth.html.

24. Bowen, *Libya and Nuclear Proliferation*, 65–66.

25. Butler Report, 21–20.

26. WMD Commission, 252.

27. Intelligence and Security Committee Annual Report 2003–2004, House of Commons, Cm 6240, June 2004, http://webarchive.nationalarchives.gov.uk/+/http://www.cabinetoffice.gov.uk/media/cabinetoffice/corp/assets/publications/reports/intelligence/annualir0304.pdf, 26.

28. Michael Evans, "Libya Knew Game Was Up before Iraq War," *The Times*, 13 March 2004, 8; Douglas Frantz and Josh Meyer, "The Deal to Disarm Kadafi," *Los Angeles Times*, March 13, 2005; Bill Gertz, "Libyan Sincerity on Arms in Doubt," *Washington Times*, 9 September 2004, http://www.washingtontimes.com.

29. Evans, "Libya Knew Game Was Up before Iraq War," 8.

30. Ronald Bruce St. John, "Libyan Foreign Policy: Newfound Flexibility," *Orbis*, 47, no.3 (Summer 2003), 463-477, 469.

31. WMD Commission, 262.

32. Butler Report, 21.

33. Andrew C. Winner, "The Proliferation Security Initiative: The New Face of Interdiction," *Washington Quarterly*, 28, no. 2 (Spring 2005), 138.

34. Ibid.

35. For more information on this issue and an informative assessment of the PSI, see Winner, "The Proliferation Security Initiative."

36. See Jonathan S. Lockwood, "Sources of Error in Indications and Warning," *Defense Intelligence Journal*, 3, no. 1 (Spring 1994), 75–78, 81, 84.

37. WMD Commission, 253.

38. Ibid., 259.

39. Ibid., 260.

40. Ibid.

41. Ibid., 253–54.

42. Ibid., 253–61.

43. Ibid., 259–61.

13 Security Assurances and the Future of Proliferation

Bruno Tertrais

One dimension of the security setting that has largely been ignored when it comes to explaining decisions to acquire weapons of mass destruction (WMD) is the role of security "assurances," commitments to act or refrain from acting in the field of security. Scholars interested in nonproliferation often speak of *negative* security assurances, but little work has been done to understand the overall concept of "security assurances."[1] This chapter will address this shortcoming by exploring the role played by *positive* and *negative* assurances with regard slowing the proliferation of weapons of mass destruction. Security assurances are extremely diverse in type and scope, but can be divided into several broad categories. *Positive* assurances are commitments to assist a state in case of aggression. When they involve a commitment to defend a country, they are frequently called "security guarantees."[2] If a security guarantee implies the possible use of nuclear weapons, it is often referred to as a "nuclear umbrella." *Negative* assurances are commitments not to attack a country or to refrain from using certain means, such as nuclear weapons. Security assurances may be given urbi et orbi (to all), either in a unilateral communication or in a multilateral framework. As Table 13.1 demonstrates, they can be given to a specific country, a certain area, or a group of states.

POSITIVE SECURITY ASSURANCES AND PROLIFERATION DYNAMICS

Security guarantees by a nuclear-armed state, potentially involving the use of nuclear weapons to protect an ally, have played an important role in preventing proliferation. Security guarantees exist in various forms, from unilateral

TABLE 13.1

Typology of Security Assurances

	Positive	Negative
General	NWS to NNWS (UNSCR 984) [assistance/nuclear] Mutual commitments by treaty members —Parties to the BTWC Convention [mutual assistance/biological] —Parties to the CWC Convention [mutual assistance/chemical]	NWS to NNWS [nonuse/nuclear] Non-NPT members to NNWS —India [nonuse/nuclear] —Pakistan [nonuse/nuclear]
Regional	Mutual commitments by treaty members —Brussels Treaty [mutual assistance/generic] —Washington Treaty [mutual assistance/generic] —Rio Treaty [mutual assistance/generic] —ANZUS Treaty [mutual assistance/generic] —SEATO Treaty [mutual assistance/generic] —Tashkent Treaty [mutual assistance/generic] —Lisbon Treaty [mutual assistance/generic]	Mutual commitments by treaty members —U.N. Charter, Helsinki Final Act, etc. [nonaggression/generic] —Tlatelolco Treaty [nondeployment/nuclear] —Pelindaba Treaty [nondeployment/nuclear] —Bangkok Treaty [nondeployment/nuclear] —Semipalatinsk Treaty [nondeployment/nuclear] NWS to NWFZ Parties —Protocols to NWFZ treaties [nonuse, nondeployment/nuclear]
National	NWS to countries having renounced WMD —P4 to Belarus, Kazakhstan, Ukraine [assistance/nuclear] —U.K. to Libya [assistance/chemical, biological, nuclear] NWS to allies —U.S. to Japan [mutual assistance/generic] —U.S. to South Korea [mutual assistance/generic] —US, UK, France —Gulf States [assistance/generic]	NWS to countries having renounced WMD —P4 to Belarus, Kazakhstan, Ukraine [nonaggression/generic, nuclear/nonuse] Nondeployment commitments —NATO to Russia [nondeployment in Eastern Europe/nuclear] —South Korea to North Korea [nondeployment/nuclear] Nonaggression commitments —U.S. to North Korea [nonaggression/generic]

statements to formal alliances backed by permanent military deployments. For instance, the North Atlantic Organization Treaty (NATO) has played the role of a nonproliferation instrument. Article 5 of the Washington Treaty (1949) creates an obligation to assist any member state that finds itself a victim of an armed attack. This article has been widely interpreted as implying the possible use of nuclear weapons by the United States, the United Kingdom, and France in defense of their allies. NATO's "internal" nonproliferation role, however, is not limited to Article 5. Over years, the organization has developed a web of collective defense cooperation and consultation mechanisms, resulting in what could be called a "security blanket" that member states feel is secure. The shadow of U.S. nuclear weapons even extended beyond NATO's borders. One of the reasons Swedish officials abandoned their nuclear weapons program, for instance, was that they believed that there was a de facto nuclear umbrella covering their territory, because of its geographical situation.[3] It also helped that a secret U.S. pledge to defend Swedish territory backed up the geographic logic of Sweden's defense posture.[4]

To bolster the credibility of the U.S. nuclear guarantee, NATO created a unique collective system of nuclear planning that provides transparency to members. Since the mid-1960s, through the Nuclear Planning Group, NATO has developed a mechanism of consultation and planning for employment doctrine, which has given all members a "nuclear culture" and a say in the deciding under what circumstances nuclear weapons might be used. The creation of the Nuclear Planning Group was largely a quid pro quo for the abandonment of the "Multi-Lateral Force," an ambitious scheme that would have given non-nuclear countries such as Germany operational control of nuclear weapons.[5]

In the Asia-Pacific region, continued U.S. protection of several key allies has helped prevent them from going nuclear despite numerous temptations. Japan is protected by the Security Treaty between the United States and Japan (1951). South Korea is covered by the Mutual Defense Treaty between the United States and the Republic of Korea (1953). Taiwan, though no longer benefiting from the same security guarantee that it enjoyed until the U.S. recognition of Beijing, is still indirectly protected by the Taiwan Relations Act (1979).[6] Australia, for its part, is covered by the ANZUS Treaty (1951).

The importance of positive security assurances in preventing proliferation can be demonstrated a contrario. The lack of a strong security guarantee, or doubts about the scope and value of an existing one, have been key drivers of nuclear proliferation since 1945. In fact, an absence of positive security guarantees is a good starting point for telling the history of many national decisions to acquire nuclear weapons. Chinese leaders, for example, realized during the first Formosa Straits crisis (1954–55) that the Soviet Union could not be counted on in the face of U.S. nuclear threats. In response, Mao launched the country's nuclear program in 1956. The second crisis (1957–58) and the breakup with the Soviet Union in 1959 confirmed Mao's decision. Israeli leaders, whose very survival was put into question the day after the Israeli state was born, were reluctant to count on any other country for their security. Ben Gurion stated in 1955, "Our security problem could have two answers: if possible, political guarantees, but this is not up to us. But what depends on us, we must invest all our power."[7] Ben Gurion tried to obtain a security guarantee, asking the John F. Kennedy administration for a "bilateral security agreement," and even raised the possibility of membership in NATO.[8] But Washington agreed only to a general commitment to Israel's security and to an informal promise to support Israel in case of an Arab surprise attack—whereas Tel Aviv wanted a real defense treaty.[9] By the late 1960s, Ben Gurion had become convinced that no Western power would give his country a security guarantee.[10]

By contrast, Charles De Gaulle did not believe that the U.S. security guarantee to France was credible. The United States did not help French forces at Dien Bien Phu (1954), nor did it support the Suez operation (1956). The U.S. push for a strategy of flexible response after 1957 was seen as a sign of U.S. reluctance to defend Europe at the risk of nuclear war. De Gaulle's decision to "operationalize" the French nuclear program when he returned to power in 1958 was in no small part based on his belief that "nobody in the world, in particular nobody in America, can say whether, where, how, or to what extent U.S. nuclear arms would be used to defend Europe."[11] In fact, he did not believe in nuclear guarantees at all: one could not expect to be protected by a state that would risk its very survival in making good on its extended deterrent threats.[12]

India tried to get formal security guarantees from the United States in the early 1960s. Washington hesitated, in particular after the 1962 India-China War.[13] There was a commitment in principle to assist New Delhi against Beijing.[14] Nevertheless, U.S. officials did not want to find themselves embroiled in a war against the Sino-Soviet bloc, and India did not want to commit itself in the U.S. fight against communism.[15] Though New Delhi justified its decision not to sign the NPT by dint of the lack of a credible security guarantee, the reality was more the other way round: New Delhi was not prepared to place its survival in the hands of Washington—or Moscow, for that matter.[16]

Pakistan also sought security guarantees before launching a nuclear program. There was a U.S.-Pakistan Agreement of Cooperation (1959), which committed Washington to the defense of its ally. But Islamabad did not trust that the United States would come to its aid in the event of a war against India because the agreement was aimed at resisting Soviet aggression. Pakistani officials noticed that Washington had supported India in 1962, and that it did not come to defend Pakistan in 1965 and 1971.[17] Zulfiqar Ali Bhutto thought that Pakistan's security was likely to be sacrificed on the altar of great power relations. Pakistan's nuclear program was launched in 1972. The next year, Bhutto denounced the 1959 agreement with the United States. He sought rapprochement with China, but held out little hope that Beijing would offer a formal military alliance.[18] After the 1974 Indian test, Islamabad tried again to get Western or Chinese security guarantees, but to no avail.[19] The nuclear program then went into full gear. After the Soviet invasion of Afghanistan, U.S. President Jimmy Carter reaffirmed the 1959 pledge and asked Congress to reaffirm it.[20] Pakistan agreed that it was a step forward, but it was not as good as a treaty commitment.[21] In 1998, after the Indian tests, Islamabad hesitated before doing the same. Some in the Pakistani elite argued that the lack of security guarantees was in itself a reason to do it.[22] Nawaz Sharif tried to obtain U.S. protection, but did not succeed.[23] Today, Pakistan possesses a nuclear arsenal.

North Korea's leader, Kim Il-Sung, had doubts about the protection given by the alliance treaties signed in 1961 with the Soviet Union and China.[24] A review of Soviet archives showed that North Korea's program was in no small part driven by the fear of being abandoned by Moscow and Beijing in case of a war with the United States.[25] After the Cold War, China reportedly made it clear to Pyongyang that it should not count on Beijing's protection in all circumstances.[26] The North Korean nuclear decision might in part be driven by a perception that with the end of the Cold War, there is minimal political support for the de facto extended deterrent guarantees it once enjoyed.

South Africa never benefited from any external security guarantee. In the early days of the Cold War, the ruling Nationalist party sought to ally itself firmly with the West but was rebuffed when it asked for membership in NATO. In the 1970s, increasing Soviet influence and Cuban military presence in the region aggravated Pretoria's sense of isolation. Simultaneously, apartheid had become increasingly unpopular throughout the world, and congressional pressures forced the United States to terminate its assistance to the regime. As a consequence, according to Roy Horton, "it seemed apparent to the South African leadership that some other means had to be applied to secure Western support in times of crisis." In response to this growing sense of isolation and threat, South Africans began to field an operational weapons capability in 1977. In 1978, Pretoria adopted a strategy of "gradual revelation" if attacked, in order to force Western intervention.[27]

The issue of security guarantees also was a key factor in the political calculus of most countries that considered acquiring nuclear weapons. South Korea, for instance, was tempted to get the bomb each time the United States seemed to diminish its security commitment.[28] In July 1969, President Richard Nixon announced the Guam doctrine: Asian allies of the United States were to take a greater part of the common defense burden. Washington began to withdraw one of the two divisions stationed on the peninsula as it initiated a rapprochement with the People's Republic of China. This led Seoul to consider going nuclear, starting a military program toward the end of 1970. In response, Washington threatened to cut off economic relations and to withdraw all remaining forces.[29] Henry Kissinger informed Park that the U.S. security guarantee would no longer be valid if Seoul persisted in developing nuclear weapons. In exchange for the renunciation of its nuclear ambitions, the United States announced that it would hold annual joint exercises with South Korea.[30] South Korea signed the NPT in 1975. Two years later, in 1977, President Carter announced that the United States would withdraw the second U.S. division and U.S. nuclear weapons from South Korea before 1982. A few months later, Seoul announced its intention to build a reprocessing plant and made it clear that it would resume its program unless Washington changed its mind. The Carter administration abandoned its conventional and nuclear withdrawal plans in 1978.

Taiwan launched its nuclear project in 1967, following Beijing's first nuclear tests.[31] Taiwanese officials felt increasingly abandoned by major powers that were in the process of recognizing the People's Republic as the legitimate government of China. The death of Chiang Kai-shek and U.S. pressures led to the abandonment of the program in 1976. In 1979, following the U.S.-China rapprochement, the Taiwan Relations Act replaced the mutual defense treaty. In response, Taipei apparently reconsidered the nuclear option. In 1987, it started constructing a uranium enrichment facility. Renewed U.S. pressure led Taiwan to give up its nuclear intentions in 1988.[32]

Several other countries that are not traditionally considered to be proliferation risks also considered nuclear weapons programs. These nations sometimes thought that they were falling outside the bipolar military system. For instance, Australia twice considered a nuclear program.[33] A key motivation was that Canberra thought that the ANZUS Treaty (1951) security guarantee appeared to be less solid than the one provided by the NATO treaty.[34] Others—Sweden, Switzerland, and Yugoslavia—had a neutral or nonaligned status, leaving them without any security guarantee deliberations.[35] Ukraine's calculations on whether or not to give up the nuclear weapons it had inherited from the former Soviet Union also were influenced by the question of security guarantees and its general vulnerability as it emerged as an independent state. Kiev had decided not to join the Commonwealth of Independent States, and Russian security guarantees were available only if Ukraine was a member of that organization. The country also was not eligible for NATO's Partnership for Peace program. Kiev agreed to give up Soviet nuclear weapons only after the Trilateral Agreement of January 1994 assuaged its security concerns. These concerns were further addressed by the nuclear weapons states in the *memoranda* of December 1994.[36]

The Expansion of Security Guarantees since1990

Although the demise of the Soviet Union brought an end to a bipolar system of alliances, a significant expansion of security guarantees has taken place since the end of the Cold War. The demise of the Soviet Union allowed for the enlargement of NATO, the disarmament of three former Soviet republics, and the creation of a new system of Russian military alliances. Growing concerns about ballistic and WMD proliferation, notably in the Middle East and Northeast Asia, also have led Western allies to increase the number and value of their national security commitments.

Reinforced security guarantees were given to countries in the Gulf region after the 1990–91 Iraq War. From 1990 to 2003, there was a U.S. military presence in Saudi Arabia designed to deter Iraqi aggression. Today, there is a de facto commitment to defend several of the smaller Gulf states, notably Qatar, which has become the new hub of U.S. military deployments in the region.[37] European powers also have given security guarantees to several Gulf states. In addition to its long-standing commitment to the security of Djibouti (1977), France has signed defense agreements with Kuwait (1992), Qatar (1994, 1998), and the United Arab Emirates (1996, 2009).[38] The United Kingdom has its own defense commitments, most notably with the United Arab Emirites (1996).[39]

Between 1999 and 2009, NATO brought in thirteen new members. It has dramatically increased the number of countries protected by the Article 5 guarantee and more specifically by U.S., U.K., and French nuclear forces. As a result, the United States now has by far the greatest number of military allies in the world (more than 50 countries).[40]

The George W. Bush administration reinforced several existing bilateral alliances, partly due to an increase in potential nuclear threats stemming from China, North Korea, and Iran. As early as 2001, President Bush declared that there was a U.S. obligation to defend Taiwan in case of Chinese attack, and pledged to do "whatever it took to help Taiwan defend herself."[41] After September 11, the defense relationship with Japan and Australia was strengthened; a new trilateral alliance seems to be in the making.[42] In 2006, Bush became the first U.S. president to state clearly that Washington would defend Israel by military force.[43] After the North Korean nuclear test, the U.S. nuclear commitment to Seoul and Japan was reaffirmed in a particularly strong way.[44] Washington also has acknowledged the importance of "nuclear umbrellas" in defusing proliferation in the 2001 and 2010 Nuclear Posture Reviews.

The creation of the European Union and the French rapprochement with NATO in the early 1990s have led Paris to affirm that its nuclear forces protect common allied interests. For instance, in 2001 President Jacques Chirac said that the French nuclear capability is part of the Atlantic Alliance's "global deterrent," and that his appreciation of any threat to French vital interests—those which are covered by nuclear deterrence—would "naturally take into account the growing solidarity of European Union countries."[45] In 2006, he stated that "the defense of allied countries" could be part of French vital interests.[46] This sentence was interpreted as signifying that French security commitments toward the Gulf region could potentially include a nuclear dimension.

Russia also has created its own military alliance through the Collective Security Treaty (1992). In 2002, the Collective Security Treaty Organization was created, with a view to establishing a parallel security framework to NATO. As of June 2007, the organization included Armenia, Belarus, Uzbekistan, Kazakhstan, Kirghizia, and Tajikistan, which now seems to be covered implicitly by a Russian nuclear guarantee. Even though Russian officials refer sometimes to all Commonwealth of Independent States countries as being protected by Moscow's nuclear forces, it is reasonable to assume that only Collective Security Treaty Organization countries are under the Russian nuclear umbrella.

How Much Do "Nuclear Umbrellas" Matter?

History suggests that positive security assurances can play a critical role in preventing WMD proliferation. Nevertheless, only strong defense commitments, especially those that include a nuclear dimension, have bolstered the nonproliferation regime. Vague promises of "assistance" are not enough to prevent proliferation. As Llewelyn Thompson noted while serving as an adviser to the Lyndon B. Johnson administration, "It is doubtful that a country which feels really threatened and is capable of building nuclear weapons will indefinitely refrain from doing so merely in exchange for general or conditional guarantees."[47] Most important, the recipient state must be convinced that the assurances given meet its security needs. Soviet and Chinese protection did not prevent North Korea from advancing on the nuclear path; existing formal U.S. guarantees did not prevent France from going nuclear, or Australia from considering doing the same. Soviet "friendship" did not prevent India from embarking on its own program. American protection did not prevent several Asian countries from embarking on a nuclear program. A U.S. commitment to the security of Saudi Arabia did not prevent Riyadh from acquiring medium-range ballistic missiles in the late 1980s. Here, the psychology of leaders and "mythmakers" probably matters a great deal. Whatever is stated in written or oral form, the beliefs of recipient governments regarding the value of security commitments, and how they transmit it to the next generation, matter significantly—for instance, a security guarantee may be judged as credible by one set of leaders but not by the next.

IS THERE A ROLE FOR
INFORMAL POSITIVE SECURITY ASSURANCES?

Informal positive security assurances are general commitments to assist countries in case of a WMD attack that often take the form of stating an intention, rather than the form of a legally binding pledge. They originate in U.S. thinking about how to best prevent further nuclear proliferation after the 1964 Chinese test. Specifically, President Johnson said that "nations that do not seek nuclear weapons can be sure that if they need our strong support against some threat of nuclear blackmail, then they will have it."[48] Such assurances were first given in 1968 in response to the concerns of Non Nuclear Weapons States (NNWS) about vulnerabilities created by the NPT. U.N. Security Council Resolution 255 (UNSCR 255) took note of these concerns and gave special responsibility to Nuclear Weapons States (NWS): "[N]uclear-weapon state permanent members would have to act immediately to provide assistance, in accordance with their obligations under the United Nations Charter" to any NNWS party to the NPT that was "a victim of an act or object of a threat of aggression in which nuclear weapons are used."[49] The vague nature of the text was a reflection of the fact that the U.S. administration "had no intention of making the United States the policeman of the world."[50] Thus, from Washington's point of view, UNSCR 255 merely reaffirmed U.S. responsibilities as stated in the UN Charter.[51] A few years later, parties to the Biological and Toxin Weapons Convention pledged to assist one another in case of a biological threat: "Each State

Party to this Convention undertakes to provide or support assistance, in accordance with the United Nations Charter, to any Party to the Convention which so requests, if the Security Council decides that such Party has been exposed to danger as a result of violation of the Convention."[52] Mutual assurances of assistance in case of a chemical attack also were provided to the signatories of the Chemical Weapons Convention (CWC): "Each State Party has the right to request and . . . to receive assistance and protection against the use or threat of use of chemical weapons if it considers that: (a) Chemical weapons have been used against it; (b) Riot control agents have been used against it as a method of warfare; or (c) It is threatened by actions or activities of any State that are prohibited for States Parties by Article I."[53]

Country-specific positive security assurances have been given to several countries as a quid pro quo for having renounced nuclear, chemical, or biological weapons. The former Soviet Republics of Belarus, Kazakhstan, and Ukraine received informal positive security assurances from France, Russia, the United Kingdom, and the United States in the form of *memoranda* in December 1994.[54] Similar informal assurances were extended to North Korea in the 1994 Agreed Framework. A country-specific informal assurance was also given by the United Kingdom to Libya in 2006. In addition to the standard language on the intention to seek "immediate Security Council action" in case of a nuclear threat, the assurance to Libya included a provision to seek "appropriate action by the Security Council" in case of a chemical or biological threat.[55]

It is unlikely that such informal, general statements to "assist" a state attacked with weapons of mass destruction have had any major role in proliferation dynamics. They are too vague to have made any real difference. The fact that most of them are mutual or multilateral does not necessarily reinforce their credibility. Such arrangements raise the well-known "free-rider" problem. And if assistance was to be directed by the U.N. Security Council, any response to an aggression by a NWS could be met by a veto of the same NWS in its capacity of permanent member.

NEGATIVE SECURITY ASSURANCES AND PROLIFERATION DYNAMICS

Calls for assurances of nonuse of nuclear weapons against non-nuclear-weapons states were first heard during the mid-1960s during the discussions that would lead to the signature of the NPT. The first Negative Security Assurances, however, were given through the creation of Nuclear Weapons Free

Zones. This concept, which can be viewed as an offspring of the Cuban Missile Crisis, was included in the NPT (Article 7). Latin American countries agreed, through the Tlatelolco Treaty (1968), to refrain from deploying nuclear weapons on their territory—as well as to avoid developing them.[56] The treaty of Tlatelolco became a template for the Rarotonga Treaty (1985), which established a nuclear-weapons-free zone in the South Pacific. These protocols were important because they restricted the right of some nuclear weapons states to deploy nuclear weapons on parts of their own national territories. As international conventions subject to ratification, they also created legally binding commitments.[57] Nuclear weapons states, in particular the United States, readily agreed to associate themselves with the initiative through separate protocols that committed them to avoid deploying nuclear weapons in the area and to refrain from using nuclear weapons against the parties, unless allied with a nuclear weapons state.

The first global, blanket negative security assurances were given through unilateral statements in response to demands by non-nuclear-weapons states made at the First U.N. Special Session on Disarmament of 1978.[58] With the exception of China, which had proclaimed in 1964 a doctrine of unconditional no-first-use, all nuclear weapons states qualified their negative security assurances by noting that they would retain the right to use nuclear weapons against a non-nuclear-weapons state if that state was allied to a nuclear weapons state.

In 1993, country-specific negative security assurances were given to three former Soviet republics. That same year, Russia's renunciation of the Soviet no-first-use policy allowed it to adopt doctrinal language similar to that of the other nuclear weapon states. In 1994, negative security assurances were promised to North Korea in the Agreed Framework. In 1995, during the run-up to the NPT Conference, many non-nuclear-weapons states demanded stronger negative security assurances as the price for their agreement to an indefinite extension of the NPT. The nuclear weapon states agreed, but the United States made it clear that the quid pro quo had to be reversed: negative security assurances would only be in force if the NPT extension occurred.[59] Finally, in the 2010 U.S. Nuclear Posture Review, Washington significantly revised and expanded its negative assurance.[60]

New nuclear-weapons-free zones have been created in Southeast Asia (Bangkok Treaty, 1995), Africa (Pelindaba Treaty, 1996), Mongolia (1998), and Central Asia (Semipalatinsk Treaty, 2006). Although some of these agreements have not yet entered force, signatories of the treaties are obliged to refrain from hosting nuclear weapons on their territories. A similar obligation was undertaken when NATO adopted the "three no's" policy of 1997. To reassure Russia, the alliance stated that it had "no intention, no plan, and no reason" to base nuclear weapons on the territory of the new Central European members. In the same vein, the Six Party Talks on North Korea produced an assurance of "non-deployment" of nuclear weapons, which was given by Seoul in 2005.[61] India and Pakistan also have stated that they would abstain from using nuclear weapons against non-nuclear-weapons states in language similar to the negative security assurances given by other nuclear weapons states.[62]

As a result of these initiatives, two emerging norms have developed regarding negative security assurances. One is a perceived tradition of nuclear nonuse against a non-nuclear-weapons state. The other is a tradition of nondeployment of nuclear weapons on other countries' soil, which emerges from the combination of the multiplication of nuclear-weapons-free zones, specific nondeployment commitments, and the gradual withdrawal of most nuclear weapons from non-nuclear-weapon states' territories.[63]

The Demand for Guarantees

Non-nuclear countries have consistently called for stronger and more explicit negative security guarantees, especially in return for nonproliferation commitments. Nuclear weapon states did not see these commitments as detrimental to their security. The "escape clause" allowing for a nuclear response in case of an attack by an ally of a nuclear weapon state was viewed as covering the most dangerous contingencies. As Joseph Pilat put it, "During the Cold War, there was little possibility that a nonnuclear state would be attacked with nuclear weapons unless it was allied with another nuclear power."[64]

Since the end of the Cold War, nuclear and non-nuclear-weapons states have hardened their positions. Representatives of non-nuclear-weapons states noted that the final documents of the 1995 NPT Review and Extension Conference should mention a possible reinforcement of existing negative security guarantees. The "Principles and Objectives" document opened the door for the reinforcement of negative security assurances: "[F]urther steps should be considered to assure non-nuclear weapons states parties to the Treaty against the use or threat of use of nuclear weapons. These steps could take the form of an internationally legally binding instrument."[65] Nevertheless, by insisting on conditional assurances, the nuclear weapons states ensured that they would retain their freedom of action. Nuclear weapons states believe that they have good reasons for opposing any reinforcement of negative security assurances. All of them have signed both the Biological and Toxin Weapons Convention and the Chemical Weapons Convention, and, with the possible exception of China, none of them maintain biological or chemical weapons capabilities, making it impossible to respond in kind. From their point of view, only the preservation of a nuclear option remains to deter chemical or biological attacks. This is the case in particular for Russia, whose unease vis-à-vis Western conventional superiority is well known.

Since the 1995 commitments, nuclear countries have qualified their negative security assurances in two different ways.[66] One is to highlight the existence of the right to self-defense, which is recognized by Article 51 of the U.N. Charter. The other is to highlight the principle of "belligerent reprisals," which allows for a previously unlawful act in response to an unlawful act (as long as the response meets the self-defense criteria of necessity and proportionality). In 1995, for instance, the French government stated that its negative security assurances "did not affect our inalienable right to self defense" and that "our deterrent covers any kind of threat against our vital interests, including of course that of WMD produced and used in spite of the international ban against them."[67] The United States has also made several statements to assert its right to be the first to use nuclear weapons. In 1996, Robert Bell, senior advisor to the president, stated: "[We] reserve the right to use nuclear weapons first in a conflict whether it's CW, BW [chemical weapons, biological weapons], or for that matter conventional." He added that the aggressor's "standing under the Non-proliferation Treaty or an equivalent international convention" would be taken into account.[68] In 1998, the British government stated that "the use of chemical or biological weapons by any state would be a grave breach of international law. A state which chose to use chemical or biological weapons against the UK should expect us to exercise our right of self defense and to make a proportionate response."[69] Other similar statements have been made by the three countries more recently. Between 2001 and 2008, for example, U.S. opposition to legally binding negative security assurances has been expressed forcefully by American diplomats at the 2004 Preparatory Committee to the 2005 NPT Review Conference.[70] Even the U.S. 2010 Nuclear Posture Review maintained caveats to the revised U.S. negative security assurance, stating that it would not be valid for Nuclear Weapon States and for non-nuclear countries violating their nuclear nonproliferation commitments.[71]

Nonaggression Commitments as Nonproliferation Tools

A new feature of nonproliferation policies is the multiplication of nonaggression commitments, which can be viewed as the mirror image of security guarantees. Belarus, Kazakhstan, and Ukraine received significant and broad assurances in December 1994 from France, Russia, the United Kingdom, and the United States. The signatories agreed to "respect the independence and sovereignty and the existing borders" of the three countries, and to "refrain from the threat or use of force against the[ir] territorial integrity or political independence."[72] Throughout the diplomatic process of normalization that took place over the Lockerbie airline bombing case, Libya sought security assurances that the United States and the United Kingdom sought a change in regime behavior, not regime change. This seems to have played a significant part in Libya's decision to abandon its clandestine nuclear program.[73] In 2003, before making a final commitment to disarm in 2003, "the Libyans asked for non-aggression pacts and other security guarantees."[74] The deal was reportedly struck only after Qadhafi was reassured that Bush would not seek "regime change," and would settle for "policy change."[75]

North Korea has long demanded negative security assurances. The 1994 Agreed Framework included a promise by the United States to give a country-specific negative security assurance (that would have been equivalent to the one given to the former Soviet republics). Pyongyang also has demanded an assurance of nonaggression. Unilateral statements to that effect by Washington in 2003–4 were formalized by the September 2005 agreement, whereby the United States affirmed that it had "no intention to attack or invade the DPRK [Democratic People's Republic of Korea] with nuclear or conventional weapons," and pledged to respect North Korea's sovereignty.[76]

These examples show that countries which fear external attack and acquire weapons of mass destruction attach value to commitments of nonaggression. These so called countries of concern have to be taken into account when thinking about the future of nonproliferation policies. Security assurances must address a nation's specific security concerns before they can influence a nation's decision to eliminate its nuclear arsenal.[77]

THE FUTURE ROLE OF SECURITY ASSURANCES
IN PREVENTING PROLIFERATION

Further efforts to limit the proliferation of nuclear weapons may require an increase in the number of security guarantees and the reinforcement of existing ones. Growing concerns about nuclear proliferation and the possible emergence of new nuclear arsenals are likely to "test" existing security commitments. Gulf countries, NATO members, and East Asian allies will ask for stronger and more explicit security guarantees, especially if Iran develops an operational nuclear capability.[78] Riyadh probably benefits from a U.S. pledge of protection, but this guarantee is based on vague statements and private assurances.[79] According to U.S. ambassador Chas Freeman, in 2003 King Fahd asked for a nuclear guarantee in case Iran produced the bomb.[80] Several sources claim that three options for the Saudi nuclear future were considered that year by Riyadh: a nuclear deterrent; a security guarantee; or a nuclear-weapons-free zone in the region.[81]

In 1991, Turkish officials expressed their dismay as some Atlantic Alliance members voiced their reluctance to deploy NATO defenses on Turkish territory, raising questions about the validity of NATO's security guarantee given to Ankara. Immediately before the invasion of Iraq, a crisis of confidence developed with NATO when several alliance members refused to invoke Article 4 of the Washington Treaty (which calls for consultations among members in case one of them believes its security is threatened), thus repeating, in the view of Turkish officials, the experience of 1991. As Ian Lesser put it, "In the absence of a predictable Western security guarantee, Ankara might consider deterrent capabilities of its own."[82]

There are several ways to reinforce existing security guarantees. Public statements can be made more explicit. The fact that it was Secretary of State Condoleezza Rice who came in person to Japan to reaffirm the U.S. nuclear umbrella after the 2006 North Korean nuclear test was seen as important by Japanese officials. Commitments can be formalized in a defense treaty. They also can be institutionalized through military engagement and "habits of cooperation."[83] Existing guarantees can be multilateralized; for instance, France, the United Kingdom, and the United States could give joint reassurances to some Gulf countries if Iran went nuclear. Missile defense—"extended deterrence through denial"—will likely be an increasingly important commitment of "reassurance" toward allies. This will be all the more important since the practice of deploying nuclear weapons on allied territory has now become marginal: today only five non-nuclear-weapons states are reported to host nuclear weapons (U.S. B-61 bombs).[84] But the potential role of stationing nuclear weapons on foreign territory should not be discarded. Precisely because it is no longer a standard practice, deployment abroad would now be one of the strongest possible signs of guaranteeing a country's security when faced with a serious threat.[85]

The Limits of Policy

Security guarantees offer no magic bullet when it comes to the prevention of proliferation. Because a clear defense commitment is likely to be accepted by a friendly state, not a potential enemy, several dilemmas reduce the effectiveness of various types of assurances. The first series of dilemmas concerns the reinforcement of existing guarantees. Countries that give a security commitment generally want to preserve a margin of maneuver and not be caught in "entangling alliances." For example, a key reason why Article 5 of the Washington Treaty is vague is that the U.S. Congress would not have sanctioned an automatic commitment to war.[86] Fear of a "commitment trap" is one reason why U.S., U.K., and French leaders have chosen to obscure the nature of their response to a chemical or biological weapons attack.[87] The CWC language on mutual assistance offers several options due to Washington's desire to avoid being bound to provide a particular type of assistance.[88]

Governments that offer a security guarantee also are aware that states can be emboldened by "umbrellas" and embark on dangerous adventures. This is why the United States never wanted to give Taiwan a complete assurance of support in any contingency, which could induce Taipei to declare its independence, leading to conflict with Beijing. It is thus no coincidence that the term "ambiguity" has been frequently associated with the expression "security commitments." Security guarantees can pose ethical problems to the "donor" and to the "recipient." Questions have been raised about the wisdom of giving protection to authoritarian regimes, such as Pakistan, or to quasi-fundamentalist states, such as Saudi Arabia. By contrast, some countries may not want to be protected by the United States. In 2003, Mexico symbolically decided to withdraw from the Rio Treaty as a protest against the Iraq War. A formal security guarantee to Saudi Arabia, which would mean open and complete reliance on the United States for Saudi security, could raise anti-American sentiment in the kingdom.[89]

Another dilemma exists regarding the possible deployment of nuclear weapons. Critics of NATO's nuclear posture have a point when they say that the alliance has established a pattern that it does not want other states to emulate.[90] In legal terms, nothing would preclude Islamabad from deploying nuclear weapons in Saudi Arabia, or forbid the presence of Chinese nuclear weapons in, say, Burma, or prohibit the stationing of Iranian nuclear weapons on Syrian soil—as long as these weapons were not under the control of the recipient country.[91] Several countries would be more than happy to use the U.S. precedent to justify this type of nuclear deployment policy.

A second series of dilemmas is created by an increase in the number of security guarantees. Growth in the number of security guarantees can decrease their individual value. As an adviser to the Johnson administration put it in 1965, "The character of our determination will be diluted if we have 20 such commitments and our fundamental image of capability to defend the free world might be impaired."[92] A large number of security guarantees would also increase the risk that one of them will sooner or later be tested in a crisis. The problem for the guarantor is that it may have to intervene *forcefully* regardless of the direct interests at stake in order to maintain its reputation as a reliable ally. The greater the number of allies, the higher the stakes. Some in the Johnson administration argued that a key reason to remain in Vietnam was that absent a U.S. victory, the credibility of U.S. guarantees in Asia would be weakened. The same argument has sometimes been made more recently about Iraq.

THE FUTURE OF NEGATIVE ASSURANCES

Would future nonproliferation efforts benefit from a reinforcement of negative security assurances? The case here is much weaker when compared with the case for positive security assurances.

Negative security assurances create their own problems. For instance, assurances of nuclear nonuse can weaken deterrence, and thus lower the costs of aggression. Countries receiving a nuclear nonuse pledge could even interpret it as implying that chemical or biological weapons can be used without any risk of nuclear retaliation. Negative security assurances also can have a negative impact on allies. The Johnson administration refused to adopt a no-first-use policy, inter alia for fears that it would weaken security guarantees given to its allies.[93] The 2010 U.S. Nuclear Posture Review maintained caveats to the revised U.S. negative assurance in order to reassure allies such as Japan, which face a significant non-nuclear threat. For these reasons, the impact of negative security assurances could run counter to the principle of "undiminished security for all" claimed in NPT Review Conference documents.

Country-specific negative security assurances are especially problematic when they are designed to have an impact on the chemical, biological, or nuclear programs of an unfriendly state. Japan has reportedly urged Washington to avoid offering Pyongyang any concession that would weaken the U.S. deterrent, including an assurance that the United States would not use nuclear weapons against North Korea.[94] The North Korean case also shows that the desire for a country-specific promise of nonuse or nonaggression can easily become an instrument of blackmail; giving security assurances can open the door to never-ending demands.[95] Negative security assurances may raise ethical problems if the price of nuclear renunciation is the recognition of the regime or at least an assurance of "no regime change," as was the case for Libya. Would Western countries want to give such an assurance to Iran without at least a clear commitment to cease support for Hezbollah and Hamas?

The value of negative security assurances also is diminished by the fact that they are not necessarily believed by recipient states. This is one of the reasons some countries actually say that they do not want Western negative security assurances. Despite frequent discussions in diplomatic circles about the relevance of security assurances to Iran, Tehran has repeatedly made it clear that it was not interested in Western promises of nonaggression.[96]

It also is possible that negative security assurances have become more important as a raison d'être of the diplomatic service of some countries, notably the Non-Aligned Movement, than as a real nonproliferation tool. Many African countries, for instance, have yet to ratify the Pelindaba Treaty. As a U.S. analyst put it, "[T]he failure to bring some NWFZs [nuclear-weapons-free zones] into force suggests to some that the goal of legally binding negative security assurances may not have the priority that they are rhetorically accorded by many states."[97] If protocols to all existing nuclear-weapons-free zones were to come into force, nearly four-fifths of the nonaligned countries would be covered by legally binding commitments of nuclear nonuse —thereby making a new, global international instrument relevant only to a handful of countries.[98] For all these reasons, the multiplication or reinforcement of generic, blanket negative security assurances have little chance of becoming a priority of the international community as a whole.

CONCLUSION

Security assurances are a key parameter of proliferation dynamics, and their analysis has often been neglected in the mainstream intellectual debate about weapons of mass destruction. If the above analysis is correct, countries which are the most likely to be tempted by a nuclear program in the coming years are those that, in light of the threats they perceive, may not be satisfied with the security guarantees they currently have. Japan, Saudi Arabia, Taiwan, Turkey, and Ukraine are states that seem to fit this category. Country-specific promises of nonaggression or nonuse may be important confidence-building measures.

Stemming proliferation may require additional negative security assurances, especially to countries that are not part of existing alliances.

Conversely, vague, generic positive and negative security assurances, such as the ones that were acknowledged by UNSCR 984, have little relevance except as symbolic gestures. Positive and negative security assurances failed to have an impact on the nuclear programs of India, Pakistan, Israel, North Korea, Iran, and Libya. There is no reason to believe that turning general assurances into legally binding instruments would bring any tangible nonproliferation benefit. If one assumes that the efficiency of deterrence supposes that the adversary is unable to calculate the exact costs and risks that would be associated with aggression, then there is an inherent limit to what it is possible to achieve in terms of strengthening security assurances for the purpose of nonproliferation without compromising deterrence. Additionally, positive and negative security assurances can potentially work at cross purposes. Stronger commitments to protect or assist a country in case of aggression run counter to the very purpose of negative security assurances, which is to reassure countries that weapons of mass destruction will not be used against them. Stronger commitments to refrain from military action run counter to the very purpose of positive security assurances, which is to reassure countries that they will be protected if chemical, biological, or nuclear weapons are used against them.

NOTES

1. Precedents include Michael Wheeler, *Positive and Negative Security Assurances*, PRAC Paper no. 9, Center for International and Security Studies at Maryland, University of Maryland, February 1994; Amy F. Woolf with Ross Kaplan, *Nuclear Weapons Proliferation: The Role of Security Assurances in Nonproliferation Policy,* CRS Report for Congress, 95-984 F, 15 September 1995; and Joseph F. Pilat, "Reassessing Security Assurances in a Unipolar World," *Washington Quarterly,* 28, no. 2 (2005), 159–70.

2. The expression "security assurance" is the one most frequently used in policy and analysis. The expression "security guarantee" generally refers to a *positive* security assurance. (Some countries or languages use both words without any clear distinction; for instance, the words "assurance" can be translated in French either by *"assurance"* or *"garantie."*) For the purpose of this paper, the expression "security guarantee" refers to a defense commitment.

3. Paul Cole, *Sweden without the Bomb. The Conduct of a Nuclear-Capable Nation without Nuclear Weapons,* MR-460, The RAND Corporation, 1994, xii.

4. NSC 6006/1 (1960) stated that the United States should *"be prepared to come to the assistance of Sweden"* in case of aggression. Another directive, dated 1962, stated that

Washington will *"undertake to come to the assistance"* of Sweden. Per T. Ohlsson, *Close Friends and Distant: Relations between the United States and Sweden over 200 Years,* Columbia University, 23 September 2003.

5. In addition to being covered by the NATO guarantee, ten European Union members are signatories of the Modified Brussels Treaty (1954), which includes a mutual defense commitment and was not superseded by the NATO treaty.

6. Thailand and the Philippines are also covered by U.S. security guarantees. Neither of these two countries, however, has ever been considered a serious WMD proliferation risk.

7. Quoted in Avner Cohen, *Israel and the Bomb* (New York: Columbia University Press, 1998), 43.

8. It is not widely known that De Gaulle had, in effect, given a security guarantee to Israel: *"[If] Israel is attacked, we will not let it be destroyed."* Press conference at the Elysée Palace, 27 November 1967, in Charles de Gaulle, *Discours & Messages,* vol. 5 (Paris: Plon, 1970), 132.

9. Cohen, *Israel and the Bomb,* 122–23.

10. Ibid., 66.

11. Press conference at the Elysée Palace, 14 January 1963, in De Gaulle, *Discours & Messages,* vol. 4, 73.

12. "You see, for a long time, one could count on the automaticity of alliances, because they were totally committing the existence of a nation. Today, atomic warfare puts all commitments into question. Can you imagine a U.S. President taking the risk of condemning to death tens of millions of Americans in application of an alliance treaty?" As reported by Alain Peyrefitte, *C'était De Gaulle* (Paris: Gallimard, 2002), 707.

13. Anand Giridharadas, "JFK Faced India-China Dilemma," *International Herald Tribune,* 26 August 2005.

14. See A. G. Noorani, "The Nuclear Guarantee Episode," *Frontline,* 18, no. 12 (June 2001), 9–22.

15. Francis J. Gavin, "Blasts from the Past: Proliferation Lessons from the 1960s," *International Security,* 29, no. 3 (Winter 2004–5), 118.

16. George Bunn, "The Legal Status of U.S. Negative Security Assurances to Nuclear Non-Nuclear Weapon States," *Nonproliferation Review,* Spring–Summer 1997, 13.

17. During the 1965 war, Pakistan invoked the 1959 agreement, but Washington chose to suspend all assistance to both countries. During the 1971 war, Islamabad saw that the deployment of a U.S. carrier group did not have any influence on Indian decision-making.

18. In 1965, China had recommended that Pakistan withdraw its forces. In 1971, Beijing had supported Islamabad, but then Moscow had issued threats to destroy the Chinese arsenal. Steve Weissman and Herbert Krosney, *The Islamic Bomb* (New York: Times Books, 1981), 51.

19. Naeem Ahmad Salik, "Regional Dynamics and Deterrence (2): South Asia," *Contemporary Security Policy,* 25, no. 1 (April 2004), 185.

20. Jimmy Carter, *State of the Union Address,* 23 January 1980.

21. Dennis Kux, *The United States and Pakistan 1947–2000: Disenchanted Allies* (Washington, DC: Woodrow Wilson Center Press, 2001), 249.

22. Hasan Askari-Rizvi, "Pakistan's Nuclear Testing," in Lowell Dittmer (ed.), *South Asia's Nuclear Security Dilemma* (New York: M. E. Sharpe, 2005), 107.

23. Owen Bennett Jones, *Pakistan: Eye of the Storm* (New Haven: Yale University Press, 2003), 192.

24. Alexandre Y. Mansourov, "The Origins, Evolution, and Current Politics of the North Korean Nuclear Program," *Nonproliferation Review,* Spring–Summer 1995, 28. Article 1 of the treaty with China stated: "Should either of the Contracting Parties suffer armed attack by any State or coalition of States and thus find itself in a state of war, the other Contracting Party shall immediately extend military and other assistance with all the means at its disposal." Article 2 of the treaty with the Soviet Union stated: "In the event of one of the Contracting Parties being subjected to the armed attack by any state or several states jointly and thus being involved in a state of war, the other Contracting Party shall immediately render military and other assistance by all means at its disposal." Nevertheless, Soviet military help during the Korean War had been limited, and Pyongyang was always wary about China, a former dominant country on the peninsula.

25. Robert S. Litwak and Kathryn Weathersby, "The Kims' Obsession," *Washington Post,* 12 June 2005.

26. Hui Zhang, "Don't Blame Beijing," *Bulletin of Atomic Scientists* (September–October 2005), 24.

27. Roy E. Horton III, *Out of (South) Africa: Pretoria's Nuclear Weapons Experience,* USAF Institute for National Security Studies, Occasional Paper no. 27, August 1999.

28. Peter Hayes, "The Republic of Korea and the Nuclear Issue," in Andrew Mack (dir.), *Asian Flashpoint: Security and the Korean Peninsula* (Canberra: Allen and Unwin, 1993); Michael J. Engelhardt, "Rewarding Nonproliferation: The South and North Korean Cases," *Nonproliferation Review,* Spring–Summer 1996.

29. Mitchell Reiss, *Without the Bomb: The Politics of Nuclear Nonproliferation* (New York: Columbia University Press, 1988), 78–108.

30. Jungmin Kang & H. A. Feiveson, "South Korea's Shifting and Controversial Interest in Spent Fuel Reprocessing," *Nonproliferation Review,* January–February 1998.

31. David Albright and Corey Gray, "Taiwan: Nuclear Nightmare Averted," *Bulletin of the Atomic Scientists,* January–February 1998; William Burr, "New Archival Evidence on Taiwanese 'Nuclear Intentions,' 1966–1976," *Electronic Briefing Book no. 19,* National Security Archive, 13 October 1999.

32. Derek J. Mitchell, "Taiwan's Hsin Chu Program: Deterrence, Abandonment, and Honor," in Kurt M. Campbell, Robert J. Einhorn, and Mitchell B. Reiss (eds.), *The*

Nuclear Tipping Point. Why States Reconsider Their Nuclear Choices (Washington, DC: Brookings Institution Press, 2004), 299–300.

33. Wayne Reynolds, *Australia's Bid for the Atom Bomb* (Melbourne: Melbourne University Press, 2000); Jacques E. C. Hymans, "Isotopes and Identity: Australia and the Nuclear Weapons Option, 1949–1999," *Nonproliferation Review,* Spring 2000, 3–23.

34. Ronald A. Walker, "Armes nucléaires et multilatéralisme," *Géopolitique,* no. 70 (July 2000,) 44. Article 4 of the ANZUS treaty stated: "Each Party recognizes that an armed attack in the Pacific Area on any of the Parties would be dangerous to its own peace and safety and declares that it would act to meet the common danger in accordance with its constitutional processes."

35. Norway, a NATO member, is sometimes wrongly added to the list of European countries that once had a nuclear weapons program. In fact, the Norwegian example bolsters the thesis presented here. Oslo had a strong nuclear research program and was a leading producer of heavy water, but there is no evidence that it ever considered a military option after it signed the Washington Treaty in 1949. The NATO guarantee was explicitly mentioned as a reason *not* to develop nuclear weapons by the Norwegian Chief of Defense Staff in 1954. See Astrid Forland, "Norway's Nuclear Odyssey: From Optimist Proponent to Nonproliferator," *Nonproliferation Review,* Winter 1997, 11.

36. See Mitchell Reiss, *Bridled Ambition: Why Countries Constrain Their Nuclear Capabilities* (Baltimore, MD: Johns Hopkins University Press, 1995), 90–129.

37. Post-1991 agreements "do not formally require the United States to come to the aid of any of the Gulf states if they are attacked, according to U.S. officials familiar with their contents." Kenneth Katzman, *The Persian Gulf States: Post-War Issues for U.S. Policy, 2003,* CRS Report for Congress, 14 July 2003.

38. The content of these agreements has not been made public. It is generally acknowledged that the one with the United Arab Emirates is particularly strong.

39. The latter is described by the UK Foreign & Commonwealth Office website as being "our largest defence commitment outside NATO" (*Country Profiles—UAE*).

40. This includes the signatories of the Rio, Washington, ANZUS, and SEATO treaties, as well as U.S. formal bilateral alliances in Asia, and informal alliances in the Middle East. These texts do not necessarily include an explicit commitment to protect allies; more often than not, it is the fact that they are interpreted in such a way that matters.

41. "Bush Pledges Whatever It Takes to Defend Taiwan," *CNN.com,* 25 April 2001.

42. A tripartite defense forum was created in 2006. A bilateral defense cooperation agreement was signed by Canberra and Tokyo in March 2007. Australia is considering a participation in a joint missile defense system with the United States and Japan. "Australia Mulls Missile Defense Cooperation with Japan, U.S.," *Japan Times,* 6 June 2007.

43. "We will rise to Israel's defense, if need be. . . . You bet, we'll defend Israel" (quoted in Glenn Kessler, "Bush Says U.S. Would Defend Israel Militarily," *Washington Post,* 2 February 2006); "I made it clear, I'll make it clear again, that we will use military

might to protect our ally, Israel" (*President Discusses War on Terror and Operation Iraqi Freedom, Cleveland,*The White House, Office of the Press Secretary 20 March 2006).

44. "Secretary Rumsfeld offered assurances of firm U.S. commitment and immediate support to the ROK, including continuation of the extended deterrence offered by the U.S. nuclear umbrella, consistent with the Mutual Defense Treaty," *38th Security Consultative Meeting Joint Communiqué,* Washington, 20 October 2006; "The United States has the will and the capability to meet the full range—and I underscore full range—of its deterrent and security commitments to Japan," Condoleezza Rice, quoted in Thom Shanker and Norimitsu Onishi, "Japan Assures Rice that It Has No Nuclear Intentions," *New York Times,* 21 October 2006.

45. *Discours de M. Jacques Chirac, Président de la République, devant l'Institut des hautes études de défense nationale,* 8 June 2001.

46. *Allocution de M. Jacques Chirac, Président de la République, lors de sa visite aux forces aériennes et océanique stratégiques,* 19 January 2006.

47. Ambassador Llewelyn Thompson, quoted in Gavin, "Blasts from the Past," 118.

48. Press statement of 16 October 1964, in U.S. Arms Control and Disarmament Agency, *Documents on Disarmament, 1964* (Washington: USGPO, 1965), 451.

49. Resolution 255 (1968), 19 June 1968, on question relating to measures to safeguard non-nuclear-weapons states parties to the Treaty on the Non-Proliferation of Nuclear Weapons.

50. Quoted in Wheeler, *Positive and Negative Security Assurances,* 10.

51. Ibid.

52. *Convention on the Prohibition of the Development, Production and Stockpiling of Bacteriological (Biological) and Toxin Weapons and on Their Destruction,* Article 7.

53. *Convention on the Prohibition of the Development, Production, Stockpiling and Use of Chemical Weapons and on Their Destruction,* Article 10.8.

54. *Memorandum on Security Assurances in connection with Ukraine's accession to the Treaty on the Non-Proliferation of Nuclear Weapons,* 5 December 1994; *Memorandum on Security Assurances in connection with the Republic of Belarus' accession to the Treaty on the Non-Proliferation of Nuclear Weapons,* 5 December 1994; *Memorandum on Security Assurances in connection with the Republic of Kazakhstan's accession to the Treaty on the Non-Proliferation of Nuclear Weapons,* 5 December 1994. France gave Ukraine security guarantees in a separate memorandum, since it is not an NPT depositary state. Initial assurances to Ukraine had been given in the *Trilateral Statement by the Presidents of United States, Russia and Ukraine,* 14 January 1994.

55. *Joint Letter on Peace and Security between the Great Socialist People's Libyan Arab Jamahiriya and the United Kingdom of Great Britain and Northern Ireland,* 26 June 2006.

56. In the broad sense of the term, the first region to be denuclearized was Antarctica (1959 treaty). Other areas free of nuclear weapons and recognized as such by international law include Outer Space (1967 treaty) and the Sea Bed (1971 treaty).

57. As of June 2007, only protocols to the Tlatelolco Treaty had been ratified by all five NWS.

58. These were reaffirmed at the Second SSOD (1982).

59. Bunn, "The Legal Status of U.S. Negative Security Assurances to Nuclear Non-Nuclear Weapon States," 8.

60. U.S. Department of Defense, Nuclear Posture Review Report, April 2010. 15–16.

61. "The ROK reaffirmed its commitment not to receive or deploy nuclear weapons in accordance with the 1992 Joint Declaration of the Denuclearization of the Korean Peninsula, while affirming that there exist no nuclear weapons within its territory," *Joint Statement of the Fourth Round of the Six-Party Talks,* Beijing, 19 September 2005.

62. India affirms a principle of "non-use of nuclear weapons against non-nuclear weapon states" (Prime Minister's Office, *Cabinet Committee on Security Reviews Operationalization of India's Nuclear Doctrine,* New Delhi, 4 January 2003); Pakistan "has made a solemn pledge that we will not use or threaten to use nuclear weapons against non-nuclear weapon states," *Statement by Ambassador Masood Khan,* Conference on Disarmament, Geneva, 3 August 2006.

63. Today only five NNWS are reported to host nuclear weapons: Belgium, Germany, Italy, the Netherlands, and Turkey. The United Kingdom is also reported to host U.S. nuclear weapons.

64. Pilat, "Reassessing Security Assurances in a Unipolar World," 163.

65. NPT/CONF.1995/32 (Part I, Annex, Decision no. 2).

66. Some of the NWS have also qualified their negative security assurances given through protocols to the treaties establishing NWFZs.

67. *Communication du ministre des affaires étrangères, M. Alain Juppé, au Sénat,* Paris, 6 April 1995.

68. Quoted in Craig Cerniello, "Clinton Issues New Guidelines on U.S. Nuclear Weapons Doctrine," *Arms Control Today,* November–December 1998, 24.

69. Lord Hoyle, Answer to Question HL3331, in *Hansard,* Written Answers, WA 224, 29 October 1998.

70. Jean du Preez, *The Demise of Nuclear Negative Security Assurances,* Paper for the Article VI Forum, 28 September 2006, 4, 10.

71. U.S. Department of Defense, Nuclear Posture Review Report, April 2010, 15–16.

72. See *memoranda* on security assurances, 1994.

73. Bruce W. Jentleson and Christopher A. Whythock, "Who 'Won' Libya? The Force-Diplomacy Debate and Its Implications for Theory and Policy," *International Security,* 30, no. 3 (Winter 2005–6), 76.

74. Gordon Corera, *Shopping for Bombs: Nuclear Proliferation, Global Insecurity and the Rise and Fall of the A. Q. Khan Network* (London: Hurst and Co., 2006), 184.

75. Michael Hirch, "Bolton's British Problem," *Newsweek,* 2 May 2006.

76. *Joint Statement of the Fourth Round of the Six-Party Talks*, Beijing, 19 September 2005.

77. Woolf, *Nuclear Weapons Proliferation*, 4.

78. See also the contribution by James Russell in this volume.

79. "Though America has never signed a formal treaty with Riyadh, since World War II the United States has made clear by its actions . . . and by informal guarantees given to Saudi leaders by American officials that it will protect the monarchy from outside threats." (Michael Levi, "Royal Pain," *New Republic*, 2 June 2003). According to one author, the Reagan administration gave a security guarantee to Saudi Arabia in return for increasing its oil production. Peter Schweizer, *Victory: The Reagan Administration's Secret Strategy that Hastened the Collapse of the Soviet Union* (New York: Atlantic Monthly Press, 1994), 141–43.

80. Selig S. Harrison, "U.S. Must Clamp Down on Pakistan Nuke Dealing," *San José Mercury News*, 30 May 2003.

81. Ewan MacAskill and Ian Traynor, "Saudis Consider Nuclear Bomb," *Guardian*, 18 September 200; Simon Henderson, *Toward a Saudi Nuclear Option: The Saudi-Pakistani Summit*, Policywatch, no. 793, Washington Institute for Near East Policy, 16 October 2003.

82. Ian O. Lesser, *Turkey, Iran and Nuclear Risks*, Nonproliferation Policy Education Center, 2004, 14.

83. According to U.S. ambassador Maynard Glitman, such "habits of cooperation" gave its real value to the U.S. extended deterrence commitment. Lewis A. Dunn, *Deterrence Today—Roles, Challenges, and Responses*, paper prepared for the Institut Français des Relations Internationales, 14 May 2007, 9.

84. Hans M. Kristensen, *U.S. Nuclear Weapons in Europe: A Review of Post-Cold War Policy, Force Levels, and War Planning*, Natural Resources Defense Council, February 2005.

85. Assuming that all existing NWFZ treaties come into force, this would be legally possible only in Europe, the Middle East, and parts of Asia.

86. Wheeler, *Positive and Negative Security Assurances*, 31.

87. The expression "commitment trap" comes from Scott D. Sagan, "The Commitment Trap: Why the United States Should Not Use Nuclear Threats to Deter Biological and Chemical Weapons Attacks," *International Security*, 24, no. 4 (Spring 2000), 85–115.

88. Woolf, *Nuclear Weapons Proliferation*, 9.

89. Levi, "Royal Pain."

90. Martin Butcher, Otfried Nassauer, Tanya Padberg, and Dan Plesch, *Questions of Command and Control: NATO, Nuclear Sharing and the NPT*, PENN Research Report 2000–1, 2000.

91. The case of Iran assumes that Tehran has withdrawn from the NPT. The case of Burma is illustrative: the country has signed the Bangkok Treaty establishing a NWFZ in South-East Asia.

92. John J. McCloy, quoted in Gavin, "Blasts from the Past," 119.

93. Ibid., 119–20.

94. Llewelyn Hughes, "Why Japan Will Not Go Nuclear (Yet)," *International Security*, 31, no. 4 (Spring 2007), 75.

95. In May 2007, Pyongyang reportedly stated that denuclearization now depended on the removal "of more than one thousand nuclear weapons deployed in and around North Korea under the US nuclear umbrella and termination of the US hostile policy toward [the country] and its nuclear threat as well." Quoted in Jim Gomez, "N. Korea Slams U.S., Japan, S. Korea," *International Business Times*, 24 May 2007.

96. Associated Press, "Iran: No Need for US Security Guarantee," *China Daily*, 14 December 2005; Reuters, "U.S. and Iran Reject Offers of Security Guarantee," *Gulf News*, 22 May 2006; IRNA, "Iran Does Not Need U.S. Security Guarantees—Larijani," *Payvand*, 3 October 2006. Note that some of these statements may be aimed at a domestic audience.

97. Pilat, "Reassessing Security Assurances in a Unipolar World," 163.

98. Leonard S. Spector and Aubrie Ohlde, "Negative Security Assurances: Revisiting the Nuclear-Weapon Free Zone," *Arms Control Today*, April 2005. As of June 2007, only Protocol II of the Pelindaba Treaty had been ratified by all NWS.

14 Options and New Dynamics: Chemical and Biological Weapons Proliferation in 2020

Michael Moodie

The proliferation of chemical and biological weapons (CBW) in 2020 will little resemble the problem that occupied policy-makers and analysts for most of the twentieth century. Today, the world is witnessing a life sciences revolution. What we know about life today is far greater than what we knew even a decade ago; what we know about life today, however, is far less than what we will know a decade hence. A National Academies of Sciences report cautions, therefore, that "tomorrow's world of proliferating threats . . . may be quite different from the twentieth century agents and indeed may not even exist at this time."[1] The growth in our knowledge about biology and life sciences could lead to the growth of new types of weapons or an increase in their availability to both state and nonstate actors.

The CBW proliferation challenge also is a function of other ongoing changes that are converging to create an environment marked by greater complexity and uncertainty, leading to heightened unpredictability and potential instability. Managing proliferation risks in this environment will constitute an unfamiliar challenge. It will not be about what potential proliferators have, but what they know, how they may try to use—or misuse—that knowledge, and what the United States and the international community can do to shape those choices.

Two factors are especially important in this more complex and uncertain environment. First, advances in science and technology are creating new and sometimes unforeseen opportunities and options for both states and nonstate actors. Second, the process of globalization is profoundly altering CBW proliferation dynamics and will create additional problems for policymakers. The remainder of this chapter will explore these developments and their implications, especially in terms of how they could create new proliferation challenges.

THE CHALLENGE OF ADVANCING SCIENCE
AND TECHNOLOGY

A key dimension of the current process of scientific and technological advance is the speed at which it is proceeding. Like science in general, the life sciences are moving incredibly fast. Certain branches of the life sciences are advancing more rapidly even than Moore's Law—the formula that describes the incredible velocity of change in information technology.[2] In the face of such rapid change, it is difficult for legal, regulatory, or even ethical systems to keep up with the scope and pace of what scientific progress makes possible.

The speed at which basic scientific discoveries are translated into "commodities" also is increasing. Many people believe that the life sciences, and biotechnology in particular, will be a key driver of their future economic growth, and their goal is to transform cutting-edge science into commercial products. One example of this "commoditization" is the worldwide explosion of "gene foundries" whose goal is to provide made-to-order DNA segments on request, for profit.[3]

Another aspect of scientific and technological trends that will have a major impact on the future proliferation environment is the convergence of various scientific fields. As analyst Alexander Kelle has noted, "[M]any of the products flowing from the biotechnology revolution . . . are basically chemical compounds."[4] A survey of many leading chemists conducted by *Nature* magazine resulted in a clear consensus that many of chemistry's most urgent questions are ones that address aspects of biology.[5]

Equally important is the convergence of biology and chemistry with other scientific and technological disciplines, particularly information technology, materials science, nanoscience and nanotechnology, and imaging and sensor technology. Not only is this convergence creating new fields such as "bioinformatics" and "bionanotechnology," but it also is combining with other technology-related developments such as automation and miniaturization to produce a transformation potentially "as powerful as the industrial revolution."[6] If this view proves correct, all of those touched by these developments, including those responsible for managing proliferation risks, must develop new understandings, skills, and tools in order to deal successfully with the challenge ahead.

An important determinant of the success of converging technologies will be the ability to integrate new knowledge and technologies to produce innovative capabilities. The importance of integration, however, extends far beyond the way in which actors are able to bring the sciences together. Integration is important because the life sciences enterprise is increasingly marked by out-sourcing and decentralization. Outsourcing results from the largely commercial desire to share business risk, exploit distributed expertise around the world, and penetrate new markets. Any successful endeavor will likely have to bring together various elements from many different places. This has led to what one assessment has described as "deinfrastructuralization,"[7] or a diminished reliance on an indigenous infrastructure in favor of one that is more geographically decentralized. Those interested in exploiting the life sciences will be reliant on neither wholly indigenous nor wholly external resources, but a combination of the two. The National Intelligence Council's study of the world in 2020 makes the key point: "[A] nation's level of technological achievement will be defined in terms of its investment in integrating and applying the new, globally available technologies."[8]

What is true in the broader scientific and economic arenas of the life sciences is also true for the security sphere. Because the security sector now relies largely on the application of technologies from the commercial sector, the advantage here also rests with those who can rapidly adapt, exploit, and integrate evolving technology.[9] Given the growing scientific and technological competence of many countries around the world, the United States should be under no illusion that it or its friends and allies are the only places where innovation in the security arena can occur.

A second implication of this rapid increase in science and technical prowess is that it creates an opportunity for a proliferator to pursue multiple routes to the same end point. It is vital for those responsible for managing CBW proliferation risks to recognize that future proliferation efforts are likely to bear little resemblance to those of the past in terms of the pathways traveled to achieve success. Former CBW programs such as those of the Soviet Union, Iraq, or South Africa began at different points on the learning curve and took distinct forms. This difference is likely to become only more pronounced.

THE IMPACT OF GLOBALIZATION

The second trend that will shape the future of CBW proliferation is globalization, which is characterized by inter-relationships and transactions among actors at various levels that are distinguished by their worldwide scope, accelerating speed, growing magnitude, thickening density, and increasing complexity. The general impact of globalization is hard to exaggerate. The National Intelligence Council's study of the trends and factors shaping the world of 2020, for example, called globalization a "force so ubiquitous that it will substantially shape all the other major trends."[10]

The life sciences have felt the impact of globalization as much as any other endeavor. The chemical industry has been a global enterprise for decades, but the explosion in the number of biotechnology enterprises around the world is more recent. It is not just in developed countries where this explosion is occurring. Many anecdotes demonstrate how globalization is also shaping trends in science and technology in the developing world.

According to the consulting firm Ernst and Young, for example, Asian biotechnology growth rates in 2005 outpaced those in all other parts of the world, including North America, which is the recognized leader in the field of biotechnology.[11] Singapore has created "Biopolis," a research and industrial park dedicated to the life sciences enterprise that will undertake both public and private corporate research and development. In Brazil, the number of biotechnology companies increased from 76 in 1993 to 354 in 2001. Today, the Brazilian government claims that as many as 1,700 groups in the public, academic, and private sectors are working on biotechnology.[12] In 1995, Mexico adopted a plan to establish and develop a genomic medical platform, including creation of a new Institute of Genomic Medicine that it hopes will become a model for wider adoption throughout Latin America.[13] In the Middle East, an area generally considered to be behind in biotechnology, Egypt now has more than 3,000 scientists active in biological research fields, and it directs $100 million annually to biotechnology research and development projects.[14]

Many other countries are making a long-term commitment to their life sciences enterprises. South Korea invested more than $4.7 billion in biotechnology between 2000 and 2007. India already has the twelfth largest biotechnology sector in the world, as measured by the number of companies,[15] and the government's Department of Biotechnology hopes to expand India's biotechnology sector fivefold.[16] South Africa hopes to use regional initiatives, such as its New Partnership for African Development, as a springboard to make it the biotechnology leader in Africa.[17]

Another key feature of globalization in the life sciences is the prevalence of international collaborations, alliances, and partnerships. Alliances, partnerships, and other forms of collaboration bring access to new technology, global distribution networks, new management skills, and broader markets. Lower labor costs, increased efficiency in the use of capital, and the pooling of business risks are among the economic incentives that push individuals, firms, and countries toward collaboration.[18] Cooperation can take many forms, including technical or licensing agreements, contract research or manufacture, or joint ventures in research and development or production. It also can take less formal forms, including academic exchanges and conferences, or reaching out to ethnic diasporas. Given that the life sciences enterprise has achieved global proportions in both science and commercialization, more and more of those cooperative relationships, whether among companies or scientists, occur across international borders.[19]

IMPLICATIONS FOR PROLIFERATION: FORGING A NEW DYNAMIC

These trends produced by globalization will have a significant impact on CBW proliferation. "Proliferation" often is conceived as a process whereby a government makes a commitment to achieve a nuclear, chemical, or biological weapons capability, and then moves systematically through a series of programmatic steps to the eventual deployment of full military systems. In the past, many state CBW programs constituted variants of this standard pattern. Today, however, the process of proliferation is moving away from this paradigm as global trends alter several elements of that classic model.

The Changing Nature of Chemical and Biological Weapons

Emerging global trends are combining to alter common conceptions of what constitutes a chemical or biological weapon. Biological weapons were traditionally defined in terms of living organisms (or the chemical byproducts of living organisms—that is, toxins) found in nature that caused diseases in people, plants, or animals. Traditional agents (such as smallpox, anthrax, tularemia, plague, botulinum toxin) cannot be dismissed as potential threats, as the experience with the anthrax letters in 2001 so clearly underlined. Nevertheless, the range of potential options is expanding.

One dimension of this expansion is the use of new science—particularly genetic engineering—to enhance traditional CBW agents. Advanced techniques might be used to bolster the pathogenicity or virulence of an organism, allow for the transfer of antibiotic resistance, boost its aerosolization, or shore up the stability of agents once they are deployed into the environment. Moreover, someone interested in doing harm need not look to nature as the source for such organisms; science is increasingly making it possible to synthesize them artificially.

Another way in which the spectrum of weapons options is expanding is through the growing ability to recover organisms from old tissues, as has been done with the 1918 Spanish influenza. Natural selection also continues to add to the potential organisms available for weaponization. The World Health Organization reported that more than 30 new infectious diseases threatening to human health appeared in the last two decades of the twentieth century, and even more new microbial diseases are likely to emerge over the next 20 years.[20]

Advancing science and technology also will shift the focus from the agent to the target, as "future biological agents could be rationally engineered to target specific human biological systems at the molecular level."[21] These advances would allow biological weapons developers, according to James Petro, "to identify biochemical pathways critical for physiological processes and engineer specific [advanced biological weapons] agents to exploit vulnerabilities .... [Such agents] will be able to target specific biological systems, such as the cardiovascular, immunological, neurological, and gastrointestinal systems ... and produce a wide range of effects including death, incapacitation, or neurological impairment."[22] Some people even believe that the development of ethnically targeted weapons is only a matter of time.[23] A 2003 unclassified Central Intelligence Agency report on these "advanced biological agents" concluded that the "resulting diversity of new BW agents could enable such a broad range of attack scenarios that it would be virtually impossible to anticipate and defend against."[24] The concept of biologically related threat agents, therefore, must now go beyond "bugs," or disease-causing microbes, to include substances such as bioregulators that make it possible to manipulate behavior or thought processes. These scientific and technological advances could potentially lead to a diffuse and fundamentally unknowable range of potential agents.[25]

Another facet of this changing concept of a chemical or biological weapon relates to delivery systems. The standard notion of "delivery" has evolved from the military context in which traditional munitions and missiles were the primary means used to place a weapon on a target. Here, too, options are expanding. As a result of efforts to find new mechanisms for drug delivery, for example, cutaneous absorption and improved aerosolization technologies are available. These new devices are intended for drug delivery to individuals, and are therefore probably not suitable for "mass effect" applications. In a context in which the perceived utility of CBW may change, however, the potential to exploit these new delivery devices and techniques should not be ignored.

Capability and Intent: A More Complex Relationship

Today's scientific advances promote a more complex relationship between capabilities and intentions than traditionally has been assumed. Conventional wisdom holds that "intent drives capability": the process of proliferation is characterized by a systematic move down a path toward specific capabilities following government policy. This assumption may no longer represent the only dynamic in play. Advancing science and technology, combined with globalization, could also generate a dynamic in which "capabilities shape intentions." Indeed, future decisions to seek CBW are likely to be driven as much by ongoing scientific and technological advances as by the threats posed by potential adversaries.

The mid-1990s scientific experiment to recover the agent responsible for the 1918 Spanish flu demonstrates how scientific advances might drive the creation of new weapons. The research team that recovered the 1918 virus had recently developed a new technique to analyze DNA in old, preserved tissues. Looking for a new application they decided on the Spanish flu. It appears that "this work was not triggered by a search for flu treatments, or the search for a new biowarfare agent, but by a rather simple motivation: [the] team could just do it."[26] According to the team leader, "[T]he 1918 flu was by far and away the most interesting thing we could think of."[27] The work went ahead because the team was curious, the issue was interesting, and they could do it.

In a security context, this combination of curiosity and capability could yield worrisome results. States or nonstate actors might be willing to explore the CBW potential of the life sciences, not because they are committed to an institutionalized program or deploying a complete weapons system, but because they are curious or because potential weapons are inadvertently discovered by researchers undertaking legitimate inquiry. They might begin such an exploration merely because the knowledge and capabilities exist somewhere in their scientific establishments, and they are interested in what possibilities these capabilities might offer. Work might go forward with no sense of an ultimate objective, certainly without the highest levels of government intent on fielding a CBW capability. "Dabbling" could become the order of the day. The challenge this dynamic poses has been identified by the Lawrence Livermore National Laboratory's Center for Global Security Research as proliferation "latency."[28] Latency is possibly the greatest conundrum confronting those responsible for addressing CBW proliferation. How does one counter proliferation in a world in which state and nonstate actors enjoy, through the diffusion of technology developed for legitimate purposes, a "break out" capability that might be activated on short notice?

Changing Views on CBW Use?

The choices potential CBW proliferators make also will be shaped by their perceptions of the utility of such capabilities and the contexts within which they might be used. History has already witnessed an expansion in thinking about CBW use, from their tactical employment on the battlefield to their exploitation at the operational level against targets such as rear-area assembly points or ports. The Soviet Union's program even called for strategic use of biological weapons against targets in the United States following an all-out nuclear attack.

Today, apprehension over the potential military use of chemical and biological weapons has been joined by concerns about terrorist CBW use, particularly to produce mass or even catastrophic numbers of casualties. As a result, perspectives on CBW use tend to assume a binary character; most thinking focuses on CBW use by either military forces in a conflict against the military forces of an adversary or by international terrorists seeking to inflict mass casualties. While both concerns are valid, this kind of binary thinking is inadequate because it fails to encompass the full range of contingencies in which CBW could be used. Indeed, these two contingencies, which continue to receive the greatest attention from security planners and the media, are probably not the most likely scenarios for CBW use.

The classic force-on-force battlefield confrontation is an increasingly rare event. Military forces now find themselves in conflicts that are not characterized by high-intensity conventional combined-arms combat. Many operations take on an unconventional character, as the wars in Iraq and Afghanistan have demonstrated. Others qualify as "operations other than war," such as peacekeeping or deployment in support of a legitimate civil authority. As the relevant science and technology continues to come within the grasp of more and more people, chemical and biological weapons could be introduced by local populations or militias in these conflict situations.

Many of the world's most recent and current conflicts do not even include formal military forces but are community-based conflicts involving competing militias, warring ethnic groups, warlords, and informal paramilitary organizations.[29] It is these internal, communal, or unconventional conflicts that hold the greatest possibility for the use of chemical and biological weapons. In almost every conflict of this type in the last decade, one side or the other, and sometimes both, have accused the adversary of using chemical weapons. In most cases, these charges are either politically motivated or the product of confusing real chemical weapons with smoke, tear gas, or some other noxious chemical introduced into the environment. As technical capabilities come within the grasp of more and more people, however, the potential risk of genuine chemical weapons use under these circumstances increases. Chlorine bomb attacks in Iraq, albeit of limited utility, may be a harbinger of future battlefield developments.

Similarly, scenarios of CBW terrorist use that have received the greatest attention are not the most likely to occur, particularly with respect to mass casualties. More probable are attacks that produce relatively few casualties but still yield significant disruptive effects. The "Amerithrax" letters killed only five people. Nevertheless, they demonstrated the enormous economic, psychological, and social impact that even a limited biological attack can generate, especially if the public becomes hypervigilant in seeking to protect itself from attack.

The "next use" of CBW, especially if successful, could have a profound impact on the perceived utility of creating and employing a chemical or biological weapon. It could change actors' calculations regarding the costs and benefits of pursuing a chemical or biological arsenal, or prompt a more serious exploration of their potential political or military utility. Moreover, concepts of use bear directly on the technical and operational requirements needed to conduct a successful attack, and, therefore, on proliferation cost-benefit calculations. For a considerable time, some measure of relief has been taken from the view that an attack producing catastrophic casualties is beyond the technical or operational capacity of most nonstate actors and even many states. The requirements for contingencies producing fewer victims, however, are less stringent. A small-scale event, by definition, would not be catastrophic, but it could nevertheless generate disastrous second- or third-order effects as people respond to "human-scale" horrors.

Outsourcing Proliferation?

Globalization is shifting the impetus for technological innovation from the military to the civilian sector. This shift means that the research and development phase of a CBW program need not be conducted in a dedicated military facility or in a specific military program directed toward the creation of an offensive capability. Significant understanding of the fundamentals of chemical or biological weapons can be achieved without violating international treaty obligations. In the biological arena, for example, drug companies are exploring improvements in aerosol technology that bear directly on what is perhaps the single most difficult technical challenge in developing an effective weapon.

Scientific and technological trends are making some traditional CBW program elements less necessary. It would be foolish, for example, for any state to produce and store large stockpiles of chemical or biological weapons. Such stockpiles are not needed in the face of a growing "just in time" production capability. In the chemical arena, the appearance of microreactors creates some very disturbing possibilities for quickly fabricating important ingredients.[30] If such technology becomes widely used, it could alter significantly the processes by which industry produces a wide range of chemicals, thereby undermining the fundamental assumptions about the chemical industry that underlie the verification provisions of the Chemical Weapons Convention.

The Central Importance of Knowledge

Traditional approaches to nonproliferation have been based on two assumptions: (1) that sensitive materials and technologies were critical to the proliferation process and could be identified as inherently dangerous; and (2) that suppliers of that material and technology could be controlled through a system of guidance regimes and national export controls without unduly hampering legitimate commercial trade.[31] In today's globalized and networked world, neither of these assumptions is warranted. Rather than material and equipment, the fulcrum for CBW proliferation has become knowledge.

Several reasons account for this shift. First, the enormous progress and accelerating rate of change in science, particularly knowledge about life, generates unexpected and even unknowable phenomena. The NAS study makes the point, for example, that scientific progress in the twentieth century was marked by successive serendipitous discoveries that had profound impacts, in some cases forcing complete revisions in how the world understood certain natural phenomena.[32] The life sciences are expected to continue to advance quickly, in a variety of directions, and previously unanticipated paradigm shifts are likely.[33] Given that history has shown that virtually all new science is explored for its potential use in the security arena, some of those surprising outcomes could well occur in the area of defense.

Moreover, innovation is not likely to come only from advanced research and development in developed countries. Today, it could emerge anywhere. Countries such as India and China are particularly well placed to achieve break-throughs, but innovations with potential security implications could occur virtually anywhere in the world. Evidence for such a possibility abounds: Cuba was the first country to produce a vaccine against meningitis B;[34] South Africa was the first country to become involved in a trial of a preventative vaccine against the HIV-C strain; and India is the world's largest producer of hepatitis B vaccine.[35] China is the first country in the world to license a gene therapy;[36] it was also the only "developing" country to participate in the Human Genome Project, mapping 1 percent of the genome with a reported 99 percent accuracy.[37]

The shift of CBW proliferation to a knowledge-based risk has also occurred because the life sciences are now a global enterprise; growing numbers of people in more places know more of relevance to this challenge. More international players are becoming scientifically productive. The United States continues to lead in the publication of academic papers, but recently the percentage of such papers authored by U.S. scientists has declined, while scientists from states such as China and Turkey have boosted their academic scientific output by 20 to 30 percent.[38] Moreover, the number of patents is dramatically increasing world-wide, with countries such as Brazil, China, and India showing "remarkable growth" in the number of patents they have been granted.[39]

Another measure of the diffusion of knowledge is the dispersion of expertise. The last 35 years have witnessed a remarkable growth in the proportion of foreign-born scientists and engineers in the United States. But many of these foreign-born experts are returning home, frequently induced by government incentives ensuring a quality of life they deem to be better than the one they would have in the United States. In addition, fewer of the most talented foreign-born science and engineering students are coming to the United States. One reason for this change is the growing two-way flow of scientific and advanced technological expertise that now characterizes relations among high-, middle-, and low-income countries.[40] A second reason, which has received very little attention, is the growing competition for the best scientific and engineering scholars. That competition is now global. In most of South Africa's major research universities, for example, foreign students in graduate programs constitute an even larger percentage of the student body than they do in the United States.[41] The impact of this trend could be that many of tomorrow's CBW scientists will be trained in institutions in Asia, Latin America, and Africa.[42]

Life sciences enterprises are some of the most knowledge-intensive activities in the today's global economy. Competition among firms is increasingly based on the production, appropriation, dissemination, and application of knowledge. The Organization for Economic Cooperation and Development, for example, argues that "knowledge churning"—the creation and disappearance of companies only to be replaced by other technologies and companies—has become the motor for advances in the life sciences.[43] Technology transfers relating to the life sciences are increasingly about knowledge—that is, "intangible" technology in the form of data, processes, and expertise. Moreover, knowledge is the currency of networks, and the interactions across those networks make possible flows of knowledge and information more than movement of materials and equipment. From a security perspective, what is most disturbing about this "knowledge churn" is how it diminishes the capabilities of governments to regulate developments in any meaningful way.[44]

ACTORS

Given that knowledge is now the fulcrum of the CBW proliferation problem, the challenge now encompasses a wider range of potential actors. At the level of governments and nation-states, the greater number of active or potential players in the global life sciences enterprise could alter proliferation dynamics significantly. What is emerging today is a more complex reality than the one captured by the distinction between technology "haves" and "have-nots" or "developed" and "developing" countries. One term that has been employed to identify those countries that should be of special concern is "innovative developing countries (IDCs)."[45] China and India are perhaps the most notable members of this group, but Brazil, Argentina, Cuba, South Africa, Singapore, South Korea, and Israel could also be included. Others will join them in the future. While the poorest developing nations may be able to achieve single or limited accomplishments, those countries are not the sources of greatest concern. It is the IDCs that bear greatest scrutiny.

How will these countries view the CBW proliferation challenge? Not all nations, including some of those who are potentially key future players in the life sciences, share the same security concerns as the United States. They have different priorities, and for them the risk of the potential deliberate misuse of the life sciences is not necessarily among their major worries. Indeed, not even some U.S. allies that are life sciences leaders share Washington's sense of urgency regarding future chemical and biological proliferation. Some of these states might even fall to the allure of the combination of capability and curiosity when it comes to the new possibilities created by scientific and technological advances.

China is of particular interest in this regard. Suspicions exist—at least in the United States—with respect to China's general commitment to nonproliferation. Not only has Beijing abetted proliferation through nuclear assistance to Pakistan, but on 19 occasions the George W. Bush administration imposed sanctions on 32 different Chinese entities for transfers related to ballistic and cruise missiles as well as to chemical weapons. The director of the Central Intelligence recently reported to Congress that China remains a "key supplier" of weapons technology, particularly missile and chemical technology.[46] Moreover, the United States has judged that China maintains a chemical weapons production mobilization capability, although there is insufficient information to determine whether it maintains an active offensive chemical weapons research and development program.[47]

The United States also contends that China maintains some elements of an offensive BW capability in violation of its BWC obligations. Given China's enormous investment in commercial biotechnology and life sciences research, Chinese leaders, or organizations within the government acting independently, may decide that little risk is attached to research activities that have implications for an offensive capability should Beijing conclude that sometime in the future such capabilities may prove useful. This is not proliferation in terms of the classic model, but an example of the potential challenges of managing proliferation latency.[48]

China is not the only country in a position to pursue latent CBW proliferation. Virtually every other innovative developing country is investing heavily in its life sciences sector on the bet that it will emerge as a driver of economic growth. Their scientific establishments are increasingly sophisticated, and they all are increasingly well versed in relevant scientific and technological developments and processes. For these countries, the ability to develop chemical and biological weapons capabilities will emerge over time. Some of them may be dabbling in military-related research and development already, or at least keeping a watch on what their life sciences enterprises are doing, with an eye to their potential security implications. Whether or not they go this far, these IDCs, and others who will join them, will all be residing close to the line of a weapons capability. The key question will be whether and under what circumstances they would choose to cross that line.

Currently, few IDCs appear to have a strong incentive to pursue a major national CBW program. For some of these countries, such as Brazil, Singapore, or South Africa, neither their national security requirements nor their geostrategic environment provides a compelling rationale to do so. Others, including India, have capabilities that meet their currently perceived needs. In the case of South Korea, the U.S. security guarantee still seems to be a major factor dampening enthusiasm for a national chemical, biological, nuclear, or radiological weapon program.

In several cases, stronger incentives may exist for at least sustaining some kind of limited research and development program housed in the nation's broader life sciences enterprise. Both Cuba and Israel, for example, have been accused of pursuing biological weapons. Given the situations in which they find themselves, discoveries of such programs would not be surprising. At the present time, however, unclassified information does not support a conclusion that they have a major national effort underway. But both countries have advanced life sciences and biotechnology sectors,[49] and it would not take much for them to initiate a small-scale CBW program.

Nevertheless, things could change. If what the National Intelligence Council 2020 study called a "fear dynamic" became the prominent feature of the security environment, a different set of considerations could come into play. This would particularly be the case if the WMD nonproliferation regimes were perceived to be collapsing. If North Korea and Iran become recognized nuclear powers, no one could be certain of the chain of consequences that would follow. More countries might feel compelled to seek a countervailing capability. Current assessments assume that if such nuclear proliferation occurs, other countries would opt for nuclear weapons. Is such an assumption warranted? Other chapters in this volume make clear that a nuclear weapons program is an expensive, technically challenging, lengthy, and politically risky option. A case could be made, then, that rather than expending the massive resources required for developing a nuclear capability and waiting decades for such an effort to come to fruition, countries might instead seek to exploit what they have on hand, which, increasingly, will be life sciences–based capabilities.

This is exactly what Syria has done vis-à-vis Israel. Damascus has responded to Israel's nuclear arsenal by developing chemical weapons, and possibly biological weapons. Syrian officials probably recognize that their chemical weapons do not truly offset Israel's nuclear capabilities, but these weapons do provide some countervailing capability that Israeli decision-makers must take into account in any confrontation. In a deteriorating security environment, other countries faced with a sense of urgency to act and limited resources might very well emulate this "Syrian option."

The Firm or Company

A key player in the global life sciences enterprise is the firm or company. Proliferation concerns emerge about firms in terms of the supply side of the proliferation equation. The globalization of the life sciences enterprise provides almost a limitless number of choices for companies regarding locales for their operations. Different countries clearly have different business environments, regulatory regimes, and track records for proliferation-related oversight. In addition, the distribution and decentralization of scientific and commercial functions, and the outsourcing, subcontracting, and cooperative agreements they foster, create a series of complex connections that can be hard to identify, let alone monitor or regulate. Such complexity would seemingly make it easier for companies to deceive governments should they choose to try to hide unscrupulous behavior.

Moreover, not every life sciences company is going to be an economic winner. As global competition intensifies or severe economic downturns threaten a firm's survival, pressures on businesses to generate income will become more acute. Economic pressure might force business executives to consider options that are unsavory from a security perspective, especially when chances are good that it will be impossible to trace the source of substances or equipment. Might they, for example, turn a blind eye to the transfer of dual-use technology even if they have doubts about its end use? It has happened before, and in an environment in which government monitoring and regulation of business activity among intensely networked players is extremely difficult, trafficking in dangerous materials might become more attractive.

Terrorists

Since Aum Shinrikyo's 1995 sarin gas attack on the Tokyo subway, the question of whether terrorists will turn increasingly to chemical and biological weapons has been the subject of intense debate. The Aum experience, however, is of only limited utility in considering the prospects of terrorists attempting to exploit chemistry or biology for malicious purposes.[50] The evidence on which participants in the debate can base their respective cases is extremely narrow, creating enormous bands of uncertainty.

Some experts contend that terrorists are both unwilling and unable to exploit the life sciences. Milton Leitenberg, for example, argues that "advanced genetic engineering capabilities are not likely to become available to real world terrorist groups in the near future. Judgments based on the prevalence of genetic engineering competence in the general academic molecular research community are still not useful guides to terrorist capabilities."[51] Other commentators are not so sure. David Relman argues, for example, that, today, "anyone with a high school education can use widely available protocols and prepackaged kits to modify the sequence of genes or replace genes within a microorganism; one can also purchase small, disposable, self-contained bioreactors for propagating viruses and microorganisms." Relman's conclusions are that (1) the full potential of past programs was never unleashed; (2) past biological weapons use by small groups was relatively unsophisticated; and (3) past use is "far from representative of what moderately well informed groups might do today."[52] The differences may be explained, at least in part, by the focus of the commentators. Leitenberg stresses "advanced" genetic engineering responsibilities. In contrast, Relman seems to be addressing simpler technologies.

Even if terrorists cannot exploit the most cutting edge scientific and technological capabilities, however, it does not mean they can do nothing. Terrorists do not need the most advanced capabilities to inflict large numbers of casualties. They do not demand the same operational performance from their technology that militaries require.[53] Their science and technology have to be just "good enough."

Given this situation, Malcolm Dando contends that terrorists pose real threats, but that their current level of threat is likely to fall short of mass impact.[54] But terrorist threats at this level must not be dismissed, particularly since their potential impact could extend well beyond limited casualties to devastating economic losses or a profound psychological effect. Dando concludes that this challenge is likely to get worse: "[We] face the threat in the coming decades of a much more systematic application of the new biology to hostile purposes .... [In] the future . . . it seems likely that sub-state groups, and perhaps even deranged individuals, may gain the capabilities to cause more human casualties."[55]

LESSONS FOR THE FUTURE

It is impossible to predict precisely what form future chemical or biological weapons proliferation will assume, or which group or nation might create a potent CBW arsenal. The goal of those responsible for addressing proliferation, therefore, must be to work across an expansive front of policy options to prepare for a wide range of contingencies. Such an approach demands building robust, flexible, and adaptive capabilities. Developing such capabilities, however, is not easy. It entails the difficult tasks of identifying requirements, establishing criteria to determine appropriate capabilities, and involving the right set of players. It also requires managing difficult trade-offs and striking effective balances between competing, but equally worthy, interests. Some of the most difficult of these tradeoffs relate to emphasizing prevention or preparedness, investing in people or technology, and giving priority to immediate requirements or longer-term needs.

Shift from Threat and Vulnerability Assessments to Risk-Management Approaches

Chemical and biological threats to security are not problems to be solved. They are risks to be managed. Work in the life sciences will continue, and should do so for important, legitimate reasons. This means, however, that the potential for the misuse of the life sciences remains a permanent reality.

Traditional threat assessments treat different potential outcomes as equally likely. By contrast, risk assessment introduces the important factor of probability. Analysis of potential proliferation pathways suggests that if the goal in using chemical or biological weapons is to produce catastrophic casualties or widespread disruption, fewer pathways are available and those that do exist are more difficult than those producing less significant results. A risk assessment approach would conclude that the degree of risk declines as the level of desired casualties or disruption increases, insofar as it becomes less likely. Such a finding could have important implications for shaping policy responses.

Current threat and vulnerability assessments tend to emphasize a potential user's technological capacity. Excessive consideration of technological requirements, however, diverts attention away from creativity. One should approach assessments of the chemical or biological weapons threat with the same caution as the military planner who noted that battle plans become irrelevant with the first shot. Events involving chemical and biological weapons are likely to proceed in ways quite different from those anticipated.

The utility of traditional policy tools is also increasingly questioned if not questionable. Chemical and especially biological export controls, for example, emerged more than 20 years ago. Whether they will continue to be of help in the years ahead is of growing concern because of the dual-use nature and global ubiquity of key components, the shift in the proliferation center of gravity from materials and equipment to knowledge, the difficulty of "controlling" intangible technology transfers, and the tension between export controls and the imperatives of economic development. The ambiguous attitude of key countries toward export controls further weakens the impact of traditional policy instruments.

Because the problem is increasingly one of managing knowledge-related risks, and because basic and commercial knowledge in the life sciences is one such risk, control is probably impossible. Too many ways exist to get around whatever control regime might be put in place. Moreover, attempts to proscribe activities, information, or artifacts often foster a black market, which would be extremely difficult to police.[56]

Work across a Wide Spectrum of Policy Options

Innovative thinking is needed to foster new approaches to curtailing the negative externalities produced by scientific and industrial innovation. Managing the risks of proliferation is a complex challenge that requires a multifaceted response including norm building, deterrence, prevention, defense, preparedness, and consequence management, mitigation, and amelioration. No single instrument will be sufficient.

One set of capabilities focuses on prevention. These include measures in such critical areas as law enforcement, intelligence, pathogen security, export controls, and cooperative threat reduction. Necessary preparedness capabilities also span a spectrum of elements such as disease surveillance and reporting, health monitoring, epidemiology, robust laboratory-based analysis, diagnostics and medical countermeasures, and medical stockpiles. A national effort to develop these capabilities also requires a robust research and development agenda and effective communications. To be most effective, this array of measures must be implemented in a context of international cooperation.

In recent years, several novel measures to stop emerging proliferation threats have been initiated, often through U.S. leadership. Several of these new measures emerged precisely because of concern over the continuing utility of traditional policy tools. Some measures—such as the nontraditional approach to strengthening the Biological Weapons Convention through an annual work plan—have been specific to issues created by the risk of chemical and biological weapons. Most of these initiatives, however, have addressed proliferation more broadly. In fact, many of the new nonproliferation measures were designed more with nuclear proliferation in mind. As a result they fall short in promoting CBW nonproliferation. The value of the Proliferation Security Initiative in impeding chemical or biological weapons proliferation, for example, should not be oversold when material can be carried in small vials or even synthesized from small bits of DNA, or when critical equipment can readily be bought on e-Bay.

Incorporate More Players into the Risk Management Process

Fighting proliferation in today's dynamic global environment is not a job for governments alone. Beyond government nonproliferation officials, the military, public health, law enforcement, industry, civil society, and academia are now involved in nonproliferation efforts in new and innovative ways. Each of these communities has some role in promoting chemical and biological nonproliferation, but none of them have that mandate as its primary responsibility. As a result, each community must reconcile its nonproliferation duties with its other responsibilities. Equally important, these communities must develop and maintain effective working relationships with one another. And they must do so on an international basis.[57]

Managing chemical and biological weapons proliferation risks demands that governments reach out to the life sciences community. Attitudes of those working in the life sciences, however, have not always facilitated cooperation. Their focus on the good they are trying to do for humanity or scientific discovery for its own sake has too often blinded them to the risks that stand alongside the benefits they seek. Such an attitude is an unaffordable luxury. As science and technology advances, industry and the academic community must understand their stake in the challenge and be fully integrated into the strategic response.

Life scientists and governments should collaborate to help strengthen the norms against chemical and biological weapons research, acquisition, and use. Codes of conduct, peer reviews and panels, and self-regulation and other measures that define appropriate restrictions in scientific research are all ways in which the scientific community can contribute to the development of the culture of responsibility that is an essential element of an effective response. For its part, governments must engage the life sciences communities in ways that take into account legitimate proliferation concerns without harming the innovation and creativity on which scientific efforts thrive. The goal is a balance between security imperatives and the requirements of the scientific process and good business practices.

A Genuine Network Approach to Nonproliferation

Jean-Francois Rischard, the World Bank's former Vice President for Europe, has noted that changes of the kind fostered by globalization "put existing human institutions (nation states, governments, ministries, international institutions, any large hierarchy), which evolve only slowly and linearly, under massive pressure—and tend to overwhelm them."[58] He argues further that "[t]raditional institutions are incapable of addressing the growing list of complex global issues."[59] Those in charge of effecting a successful response to the proliferation challenge may be approaching that point of being overwhelmed. Many policy options are unattractive and are often derived from slow, linear processes that are likely to be neither sufficiently timely nor adequately effective to prevent a dangerous biological or chemical weapons threat from emerging.

One means of overcoming these problems is to create a novel mechanism for bringing critical stakeholders together as partners in managing potential risks. As Anne-Marie Slaughter points out, "Networked threats require a networked response."[60] Global networks that are greater in number, deeper in reach, and more rapid in response can take the raw material of national action and process it into a collaborative international effort that will have a better chance of dealing effectively with the complex challenges posed by CBW proliferation. So far, however, "using networks to fight networks" is a mere mantra, a slogan without content. New thinking is needed about how this networking approach can be put into action.

Each of the communities mentioned above represents a node in a nonproliferation network. The basis thus exists for a disaggregated and distributed response to a disaggregated and distributed problem. Promoting a networked, disaggregated approach to the proliferation problem facilitates the local, national, regional, ad hoc, multilateral, global, formal, and informal responses that are needed to slow chemical and biological weapons proliferation.

FINAL THOUGHTS

The chemical and biological weapons proliferation challenge in 2020 will be marked by uncertainty and unpredictability. It will be an issue about an interaction between intent and capability that is much less straightforward than the standard proliferation model suggests, and it will span a spectrum from traditional military programs to latent capabilities that could be quickly mobilized to achieve an operational capability.

In recent years, U.S. nonproliferation efforts have focused more on address
ing compliance concerns than on the more abstract notion of the appropriate
nonproliferation "architecture."[61] But if that emphasis on noncompliance con
tinues to the exclusion of U.S. leadership promoting badly needed conceptua
and policy innovations, the danger emerges of pursuit of a narrow agenda in
sensitive to the challenges produced by a rapidly changing world. "Winning
the proliferation contest must be more than preventing the next country from
deploying an offensive CBW program. It must also include preventing the los
of hope that success can be achieved and ensuring that if risks do materialize
their potential damage is minimized. Perhaps most important, however, "win
ning" is about shaping the choices made by state and nonstate actors that migh
be inclined to explore and exploit opportunities that an evolving scientific
technological, and security landscape provides.[62] Channeling those choices ir
positive directions will not occur without the options provided by robust non
proliferation networks. Building those networks and operating them effectively
is today's key nonproliferation challenge.

NOTES

1. National Academies of Science, *Globalization, Biosecurity, and the Future of the
Life Sciences* (Washington, DC: National Academies Press, 2006), 59.

2. "Moore's Law" holds that the number of transistors on a microchip doubles ap
proximately every eighteen months. Another way to formulate this "law" is that compu
tational resources for a fixed price double every eighteen months. Robert Carlson argues
that today "we see the beginnings of a similar effect in the development of biologica
technology." Robert Carlson, "The Pace and Proliferation of Biological Technologies,"
Biosecurity and Bioterrorism: Biodefense Strategy, Practice, and Science 1, no. 3 (2003)
1–3.

3. See, for example, Emily Singer, "DNA Factories," *Technology Review*, April 4, 2007
and Rob Carlson, "Global Distribution of Commercial DNA Foundries," *Synthesis*
http://synthesis.typepad.com/2005/07/global_distribu.html.

4. Alexander Kelle, *The Changing Scientific and Technological Basis of the CBW Proliferation Problem*, Bradford Science and Technology Reports no. 7, University of Bradford, 2007, 7.

5. Richard Zare commented, "To me, the big unanswered question concerns the
chemistry of life processes." Philip Ball, "What Chemists Want to Know," *Nature* 442
(August 3, 2006), 501.

6. National Academies of Science, *Globalization, Biosecurity, and the Future of the
Life Sciences*, 195.

7. Ronald F. Lehman and Eileen S. Vergino, "Unclear and Present Danger: Under-standing and Responding to WMD Latency," Presentation to the 2005/6 CGSR Futures Roundtable, Center for Global Security Research, Lawrence Livermore National Labora-tory, January 19–20, 2006.

8. National Intelligence Council, *Mapping the Global Future,* Report of the National Intelligence Council's 2020 Project, December 2004, 11.

9. Ibid., 13.

10. Ibid., 10.

11. "Biotechnology Industry Growth in Asia-Pacific: Findings of a Study," *Nandini Chemical Journal* 13, no. 8 (May 6–31), 34.

12. "Brazil to Seek Global Leadership in Biotechnology," Brazil-Arab News Agency, February 8, 2007, http://www.anba.com.br/ingles/imprimir.php?tipo_referencia=ID ref.

13. Institute of Medicine and National Research Council of the National Academies, *An International Perspective on Advancing Technologies and Strategies for Managing Dual-Use Risks: Report of a Workshop* (hereafter referred to as the NAS Workshop Re-port) (Washington, DC: National Academies Press, 2005), 6.

14. John Mugabe, *International Trends in Modern Biotechnology: Entry by and Impli-cations for African Countries,* African Technology Policy Studies Network, ATPS Special Paper Series no. 15, 2003, 10.

15. Nandini K. Kumar, Uyen Quach, Halla Thorsteinsdottiir, Hemlatha Somsekhar, Abdallah S. Daar, and Peter A. Singer, "Indian Biotechnology—Rapidly Evolving and In-dustry Led," in *Health Biotechnology Innovation in Developing Countries,* Global Partners Symposium, Vienna March 3-4, 2005, http://www.unido.org/fileadmin/import/35240_Panelo204 Thorsteinsdottiir CANADIANgenomics.8.pdf DC31. See also Parveen Arora, "Healthcare Biotechnology Firms in India: Evolution, Structure and Growth," *Current Science* 89, no. 3 (August 2005), 458–63.

16. David Kang and Adam Segal, "The Siren Song of Techno-nationalism," *Far East-ern Economic Review,* March 2006, http://www.feer.com/articles1/2006/0603/free/p005.html.

17. Helen E. Purkitt, *Biowarfare Lessons, Emerging Biosecurity Issues, and Ways to Monitor Dual-Use Biotechnology Trends in the Future,* U.S. Air Force Institute for Na-tional Security Studies, INSS Occasional Paper 61, September 2005, 40–41.

18. Gerald L. Epstein, *Global Evolution of Dual-use Biotechnology,* A Report of the Project on Technology Futures and Global Power, Wealth, and Conflict (Washington, DC: Center for Strategic and International Studies, April 2005), 9.

19. "Science and Technology Minister Discusses Nuclear, Space, and Other Priori-ties," Open Source Center, original published in *Brasilia InfoReal* in Portuguese, April 6, 2006, "Experts Meet in Tehran for Establishment of ECO Agricultural Biotechnology Network," Islamic Republic News Agency, April 25, 2006.

20. Michael Moodie and William J. Taylor, *Contagion and Conflict: Health as a Global Security Challenge*, Center for Strategic and International Studies, 2000, 3.

21. James B. Petro, Theodore R. Plasse, and Jack A. McNulty, "Biotechnology: Impact on Biological Warfare and Biodefense," *Biosecurity and Bioterrorism: Biodefense Strategy, Practice, and Science* 1, no. 3 (2003), 162.

22. Ibid.

23. The Sunshine Project, "Emerging Technologies: Genetic Engineering and Biological Weapons," Background Paper no. 12, November 2003, http://www.sunshine-project.org/publications/bk/bk12.html, 11–16.

24. Central Intelligence Agency, "The Darker Biological Weapons Future," November 3, 2003, 2.

25. Kathryn Nixdorff, Neil Davision, Piers Millett, and Simon Whitby, "Technology and Biological Weapons: Future Threats," Bradford Science and Technology Reports no. 2, University of Bradford, 1.

26. The Sunshine Project, "Emerging Technologies," 7.

27. Ibid.

28. Lehman and Vergino, "Unclear and Present Danger."

29. Michael Moodie, "Conflict," in *Fighting Chance: Global Trends and Shocks in the National Security Environment*, edited by Naylan Arnas (Washington, DC: National Defense University Press, 2009), 9–29.

30. Tuan Nguyen, "Microchallenges of CW Proliferation," *Science*, August 12, 2005.

31. Julie Fischer, *Dual-Use Technologies: Inexorable Progress, Inseparable Peril*, A Report of the Project on Technology Futures and Global Power, Wealth, and Conflict (Washington, DC: Center for Strategic and International Studies, April 2005), 3.

32. National Academies of Science, *Globalization, Biosecurity, and the Future of the Life Sciences*, 24.

33. Ibid.

34. NAS, Workshop Report, 32.

35. Marion Motari, Uyen Quach, Hall Thorsteinsdottir, Douglas K. Martin, Abdallah S. Dasr, and Peter A. Singer, "South Africa—Blazing a Trail for African Biotechnology," in *Health Biotechnology Innovation in Developing Countries*, nature biotechnology volume 22 supplement, December 2004, DC 37.

36. Epstein, *Global Evolution of Dual-use Biotechnology*, 10.

37. Li Zhenshen, Zhang Jiuchun, Wen Ke, Halla Thorsteinsdottir, Uyen Quach, Peter A. Singer, and Abdalla Dahr, "Health Biotechnology in China—Reawakening of a Giant," in *Health Biotechnology Innovation in Developing Countries*, nature biotechnology volume 22 supplement, December 2004, DC 13.

38. National Academies of Science, *Globalization, Biosecurity, and the Future of the Life Sciences*, 99.

39. Ibid., 102.

40. Ibid., 116.

41. Purkitt, *Biowarfare Lessons, Emerging Biosecurity Issues, and Ways to Monitor Dual-Use Biotechnology Trends in the Future*, 34.

42. Ibid., 7.

43. Organization for Economic Cooperation and Development, *The Bioeconomy to 2030: Designing a Policy Agenda*, OECD International Futures Program, 5.

44. Anne G. K. Solomon, "Introduction," in *Technology Futures, and Global Power, Wealth, and Conflict*, edited by Anne G. K. Solomon, A Report of the Project on Technology Futures and Global Power, Wealth, and Conflict, Center for Strategic and International Studies, May 2005.

45. Hall Thorsteinstdottir, Uyen Quach, Douglas K. Martin, Abdallah S. Daar, and Peter A. Singer, "Introduction: Promoting Global Health through Biotechnology," in *Health Biotechnology Innovation in Developing Countries*, nature biotechnology volume 22 supplement, December 2004, DC3

46. Shirley A. Kan, *China and Proliferation of Weapons of Mass Destruction and Missiles: Policy Issues*, Congressional Research Service, May 9, 2007, 1.

47. Bureau of Verification and Compliance, "Adherence to and Compliance with Arms Control, Nonproliferation, and Disarmament Agreements and Commitments," U.S. Department of State, August 30, 2005.

48. A different view, however, holds that China is doing better with respect to nonproliferation. Over the last five years, China's nonproliferation policy has become increasingly compliant with international and multilateral conventions and regimes. See Dr. Juan-dong Yuan, "China's Proliferation and the Impact of Trade Police on Defense Industries in the United States and China," Testimony before the U.S.-China Economic and Security Commission, July 12, 2007. See also Evan S. Medeiros, *Reluctant Restraint: The Evolution of China's Nonproliferation Policies and Practices, 1980–2004* (Stanford: Stanford University Press, 2007); Bates Gill, *Rising Star: China's New Security Diplomacy* (Washington, DC: Brookings Institution Press, 2007), chap. 3; Wendy Frieman, *China, Arms Control, and Nonproliferation* (London and New York: Routledge, 2004).

49. In an interview with the author, for example, when asked what developing country had the most capable biotechnology sector, the chief executive officer of a major European biotechnology company immediately responded, "Cuba."

50. James A. Russell and Christopher Clary, *Globalization and WMD Proliferation Networks: Challenges to U.S. Security*, Report of a Conference sponsored by the Naval Postgraduate School, June 29 –July 1, 2005, 9.

51. Milton Leitenberg, *Assessing the Biological Weapons and Bioterrorism Threat*, Strategic Studies Institute, U.S. Army War College, December 2005, 64.

52. David A. Relman, M.D., "Bioterrorism—Preparing to Fight the Next War," *New England Journal of Medicine* 354, no. 2, 2006, 113.

53. Gary A. Ackerman and Kevin S. Moran, "Bioterrorism and Threat Assessment,"

Paper no. 22, The Weapons of Mass Destruction Committee (The Blix Commission), November 2004, www.wmdcommission.org, 3.

54. Malcolm Dando, "Bioterrorism: What Is the Real Threat?" Risk Case Studies, Nuffield Trust Global Programme on Health, Foreign Policy and Security, 3.

55. Ibid., 35.

56. Carlson, "The Pace and Proliferation of Biological Technologies," 1.

57. Gerald Epstein, David Hamon, and Michael Moodie, *The Global Forum on Biorisks: Toward Effective Management and Governance of Biological Risks* (Washington, DC: Center for Strategic and International Studies, December 2009).

58. Jean-Francois Rischard, "My Views on What the Helsinki Process Should Stand For: Accelerated Global Problem-Solving," Personal Contribution to the Helsinki Process on Globalization and Democracy, 1.

59. Jean-Francois Rischard, "Global Issue Networks," *Washington Quarterly* 26, no. 1 (Winter 2002–3), 17.

60. Anne-Marie Slaughter, "Government Networks, World Order, and the G20," prepared for the meeting on *The G20 at Leader's Level*, Ottawa, February 29, 2004, 2.

61. Brad Roberts, "Nonproliferation—Challenges Old and New," in *Avoiding the Abyss: Progress, Shortfalls, and the Way Ahead in Controlling the WMD Threat*, edited by Barry Schneider and Jim A. Davis (Westport, CT: Praeger, 2006).

62. Ibid.

15 Conclusion

Jeffrey W. Knopf

Research on proliferation has evolved. Initially, theorizing about proliferation sought to explain why certain countries built nuclear weapons. Over time, however, the number of states that considered building or actually acquired nuclear weapons but later changed course came to outnumber those that developed and kept a nuclear arsenal.[1] As a result, proliferation research broadened to focus as much on explaining cases of nuclear restraint as on explaining cases of proliferation. Our volume is part of this emerging trend because it poses logical follow-on questions to the proliferation puzzle. For example, among states that have renounced nuclear weapons, might that decision ever be reconsidered? Under what conditions might nuclear reversal itself be reversed?

These questions are especially pertinent because every state that currently lacks nuclear weapons is also a non-nuclear state party to the Non-proliferation Treaty (NPT). This means that any future cases of nuclear proliferation will have to result from cheating within or withdrawal from the NPT. Understanding whether countries that have formally committed to a permanent non-nuclear status might later defect from the nonproliferation regime has become the central analytical issue in forecasting future proliferation.

The goal of this volume is to consider over-the-horizon threats that could materialize by 2020. Part of the effort has involved examining countries that are not necessarily among the usual suspects for potential future proliferation. Some chapters deal with countries, such as Venezuela and Myanmar, that were until recently never considered serious proliferation risks. The findings point to the dangers of any single-factor analysis. Many studies of the causes of proliferation argue for the superiority of one explanatory variable over the alternatives. In contrast, this study shows that decisions about proliferation result from a complex interplay of factors. Rather than mine cases for evidence that supports a favored general theory, it traces how all the many relevant variables combine in each particular case. The current volume also goes into greater detail than earlier studies on a range of possible policy tools to counter potential future proliferation. In sum, this project has sought not only to help forecast the future of proliferation, but also to help shape that future.

THE FINDINGS: MOSTLY GOOD NEWS, WITH IMPORTANT EXCEPTIONS

Eight chapters in this volume address the prospects for a nuclear breakout in a total of eleven countries. The findings are mostly encouraging. On balance, state motivations and technical constraints lead to a forecast of continued nuclear restraint in 10 of the 11 nations. The factors favoring restraint are stronger in some of these cases than in others. Among the cases studied, Taiwan, Indonesia, Vietnam, Argentina, and Ukraine appear to be the least likely candidates to seek nuclear weapons. It is somewhat more possible to imagine scenarios in which Japan, Brazil, or South Africa would go nuclear, but it would likely take a major external shock or series of shocks to prompt any of these countries to seriously reconsider their present non-nuclear status. Among countries still likely to be in the restraint column, Venezuela and Myanmar appear to have the most potential motivation to seek nuclear weapons, and current trends suggest there may be real reasons for concern about Myanmar.[2] Both countries lack the technological capability to develop nuclear arms on their own, however, so any effort by either to acquire nuclear weapons will likely require outside assistance and take a long time to complete. These constraints will create opportunities for the nonproliferation community to discover and perhaps halt any effort to obtain a nuclear weapon. In 10 of the 11 countries analyzed in detail, therefore, there is little reason at present for alarm.

The one exception in this positive assessment is Saudi Arabia. As James Russell notes in his chapter, many of the forces that helped preserve nuclear restraint in the Persian Gulf and the broader Middle East have weakened. The potential threat of a nuclear-armed Iran is the most direct driver of potential proliferation among the Arab states, but several other factors could reinforce the proliferation pressures arising from the Iranian nuclear program. There are long-standing frustrations over Israel's nuclear weapons and the lack of progress in the Israeli-Palestinian peace process. U.S. standing with the Saudis and other Arab states also has been greatly diminished. To the extent that Arab leaders believe they have to take anti-American public sentiment into account, they may be increasingly reluctant to rely on U.S. security guarantees—though Saudi leaders have demonstrated an ability to recognize and follow their national interests in private regardless of what they say in public. Russell stops short of predicting that Saudi Arabia or other Arab states will actually go nuclear, but this is the one region in which the balance of forces at work no longer clearly favors continued nuclear restraint.

Taken as a scorecard, a forecast of continued nonproliferation in 10 out of 11 cases sounds reassuring, but the one exception involves a particularly serious case. The factors that might stimulate a Saudi nuclear program apply to much of the Middle East, and a Saudi bomb program could be followed by similar efforts in Egypt, some of the Persian Gulf states, and perhaps even Turkey. Given the volatility of the Middle East, extensive nuclear proliferation there would be especially dangerous. Although there is a basis for optimism in proliferation forecasts for most regions, the potential for further proliferation in the Middle East makes it impossible to be completely sanguine about where the world may be headed by 2020.

A comparison across cases considered in the volume reveals another problematic trend—the continued diffusion of nuclear technology. For example, the number of countries that have an interest in nuclear energy is increasing. Even the Persian Gulf states, which are among the world's leading oil exporters, have begun a strong push to develop nuclear power plants. As Michael Malley and Tanya Ogilvie-White observe in their chapter, at least six countries in Southeast Asia have also started seeking the ability to produce nuclear energy. Moreover, there are good reasons to expect commercial nuclear energy production to become more common throughout the world, both to meet growing energy needs and to slow the rate of global warming. Although this trend will not automatically lead to proliferation, greater access to nuclear materials and know-how will lower the technical barriers to proliferation. This will make it increasingly difficult to rely on supply-side measures, such as export controls and interdiction, to prevent the proliferation of nuclear weapons.

DON'T OVERLOOK CHEMICAL AND BIOLOGICAL WEAPONS

Most of the chapters in this volume focus on the dangers of nuclear proliferation. The most sobering analysis, however, is contained in Michael Moodie's chapter on chemical and biological weapons. Moodie makes it clear that we need to stop thinking of chemical and biological weapons (CBW) as analogous to nuclear weapons, only less destructive. In many ways, the CBW proliferation problem differs from its nuclear counterpart.

Just as the spread of nuclear energy technology contributes to the risk of nuclear weapons proliferation, technology diffusion makes CBW proliferation more likely. In this case, however, the diffusion of technology—and, even more so, of knowledge—is the heart of the problem. Moodie cautions that the classic pattern of nuclear proliferation—from state intentions to a development program to a weapon—will not necessarily be replicated in the CBW area. It is possible that scientific researchers, motivated mainly by scientific curiosity, will create a dangerous pathogen in their research lab. Or a rogue company, seeking profits after a failure to develop a commercial product, might deliberately engineer chemical or biological agents, but without its host government's knowledge. Because CBW development does not necessarily require industrial-scale facilities, it is harder to detect traditional state-run chemical and biological weapons programs than efforts to manufacture nuclear weapons. A remarkably wide range of pathways might lead to CBW proliferation. Although nuclear proliferation continues to merit urgent attention, Moodie shows that it is important not to let CBW proliferation fall through the cracks.

FINDINGS RELEVANT TO FORECASTING

The research in this volume both reinforces and adds to the wisdom derived from previous studies. In an earlier project to forecast proliferation in 2016, Peter Lavoy argued that it is important for intelligence agencies to pay attention to more than just the technical capabilities of potential proliferators. The public statements of top leaders and internal policy debates are also important for what they indicate about possible intentions.[3] Sometimes, political rhetoric can be fairly explicit. In countries that have committed to a non-nuclear course, politicians or military officers who want to reopen debate on the subject will state publicly that their country should reconsider nuclear weapons. Katsuhisa Furukawa identifies a subtle shift in such rhetoric in Japan. In the past, political officeholders who made such statements were rebuked and forced to resign, but in recent years the Japanese have been more willing to tolerate such open talk about nuclear weapons.

The Japan case also demonstrates that policy studies and debates can be useful indicators of non-nuclear intentions. As Furukawa notes, in the 1960s and 1970s, a series of policy reviews all concluded that Japanese interests would best be served by remaining non-nuclear. The consistency with which various studies reached this conclusion showed that they were a reliable indicator of Japan's intentions. More recently, outside observers have widely assumed that North Korea's nuclear efforts will eventually lead Japan to follow suit. Yet, Furukawa argues convincingly that most of the forces that have inclined Japan to forgo nuclear weapons are still in place, meaning that Japan is unlikely to initiate a nuclear weapons program in the near future. Rather than rely on a casual assumption that proliferation in one country must beget proliferation in its neighbors, it is better, as the Japan case shows, to track internal debates for indicators of which way a country's leaders are tilting on the nuclear issue.

SECURITY AND NONSECURITY CONSIDERATIONS BOTH MATTER

The cases in this volume show the importance of understanding the wide range of causes that can affect a country's decisions about nuclear weapons. Conventional wisdom has long emphasized security as the primary motivation for nuclear weapon programs. This perspective receives some confirmation from the present volume; security considerations are a factor in several of the cases examined in this study. Using security concerns as an indicator of proliferation risk, however, is not always straightforward. As Etel Solingen has pointed out, sometimes the security of a ruling regime's hold on power is what matters, rather than traditional threats to national security.[4] Andrew Selth's chapter suggests this is likely the case for Burma, where the military rulers appear to fear outside intervention to promote regime change.

Developments that could cause a change in a state's security environment are also potentially relevant. In terms of Japan and Taiwan, perceptions of the strength of the U.S. commitment to their defense remain quite important. In other cases, regional developments are likely to be key. This may be the case in Southeast Asia, where, as Malley and Ogilvie-White observe, countries are hoping the Association of South East Asian Nations can develop a security architecture for the region. This example suggests that proliferation analysts should devote more attention to regional organizations and agreements. Where countries are satisfied with regional arrangements, proliferation is less likely. But if regional organizations go into sudden decline, security perceptions may change in ways that increase the risks of proliferation.

Several cases in this volume also show that nonsecurity considerations can have a significant impact on the decision to acquire a nuclear weapon. Concerns about safety, potential environmental impacts, or public health effects appear as a factor in deliberations about nuclear programs. Although Japan's reputed "nuclear allergy" arises mainly from the fact that Japan is the only country to have had atomic bombs used against it, Furukawa notes that when the crew of a Japanese fishing boat was contaminated by radioactive fallout from a 1954 nuclear test, this further enhanced the public's antinuclear sentiments. In her chapter on Ukraine, Isabelle Facon observes that memories of the 1986 Chernobyl disaster gave the public another reason to favor giving up nuclear weapons. Malley and Ogilvie-White suggest that a similar dynamic may be at work in Indonesia. There, the government's poor track record on public safety leads Indonesians to doubt whether the government could ensure that any nuclear reactors built in the country would be operated safely.

In addition to security concerns, proliferation specialists have long recognized that considerations of prestige or status can be a factor in how states view the desirability of developing nuclear capabilities. Theories of proliferation initially assumed that nuclear weapons would provide prestige and great power status. Over time, however, nonproliferation norms associated with the Nuclear Non-proliferation Treaty (NPT) have provided an alternative understanding of what provides a state with international standing.[5] Membership in the NPT has become an important marker of what makes a state a good international citizen. As a result, concerns about status can be a driver of either proliferation or restraint.

This means that actor-specific knowledge will be important to forecasting how prestige concerns might affect proliferation. Most relevant will be the aspirations of a state's leaders for the role or identity they seek for their state. For Taiwan's rulers, as Arthur Ding notes in his chapter, simply gaining diplomatic recognition has been a long-standing objective. In the Taiwan case, therefore, status considerations strongly favor nuclear restraint. To pursue nuclear weapons in defiance of nonproliferation norms would only relegate Taiwan to the "pariah" status it has long sought to escape. Nonproliferation norms had a similar effect on Ukraine. According to Facon, Kiev's initial signals of a willingness to give up nuclear weapons reflected the desire to demonstrate that the newly independent country would be a responsible actor. For other countries, especially those that were former colonies of the European powers, mastering nuclear technology can be valued as a signal of modernity and development. According to Malley and Ogilvie-White, this has been a reason why Southeast

Asian countries are attracted to nuclear power. This is likely also a factor in Iran's nuclear weapons ambitions.

For forecasting purposes, expressions of defiance toward and active disregard of existing norms are obvious indicators that a state's leaders might find nuclear weapons attractive. But expressions of desire to prove that a state can be the equal of the great powers, and accomplish anything the existing great powers have achieved, should also be taken as a possible warning sign even if the state in question does not otherwise act like a rogue. In contrast, evidence that a state wants to demonstrate that it can play by the rules and fit into the international community indicates that the state is likely to favor nuclear restraint.

Finally, the cases in this volume highlight the importance of domestic political factors. Different domestic factions can have different views about the advisability of seeking nuclear weapons. As a result, changes in the ruling coalition or regime, or in the balance of power between competing factions, can lead to changes in policy, either toward or away from an interest in developing nuclear weapons. Incentives arising from a state's external environment remain relevant, but state decisions about how to respond to those incentives are determined by internal political processes. Hence, it is important to monitor domestic politics for possible indicators about whether a state is likely to maintain or reverse nuclear restraint. Collectively, these results make it clear that it is unwise to rely on any single factor as the supposedly dominant explanation of proliferation or restraint. Forecasting will require tracking the interplay of multiple factors in individual cases.

POLICY TOOLS: MANY USEFUL OPTIONS, BUT NO SILVER BULLETS

One reason for sharpening proliferation forecasts is the hope of being able to do something to stop nuclear weapons programs before they get started. Several chapters in this volume examine various nonproliferation tools. The basic finding is similar in every case. Each tool has the potential to make a positive contribution to stemming proliferation, but no individual tool is always effective. There is no silver bullet that can prevent proliferation. Nevertheless, the ability to use several tools in combination has made it possible to slow proliferation. Thinking now about possible new policy measures could become valuable later. As Lew Dunn observes in his chapter, past proliferation shocks have often opened the door for the adoption of new nonproliferation tools.

Among existing policy instruments, the NPT remains the centerpiece of the effort to prevent nuclear proliferation. In his chapter on the NPT regime, Christopher Ford reaches a balanced judgment that could provide a basis for consensus on how to ensure that the NPT has a future. On the one hand, Ford concludes that the NPT has made a difference and is worth preserving and bolstering. On the other hand, Ford observes that the NPT has real weaknesses, especially with respect to timely detection of violations and procedures for enforcing compliance. These weaknesses need to be addressed if the treaty regime is to continue to work as an anchor to nonproliferation efforts.

Although Ford argues for reemphasizing the centrality of nonproliferation in the NPT mission, it is important to remember that most non-nuclear states view the NPT as involving a bargain with the nuclear-armed states. Even if, as Ford claims, Article VI does not legally oblige the nuclear weapons states to achieve nuclear disarmament, there is a clear expectation on the part of non-nuclear states that the nuclear states will seek to reduce their nuclear arsenals. As Noel Stott notes in his chapter on South Africa, there are some states that might revisit decisions to renounce nuclear weapons if they become convinced that the nuclear weapons states have no intention of living up to their side of the NPT bargain. Non-nuclear states, as codified in Article IV, also expected continued access to the potential benefits of peaceful uses of nuclear technology. Given renewed interest in nuclear energy, it is more critical than ever to make available the most proliferation-resistant possible forms of technology assistance, a point that Ford also stresses.

As a final element of their bargain with nuclear weapons states, non-nuclear states sought security assurances. They wanted to know that, if they gave up the option of developing nuclear weapons, they would not be threatened or attacked by nuclear weapons in the hands of other states. Security assurances can be negative, involving promises by nuclear states not to use or threaten to use their weapons against non-nuclear states, or positive, involving promises by nuclear states to assist non-nuclear states that are threatened by a nuclear-armed third party. In his chapter Bruno Tertrais has provided the first attempt to assess the effectiveness of security assurances across a large number of cases. He finds that positive assurances in the form of bilateral security guarantees have played a significant role in discouraging proliferation. The chapters on Japan, Taiwan, Saudi Arabia, and Ukraine provide additional support for this conclusion. Tertrais also concludes that negative security assurances, and positive assurances that are vague or multilateral, are unlikely to have an impact on proliferation.

These conclusions represent a valuable first cut at estimating the value of security assurances. However, because the motivations for proliferation can differ, the effectiveness of security assurances is likely to vary across cases. This makes it important to explore the conditions under which different forms of security assurance are more or less likely to be effective.[6]

Other policy tools include intelligence and interdiction, which are the subjects of the chapter by Wyn Bowen. These tools have enjoyed some apparent successes. Bowen notes that the interception in October 2003 of the *BBC China*, with its nuclear-related cargo bound for Libya, was an important catalyst in convincing Col. Mua'mar Qadhafi to give up Libya's WMD programs. In the best case, interdiction and intelligence are synergistic. Intelligence makes interdiction possible, which then provides additional intelligence information. Of the two, intelligence is the primary source of leverage. If the United States or the international community demonstrates that countries cannot keep clandestine weapons programs hidden, the likelihood that secret programs will be discovered before they are completed may dissuade some countries from taking the risk involved in pursuing a clandestine effort to manufacture weapons.

Other chapters in this volume suggest a wider variety of policy tools that might be able to contribute to nonproliferation. Stott points to the potential value of providing education and training in nonproliferation, especially to government personnel in states that do not have much prior involvement in these issues. Individuals who receive such training can operate in the bureaucracy of their home country to help ensure that their state understands and does not drift away from its nonproliferation commitments.

In the CBW area, Moodie emphasizes that using a broad range of tools will be essential. Some options are rather different from the traditional nonproliferation tools. It could be useful, for example, to build up norms among scientists against working on CBW. Efforts to improve public health capabilities are also relevant. They will improve the odds of identifying a disease outbreak resulting from a biological agent, and they may reduce the deaths that result. Improving consequence management abilities more generally, beyond aiding in the direct goal of saving lives, could also have deterrent effects. If it becomes less likely that a CBW attack would cause mass fatalities, other actors may become less interested in using or even acquiring CBW.

Creativity in identifying and using a diverse set of policy tools hence offers some hope that further proliferation can be prevented. One caveat applies, however. Policymakers should be careful not simply to throw every tool available at the problem. There can be circumstances when using a particular tool might backfire, and there can be tradeoffs between different nonproliferation measures. Bowen observes, for example, that interdiction could be seen as an act of bad faith if there are already diplomatic negotiations underway to convince a country to give up its WMD programs. And Tertrais points out that positive security assurances are in tension with some nonproliferation tools. Positive assurances often involve extending a nuclear umbrella over an ally. This creates an incentive to maintain certain nuclear capabilities, which can work at cross purposes with both negative security assurances and the Article VI promise to seek nuclear disarmament. Thus, just as it is valuable to understand as much as possible about other actors, it is useful to understand the potential and the limitations of each policy tool.

Beyond the policy tools explicitly discussed in this volume, the research presented here contains other policy-relevant implications. It suggests, for example, that strategic dialogue, academic exchange programs, and public education efforts could all contribute to nonproliferation. First, they offer valuable ways to draw attention to the possible security risks of going down the nuclear path. New nuclear states are likely to be added to the nuclear targeting lists of states that already possess nuclear weapons, which may increase the threat of a nuclear attack on them in ways they would not have anticipated. Nuclear programs can also provoke neighboring states to seek their own nuclear deterrent, which can leave the first state less secure than it was beforehand. Policy studies in Japan, summarized by Furukawa, showed awareness of this security dilemma, and desire to avoid triggering regional responses was one factor that convinced Japan to remain non-nuclear.[7] Anything that increases information about the possible negative impact of nuclear programs on national security could help tilt internal debates in potential proliferators back in favor of continued restraint.

Second, nuclear programs can have consequences beyond their implications for national security as traditionally construed. Their budgetary cost can be unexpectedly large, especially for developing countries. Among existing nuclear weapons states, there is also an unfortunate history of accidents at nuclear production sites that have released radioactivity and toxic materials, causing death or illness to workers and nearby residents.[8] Disseminating information about the possible nonsecurity costs and dangers of nuclear weapons development could hence usefully supplement other nonproliferation measures.

Another potentially useful step would be to strengthen relevant norms.

For states concerned about their international standing, such norms can be a factor in whether states view nuclear weapons possession as advancing their interests. Norms against acquiring nuclear weapons do not appear to be as strong, however, as those against using such weapons. The widely discussed concept of a "nuclear taboo" indicates that, relative to proliferation, actual use of nuclear weapons would be more broadly condemned as a major violation of international standards.[9] Because further proliferation of chemical, biological, and perhaps nuclear weapons remains possible and maybe even likely, more attention needs to be devoted to preventing such weapons from being used if they spread to new actors. A number of policy tools, including deterrence and defenses, will potentially be relevant. Given the stakes, however, it would be unwise to dismiss the potential contribution of norms to inhibiting WMD use. The research in this volume suggests that there may be value in reemphasizing taboos against the use of chemical, biological, and nuclear weapons.

In thinking ahead, it is worth keeping in mind Lew Dunn's sage advice. Future shocks and surprises are likely, but they could sometimes have a silver lining. New, negative proliferation developments could provide opportunities to advance nonproliferation proposals that today appear politically infeasible. Planning ahead will improve the odds of being able to leverage proliferation shocks in this way. The research presented here suggests that a remarkably diverse range of tools have the potential to contribute to combating proliferation.

FINAL THOUGHTS

The findings of this volume provide a basis for cautious optimism. In most of the cases and regions studied, the most likely forecast for 2020 is continued nuclear restraint. The forecast for Saudi Arabia and the broader Middle East, however, is less optimistic. Here, there are several forces at work that could encourage proliferation, and while proliferation is not inevitable, it is also not possible to forecast a high probability of continued restraint.

The attempt to forecast chemical and biological weapons proliferation raises additional reasons for serious concern. The rapid advance of knowledge and spread of technology are on the brink of making CBW proliferation incredibly easy, if that is not the case already. More creative thinking about how to counter CBW proliferation and a renewed policy commitment to managing this problem, as a separate issue from nuclear proliferation, are clearly in order.

Because proliferation risks remain, finding policies that can reduce the likelihood of proliferation will continue to be a challenge. In the short term, efforts to deal with Iran and North Korea are likely to remain central. Success in getting these countries to commit convincingly to a non-nuclear future would be a tremendous boon to future nonproliferation efforts. But even if these countries end up in the loss column for nonproliferation, that need not open the proliferation floodgates. There are still opportunities to slow or halt the further spread of WMD, even if one or two more aspirants join the nuclear club. No individual policy tool is 100 percent effective, meaning that nonproliferation success will likely require a combination of policy measures. Finding ways to integrate the tools so that they are mutually reinforcing rather than working at cross purposes will be an important task.

Treaties such as the NPT remain the centerpiece of nonproliferation efforts. These treaties have weaknesses, but, in the absence of a better alternative, their flaws should not be seen as a reason to abandon them. Neither should their weaknesses be ignored. For future nonproliferation efforts to succeed, the international community will have to patch problem areas in the existing nonproliferation regimes.

Treaty regimes are increasingly being supplemented by other nonproliferation policy measures. This volume has shown that security assurances, intelligence activities, and interdiction can all contribute to nonproliferation. More generally, the research presented here has suggested that there is also potential value in promoting norms for nonproliferation and non-use, and in seeking to bolster regionally based efforts.

The most effective approach will combine generic global and regional measures with efforts to identify and respond to actor-specific motivations. The cases in this volume suggest that proliferation decisions are often affected by a complicated mix of security and nonsecurity considerations, with the impact of those factors often depending on domestic politics. Nonproliferation policies derived from a generic, single-factor model of proliferation will not be able to address these types of nuances. Efforts to track and understand internal debates and perceptions will increase the chances of correctly identifying cases where there is a risk of proliferation. They will also improve the chances of crafting an effective policy response.

Given the inherent difficulty of forecasting, perhaps the only forecast that can be made with confidence is that the policies and actions of today will affect the likelihood of further proliferation. If policymakers take advantage of available knowledge about the causes of proliferation and restraint, the factors at work in individual cases, and the range of policy measures available for combating proliferation, they can shift the odds in favor of a less dangerous world.

NOTES

1. Proliferation researchers have identified more than twenty countries that pursued or acquired nuclear weapons but ultimately decided to forswear nuclear arms. See Ariel E. Levite, "Never Say Never Again: Nuclear Reversal Revisited," *International Security*, 27, no. 3 (Winter 2002/3): 62, Table 1; Harald Mueller and Andreas Schmidt, "The Little Known Story of De-Proliferation: Why States Give up Nuclear Weapon Activities," in William C. Potter and Gaukhar Mukhatzhanova, eds., *Forecasting Nuclear Proliferation in the 21st Century*, vol. 1 (Stanford: Stanford University Press, 2010).

2. The evidence in this case remains controversial. See Stephen Engelberg and Natan Dotan, "Experts, Intelligence Agencies Question a Defector's Claims about Burma's Nuclear Ambitions," ProPublica, November 12, 2010, http://www.propublica.org/article/experts-intel-agencies-question-a-defectors-claims-about-burmas-nuclear.

3. Peter R. Lavoy, "Nuclear Proliferation over the Next Decade: Causes, Warning Signs, and Policy Responses," *Nonproliferation Review*, 13, no. 3 (November 2006).

4. In addition to her chapter for this volume, see Etel Solingen, *Nuclear Logics: Contrasting Paths in East Asia and the Middle East* (Princeton: Princeton University Press, 2007).

5. Scott D. Sagan, "Why Do States Build Nuclear Weapons? Three Models in Search of a Bomb," *International Security*, 21, no. 3 (Winter 1996/97): 76; Maria Rost Rublee, *Nonproliferation Norms: Why States Choose Nuclear Restraint* (Athens: University of Georgia Press, 2009).

6. I have led a follow-on project to assess in more detail the factors associated with the success or failure of security assurances. The findings will be reported in Jeffrey W. Knopf, ed., *Security Assurances and Nuclear Nonproliferation*, forthcoming.

7. According to T. V. Paul, *Power versus Prudence: Why Nations Forgo Nuclear Weapons* (Montreal: McGill-Queens University Press, 2000), concern about regional security dilemmas helps account for several cases of nuclear restraint.

8. Jeffrey W. Knopf, "Recasting the Proliferation Optimism-Pessimism Debate," *Security Studies*, 12, no. 1 (Autumn 2002).

9. Nina Tannenwald, *The Nuclear Taboo: The United States and the Non-Use of Nuclear Weapons since 1945* (Cambridge: Cambridge University Press, 2007); T. V. Paul, *The Tradition of Non-Use of Nuclear Weapons* (Stanford: Stanford University Press, 2009).

Index

Index

Made in the USA
Middletown, DE
17 January 2021